D1555608

# THE GIFT OF PROPERTY

# THE GIFT OF PROPERTY

## HAVING THE GOOD

*STEPHEN DAVID ROSS*

betraying genitivity,
economy and ecology,
an ethic of the earth

STATE UNIVERSITY OF NEW YORK PRESS

Published by
State University of New York Press, Albany

© 2001 State University of New York

For information, address State University of New York Press,
90 State Street, Suite 700, Albany, NY 12207

Production by Marilyn P. Semerad
Marketing by Dana E. Yanulavich

**Library of Congress Cataloging-in-Publication Data**

Ross, Stephen David.
    The gift of property : having the good : betraying genitivity : economy and ecology : an
ethic of the earth / Stephen David Ross.
        p. cm.
    Includes bibliographical references and index.
    ISBN 0-7914-4865-7 (alk. paper) — ISBN 0-7914-4866-5 (pbk. : alk. paper)
    1. Ethics. 2. Property—Moral and ethical aspects. 3. Philosophy of nature. I. Title.

BJ1031 .R673 2001
170—dc21                                                                    00-039480

                        10  9  8  7  6  5  4  3  2  1

# Contents

Derrida on property. Heidegger on sexual difference. Property, genitivity. *Specters of Marx*. Genitality and propriety. Production and reproduction. Life and death. Blood, sex, kin, class, food, desire, and power. Property, *propriéte, le propre*. *Epekeina tes ousias*: beyond property. *Ek-stasis*. *L'écarte*. *Mimēsis*. *Hamlet*: more things on heaven and earth. Your, my, our philosophy, in the genitive. Heidegger on jointure, giving without having. Derrida. Heidegger favors jointure. Scholars and ghosts. Gift of *Dikē*. Sacrifice sacrifice. Assume inheritance of Marx. Bear witness. Impossibility, giving without taking, responsibility. Kojève. Sacrificing animals. Genitivity of Marx, Marxism. Inheritance. Witness. Call to excessive, incalculable responsibility. Property without genitivity. Props of property. *Mimēsis*. Table comes on stage, becomes commodity. Automaton, simulacrum, specter. Promised to iterability. Use-value promised to exchange and beyond. Betrayal. Marx glorious, sacred immigrant. Property's *mimēsis* on stage.

*Ousia, parousia*. Aristotle. Thing with properties. *Oikos*, household. Genitivity in the home. As genitality. Blood, sex, kin, class, food, desire, and power. Plato. *Republic*. City of pigs. Economy, ecology, of soul. Without genitivity. Cephalus. Justice, property, advantage. *Apology, Phaedrus*. Possession and being possessed. Divine madness, *mimēsis*, gifts from gods. Writing, wandering. *Theaetetus*. Knowledge impossible to possess. *Laws*. Abolishing genitivity. *Gorgias*. Callicles. Philosophers helpless, others steal their property. Slavery. Virtue not owning or having. Callicles. Let appetites' desire grow without restriction, satisfy every craving. Socrates. Better to suffer than to commit injustice. Better to give than to have. Live for sake of the good, without owning or having.

Hobbes. Desire to have forever, desire for power. Ecolonomy. Smith. Division of labor. Exchange and trade. Labor foundation of property. Trade and exchange. Beyond restricted economy. Rousseau. Freedom, general will. Social contract as unqualified gift. Inequality. Having as injustice. Life and liberty gifts that cannot be given away. *Oikos, oeconomy*. Public, private economy. Right to property most sacred right. Dewey. Experience not owned. Nothing in nature belongs absolutely. Foucault. Author. Proper name.

Locke. Possessing truths. God gives world to human beings in common. Appropriate through labor. Right to enclose for oneself, provided leave enough for others. Not licence to destroy. Owning as responsibility. Labor right to property. In the hands. Human beings proprietors of themselves. Giving, taking, as property. Hegel. Freedom, will. Embodiment in external things as property. *Lowliness: onlyness, loneliness, ownliness.* Kant. Desire. Right. Genealogy, genitivity, and genitality. Household. Wife, child, servant. Rights to persons. Sexual union as property. Hegel. Contract. Sexual difference. Family and property. Economic classes. Proudhon. Property theft. Property impossible. Political economy. Anarchy as dispossession, disowning genitivity.

Engels. *Origin of the Family, Private Property and the State.* Production and reproduction. Property linked with blood, sex, wealth, food, desire, and power. Genitality of genitivity. Written history, *mimēsis.* Mother right. The curse. Animal domestication. Family. Division of labor. Monogamy. Prostitution. Genitivity of genitality. Capitalism creates "free" and "equal" persons. State power. Private property. Commodities. Producer loses control over products. Products wander. *Phaedrus.* Writing wanders. *Mimēsis.* Social division of labor. Emancipation of women. Emancipation of cattle. Money. Jacoby. Animal domestication. Slavery. Marx's critique of Proudhon. Althusser on Marx. Construction of political economy. As science. Construction of genitivity. As property. Marx on Jews. Why such hatred? Communism as anti-Semitism. Use-value. Commodities. Excess. Household. *Ethicoeconomoecology, economology, ecolonomics, economology\ecolonomics.* Grip of household on every thing. Excessive circulation. Fetish. General economy. Genitivity as genitality. Excesses of desire. Phantasmagoria of fetish. *Mimēsis* of *mimēsis.* Foucault. Money. Representation. Value. Sacrifice. Marx. Commodities as circumcised Jews. Economology. Giving without having. Cherishment, sacrifice, plenishment.

Living in the earth before genitivity. Without enclosure. Stirner. Right, freedom, as power. Ethics as theft. Enclosure of land, enclosure of women, children, and animals. Schleuning. Freedom as genitivity. An ethic of inclusion,

*Contents*

without enclosure. Fetishism as phantasmagoric desire. Fetishism as *mimēsis*. Leopold. Mountain and deer. Double gesture. Game management. Land ethic. Brueggemann. Homelessness and home. Biblical faith and land. Israel, landlessness, wilderness, promise of the land. Botkin, Buffon. Nature as wilderness, to be tamed. *Aporia* as wandering, *mimēsis*. Brueggemann. Israel. Wanders in the desert. Tempted to hoard, to covet. Giving becomes having, taking. Betraying abundance beyond possessing.

Chapter 7    Domestic Properties                                    105

Aboriginal peoples disenfranchised in relation to land. Double exclusion: in property itself, mine not yours; certain peoples excluded from owning land. Stirner. Negroidity. Wilmsen. Aboriginal peoples, hunter-gatherers, foragers. Unfit to own land. Harris. Whiteness as property. Property rights and race. Affirmative action as distributive justice, equal rights to property. In the genitive. Singer. History of broken treaties with American Indian nations. Sovereignty and property rights used against Indian nations. Regarded as primitive peoples, without rights in property or in sovereignty.

Chapter 8    Gender Properties                                      115

Human relations to themselves and world as property. Property relations as seizing the goods of other peoples. Human identity and property relations. Human life and being as having, taking, accumulating, consuming. Gender. Men require house, woman, and ox. Irigaray. Woman as place for man. Change in economy of space-time. *Genre*. Kinship. Human kind as masculine. Angels. Intermediary figures. Differential genitive relationships for men and women. Women as property. Women and property. Dworkin. Power of owning as power of self who takes. Male power. Women chattel property. The curse. MacKinnon. Systematic gender inequality. Sexual objectification. Irigaray. Wittig. Society based on exchange of women. Rubin. Production, reproduction. Culturally determined. Political economy of sex and gender. Hirschon. Women as things. Equated with wealth. Exchanged for things. Resisting genitivity in kinship and property. Difference between Western and non-Western, capitalist and noncapitalist views of property, persons, and objects. Rubin. Political economy of sex and gender. Exchange of women. Women for women, women for things. Abusing animals as animals, not as things. Abusing women, children, and slaves as human beings, not as things. Things not just things. Things and persons in complex social relationships of having and meaning. Separability of individuals and things from other individuals and things. Defining condition of individuality.

Freedom as infinite desire to accumulate. As having and owning. Individual autonomy. Free will. Minogue. Anything can become active property. Anything can be desired. Infinite will. Schleuning. Property rights. Macpherson. Reich. Freedom and equality. Stirner. Infinite freedom, infinite owning, Becker. Elements of ownership. Locke. Accumulating beyond personal needs. Household management. Use-value. Distinction between public and private spheres. Radin. Personhood and property. Genitivity not generosity. Alienability and inalienability. The curse. Grunebaum. Autonomy principle. Right to have what maximizes autonomy. Sphere of private property rights in labor. Collective rights to land and resources.

Stirner. Ego, self, as owner. Abjection. Mineness. My power is my property. I am my power as my property. Marx's critique of Stirner. Material production. Production and reproduction. Saint Max. Saints Ma(r)x. Definite modes of life. Derrida. Disappearance of ghost. Phantasmagoria of commerce between commodities. Wooden table on stage. *Mimēsis*. Not only human. Wikse. Modern identity, authenticity, as self possession. Self as owner. Deleuze and Guattari. Producing-machines, desiring-machines, writing-machines. Capitalism as schizophrenia: production of production. Falling back down on *(se rabat sur)* production. Body without organs. Wikse. Pathos and poetry of self as private property. Behavior as having oneself. Self as fetish. As sacrifice. Inheritance as genitivity.

Wikse and Stirner. Ecstasy is possession by ghosts. Slavery. Wikse. *Extasis* as separation from others. *Ekstasis* as madness, withdrawal of soul. Heidegger. *Ek-stasis* as interruption. Out of place, displaced. Betrays genitivity. Clément. Syncope, rapture, ecstasy. As disowning. Women and syncope. Fainting. Tremors. Sneezes. Laughter. Epilepsy. Orgasm. Irigaray. "*La mystérique.*" Soul, *l'âme, jouissance.* Woman as fluidity. Resisting genitivity. Bataille. Ecstasy. Expenditure. General economy. Lyotard. Libidi-

nal economy. Theatricality. Desire's *mimēsis*. Cry and labyrinth. Big fat
Marx. Little girl Marx. *Jouissance*, desire, body. Capitalism as prostitution.
Capital as general economy. *Mimēsis*. Ecstasy as betrayal.

Accumulation. Standing reserve. Consumption. Derrida. Heidegger. Singu-
larity. Nietzsche. Learn to laugh! Squander. Derrida. *Yes, yes!* Affirmation.
Bataille. Expenditure. General economy, restricted economy. Squander as
giving without return. Intimacy. Genitality and genitivity. Derrida. Virility.
Flesh. Adams. Women and meat. Absent referents. Thrownness as *mimēsis*.
Betrayal. Derrida. Hospitality. Not only human. Giving without gifts.

Stirner. Having oneself. In the genitive. Heidegger. Genitivity of Being.
Levinas. Sedentary peoples. Being here. Hospitality. Generosity. Femininity.
The home. Dwelling. In the genitive. I myself. In the home. Recollection,
intimacy, welcome. Feminine. Betrayals of women and animals. Dwelling
site of danger and betrayal. Face. Animal face. Nancy. Return to being.
Freedom. Surprising generosity of being. Ontotheology. Secret of being.
Freedom without causality. Being there. Levinas. Being here. As accusation.
Exposed as hostage. In the genitive. *Mimēsis* not only human. Exposure as
*mimēsis*.

Sustainable practices. Environmental, ecological fascism. Authoritarianism.
Betrayal. The greatest values become the worst. Naess. *Friluftsliv*. Touching
the earth lightly. Schumacher. Sustenance as permanence. Small is beautiful. Choosing sustenance. Living like the bee. Waste. Monsters. Global
economy. Berry. Proper human scale. Natural scale. Goodness and wickedness. Economics of betrayal. Ecolonomics. Schumacher. Global economy.
Dual economy. Nobler economics. Buddhism. Local practices. Intermediate
technology. Large-scale organization. Economics of human scale. Berry.
Sustainability. Otherwise. Resistant to propriety. Middle, intermediariness.
Wilderness as intermediariness. Harmony. Love and care. Anything but
propriety.

Chapter 15  Giving                                                 211

Berry. Two economies, great and small. Vernacular of general and restricted economy. Kingdom of God. Topsoil. Limits. Authority. Prescription. Sacrificing sacrifice. Betrayal. Derrida. *Gift of Death*. Arrival of responsibility. Responsibility, liberty, singularity, infinite goodness. Giving as taking. Platonic incorporation of death. *Phaedo*. Assembling of self. Philosophy as obsession with death. Question of the obsession. Its Christianity. Economy of sacrifice. *Mysterium tremendum*. Irresponsibility in responsibility. Betrayal. Secret of the secret. *Dasein*'s singularity. Aporia of responsibility, betraying having. Woman. Interrupting masculine economy of sacrifice. *Oikos*. Disowning genitivity. Economology. *Tout autre est tout autre*. Betraying *les autres*.

Chapter 16  Betraying                                              227

Promised to iterability. As betrayal. Betraying betrayal as sacrifice, (the step) (not) (beyond) having, as (for) giving. *Ousia* in *parousia*. *Mimēsis*. Property on stage. *Be* and *bet* of betrayal. *Beyond* as mimêsis. *As, as, as*. Promised to *mimēsis*, *as mimēsis*, betrayed in betrayal. Beauty, truth, goodness *as* gifts. Cannot be had. Call. *Zusage*. Cherishment, sacrifice, plenishment. Expressivity and responsivity. Three concluding gestures, mimetic betrayals. First, rewriting guidelines for plenishment in exuberance of betrayal. Second, *philanthropy, philogyny, philogeny, philokyny*. Ecolonomics, economology.

Chapter 17  Forgiving                                              245

Forgiveness as extreme giving. Betraying authority. Otherwise. *For*-giving *as not beyond*. Beyond transgression, without holding onto sin. Without insisting on knowing and having the sin. As betrayal. Betraying the beyond. Spinoza's *gaudeo* and *laetitia*. Unrestrained gladness. Derrida's yes, yes! Joy *as not beyond* itself. Locke. Mother's grief at death of her child. Mother's forgiveness, betraying the loss. Surpassing having. Betrayal betrayed.

# General Preface to the Project:
## Gifts of the Good*

This volume is the fifth devoted to the good,[1] understanding human and natural worlds to be filled with gifts,[2] exposing human beings everywhere to other individuals and kinds,[3] calling us and others to respond with endless movements in and out of every place.[4] The works we know, their precious ingredients, all possessions, dwelling places, and natural kinds, come as gifts in the name of something other than themselves, unlike any thing, interrupting the limits of places and worlds, resisting authority. I speak of the circulation of these local and contingent gifts as the giving of the good everywhere in nature, understanding nature as the general economy

*This general preface, with ensuing changes, begins each volume of the project, reaching toward those without prior knowledge of the undertaking, to call their attention to giving and the good. The preceding volumes of the project are: *The Gift of Beauty: The Good as Art; The Gift of Truth: Gathering the Good; The Gift of Touch: Embodying the Good; The Gift of Kinds: The Good in Abundance.* I hope to trace gifts from the good in other places, multiplying their profusion.

Each volume may be read independently, in its terms. Each may benefit from other volumes. Here I address the ecology of human and natural worlds in the heterogeneous economy of abundance, the immeasurable giving of the good, in a world where human beings have largely forgotten generosity in the impetus to have and own. I think of gifts and giving in a world of taking, acquiring, and possessing, of accumulating and consuming, of property. I hope to think of giving beyond having, of abundance beyond genitivity.

In order of their anticipated production, additional volumes are planned as *The Gift of Self, The Gift of Memory, The Gift of Life, The Gift of Work, The Gift of Love, The Gift of Strangeness, The Gift of Time, The Gift of Place, The Gift of Peace, The Gift of Evil, The Gift of Law, The Gift of Authority*, and finally, perhaps, in retrospection, *The Gift of the Good.*

of the good, the circulation of goods beyond acquisition, abundance in the earth, interrupting measure, resisting property and totality.[5] An ethic of inclusion, bearing responsibility to supplement the goodness of things everywhere, however impossibly, in memory of disaster.

I speak of the good in memory of Plato, who recalled Socrates' death as a disaster.[6] I read every word he wrote in memory of such disasters, echoes of the good. Yet we do not find it congenial today to speak of the good. We prefer to speak of value, or virtue, or the good life, and God.[7] We pursue being in the neuter as if it bore no ethical exposure.[8] I hope to rehabilitate the good in relation to each of these and more, as what calls us to them and what disturbs our relation to them, what impels them in circulation. But the good is not any of them, is not a thing, or event, or being; does not belong to human beings; and is not God—though many have spoken of the good in terms of the divine. It is neither in this world nor out, inhabits no immanent or transcendent place, but is giving in abundance, beyond having, the unlimiting of every limit and the displacement of every place, exposing each creature and thing to others. The good of which I speak is not a category, does not oppose the bad or depart from the beautiful, does not war with evil, but interrupts the authority of judgment. The good is not good opposed to bad, right opposed to wrong, justice opposed to injustice.[9] It expresses what is priceless, irreplaceable, beautiful or lovely in local, contingent, heterogeneous things and kinds, worth cherishing throughout nature, all born in immeasurable exposure to others, imposing a debt to foster them and to pursue ideality, instituting the good in place. It haunts the limits of individual things in their identities and relations and of the kinds and collectives of the earth, belongs to nature everywhere, composing the circulation of goods beyond having.[10]

To speak of the good is to speak of an exposure given from no place or thing, which circulates everywhere, in every place, a giving without a giver, without a receiver, everywhere in proximity. In this sense, it is impossible to speak of the good, impossible to fix its limits, not because the good is something we cannot know but because expressing it is endless interruption. My efforts are endeavors in an ongoing struggle to understand and to participate in working to make things better where every such effort is a betrayal.[11] The struggle is to interrupt the flow of continuities and identities that do the work of the good in nature. It is a struggle to keep the gifts moving, not to let them come to rest in a better that denies its own betrayal, insisting on possessing authority.

I call exposure to the good everywhere in generosity *cherishment*; I call the impossibility of fulfilling conflicting demands everywhere *sacrifice*, wounding and disaster, betrayal without honor;[12] I call work in response to the good *plenishment*, the crossing of cherishment and sacrifice, inexhaustible exposure to the good. These make it possible to undertake and to resist binary divisions between good and bad, true and false, high and low, make it possible to give goods in circulation, unlimiting every limit, dwelling in and crossing every threshold, in the endless responsiveness in which we do ethical work, calling us to work for justice and to resist injustice by struggling against the authority of every category and identity, including every authority that would justify sacrifice.

This thought pursues Socrates' suggestion that the good grants authority to knowledge and truth, gives being to all things and kinds—giving without an origin: "This reality, then, that gives their truth to the objects of knowledge and the power of knowing to the knower, you must say is the idea of the good, and you must conceive it as being the cause *[aitian]* of knowledge, and of truth in so far as known" (Plato, *Republic*, 508e), described by Glaucon as "[a]n inconceivable beauty *[kallos]*" (509a). This beautiful idea of the good, giving knowledge and truth, and more, meets and surpasses the idea of being as its expressiveness, as *mimēsis*: sonance, radiance, and glory beyond neutrality.[13] Plato expresses it in Diotima's voice as a "nature of wondrous beauty *[phusin kalon]*" (*Symposium*, 211). The good touches the mundane with beauty, disturbs the hold of categories and distinctions, ecstatically displaces every place, answers to the profane. The good touches the earth with a call to resist endless injustices perpetrated in the name of the Good and God. For the good resists every authority, including its own. In the institution of authority, it resists authority. In betraying it betrays betrayal.

Socrates' words evoke Anaximander, who understands all things to bear the mark of the good, demanding restitution for endless injustices. All things "make reparation to one another for their injustice according to the ordinance of time."[14] This debt incurred by being is remembrance of the good, lacking any possibility of instituting justice, of inaugurating the good without injustice. All things are charged by the good with their truth and being, responsible for who and what they are, the sacrifices of their birth. The sense of *aitia* here is *for the sake of which*, responsive and responsible for and to, exposed in heterogeneity. Knowledge and truth are for the sake of the good, demanding responsiveness everywhere and always, resistant to neutrality. The giving of the good is that within each thing, for the sake of which it is and for which it moves, interrupts the fixing of its identity.

This giving, as I understand it in Plato, does not measure up the goal for which things strive, does not mark them for possession, but undercuts the inescapable wound of measure. I pursue Levinas's thought that the good does not rule over being, does not reassemble being in its place together with the authority of identity and difference, but interrupts the order of being. The giving of the good interrupts the rule of identity, undermines the domination of being and law, challenges the authority of every propriety and rule, disrupts the totality of truths. In immeasurable exposure. In proximity, in propinquity, in kind. Face to face with heterogeneity, with other beings of other kinds, touched everywhere with strangeness. The good is less encounter with the face of the singular other, something that only humans may know, than touching another, exposure to others in skin and flesh and kind, reaching beyond one's limits to others, known to every thing in every place.

I believe that the forms of thought around which philosophy has traditionally coalesced have been sites of interruption, where the good displaces the hold of work upon us. The work of human life, the promulgation of rules, the coercion of political powers, the exclusive right to own, all institute excessive authorities against which life repeatedly struggles to recapture a freedom it never had. This mobilization against the claims of authority, legitimate and otherwise, fills the world of disciplines, including Western philosophy, themselves filled with clashes of authority and propriety, with coercion and exclusion. The possibility that an authority might claim legitimacy, or that it might be resisted, both draw sustenance from the good, not a good with overarching authority, preempting this clash of power and resistance, but a good that resists authority yet demands it for its work. The space of this ceaseless struggle with possession echoes the call of the good,[15] demands from us endless responses to the injustices of every authority.

I understand beauty, truth, and justice to come from the good as gifts, displaced, unplaced, in Heidegger's words, *ek-static*: out of place. The good ecstatically places things outside themselves, interrupts the hold of being everywhere in nature, in every kind. Such a thought pursues the challenge posed by Nietzsche, then by Heidegger and Levinas, that the thought of Being, however forgotten, remains gathered neutrally in truth under the sign of *legein*.[16] It evokes several questions that follow the course of this project: What if the Western philosophic tradition, from the beginning and nearly always, gave precedence to being and truth, precedence to gathering, assembling, and having being; and what if that privilege gestured toward—betrayed—something that was neither truth nor being, but gave them forth as gifts, interrupting the gathering, deneutering neutrality? What if the Western philosophic tradition gave precedence to spirit, to gathering and assembling being in a disembodied truth; and what if that privilege gestured toward and betrayed something that was neither truth nor being nor spirit, but gave them forth as corporeal gifts? What if the Western philosophic tradition insisted on subordinating singular things to kinds, ranking kinds from high to low, so that kinds betrayed singularity as if that were extreme betrayal? And again, what if the Western philosophic tradition took the destiny of things to be owned, the destiny of human beings to own; gathering, accumulating things to possess them or their truth, instituting authority over things and other human beings, striving to possess the earth, genitively?[17]

The provocation I undertake in this volume is to explore a giving without having, without authority, ecology beyond economy, owning as owing, beyond property and possession,[18] an ethic responsive to the heterogeneous abundance of things in the earth, resistant to the genitive.

If the Western tradition, from its beginning with the Greeks, followed the trajectory I have described, instituting the rule of spirit within the gathering of being, and if this sovereignty and rule are to be understood as I have suggested, as ethical|political, or ethical|political|economic|ecological,[19] in memory of the good, then this volume undertakes a movement of the project incongruous in many ways with traditional philosophy. Yet I hope to show that this departure can be understood from within that same tradition, that the most fervent defenders of property, in their ardor, betray the abundance of earthly things beyond owning and having.

This book, however long, is shorter than the topic of property demands, which could be as long as human history. I have said much in framing the discussion here of giving and having in other places, beginning with *The Ring of Representation* through *Injustice and Restitution: The Ordinance of Time* and *Plenishment in the Earth: An Ethic of Inclusion*. My project of generosity and abundance pursues this ethic of inclusion, an ethic that includes all things, mourning its impossibility. All these different works come together in the name of the good, remembering countless injustices, sorrows and joys.

With this immeasurability before us, I undertake the impossible project of working toward the good without impeding its circulation. Endless interruptions and betrayals.

# Introduction:
# Giving and Taking in the Genitive

**ousia:** *that which is one's own, one's substance, property; being, exist-ence; the being, essence, nature* of a thing.

**parousia:** *being present, presence; arrival, advent.* (Liddell & Scott, *IGEL*)

> Property is the root of all evil: and, at the same time, property is that toward which all the activity of our modern world is directed, and that which directs the activity of the world. . . .
> Property is the root of all evil; and now all the world is busy with the distribution and protection of wealth. (Tolstoi, *WD*, 243–44)

*In the beginning* was property, so it is said. In the genitive.[1] Yours, mine, ours, theirs. Claiming divine authority. Or if not the very beginning, with darkness on the face of the deep, then soon after, on the second day, with the tree yielding fruit *after its kind*; or perhaps not long after that, on the fifth day, with every living creature, every plant and beast, *after its kind*, a kind that insists on the genitive; surely soon after that, when humanity arrived on the scene, in the greatest production known to the earth, when God created man *in his own image*. The institution of owning and having comes to pass as the appearance of an image: property and *mimēsis* to-gether, at the beginning. Genitivity as *mimēsis*. Props of property. Betrayals to which I will come in due course.

Immediately after their appearance in the genitive image of God, hu-man beings were given dominion over all things of the earth, theirs to subdue, to possess, to own, to betray. All genitive marks of property, I would say. *Mimēsis* again. Culminating in the epochal event of history: the cov-enant in which Abraham together with his progeny are to be given the land wherein they are strangers, all the land of Canaan, *for an everlasting possession*. Genitivity forever. All things in the earth become the rightful possessions of human beings, always. In the Judeo-Christian tradition, at least, if not in other traditions. Who could speak of all? Yet I would speak of at least one other in the name of philosophy—at least in a Greek-Judeo-Christian voice. And I will pay attention later to others, to the limits of my abilities and qualifications—of my *properties*. For a moment, property in Greek.

For if the arrival of which I have spoken appeared in Hebrew, something similar—or perhaps different—can be heard in Greek. The founding event of Greek philosophy—the arrival of Western, Judeo-Greek-Christian philosophy—took place as *parousia*, the arrival of what is present, *ousia*, as being, existence, substance, anything whatever, composing heaven and earth; and as property, that which is one's own, what makes something what it is. Existence arrives in the genitive. Passing properly from Greek to Latin, where *proprius*, that which is one's own, becomes *proprete*, that which one owns. Long before capitalism and Marx, if not right at the very beginning. Perhaps what we may say, in commencing here, is that the arrival of being and the earth brings with it the advent of the genitive, God's or humanity's. Being as owning, having, possessing; as accumulating, expending, consuming; perhaps also as giving, owing, responding, as responsibility, hospitality, and generosity: an advent that remains to be received.

Granted that Marx said much of this before—or something similar. Yet perhaps the having, possessing, and owning of which I speak, the universality of genitivity, are not exactly what Marx said or meant, though it would be impossible to examine property and owning without Marx, and those who followed in his name. In this way, and others, what I have to say here may be understood as "after Marx," as well as after many other Europeans, non-Europeans, and others: after Marx in acknowledging a debt, insisting or demanding that philosophy and humanity may never be the same. Genitivity again, in the name of Marx. Marx's debt; Marx's discovery; Marx's authority.

Yet to many, the debt will seem a betrayal. For I believe that in *ousia* and *proprius*—in the genitive—we find nothing in particular of base and superstructure, nothing of the supremacy of materiality—though matter is everywhere. The genitive appears in Greek philosophy frequently in relation to the soul: my soul or yours, which may travel on its journeys after my body's death. If that is what we find in Greek philosophy. The genitive cares not for body or soul, it can make either mine or yours or theirs: someone's or something's. The question is whether we can think of being, the earth, arrival, whatever, except in terms of making it or something else our own. *Know thyself!* as *Have thyself!* or *Take what you need!* Certainly not *Give what you do not have!*

In an earlier volume of this project of giving in memory of the good,[2] I read *Phaedo* as evoking the possibility that philosophy's truth of death is a lie. Socrates' truth of the life of the soul beyond the body, told in grief and mourning in the face of death, is a lie. Philosophy—always half dead—has the burden of bearing witness to death, which can never be witnessed in truth without misrepresentation—without *mimēsis*, betrayal. After Nietzsche, the truth of death—philosophy—is a lie, perhaps in an extra-moral, an extra-something sense. The greatest lie of *Phaedo* is to suggest that there is a truth of death—Socrates' death, for example. Untruth is at the heart of truth—of life and death, of everything that matters, of being beyond neutrality. Misrepresentation is at the heart of representation; the dividedness of truth is at the heart of responsibility, of the good, interrupting neutrality.

Here I would evoke a comparable movement in Greek philosophy, including *Phaedo*, where the answer to the question for those who think that death is better than life—why not then kill ourselves?—is that human beings are the property *(ktēmatōn)* of the gods, who would not like to see their possessions destroyed (Plato, *Phaedo*, 62bc). Property lies on the surface of humanity and divinity, of matter and soul, of being and knowing. On the surface and, in traditional philosophy, largely ignored.

I read *Gorgias* as reminiscent of Anaximander, where philosophy's truth—still a lie—is understood not as a truth of life, the truth|untruth that would allow us to think responsibly of death, but of property, genitivity:[3] owning, possessing, exchanging; having, taking, giving, belonging; eating, consuming, stockpiling, storing, circulating, accumulating; mine, yours, ours, theirs; generically, of possession and the earth, of authority over natural creatures and things. Economy and ecology, all terms we have heard before, frequently absent from *the metaphysical tradition*; from philosophy in the neuter. The greatest betrayal of this metaphysical tradition is its suggestion of a truth of being in the neuter, as if neutrality were essential to truth. In the name of *property*—a term I offer to gather things under the genitive— I suggest that the secret of the metaphysical tradition is that it denies that philosophy hopes to make the world its own, to gather its truth and being into its territory, to claim its authority in the name of truth.[4] I would consider the possibility that the task of philosophy has always been to own, to possess, to make the earth its own, to work in the genitive. These two tasks of philosophy, in the genitive, are to make life its own by lying about death—life and death and disaster—as if it might tell a neutral truth of death. Property and death know no neutrality.

What then if philosophy were bound up with the genitive—*my* philosophy or *his* (too seldom *hers*); with the pronouns and possessives that define every thought as property, instituting authority, what kind of philosophy might we hope to undertake? I do not doubt for a moment that I am writing philosophy, although I hope to betray a philosophy that does not hope to enclose the earth in the categories of propriety, that does not claim its own authority in the name of neutrality. Enclosure is the name of philosophy's game, the name whereby the earth became landed property.

But I am far ahead of myself. I will return to the enclosure of the commons in later chapters. Here I wish to explore more closely the link of philosophy with genitivity, later turning to other narratives of wealth and exchange. Economy and ecology, I have said, where the earth becomes human property. Economy and ecology, we may hope to say, as abundance in the earth, dispossessing genitivity.

I disavow all philosophy in the genitive: Plato's, Kant's, Heidegger's, and mine. I believe the insistence of philosophy—and literature, and art, and history—on its great names—almost always European men—is a form of owning. We own the philosophical concepts and issues we have in the name of the philosophers who most fully possess them. I would resist this genitive, possessive sense of philosophy, in the name of giving. The question is how to explore this giving without presupposing having.

This question leads back to early Greek philosophy, perhaps with Heidegger, who undertakes a movement of thought back to a beginning that never took place to institute interruptions that threaten to turn history upside down. He reads the Anaximander fragment in terms of having and giving: all things that come into being and pass away "make reparation to one another for their injustice according to the ordinance of time."[5] No having, owning, or belonging, no marks of the genitive, except as owing and restitution, in debt. Yet Heidegger's German translation, retranslated into English, barely touches the genitive: "along the lines of usage *(Brauch)*; for they let order *(Fug)* and thereby also reck belong to one another (in the surmounting) of disorder *(Un-Fug)*" (Heidegger, *AF*, 57).

We remind ourselves that in German, being is giving and belonging is having. Heidegger asks the question that underlies this entire project of giving without having.[6] Does giving presuppose having? Must one (or it) first have or own in order to give? Did God own the earth before he gave it to Adam—if he did?[7] Can we think, imagine, live together in a generosity without possession, without genitivity? Heidegger asks the question but rejects an affirmative answer. "Giving is not only giving-away; originally, giving has the sense of acceding or giving-to. Such giving lets something belong to another which properly belongs to him" (p. 43). Giving allows belonging to, properly, proprietarily. Not generosity toward or with, beyond having.

Derrida responds: "is there not a risk of inscribing this whole movement of justice under the sign of presence?" (Derrida, *SM*, 27).[8] Does Heidegger favor presence and order, does he privilege jointure in the coming to presence of disjointure? As I would rephrase this question: Does Heidegger skew the asymmetry of giving in favor of that which properly belongs, is possessed, in the genitive? In favor of those who properly possess? Is there a risk of inscribing the whole movement of justice, ethics, and the good under the sign of human property? Are belonging-together, letting-be, and releasement toward things—*sein lassen, Gelassenheit*—to be understood as allowing things to come to presence in what is proper to their own being? Properly in the genitive. Perhaps Heidegger resists the possibility that *we*, human beings, should possess these things, but not possessing and owning. They and we should possess themselves, properly. He continues to insist on having properly, on proper property, on primordial genitivity.

For example, two passages from *Being and Time* displaying genitivity:

> We are ourselves the entities to be analysed. The Being of any such entity *is in each case mine* [Tr. of a sort which any of us may call his own]. (Heidegger, *BT*, 67)

> In each case Dasein *is* its possibility, and it "has" this possibility, but not just as a property *[eigenschaftlich]*, as something present-at-hand would. . . . But only in so far as it is essentially something which can be *authentic [eigentlich]*—that is, something of its own *[zueigen]*—can it have lost itself and yet won itself. . . . [A]ny Dasein whatsoever is characterized by mineness *(Jemeinigkeit)*. (p. 68)

Here is having, owning, taking in the genitive, without giving;[9] silent on possession, yet by no means silent on genitivity. Derrida's question, the questions above, may be heard in a different register: Does Heidegger, along with almost everyone in Western life and thought, understand being-in-the-world, *Dasein*'s being there, being thrown *(Geworfenheit)*, in terms of *Jemeinigkeit*, mineness and genitivity? Thrownness and thereness are to be lived and understood in the genitive, in terms of what is *properly mine, proper to me*. Evoking the possibility, as Levinas suggests, that thrownness be understood instead as owing, giving, without having, thrown into the world in debt, face to face with others, among others without genitivity. Being here, thrown here, beyond genitivity.[10]

I follow a passage from Heidegger to Levinas, with a remainder. For although I pursue Levinas's critique of the neutral assembling of being in Heidegger, would build upon Levinas's sense of generosity and hospitality, I began with Heidegger not to dismiss him, but to present questions of giving without having that haunt the ethical critique of ontology—in debt. I mean especially to say that *even in Heidegger*, who offers a way of thinking of philosophy and the earth that I think we cannot do without, we find

subtle privileges and hierarchies—betrayals—as well as affinities with National Socialism, that mark and remark our world with that which we hope
to resist. I mean also to say that *even in Levinas*, who despite his aversion
to National Socialism, despite his ethical critique of Heidegger as betraying
responsibility and generosity, who insists that the good gives without having or possessing, who tells us repeatedly to beware of betrayal, we find
subtle privileges and hierarchies—betrayals—that mark and remark our
world with that which we hope to resist: the favor and privilege accorded
to subjectivity, thereby to humanity alone. On the one hand and the other:
"Heidegger, with the whole of Western history, takes the relation with the
Other as enacted in the destiny of sedentary peoples, the possessors and
builders of the earth" (Levinas, *TI*, 46); "Is man not the living being capable
of the longest breath in inspiration, without a stopping point, and in expi-
ration, without return?" (Levinas, *OB*, 181–82).

Knowing that my entire project is inspired by the giving of being and
the impersonal destiny of sedentary peoples, I would insist on betrayal *even
in Heidegger and Levinas and others*. In Derrida's words: "Discourses as
original as those of Heidegger and Levinas disrupt, of course, a certain
traditional humanism. In spite of the differences separating them, they
nonetheless remain profound humanisms *to the extent that they do not
sacrifice sacrifice*" (Derrida, *EW*, 276).[11]

Even in Levinas. And others. Perhaps everywhere we find a genitive:
Heidegger's, Levinas's, Derrida's, mine, or yours, we insist on owning or
possessing that which cannot, must not, be owned; or if owned, possessed,
must be cared for with endless responsibility, given away. Responsibility in
Levinas is boundless, beyond limit. "The infinity of the infinite lives in
going backwards. The debt increases in the measures that it is paid" (Levinas,
*OB*, 12); "The more I answer the more I am responsible; the more I approach the neighbor with which I am encharged the further away I am.
This debit which increases is infinity as an infinition of the infinite, as
glory" (p. 93).[12] Being is generosity, not possession. Face to face, as Levinas
says, with the neighbor. In exposure and proximity. Exposure *(exposition)*
and proximity are ethical terms that bear no marks of genitivity, of possession or propriety. I do not have or own a neighbor—or my lover or my
child. I live with them in proximity, exposed to them, responsible to and for
them, where this exposure—*exposition*—is expression, saying, generosity.

Yet property is said to belong to human beings in the very nature of
being there. Expressed as clearly as possible by Hegel: the destiny of things
is to be owned, that of human beings to own.[13] In more contemporary
terms, the destiny of human beings is to possess and claim rights vis-à-vis
other human beings; the destiny of all else, natural things and creatures,
parts and properties of human beings, is to be claimed.[14]

I understand this destiny to be avowed under what Bataille calls the *curse*, where humanity insists not just on possessing what human beings need to live, even to live well, but the right, the necessity, the obligation to own, to possess, to have, in the genitive, artifacts, things, creatures, everything in the earth. Humanity marks its superiority in the inferiority of natural things—the curse—thereby cursing itself, throwing itself down into the abjection of its nature.[15] I hope to examine in detail the ways in which the destiny of natural things is to be owned even where nature itself is understood to entail no moral or political rules. Slavery is by no means irrelevant, nor the domestication of animals. Humanity marks its own abjection in the domination of everything nonhuman, marks human freedom in the unfreedom of everything nonhuman, thereby mocking human unfreedom.

The point on which I am insisting is that the curse is imposed in the genitive, that genitivity defines humanity's relation to the earth under the curse. The curse is ours. Sovereignty, though NOTHING (Bataille says), is ours—or "OURS." More of this later.

I return from this interval under the curse to the theme with which I hope to conclude this introduction: the possibility of resisting the genitive. I return to Levinas's resistance to possession, virtually the only such resistance in contemporary philosophy that goes back to the pervasive link of being and truth with having. In some ways beyond Marx, who remains Hegelian in insisting on genitivity, on putting one's will into things through one's own labor. Levinas resists property in the genitive almost as far as it can be resisted. Though perhaps he does not resist humanism.

He speaks of generosity and hospitality—of giving; of a giving without possession, perhaps without having. At the heart of the thought of being is generosity beyond possession: "impassive contemplation is defined by gift, by the abolition of inalienable property" (Levinas, *TI*, 75); "I am at home with myself in the world because it offers itself to us or resists possession" (p. 38). In the extreme, giving and the good resist even the overturning of possession, which retains the genitive—for example, two glorious passages that resist the ownership of the earth but insist on genitivity: "Freedom comes from an obedience to Being: it is not man who possesses freedom; it is freedom that possesses man" (p. 45); "This we know: the earth does not belong to man, man belongs to the earth."[16] Almost alone in philosophical writing, Levinas considers the possibility that having, owning, and possessing have occupied a place of honor in the thought of being, that gathering and assembling being in truth are profoundly territorial, that the mark of *legein* is the genitive. In the destiny of sedentary peoples. In the whole of Western philosophy, of Greek-Judeo-Christian life and history. In the history of the earth—if any are competent to tell. I hold this thought in abeyance for later discussion with hunter-gathering-foraging peoples in mind.[17]

As stake is generosity, giving without having, owning, or possessing; living for the sake of the good, in exposure and proximity. Resisting genitivity, Levinas insists repeatedly, in the name of the face—I insist, beyond the face—interrupting the neuter and the genitive. "The face resists possession, resists my powers" (*TI*, 197). Humanity's being in the world insists on genitivity, philosophy demands possession, requires property, reasoning is owning: "in knowledge there appears the notion of . . . seizing something and making it one's own, . . . an activity which *appropriates* and *grasps* the otherness of the known. . . . *Auffassen (understanding)* is also, and always has been, a *Fassen (gripping)*" (Levinas, *EFP*, 76). Being becomes present by appropriating and grasping the other. As I would put it, the goal of knowledge is to make the other one's own, to make the properties of the thing one's property.

Levinas responds with responsibility, proximity and exposure, destitution and vulnerability in the face of the other.

> Prior to any particular expression and beneath all particular expressions, which cover over and protect with an immediately adopted face or countenance, there is the nakedness and destitution of the expression as such, that is to say, extreme exposure, defencelessness, vulnerability itself. (*EFP*, 82)

> The Other becomes my neighbour precisely through the way the face summons me, calls for me, begs for me, and in so doing recalls my responsibility, and calls me into question.
> . . . as if I had to answer for the other's death even before *being*. (p. 83)

He speaks of a responsibility beyond possession and property, before being, having, and owning, giving to the other in the face, exposed by proximity. I insist on the face and skin of every thing, on exposure and proximity throughout the earth, resist holding the face hostage to subjectivity. More of that later. Here the priority of responsibility, exposure, proximity, and vulnerability to being is a priority that disrupts every claim of possession, undercuts every genitive. The only genitive—perhaps no genitive at all—is responsibility for my neighbor, to the other, and the others, a genitive that is not mine to own, not even mine to be, but mine to bear. Genitivity is a relationship of responsivity. Still, perhaps, bearing too Hegelian a tone, reminiscent of the master. "It is the responsibility of a hostage which can be carried to the point of being substituted for the other person and demands an infinite subjection of subjectivity" (p. 84).

I understand the task Levinas sets himself in *Totality and Infinity*— unlike many of his other writings—as tracing a movement from being to responsibility, from totality to infinity, in and from traditional proprietary discourses of being and knowing, in the genitive. It is a movement from the genitive of the Ego that insists that being and knowing are *Mine* to an ethical relation to the Other, still perhaps in the genitive—*yours, hers,* or *his*—given over to generosity and hospitality, to giving rather than having or owning.

A crucial moment of this movement, explicitly addressing possession and owning, is the dwelling *(la demeure),* reminiscent of the *oikos*—the economy and ecology that form the core of this discussion. "Concretely speaking the dwelling is not situated in the objective world, but the objective world is situated by relation to my dwelling" (Levinas, *TI,* 153). I interpose a brief interruption to gather *oikos* in its betrayal, linking dwelling, the household and household management, with slavery, domestication, and the subordination of women.

> he who is by nature not his own but another's man, is by nature a slave; and he may be said to be another's man who, being a human being, is also a possession. (Aristotle, *Politics,* 1254a)

> Where then there is such a difference as that between soul and body, or between men and animals . . . the lower sort are by nature slaves, and it is better for them as for all inferiors that they should be under the rule of a master. (1254b)

> A question may indeed be raised, whether there is any excellence at all in a slave beyond those of an instrument and of a servant . . . . A similar question may be raised about women and children, whether they too have excellences; . . . excellence of character belongs to all of them; but the temperance of a man and of a woman, or the courage and justice of a man and of a woman, are not, as Socrates maintained, the same; the courage of a man is shown in commanding, of a woman in obeying. (1259b-1260b)

Ecology and economy in the *oikos* are always under the rule of authority, the property of the head of the household—though Aristotle agrees with Plato that the owner must not act for his own good but for the good of others, that the shepherd's responsibility is to act for the good of his sheep. How easy to forget![18]

I return to the place of dwelling in Levinas, where the betrayal is betrayed, if not in its full abjection. Dwelling appears repeatedly in the genitive. "Man abides in the world as having come to it from a private domain, from being at home with himself, to which at each moment he can retire. He does not come to it from an intersideral space where he would already be in possession of himself. . . . He does not find himself brutally

cast forth and forsaken in the world" (Levinas, *TI*, 152). Being there, belonging to a world is, for an ego, a consciousness, in the genitive, not an
ego given possession of self from the first, but dwelling in a private domain.
The world is available to me in virtue of a place I can call my own. Not
perhaps possessing self and things as subjects and objects, but a more
intimate dwelling of husband and wife, man and woman, in the home.
Genitality as genitivity. Always at the expense of women and children in the
home—together with animals and slaves.

In the name of dwelling, where property gains its intimate meaning,
we find the feminine given over to the task of hospitality. Always for men.

> To dwell is not the simple fact of the anonymous reality of a being cast
> into existence as a stone one casts behind oneself; it . . . answers to a
> hospitality, an expectancy, a human welcome. . . . Those silent comings
> and goings of the feminine being whose footsteps reverberate the secret
> depths of being are not the turbid mystery of the animal. (Levinas, *TI*,
> 156)

Familiarity and intimacy resist possession and authority, resist the reign of
genitivity—still betraying other genitives, other authorities. For dwelling,
the habitation, home, is already human, a welcome and intimacy with someone—not an animal or stone. And familiarity belongs to human beings
among human beings—in the feminine, history's task for women. In the
genital.

Irigaray responds that "The beloved woman would be she who keeps
herself available in this way. Offering to the other what he can put to his own
use? Opening the path of his return to himself, of his open future? Giving
him back time?" (Irigaray, *FC*, 201–2). I respond that the woman, the femi-
nine, remains in the genitive—more truthfully, in the genital|genitive. Inti-
macy is for the man, the man's. The feminine is welcome, hospitality, not for
the woman but for the man, the man's. Not the animal's, the cat's. Not the
animal or cat, dispossessing genitivity. Not the stone, who some say knows
nothing of genitivity, perhaps knows nothing at all. I hold stones in abeyance,
interrupting briefly to insist that we are in proximity to stones, exposed in
proximity, as they are exposed to us. Expressive in proximity.[19]

May we ask Levinas, who forcibly resists the neuter, to resist the genitive
in the gesture of welcome, hospitality, and giving? To resist the authority
of the face? "The face . . . is not the disclosure of an impersonal Neuter
*(Neutre)*, but *expression*" (Levinas, *TI*, 51). May we understand expression
as giving without having? What one does not and cannot have, interrupting
every propriety, crossing every border, including the borders between man
and woman, human and animal? No one owns expression, it exceeds every

authority. Expression is *exposition*, exposure and proximity: betrayal, debt, responsibility, owing, giving beyond having. Never giving to, never giving by, never owned or possessed or had, even or especially in the home.

I hope to take a step with Levinas (not) (beyond), who retains the genitive in the home in a gesture that insists on generosity. Still in the feminine. Still in the genitive for men. "The home that founds possession . . . refers us to its essential interiority, . . . welcome in itself—the feminine being" (*TI*, 157). Not the possession of tangible goods but possession founded on hospitality and interiority—still in the genitive|genital, still the feminine being for the masculine. I would elicit the possibility of a generosity neither in the home nor out, neither the woman's nor the man's, neither human nor inhuman. Giving without having, had by no one and by nothing, still giving. As general economy.[20] In the *oikos*. Levinas insists, however gloriously, on restricted economy. "The access to the world is produced in a movement that starts from the utopia of the dwelling and traverses a space to effect a primordial grasp, to seize and to take away. . . . This grasp operated on the elemental is labor" (p. 158). Returning us to the hand, supremely authoritative in the genitive. Man takes possession of animals and things by labor through the hand. Genitivity has its proper organ, the genitivity of genitivity, possessed in the hand. "Possession is accomplished in taking-possession or labor, the destiny of the hand. . . . Labor is the very *en-ergy* of acquisition" (p. 159). I am reminded of Heidegger's hand. "Only a being who can speak, that is, think can have hands and can handily achieve works of handicraft" (Heidegger, *WCT*, 357).[21] The hand is the hand in virtue of the gift of language. The gift of language is given to Us, we Humans, thereby also giving us a Hand. The Hand differs from all grasping organs by an abyss of essence—The Hand that authorizes our dominion over the earth. The gift and the hand are Ours, in the genitive, belong to humans. The genitive is taken by Us even where the hand does not take.

Derrida says of Heidegger's and Levinas's humanism that they do not sacrifice sacrifice. I would say something similar of giving and taking.[22] Heidegger and Levinas ask us to think of giving without taking but do not give up taking, do not abandon the genitive, the propriety of property, the authority of sacrifice. Giving as sacrifice remains within the rule of authority even where it would resist neutrality. Even within Heidegger's and Levinas's revulsion against the grasping hand, there remains the hand and body that possess authority in the home, *my* home in the genitive. Interiority is genitivity, thereby making exteriority mine as well—a Hegelian movement. "The body is my possession according as my being maintains itself in a home at the limit of interiority and exteriority. The extraterritoriality of a home conditions the very possession of my body" (Levinas, *TI*,

162). Inhabiting and dwelling undermine the grasp of the genitive, but they remain genitive, bound without betrayal to possession. I would add that they remain genital, bound by betrayal to sexual difference. The genitivity of genitality. What would we expect from so territorial a language, realms to occupy and make our own?

"The Other—the absolutely other—paralyzes possession, which he contests by his epiphany in the face. . . . I welcome the Other who presents himself in my home by opening my home to him" (Levinas, *TI*, 171). I insist on paralyzing paralysis to an extreme where the Other—every other, absolutely other[23]—dispossesses possession, gives what it does not have, betrays the authority it cannot avoid, where we give and are given—given in giving—what can never be had. I welcome the Other where I may possess neither place nor home. In proximity and exposure to the Other, any and every other, the *I* ceases to possess and own itself, ceases to be *myself*, in the genitive. The *I*, the *self*, remains a self, an agent, an ethical agent in the work it does for others, giving in response to others, in responsibility and debt, interrupting genitivity.

Giving without having. Living without authority. Generosity beyond genitivity. Gender beyond genitality. Genitivity|genitality as genealogy. All dreams. Beginning and ending with the dream of giving without having, of being without owning. As Derrida says, ghosts of Marx.

# CHAPTER 1

## Stage Properties

*To learn to live*: a strange watchword. Who would learn? From whom? To teach to live, but to whom? Will we ever know? Will we ever know how to live and first of all what "to learn to live" means? (Derrida, *SM*, xvii)

> It would be easy, too easy, to show that such a hospitality without reserve . . . is the impossible itself, and that this *condition of possibility* of the event is also its *condition of impossibility*, . . . but it would be just as easy to show that without this experience of the impossible, one might as well give up on both justice and the event. (p. 65)

Of property, one may say that Derrida says very little. Even reading Marx. Of the possessive marks of life and experience: blood, sex, kin, class, food, desire, and power. The props of property. More of these later. More of the possessions that make humans human. In the genitive. Insisting on authority. Sacrifices in memory of Marx. For the moment, I explore the possibility that in saying little of property, Derrida speaks of nothing more, writes endlessly of having and owning, betrays the wealth of possessions that mark life and experience with genitivity.[1] The specters of property in the name of Marx. I approach the subject of property and genitivity obliquely, Derrida's obliqueness and mine, hoping to betray the multifarious marks of genitivity. Props of property. Genies of genitivity.

I echo the words in which Derrida suggests that perhaps, in almost never speaking of sexual difference, Heidegger speaks of it always, speaks of nothing more than sex. Together with "all the philosophers in the tradition who have done so, from Plato to Nietzsche, who for their part were irrepressible on the subject" (Derrida, *G1*, 66). Perhaps also on the subject of property, possession, ownership, genitivity. In speaking irrepressibly on sex. Derrida links genitivity and sex, speaking of Heidegger and the possibility that "[e]very proper body of one's own is sexed, and there is no *Dasein* without its own body" (p. 75). The genitive together with the genital. Posterity

13

and genitivity. Property and the propriety of sex, the sacrificial subjects of life and death. Production and reproduction.

Where Derrida speaks of property and life he speaks of lineage, descent, and blood. "[I]t is most often a question of *the property and proper nature of life [la propriété de la vie]*, of its inheritance, and of its generations (the scientific, juridical, economic, and political problems of the so-called human genome, gene therapy, organ transplants, surrogate mothers, frozen embryos, and so forth)" (Derrida, *SM*, 184). A matter of life and death, production and reproduction. For human beings—mortals—matters of generations, flesh and blood, sex and sacrifice. Genitivity as life itself, linked sacrificially with flesh and blood, sex, class, and kin—with generations and genealogy. Genies of genealogy.

In *Specters of Marx*, Derrida alludes to blood in two ways, both linked with genitivity. One appears in relation to ghosts, who "can never *present themselves* in flesh and blood" (Derrida, *SM*, 21). Or so it would seem. The flesh and blood of property, of kin and kind. The other allusion appears in relation to the "messianic opening to what is coming" (p. 65): "the domestic contracts of any welcoming power (family, State, nation, territory, native soil or blood, language, culture in general, even humanity)" (p. 65). Derrida suggests that nation, blood, language, and culture may be—or are claimed to be—fully present like possessions, held in the hand, reserved for use, instituted with authority. And he returns to them later in the context of inter-ethnic wars "of community, the nation-State, sovereignty, borders, native soil and blood" (p. 82). All identities claimed, possessed—the subject of my discussion here: owned as if they might be grasped in hand, linked with other spectral presences. Domestic contracts. Public and private authority. Class and posterity, joined with blood, sex, kin, desire, and power, always in the genitive.

Almost everywhere that Derrida names *property* with its proper name, *propriété*, he speaks of *le propre*, the proper of property and the name, the institution of authority.[2] His first reference to property in *Specters of Marx* is to "the *disparate itself*" as "a sameness without property" (Derrida, *SM*, 17), which may hold itself together without propriety and gathering, without authority, perhaps without sacrifice and betrayal. I hope to explore the disparate itself as property, disowned, dispossessed, betrayed, the props of property interrupting the genitive with its authority. This leads to another example, Derrida's reference to the "little connection," "known to Shakespeare" between "money, the most general form of property, and personal peculiarity" (p. 41), alluding to the most proper of all properties, acquired under the name of *ousia*: substance as that which has, possesses, owns whatever composes its identity. The authority of ontology, instituted in the genitive, returning in Derrida as renunciation, renouncing property, any right in general (p. 65), and the specter, named in Greek as *epekeina tes ousias*, "beyond the phenomenon or beyond being" (p. 100). With a twist of memory we may understand *ousia* as property, in the genitive, *epekeina* as beyond property on the stage of being, the props of property as *epekeina*, otherwise and beyond. *Ek-stasis. L'écarte. Mimēsis.* Beyond alienation. With ethics and politics in mind, together with sex and blood, and more, the props of property beyond. *Mimēsis* interrupting genitivity, betraying the rule of the father who insists on owning his works forever, no matter how widely they may circulate.[3] Bound without gathering, servitude, or sacrifice to property as *appropriation*; to renunciation as *expropriation*; to commerce as circulation beyond possession. "What we have said here or elsewhere about *exappropriation* (the radical contradiction of all 'capital,' of all property or appropriation, as well as all the concepts that depend on it . . .) does not justify any bondage. It is, if we may say so, exactly the opposite. Servitude binds (itself) to appropriation" (p. 90). Subjection binds itself to genitivity.

The radical contradiction appears as property itself, owned and possessed, authorized, appropriated; always expropriated, betrayed, *epekeina*, disparate in and toward itself. The disparate contradicts itself as property. Owed, in debt, an obligation everywhere to genitivity. Property always arrives on the stage. Propped up, standing upright, performing, assumed. My property, not yours. Mine, mine, mine: in Marx, Derrida says, "the body proper of the I, the mine, my property *(als de Meinige, als Mein Eigentum)*" (*SM*, 129). Propriety at the core of class, linked with blood, sex, kin, desire, and power, devoted to posterity, to what is to come. Center and margins in the genitive. In the name of the father.

Which again may be to say that in speaking so little of property, Derrida speaks endlessly of it, of possession, ownership, and sacrifice. Of genitivity. Together with sex, reproduction and genitality. Haunted by specters of blood, kin, and class, matters of justice, ethical and political matters of life and death. That is, of women and children, the foundation of posterity—I mean the objects of property and sex, production and reproduction.[4] I hold sex and sacrifice in abeyance for a while to speak of property, keeping women and children in mind, for most of history owned by men, betrayed by men, posterity as the genitivity of men. I hope to speak as a scholar, a philosopher, of the arrival of property, echoing *Hamlet*, speak to the ghosts of the impropriety of property, the *epekeina tes ousias*. Still in the genitive. "Thou art a scholar; speak to it Horatio"; "There are more things in heaven and earth, Horatio, / Than are dreamt of in your philosophy." *Your, my, our* philosophy. Philosophy and politics in the genitive: geophilosophy and geopolitics. The authority of philosophy. Rochelle reminds us of more things of which to dream.[5]

For a while I would dream of the advent of property.[6] Genealogically. Perhaps of specters, ghosts, of property, if dreams are disincarnate. If *parousia* is disincarnate. Or carnate, the arrival of the incarnation. I read *Specters of Marx* as an extended meditation on *parousia* as arrival, as event. In the name of Marx, however strange that may be. In the name of property, however stranger. The *parousia* of the being that arrives, the ghostly visitor whose presence is proclaimed, the annunciation and the promise, name the to and fro, the coming and going, interruption and betrayal, of one's own, one's property, nature, authority. In Greek, one's being arrives in coming and going, arrives as genitivity. The *ousia* that arrives is property, possessor or possessed. However strange. Arrives a stranger, *xenos*. The enigmatic subject of my discussion, interrupting the abject sacrificial movement of destiny. I would speak of the strangeness of property without time, interrupting Derrida's insistence on the *to come* as time, the promise as descent in kin and kind. Anachrony beyond time, not another, phantasmic time. I hold this strange thought in abeyance.

I interrupt to draw upon two moments of the spectral text where Derrida does not speak the name of property but may, perhaps, be speaking of nothing else, nothing but the being of *ousia* known to us as property. In the name of Heidegger rather than Marx. Having, possessing, owning as stockpiling and reserving, holding for posterity, together with the propriety of the gift.

> What the one does not have, what the one therefore does not have to give away, but what the one gives to the other, . . . is to leave to the other this accord with himself that is *proper* to him *(ihm eignet)* and gives him presence. If one still translates *Dikē* with this word "justice," and if, as Heidegger does, *Dikē* is thought on the basis of Being as presence, then it would turn out that "justice" is first of all, and finally, and especially *properly*, the jointure of the accord: the proper jointure to the other given by one who does not have it. (Derrida, *SM*, 26–27)

The just jointure as property, given as the gift one does not possess, the sacrifice one does not own. As Heidegger asks and Derrida responds: "Can it give what it doesn't have?" (Heidegger, *AF*, 43),[7] speaking of lingering awhile, perhaps of the It of *es gibt*. Leading Derrida to ask, perhaps a different question, perhaps the same: "is it possible to give what one doesn't have? . . . Heidegger's answer: giving rests here only in presence *(Anwesen)*. . . . The offering consists in leaving: in leaving to the other what properly belongs to him or her" (*SM*, 26). Given in an untimely and sacrificial welcome that returns us to gathering and collecting, marks of property. "Has not Heidegger, as he always does, skewed the asymmetry *in favor* of what he in effect interprets as the possibility of *favor* itself, of the accorded favor, namely, of the accord that gathers or collects while harmonizing *(Versammlung, Fug),* . . . is there not a risk of inscribing this whole movement of justice under the sign of presence . . . ?" (pp. 27–28). Arriving as property, improperly, *Un-Fug,* the thought I would interpose here between the favor Heidegger insists on and the favor Derrida refuses. The impropriety, disjointure, *Un-Fug, ek-stasis,* of property. Interrupting the authority of what lingers awhile. Propriety as prop, on the stage, insisting on gathering, stockpiling, fixing in place, holding in reserve, grasping for sacrifice. Insisting on what cannot be owned in the name of *parousia,* of the event. Insisting on having with authority, on genitivity. Property without props, without *mimēsis.* As if property could circulate without money and as if printing money might be anything but *mimēsis,* anything but the spooking of wealth. As if authority might be anything but *mimēsis,* anything but personification, genitivity, and representation. The coming of the event as real property. Otherwise than giving without gathering, without stockpiling against the passage of time. Giving as interruption, interrupting gathering as presence.[8] Linked to *parousia,* the advent of the event as justice. "Awaiting without horizon of the wait, awaiting what one does not expect yet or any longer, hospitality without reserve, welcoming salutation accorded in advance to the absolute surprise of the *arrivant* from whom or from which one will not ask anything in return" (p. 65). The impossible itself as hospitality without reserve. Relinquishing any right to property. A hospitality, a giving, that cannot be thought or lived—originarily or finally—without genitivity or authority, I would say without domestic and other contracts. The impossible itself as impossible property, giving property that one does not have or own or possess.

I hope to dream of the impossible without property. Possibly not easy at all. Life without genitivity. Resistance to neutrality. As sacrificing sacrifice, betraying betrayal.[9] I hope to interrupt possession and property by sacrificing sacrifice against all instituted authority. By *mimēsis* as betrayal, interruption, beyond humanity. Giving for the sake of the good knows no authority, betrays authority, resists genitivity. Especially humanity's authority.

I return from this interruption in the name of sacrifice—a name betraying endless betrayals—to genitivity, keeping blood, sex, kin, food, class, desire, and power in the foreground of propriety, the props of property. I turn to the question of what comes after—after the subject, after Marx, after authority, after property and genitivity. In the name of Marx, I ask what comes after genitivity, if we beware the propriety of the subject who possesses property, who implicitly or explicitly owns, or insists on owning up to propriety, possessing either to stockpile and reserve for use, or to sacrifice, consume, and devour. Betraying the advent, the *parousia* of property as if it might be owned, possessed, or consumed with propriety rather than always arriving and departing like a ghost. Betraying and betrayed.

Returning to *Specters of Marx*. Attending to the arrival of genitivity. "If it—learning to live—remains to be done, it can happen only between life and death. . . . And this being-with specters would also be, not only but also, a *politics* of memory, of inheritance, and of generations" (Derrida, *SM*, xviii–xix). Generations descending along sacrificial lines of blood, kin, sex, desire, and class, women and children especially, held as property. Arriving in the advent of property. "Beyond all living present" (p. xix). Betraying what is to come. "This question ['whither?'] *arrives*, if it arrives, it questions with regard to what will come in the future-to-come. Turned toward the future, going toward it, it also comes from it, it proceeds *from [previent de] the future*. It must therefore exceed any presence as presence to itself" (p. xix). Property exceeding any presence to itself, any identity. Consuming and stockpiling as excessive circulation. As betrayal.

Derrida speaks of this excess in *Specters of Marx* as the circulation of ghosts. I speak of it as the circulation of property, capital and capitalism, the specter of genitivity but also the possessedness of the specter. The props of property, the *mimēsis* of genitivity, the betrayal of authority, as the genitivity of ghosts. The fiction of living well is haunted by genies, together with the props of property. All in the family, descending along lines of genealogy, from generation to generation:[10] domination and violence.[11] Another name for the event.

As I said, *parousia*. The advent of property as *ousia*, hauntology. "Repetition *and* first time, but also repetition *and* last time, since the singularity of any *first time* makes of it also a *last time*. Each time it is the event itself, a first time is a last time. Altogether other. Staging for the end of history. Let us call it a *hauntology*" (Derrida, *SM*, 10). The arrival of philosophy together with property. With the possibility that philosophy like property never arrives. On which Derrida takes a stand: "A traditional scholar does not believe in ghosts—nor in all that could be called the virtual space of spectrality. There has never been a scholar who, as such, does not believe in the sharp distinction between the real and the unreal, the actual and the inactual, the living and the non-living, being and non-being" (p. 11). The philosopher takes the props of property for the thing itself, as if it were not haunted by ghosts, as if they were not props, as if without betrayal. The philosopher insists on the genitive without geophilosophy, as if it were not haunted by geopolitics, insists on authority.

We return to the gift that arrives rather than the endless giving without having. "What is this gift of the *Dikē*? What is this justice beyond right? Does it come along simply to compensate a wrong, restitute something due, to do right or do justice? Does it come along simply to render justice or, on the contrary, to give *beyond* the due *(au-delà du devoir)*, the debt, the crime, or the fault?" (p. 25). Does justice arrive to be held in hand, together with women and children, in the home? Or does it circulate too quickly, too exuberantly, to hold, to hold on to, to stockpile, even to consume? To give beyond authority?

These are questions to be asked in other ways: What is it to sacrifice sacrifice, to resist humanism's authority? Is it restitution, retribution, restoration? Is it something we may hope to achieve, to possess, to give forth with authority? Or might it be the disjointure, the *Un-Fug*, of which Heidegger speaks in the name of property, giving what one does not have, giving what one does not have to give, giving without genitivity or authority? As if capitalism might evoke the advent, arrival, of the possibility of another humanity and another economy, without having, possessing, or owning, including self, family, kin, knowledge, truth, life, and death. All lived, circulated, dwelled in for a while, without authority, without genitivity, without finality. Giving as the arrival of what never arrives. As property. Unowned yet owed, in debt. Derrida insists that giving is not jointure or lingering, but disjointure and impropriety, the props of property, always improper, always betraying and betrayed.

Including every inheritance, every lineage, descent, and genealogy, resisting genitivity. One must inherit the earth in the form of betrayal. And its betrayal. Which we might say that Marx and Engels, together with Heidegger, Levinas, and countless others refuse. Sacrifice Marx. And with that sacrifice sacrifice sacrifice. Betray betrayal. As inheritance, genealogy and genitivity. For humans. Perhaps betraying Derrida's obligatory gesture, however messianic, in the name of property, without possession. Disowning owning in the genitive.

> That we *are* heirs does not mean that we *have* or that we *receive* this or that, some inheritance that enriches us one day with this or that, but that the *being* of what we are *is* first of all inheritance, whether we like it or know it or not.... To bear witness to what we *are* insofar as we *inherit*, and that—here is the circle, here is the chance, or the finitude—we inherit the very thing that allows us to bear witness to it. (Derridas, *SM*, 54)

We are heirs, bear witness to our inheritance, insofar as we betray it. We do not have or receive, do not own the inheritance, yet still we bear witness to it, constituting the being of what and who we are. Who and which we? We humans? We Europeans? We men? As patrimony? Prodigal sons indeed. In the genitive. Assuming the props of history as one's own.[12]

Those who would be heirs to economic liberalism, even in resistance, must bear witness to what they inherit, must assume the inheritance of Marx as mourning and betrayal. I am not sure of others. I think I must assume that inheritance. Refusing to be its heir, its son, owning up to it as mine. I would disown the very thing that marks it as an inheritance—having and receiving. Without the genitive, therefore receiving nothing. Bearing witness by disowning. Owning property by disowning. Betraying genitivity.

The impossibility that gives responsibility is giving without taking—the impossibly impossible condition of possibility. The heart of life and experience, without which one might as well give up on both justice and the event. The condition of ethics and politics as the experience of the impossible—by no means an impossible experience—resisting and betraying genitivity. Speaking of Nietzsche, Bataille, Blanchot, and Klossowski—but not Marx—Foucault says something similar, something perhaps essential to thought in French—I would say geophilosophy, though that remains in abeyance. "What most struck and fascinated me about them is the fact that they didn't have the problem of constructing systems, but of having direct, personal experiences" (Foucault, *RM*, 30); "Nietzsche, Bataille, and Blanchot . . . try through experience to reach that point of life which lies as close as possible to the impossibility of living, which lies at the limit or extreme" (p. 31). Experiences that transform life itself. Ethics and politics. At the limit or extreme of law or life or property. The genitive in the extreme. Betraying life itself.

Who would wish to deny that Marx and Marxism evoke such impossibilities of experience *and make them possible*!? Which is to say in a different register that the end of Marxism is no end at all, but a beginning, facing another impossible arrival on the stage surrounded by props. As property. Another impossibility. Always arriving. Betraying the genitive.

Derrida contrasts this impossible impossibility with something entirely different, duty as necessity, repeated twice. As he says of Kojève, with Fukuyama in mind, perhaps also Marx and Engels. Endlessly repeating the curse, sacrificing everything not human—including many human beings—without a thought of betrayal. Another interruption, insisting on its *mimēsis*. "According to Kojève, the final stage of communism in the postwar United States does indeed, as it must, reduce man to animality. . . . An extravagant description, not because it compares man to animals, but in the first place because it puts an imperturbable and arrogant ignorance to work" (Derrida, *SM*, 71). Sacrificing animals without questioning its necessity, without a hint of sacrificing sacrifice. "And provisionally, but with regret, we must leave aside here the nevertheless indissociable question of what is becoming of so-called 'animal' life, the life and existence of 'animals' in this history. This question has always been a serious one, but it will become massively unavoidable" (p. 85). Humanity appears in the genitive without a thought of post-genitivity. " 'Post-historical man *doit* . . . ,' writes Kojève. . . . *Whatever may be the case concerning the modality of the con-*

*tent* of this 'devoir,' . . . there is an 'it is necessary' for the future. . . . *this 'it is necessary' is necessary and that is the law"* (p. 73). It is necessary, it is the law, to sacrifice—to stockpile and consume—property, everything we own that is sacrificed so that we may have our humanity. Always in the genitive. So that we may grasp our future. Always betrayed.

I insist on another arrival, another betrayal, insist on giving up genitivity, giving away its authority. Post-sacrifice is sacrificing sacrifice, still sacrifice, resisting its authority. Post-authority and post-genitivity still are authority and genitivity, betray their authority and genitivity. *Post*-arrives as the arrival that never arrives, that never institutes authority, that never claims possession. The impossible arrives as genitivity, betraying genitivity.

I do not think of arrival as uniquely historical, directed toward the future. I struggle with holding and circulating things and creatures of the earth as property. Impossibly. Derrida's words, keeping betrayal in mind: "this onto-theo-archeo-teleology [in Hegel, Marx, and Heidegger] locks up, neutralizes, and finally cancels historicity" (Derrida, *SM*, 80). Locks up by owning, possessing, insisting on property. Without impropriety. Owning, stockpiling, locking up the truth of history against the testimony of the present. I allude to the plagues of the new world order and the threat of another, newer world order against which we are constantly being warned at the moment of victory. Plagues of humanity, plagues of property and economy, plagues of the earth. Plagues of genitivity. Plagues of betrayal. Plagues and ghosts.[13]

I return to the genitivity of Marx. We, all of us, Derrida says repeatedly, are heirs. "Whether they know it or not, all men and women, all over the earth, are today to a certain extent the heirs of Marx and Marxism" (*SM*, 91). All men and women, all over the earth. Marx's heirs, Marxism's posterity, genitivity. Heirs of Marx and Marxism, of the Enlightenment. Heirs of Heidegger? Derrida says so frequently. From this moment, philosophy must and will be heir of Heidegger, Heidegger's posterity. Henceforth that will be our destiny. Under the heading of Marx the father's genitivity: "whether we like it or not, whatever consciousness we have of it, we cannot not be its heirs. There is no inheritance without a call to responsibility" (p. 91). No inheritance without responsibility. No life or experience without genitivity. No property without debt and call. All questions of how to inherit, as if it were impossible to refuse the debt, to disown the inheritance.[14]

The spirit of Marxism, of past, present, and future philosophy, the spirit that Derrida insists we are haunted by, the ghosts that keep returning and never arrive, the insistence of the non-arrival, is of what can never be owned: impossibility itself. As responsibility. Always seized and held as if owned and possessed. Always betrayed. Even by Derrida. "Deconstruction has never had any sense of interest, in my view at least, except as a radicalization, which is to say also *in the tradition* of a certain Marxism, in a certain *spirit of Marxism*. . . . But a radicalization is always indebted to the very thing it radicalizes" (Derrida, *SM*, 92). I suspect that readers may understand this debt as something rather than nothing, as property rather than as impropriety, as instituting rather than betraying. I insist on Derrida's insistence that to inherit is not to receive or have. I would say it is to give in memory, bearing witness, giving beyond return, a hospitality without reserve, disowning every property, betraying every tradition in the genitive. Property without a genitive.

How would you think of Marx himself and his bequest, betraying the absence of the genitive?

> *Specters of Marx*: The title of this lecture would commit one to speak first of all about Marx. About Marx himself. About his testament or his inheritance. (Derrida, *SM*, 96)

> The century of "Marxism" will have been that of the techno-scientific and effective decentering of the earth, of geopolitics, of the *anthropos* in its onto-theological identity. . . .
> But the specters of Marx come on stage from the other side. They are named according to the other path of the genitive—and this other grammar says more than grammar. The specters *of* Marx are also his. (p. 98)

Worrying on both sides of the genitive, about stockpiling, reserving, holding, owning, consuming and destroying property—things and creatures of the earth, other human beings—and of haunting, binding, betraying, what constitutes us and others as Us and Others.[15] Kin, kinds, class; always in sex and blood; intimately linked with power. Ghosts may not be forceful enough to produce this much sex and blood. Property beyond property and propriety: *epekeina tes ousias*. Sacrificing sacrifice. Philosophy as the hunt for the specter.[16] "The specter, as its name indicates, is the *frequency* of a certain visibility. But the visibility of the invisible. And visibility, by its essence, is not seen, which is why it remains *epekeina tes ousias*, beyond the phenomenon or beyond being" (p. 100). Beyond genitivity. Arriving on the stage, as *mimēsis*, in betrayal.

In the end, Derrida arrives at property, seizes upon it, for how can one speak of Marx without marking the props of property? How can one speak in the genitive without *mimēsis*? The enigmatic table become a fetish, as if some other property were not riven by desire. I would recall Engels's genealogy, where the advent of humanity arrives as the perpetuation of desire, sex, blood, and things all intimately bound together.[17] But I stay with Derrida:

If one keeps to use-value, the properties *(Eigenschaften)* of the thing (and it is going to be a question of property) are always very human, at bottom, reassuring for this very reason. They always relate to what is proper to man, to the properties of man: either they respond to men's needs, and that is precisely their use-value, or else they are the product of a human activity that seems to intend them for those needs." *(SM, 150)*

Authentic property does not arrive, belongs to the properties of the thing in relation to the properties of man. Exchange-value arrives, steps on the stage, bears props. As if use-value knew nothing of props, nothing of *mimēsis*, were an ordinary, pure, unambiguous thing.

For example—and here is where the table comes on stage—the wood remains wooden when it is made into a table: it is then "an ordinary, sensuous thing." It is quite different when it becomes a commodity, when the curtain goes up on the market and the table plays actor and character at the same time, when the commodity-table, says Marx, comes on stage *(auftritt)*, begins to walk around and to put itself forward as a market value. *Coup de théâtre*, the ordinary, sensuous thing is transfigured *(verwandelt sich)*, it becomes someone, it assumes a figure. (p. 150)

It is not enough for this wooden table to stand up, its feet on the ground . . . —it also stands on its head, a wooden head, for it has become a kind of headstrong, pigheaded, obstinate animal that, standing, faces other commodities. Facing up to the others, before the others, its fellows, here then is the apparition of a strange creature: at the same time Life, Thing, Beast, Object, Commodity, Automaton—in a word, specter. (p. 152)[18]

A monster, beast, or automaton standing on its head, on the stage, performing like an artifact, insisting on *mimēsis*. The *mimēsis* of the thing, beast, or commodity, the apparition of every thing, the props of property. A specter haunted by the name of matter—one might say, mattering greatly yet not at all. "Whoever understands Greek and philosophy could say of this genealogy . . . that it also gives a tableau of the becoming-immaterial of matter. . . . The wood comes alive and is peopled with spirits" (p. 152). Given over to exchange, promised to the market: "The commodity table, the headstrong dog, the wooden head faces up, we recall, *to all other commodities.* . . . Commodities have business with other commodities, these hardhead specters have commerce among themselves" (p. 155). This strange animal or beast haunts the propriety of property, the very properties of the thing and the human. Derrida speaks of capital contradiction. I think of betrayal, simulation.

The capital contradiction does not have to do simply with the incredible conjunction of the sensuous and the supersensible in the same Thing; it

> is the contradiction of *automatic autonomy*, mechanical freedom, techni-
> cal life. . . . Autonomy *and* automatism, *but* automatism of this wooden
> table that spontaneously puts itself into motion, to be sure, and seems
> thus to animate, animalize, spiritualize, *spiritize* itself, but while remain-
> ing an artifactual body, a sort of automaton, a puppet. (pp. 152–53)

I think of capitalism as the schizophrenia of property, wild and endless
circulation beyond restriction: general economy.[19] Beyond any origin, any
genitive.

The answer to how things become commodities is not paradoxical or
impossible but expressive beyond containment. That is the truth of the ten
plagues and ghosts:[20] betrayal beyond containment. Restricted economy is
impossible, betrayed by general economy. General economy is the impossibility in restricted economy, including every economy of property, use-
value and exchange-value, every property of property, humanity, society, or
nature. All props. All *mimēsis*. Resisting neutrality and purity. Ecology as
the *mimēsis* of economy, as the circulation of the circulation of goods,
betrayed beyond limit. "In its originary iterability, a use-value is in advance
promised, promised to exchange and beyond exchange. . . . This is not simply a bad thing, even if the use-value is always *at risk* of losing its soul in
the commodity" (Derrida, *SM*, 162). I understand this debt and promise as
betrayal. The infinite risk of losing the soul that does not exist. The infinite
risk, one might say, of losing the inheritance that cannot be had.

> Marx remains an immigrant *chez nous*, a glorious, sacred, accursed but
> still a clandestine immigrant as he was all of his life. He belongs to a time
> of disjunction, . . . between earth and sky. One should not rush to make of
> the clandestine immigrant an illegal alien or, what always risks coming
> down to the same thing, to domesticate him. To neutralize him through
> naturalization. To assimilate him so as to stop frightening oneself (making
> oneself fear) with him. He is not part of the family, but one should not
> send him back, once again, him too, to the border. (p. 174)

Always, I would say, at the border, with philosophy, frightening oneself,
hoping to frighten fright away with sacrifice. Or with genitivity.

What if property were the sacrifice of sacrifice rather than the fear of
fear? What if betrayal betrayed itself as property? What if philosophy were
the *mimēsis* of the *of*, genitivity as betrayal, endlessly propping up the
props of property? "The stake that is serving as our guiding thread here,
namely, the concept or the schema of the ghost, was heralded long ago, and
in its own name, across the problematics of the work of mourning, ideali-
zation, simulacrum, *mimesis*, iterability, the double injunction, the 'double
bind,' and undecidability as condition of responsible decision, and so forth"

(Derrida, *SM*, 184). Derrida reminds us of *Hamlet* and Hamlet's father's ghost, perhaps to remind us of philosophy. "Thou art a scholar; speak to it Horatio." You are a philosopher, Horatio, who does not know that there is more on heaven and earth than is dreamt of in any philosophy. Including ghosts, *fantômes, spectres*. Any philosophy, including yours and mine. Marx's and Derrida's. The specter of ghosts.

I am reminded of another meeting face to face with ghosts. In the Paris version of *Orpheus and Eurydice* where Orpheus descends into Hell to retrieve his property, a crucial figure, perhaps, of falling into and disowning the earth, he sings to the Furies in French: *spectres, larves, ombres terribles*.[21] Sings to them and calms them, perhaps without redemption or eschatology. Sings to them in their own place. Keeps them and him on the move, avoids disaster until he stops to gaze at his beloved Eurydice. *If you are a musician, sing to them, Derrida, of the good. If you are a philosopher, disown them, give them something to give away.* Sing of the giving that interrupts the stockpiling and consuming of property.

Eurydice's shade. Interrupting the genitive. On stage. Orpheus's *mimēsis* before his gaze.

Dreaming of genitivity, property's *mimēsis* on stage.

# CHAPTER 2

## Genitive Properties

And indeed the question which, both now and of old, has always been raised, and always been the subject of doubt, viz. what being is, is just the question, what is substance *(ousia)*? (Aristotle, *Metaphysics*, 1028b3–1028b8)

Luxury and intemperance and license, when they have sufficient backing, are virtue and happiness, and all the rest is tinsel, the unnatural catchwords of mankind, mere nonsense and of no account. (Plato, *Gorgias*, 492d)

What is, what being is—*ousia, parousia*—arrives as property: that which properly gives a being its existence and essence, makes it what it is, the genitivity of its origin. A thing is what it is because of what it has, because of the properties it possesses. In the Western tradition and other places.

Aristotle dreams of property as the mark of being.[1] "A property in its own right is one which is ascribed to a thing in comparison with everything else and distinguishes it from everything else" (Aristotle, *Topics*, 128b33–129a5), properly dividing one thing from another as if the earth were dismembered neutrally in its very being, given to some more than to others. Leading to household management, to economy and ecology in memory of the *oikos*, where the properties that make humans human meet the goods of life. The soul of human excellence is owning and giving property. Properly. "[T]he liberal man will give for the sake of the noble, and rightly; for he will give to the right people, the right amounts, and at the right time, with all the other qualifications that accompany right giving. . . . It is highly characteristic of a liberal man also to go to excess in giving, so that he leaves too little for himself" (Aristotle, *Nicomachean Ethics*, 1120a23–1121a7). It is good to give, even to give too much, always with one's property in mind. A good man does not look to himself, still giving and receiving in the genitive.

In public, among friends (1169b29–1170a3), the noble man—always the man, seldom the woman who is permitted neither to be out in public nor to have true and liberal friends—should give his goods away, properly, but should not procure them. "That sort of thing is not the business of any excellence at all" (Aristotle, *Magna Moralia*, 1192a15–1192a20). In private, the business of the household is the acquisition of property. Including human beings. "Property is a part of the household, and the art of acquiring property is a part of the art of managing the household; for no man can live well, or indeed live at all, unless he is provided with necessaries. . . . And so, in the arrangement of the family, a slave is a living possession, and property a number of such instruments; and the servant is himself an instrument for instruments" (Aristotle, *Politics*, 1253b24–1254a17). In the household, there are natural limits to the acquisition of wealth, though in public there are none (1257b). The household, limited by nature, imposes limits on possession but insists on having everything in the name of the genitive: owning slaves and animals, ruling women and children.[2]

*Ousia* evokes property and possession in the gathering of being in truth, assembling things for use in the household under the rule of the genitive. Human life is one of possessing, having. Rochelle bides her time. Stones endure, possessing nothing.

To Aristotle, the concern of the state is one of property, still our concern today. "Great then is the good fortune of a state in which the citizens have a moderate and sufficient property."[3] In consequence, economics, household management, the production of moderate and sufficient property, is the soul of the state.

> Now a city is an aggregate made up of households and land and property, self-sufficient with regard to a good life. . . . It is for this end that they associate together. . . . It is evident, therefore, that economics is prior in origin to politics; for its function is prior, since a household is part of a city. (Aristotle, *Economics*, 1343a10–1343a17)

> The parts of a household are man and property. . . . According to Hesiod, it would be necessary that there should be "First and foremost a house, a woman, and an ox for the plough. . . ." (1343a18–1343a24)

Throughout Aristotle, in the *oikos*, where human beings live, we find the constellation that marks human life in the genitive—blood, sex, kin, class, food, desire, and power, the props of property: the genitive framed on both sides by *mimēsis* and authority. We find this constellation in Western philosophy from the beginning, and throughout.[4]

This is betrayal to the extreme of everything Aristotle describes as happiness—not every thing, every component, but the genitivity that defines it.

We may define happiness as prosperity combined with excellence; or as independence of life; or as the secure enjoyment of the maximum of pleasure; or as a good condition of property and body, together with the power of guarding one's property and body and making use of them. . . .

From this definition of happiness it follows that its constituent parts are: good birth, plenty of friends, good friends, wealth, good children, plenty of children, a happy old age, also such bodily excellences as health, beauty, strength, large stature, athletic powers, together with fame, honour, good luck, and excellence. (Aristotle, *Rhetoric*, 1360b14–31)[5]

Happiness is to be grasped genitively and genitally, in terms of expenditure, including human beings. "The constituents of wealth are: plenty of coined money and territory; the ownership of numerous, large, and beautiful estates; also the ownership of numerous and beautiful implements, live stock, and slaves. . . . It is really the activity—that is, the use—of property that constitutes wealth" (1361a13–1361a25). Rochelle insists on useless expenditure, reminds us of the joys of squander, not having to make every bit count.[6]

Many of Aristotle's views of possession—especially against common property—consist of replies to Plato in *Republic* and *Laws*. I interrupt to consider some of Plato's views of genitivity, to suggest that they be regarded as sites of interruption more than support for having, including property in common. I read *mimēsis* in Plato always in interruption. I begin with words from Plato's *Republic*, frequently taken to express his predominant views in the genitive. I would remember the advent of property, perhaps dreaming all the while. I revert to the city of pigs, where we may say that, in Greek philosophy, property arrives for the first time, together with the social contract, the ownership and exchange of women together with pigs and other animals. For when Socrates proposes to "create a city from the beginning" (Plato, *Republic*, 369c), he suggests that: "Now the first and chief of our needs is the provision of food for existence and life. . . . The second is housing and the third is raiment and that sort of thing" (369d); asking with respect to the citizens, "Shall each of these contribute his work for the common use of all?" (369de). He imagines the common living use of all as if without ownership, giving without having, resisting the genitive. Instead, he describes labor and trade, buying and selling: "A market place, then, and money as a token for the purpose of exchange" (371b), the exchange of goods to meet needs, to live, perhaps without accumulation. Not bad, perhaps, for men. "[L]et us consider what will be the manner of life of men thus provided. . . . Reclined on rustic beds strewed with bryony and myrtle, they will feast with their children, drinking of their wine thereto, garlanded and singing hymns to the gods in pleasant fellowship, not begetting offspring beyond their means lest they fall into poverty or war" (372ac). Not begetting property, not seeking things beyond a life "in peace and health" (372d) lest they fall into disaster. Joyful life without genitivity. To which Glaucon responds: "If you were founding a city of pigs, Socrates, what other fodder than this would you provide?" (372d). Life without genitivity is unfit for humans and for pigs.

This thought calls for an interruption, a reminder that the leading question of the dialogue, that of justice, arises in the genitive. Justice arrives in Plato's *Republic* with Cephalus's claim that the greatest benefit of property is to enable a man to live in justice and piety (Plato, *Republic*, 330d–331c). I would not be alone in supposing that the entire *Republic* answers to this claim, leading to the division of labor on which the famous truth of justice is based, entirely in the genitive:

> that he should dispose well of what in the true sense of the word is properly his own, and having first attained to self-mastery and beautiful order within himself, and having harmonized these three principles, the notes or intervals of three terms quite literally the lowest, the highest, and the mean, and all others there may be between them, and having linked and bound all three together and made of himself a unit, one man instead of many, self-controlled and in unison, he should then and then only turn to practice if he find aught to do either in the getting of wealth or the tendance of the body or it may be in political action or private business. . . . (443ce)

Justice is the economy or ecology of the soul, taking the division of labor within for granted, a unison of parts, each and all and together in the genitive as what in the true sense is properly one's own—without a doubt, human *ousia*. The entire *Republic* turns on the link between justice and genitivity. Justice is an ecology, or economy, of that which, properly one's own, cannot be accumulated, exchanged, or consumed. An ecology that arrives on stage, as *mimēsis*, in the midst of economy.

Arriving, I continue to insist, after we have abandoned a human world without genitivity, evoking the possibility that to the extent that we are responsible to and for the good, property and possession—all forms of genitivity—must be regarded with suspicion, including every sense of what is properly one's own. Either property in common or no property at all. Touching upon the utmost dream, perhaps, of an earth without possession, neither of women and children, of creatures and things, of earth and sky and water and gods, even of our selves and proprieties. Perhaps we neither have nor own our properties but dwell in them, or together with them, in proximity and responsibility. And exposure. We dream a strangely Platonic dream in memory of the good. A genealogy. Linking human life with descent along lines of blood and kin and food, together with animals. And property. A genealogy of responsibility without property or class.

Socrates asks Cephalus right at the beginning, who boasts of having acquired property, "What do you regard as the greatest benefit you have enjoyed from the possession of property?" (Plato, *Republic*, 330d). The answer is said to be justice. Yet the arrival of the city of pigs, together with property, may be understood to suggest that the best life for human beings—of justice, virtue, happiness—comes before that arrival, before the ownership of animals and things, arrives without genitivity. Human beings live best without owning or having. Cephalus hopes to have and own justice, in virtue of his other possessions. An impossibility, one might say, Jesus said.

I have noted where, in *Phaedo*, Socrates says that human beings are property of the gods, that human beings and their gifts are possessed, not possessors. The gods possess; human beings are divine possessions. I understand this figure as evoking the possibility that the genitivity of being possessed is not having but giving, in debt. "But the truth of the matter, gentlemen, is pretty certainly this, that real wisdom is the property of God, and this oracle is his way of telling us that human wisdom has little or no value" (Plato, *Apology*, 23a). Plato presents the possibility that the good is not having but giving. "So whenever soul takes possession of a body, it always brings life with it?" (Plato, *Phaedo*, 105d); "All soul has the care of all that is inanimate, and traverses the whole universe, though in ever-changing forms" (Plato, *Phaedrus*, 246d). The way to justice and the good is not by possessing—Cephalus's way—but by being possessed, by being given. *Mimēsis* again. The Muse "first makes men inspired, and then through these inspired ones others share in the enthusiasm, and a chain is formed, for the epic poets, all the good ones, have their excellence, not from art, but are inspired, possessed, and thus they utter all these admirable poems" (Plato, *Ion*, 533c–534b). I laugh to think that Plato said it first. Though he said many other things as well on property and genitivity. Plato the master of *mimēsis*, that which cannot be owned. Rochelle laughs—if she laughs—that Plato and Euripides speak of divine powers in stones.

What can be owned gives us advantage over things and people. In the interrogative. Perhaps. For with respect to "matters of which we have a good idea," "we shall be lords over others, and they will be in fact our property"; "[w]ith regard to matters, on the other hand, into which we have acquired no insight, . . . we ourselves, in these matters, shall be subject to others, and they will be, in fact, the property of others" (Plato, *Lysis*, 210ac). Either we own or are owned; either have the advantage or are taken advantage of. Perhaps. Yet the blasphemy of which Socrates repents in *Phaedrus* is of treating love as something that provides advantage, that can be possessed. To think of advantage in relation to things ethical and immortal is blasphemy.[7] As if we might give up all genitivity, might resist all desire to have.

The blasphemy suggests that the *common property* to which Socrates leads us in *Republic* is still property, still insists on genitivity[8]—evoking the possibility that owning in common is next best to not owning at all but that being possessed is the mark of the good—giving rather than having. Aristotle and others respond that owning in common is still owning, and practically speaking private property is good for household management. Keeping women and slaves in the home for the advantage of men.

I do not mean to deny that Plato speaks of possessing the good, if somewhat ambiguously. For example, "if we do not know it, then, even if without the knowledge of this we should know all other things never so well, you are aware that it would avail us nothing, just as no possession either is of any avail without the possession of the good" (Plato, *Republic*, 505ab). I read this passage as suggesting that nothing is worth possessing without being possessed by the good. Perhaps that is too extreme. Yet consider the discussion of possessing and having knowledge in *Theaetetus*:

> "Having" seems to me different from "possessing." If a man has bought a coat and owns it, but is not wearing it, we should say he possesses it without having it about him. (Plato, *Theaetetus*, 197c)

> Now consider whether knowledge is a thing you can possess in that way without having it about you, like a man who has caught some wild birds—pigeons or what not—and keeps them in an aviary he has made for them at home. In a sense, of course, we might say he "has" them all the time inasmuch as he possesses them, mightn't we? (198b)

> And when he hands them over, we call it "teaching," and when the other takes them from him, that is "learning," and when he has them in the sense of possessing them in that aviary of his, that is "knowing." (198b)

> [A]re you going to tell me that there are yet further pieces of knowledge about your pieces of knowledge and ignorance, and that their owner keeps these shut up in yet another of your ridiculous aviaries or waxen blocks, knowing them so long as he possesses them, although he may not have them at hand in his mind? (199ab)

I read the entire discussion as showing that knowledge cannot be under-stood genitively, for one can never possess enough to know, to have in hand. The one who knows does not possess, but may perhaps be possessed, be given, a knowledge and truth that never accumulates. The one who knows may give away his knowledge but can never hold onto it.

One might say, on this reading, that the difference between *Republic* and *Laws* concerning *nomos*, law, lies in the genitive, that *Republic* begins with questions of possession, property, genitivity, and evokes the possibility of a life without having; evokes it and betrays it—transforms it—into state authority where we cannot live without genitivity or authority. Even so, where the ruler is philosopher, modeled on ship's pilot and shepherd, he does not own his people, but gives them guidance without having. Ruling is giving, not possessing.

In contrast, *Laws* is framed in genitivity, possessing that which makes life good. Here soul is not in care of all things everywhere, giving them their goodness, but is possessed by its owner. "[E]very man's most precious possession, as we said, is his soul; no man, then, we may be sure, will of set purpose receive the supreme evil into this most precious thing and live with it there all his life through" (Plato, *Laws*, 731b). Or consider where the distinction is blurred between owning in common and disowning—still marked as a possibility.

> If there is now on earth, or ever should be, such a society—a community in womenfolk, in children, in all possessions whatsoever—if all means have been taken to eliminate everything we mean by the word ownership from life; if all possible means have been taken to make even what nature has made our own in some sense common property, I mean, if our eyes, ears, and hands seem to see, hear, act, in the common service; if, moreover, we all approve and condemn in perfect unison and derive pleasure and pain from the same sources—in a word, when the institutions of a society make it most utterly one, that is a criterion of their excellence than which no truer or better will ever be found. (739be)

One might imagine that property is the foundation of law. Law exists to institute possession, is society's insistence on genitivity. But even within such inescapable genitivity—always linked with genitality, kinship and genealogy, men owning women and children—Plato evokes the possibility of eliminating ownership, abolishing genitivity—still in the genitive.[9] In many places Plato asks us to imagine a life of giving without having, abolishing genitivity.

I return from these places to *Gorgias*, a work that does not seem to concern genitivity. Yet we have seen that the good cannot be given without the genitive in the redoubled gesture in which it must resist genitivity. Justice and injustice appear in finite conditions under the marks of genitivity, the law of the father: the man who must not act like a child; who cares for his children.

I have come to *Gorgias*, as I promised, interested in its relation to property. Gorgias speaks in the voice of the father, after the discussion is under way, at the point where property is first taken seriously—though I would say that it was present from the first. For the question concerning Gorgias's art, of rhetoric, is in Plato the question of philosophy, always a question of how to live. In the words of the father—or if not Gorgias himself, then Callicles the son who would take the place of the father:

> I feel toward philosophers very much as I do toward those who lisp and play the child. . . . if anyone should seize you or any others like you and drag you off to prison, claiming you are guilty when you are not, . . . you would reel to and fro and gape openmouthed, without a word to say, and . . . you would be put to death . . . . And yet what wisdom is there in this [in which a man is] fated to be robbed by his enemies of all his property and to live literally like one disfranchised in his own city? (Plato, *Gorgias*, 484c–486c)

Philosophers are so helpless that others may steal their property with impunity as if they were children, as if holding onto one's property were the highest goal of life.

At the beginning of the dialogue, the father claims that rhetoric is good because it secures wealth, property, and life,

> the power to convince by your words the judges in court, the senators in Council, the people in the Assembly, or in any other gathering of a citizen body. And yet possessed of such power you will make the doctor, you will make the trainer your slave, and your businessman will prove to be making money, not for himself, but for another, for you who can speak and persuade multitudes. (*Gorgias,* 452e)

In his exchange with Polus, Socrates gives recurrent examples of what powerful men think are good, are to their advantage, as property

> And do we not kill a man, when we do so, or banish him or confiscate his property, because we think it better so to act than not? (468b)

> Then when we slaughter or banish from the city or deprive of property, we do not thus simply will these acts. But if they are advantageous to us, we will them; if harmful, we do not. For as you say, we will the good, not what is neither good nor evil, nor what is evil. (468c)

Polus assumes that being able to seize others' property with impunity is good in itself, to which Socrates responds by asking, what is the relation of owning, possessing, and having to justice and the good? The answer appears to be, no relation at all. Nor is it just and good to pursue our own advantage. Advantage is something we may hope to gain, to have. Having is sometimes good and sometimes not, together with being and living. The good, goodness, beauty, and justice are all inspired and mad, ungatherable into being and having. And this is so even if we cannot live, cannot pursue the good, without having, owning, or possessing. Not as common property, perhaps not property at all, or at least, not property as a good. Who other than Plato comes so close to this heretical thought? As I said, in *Gorgias* and elsewhere.

In the extreme, all things that might be had or owned—objects, animals, land, wealth, property, but also knowledge, truth, persuasion, authority—are of themselves, as had, not good at all—and not bad at all—but concomitants of life with which we may pursue justice—or not. And among the greatest of all injustices is persuasion without truth, suggesting that we may receive knowledge and truth but not possess them. Possession and authority belong to each other in the injustice of being. What more than this can be the fault of rhetoric, against which philosophy seems so incompetent, lacking authority and property? The good life for Socrates and Plato is a life resistant to property and authority, to having and taking: giving without genitivity.[10]

In Socrates' words, repeated in *Gorgias*, knowledge is nothing to own: the highest good, the greatest purification, of philosophy is to be refuted (*Gorgias*, 458a; *Sophist*, 230e). It is better to be refuted than to refute—reminding us that the issue of *Gorgias*, beyond the difference between philosophy and rhetoric—perhaps no difference at all—is whether it is better to do than to suffer injustice. What if injustice were like refutation, always better to receive than to give? What if giving were for the sake of a justice and truth that never arrived, that could never be had, possessed, or owned, whose arrival was betrayal? What if refutation were the mark of this lack of possession, disowning without owning, expropriation without appropriation: doubly betrayed within a double genitive? Dreaming of a philosophy that did not hope to own wisdom or the good, yet hoped to be good and wise, hoping for betrayal, always betrayed. Giving as the arrival of what never arrives, betraying the arrival. All the distinctions required of the philosopher or the sophist—between right and wrong, goodness and evil, beauty and ugliness, justice and injustice—*agathon-kakon, kallon-aischron, dikē-adikia*—circulate without accumulating, in betrayal. Life cannot be lived without them. Life cannot be lived with them held in hand.

The sophist claims to have them in hand, under his thumb. The philosopher who makes a similar claim is indistinguishable from a sophist or rhetorician. If beauty and justice cannot be had, if the good—*agathon*—

cannot be owned, then every claim to have it, every insistence on control-ling it, is betrayal. I read Socrates' suggestion that one might find an expert in the good as a rhetorical strategy, presenting the appearance of the pos-sibility of having what cannot be had, as he suggests elsewhere in *Phaedrus*, where all these distinctions remain contested even within ourselves, await-ing refutation.

Put another way, if rhetoric is a part, a semblance *(eidōlon)*, of politics, that of flattery, as Socrates suggests to Polus, then property—possessing, owning, and having what cannot be owned—is a simulacrum of the good, the worst kind of simulacrum, that which passes itself off as the real thing—not *mimēsis*, for example, which always simulates itself, insists on more *mimēsis*, interrupting its authority, possesses no authority at all. Owning, possessing, genitivity either accumulate or find themselves circulating so quickly as to lose all authority—the circulation I call *betrayal*.

Rhetoric and sophistry take for granted what human beings appear to insist on in the nature of their being: that they are there to have, if not goods and things, then goods as not-things, spiritual goods, still had, owned, possessed. Being there, being thrown, is genitivity, insisting on authority. On this score, the best human life is that which most completely masters—owns—genitivity. Allowing us to understand Socrates' words in the extreme,

> Does it not seem to you . . . that when a man does what he pleases, if his action is accompanied by advantage, it is a good thing and this apparently is the meaning of great power, but otherwise, it is an evil thing and implies small power? . . . Do we not admit that sometimes it is better to do the things we have just mentioned, to kill men and banish and confiscate their property, and sometimes not? (470b)

These words are addressed to Polus, Socrates' "strange friend," suggesting that we may understand them as refutation, betrayal, *mimēsis*. When Socrates speaks of advantage, profit *(ōphelimōs)*, he is speaking indirectly of the good to one who takes a simulacrum for it; when he speaks of confiscating property as sometimes good and sometimes not, he is speaking of genitivity. On this reading, advantage has nothing to do with the good, but simulates it; and genitivity has nothing to do with the good—nor have life and prop-erty as such—but takes its place. Which is not to imagine a good without simulation or betrayal, or a life without genitivity.

I would return to the simulated father, not Gorgias but Callicles, of fame and beauty, who owns the house at which Socrates is guest, who begins the dialogue and occupies the rest of the dialogue beginning with the center. Callicles the prodigal father takes the place of the son to speak with Socrates the son who arrives. The center of the dialogue is occupied by the speech on philosophy, fathers and children, followed by Socrates' reference to Callicles as a touchstone *(basanos)* of truth, reminding us that slaves were tortured in the name of such a truth.[11] I will stay here with the question Callicles poses that represents the heart of the dialogue, interpreted in terms of genitivity. First Callicles, then Socrates:

> But in my view nature herself makes it plain that it is right for the better to have the advantage over the worse, the more able over the less. And both among all animals and in entire states and races of mankind it is plain that this is the case—that right is recognized to be the sovereignty and advantage of the stronger over the weaker.... If a man arises endowed with a nature sufficiently strong, he will, I believe, shake off all these controls, burst his fetters, and break loose.... He rises up and reveals himself our master who was once our slave, and there shines forth nature's true justice. (483a–484a)

> The more powerful carries off by force the property of the weaker, the better rules over the worse, and the nobler takes more than the meaner? Have you any other conception of justice than this . . . ? (488ab)

Genitivity again, the stronger claiming the property of the weaker as justice itself.[12] Justice as genitivity—or is it injustice, as Anaximander says? *Basanos*, the torture of slaves when their owners are accused—the very essence of injustice. Perhaps we are to understand Callicles' account of natural justice as the very essence of injustice. "That is what I mean, for natural justice I consider to be this, that the better and wiser man should rule over and have more than the inferior" (490a). Ruling and having again, justice and genitivity. Is it the best life for human beings to be able to satisfy their every wish, able to compel others to their will, able to possess anything whatever? Only if what they do is for the sake of the good. Perhaps without owning or having.

Against the familiar genitive image of desert, goodness as the superior deserving and having more than the inferior, Socrates offers the extreme possibility that having has nothing to do with justice or the good. Nor has deserving.[13] It is always better, deserved or not, to suffer injustice than to do it; and it is always better, deserved or not, to give rather than to take. The issue is genitivity, understanding accounting and justifying based on deserving in the genitive.

Greek life and thought present this issue in extreme. Is it better to be able to persuade the multitude to give you what you do not deserve—or perhaps to make you deserving? Is it better to be able to compel or cheat others into giving you what you otherwise do not deserve? The unlikely answer is that fraud, force, and deception make one deserving, that tyrants and cheats are better and wiser than those they compel to do their will. Life in justice remains injustice, to be resisted. Here in *Gorgias*, Socrates appears at the opposite extreme, perhaps as implausible as the other. If it is strange to think that a tyrant is more just than those he tyrannizes, it is stranger to think that it is better to suffer than to do injustice. Justice is doing and getting what you deserve. In the genitive.

That is what Callicles says, once issues of tyranny and rhetoric are out of the way. In almost every culture—every culture with surplus wealth— it is good and right for those who are better and wiser to have more. Frequently this means that those who have more are regarded as better. Frequently this means that those who have less are regarded as worse. Democratic, industrial societies have not resolved this issue, typically expressed in terms of equality.[14] Here in Plato, it is given a deeper questioning in terms of having and taking—so far-reaching that Callicles' cannot believe that Socrates is serious. All of human life, he says, would be turned upside down (481bc). I would suppose Callicles to be truthful and sincere, not the sophist or rhetorician he is frequently taken to be. That is how I understand Socrates' reference to him as the touchstone of truth—with slavery and torture lurking in the background. I take Callicles to represent the highest values possible in Athenian society, expressed in his name: beauty, goodness, and fame.[15]

The question here, more explicit I believe than anywhere else in Plato's dialogues, concerns the nature of virtue, *agathon* and *kallon*. Whatever answer Socrates gives, it is that virtue is not having or taking. If it is governing, it is as giving. The best do not take but give their wisdom and goodness to others. Socrates is in earnest because our understanding of the good is at stake. The good gives without genitivity and without authority.

What Callicles says, if we take him at his word and leave Polus and Gorgias aside, is that Socrates is advocating a life of weakness and helplessness. Why not read such a claim as foreshadowing Nietzsche? This is Greek or Socratic if not Christian weakness, filled with *ressentiment*—if there is such a thing as Greek *ressentiment*. Life is a play of forces, agonistic, and those who are active and powerful deserve to triumph. To all post-Nietzscheans, Callicles' words must evoke fear and trembling, that the highest values Nietzsche expounds are in the genitive. Yet one must beware of genitivity in reading Nietzsche. The *übermensch* does not display his overcoming by having but by overcoming having.[16]

Callicles can be read as taking Polus's position, that the stronger takes the property from the weaker by force. This may be said to be better, as if dominance were the good, as if taking and having were goodness despite all ethical maxims contravening it. Most people appear to believe it despite saying otherwise. I have been suggesting that what many people believe is that the better should rule over and take from the worse—the stronger, wiser, quicker; natural leaders should have more than natural followers. If there be such. Sometimes it does not work out that way, and we may regard some inequities as unjust. But inequity is just, and justice is having more than others by those who deserve it. Having and ruling as taking.

Perhaps I should qualify my reading, withholding some of my admiration for Callicles. For he does not acknowledge the difference between having the better from having the stronger until he is forced to do so (489bc–490ab): "natural justice I consider to be this, that the better and wiser man should rule over and have more than the inferior" (490ab). He reminds us of Thrasymachus, except that the latter is brought to silence by this distinction. Callicles pursues it into the heart of genitivity. He goes from Polus's indefensible claim that power and goodness are the same to the genitivity that underlies Greek, perhaps every, society. Goodness is having; the social contract guards possession. The possibility Plato evokes through the rest of the discussion is that genitivity is injustice, that the social contract is founded on this injustice, and that equal property remains within genitivity. Acting for the sake of the good is not taking but something else, resistant to genitivity and neutrality.

Callicles insists on taking and consuming in the name of slavery. Genitivity in the extreme.

> Why, how could a man be happy when a slave to anybody at all? No, but the naturally noble and just is what I now describe to you with all frankness—namely that anyone who is to live aright should suffer his appetites to grow to the greatest extent and not check them, and through courage and intelligence should be competent to minister to them at their greatest and to satisfy every appetite with what it craves. . . . Luxury and intemperance and license, when they have sufficient backing, are virtue and happiness. . . . (491e–492d)

It is certainly bad to be a slave, though perhaps not much better to be the slave's master. Mastery and slavery circle the orbit of owning and having. If the highest human life is to have, then having more is better, including other human beings, having and owning and desiring to have and own more, beyond limit. Infinite desire, beyond measure, is infinite coveting, taking, and having. The only question is which kinds of things, ordinary things, wives and children, slaves, or something else—for example, God's mercy and love. Giving becomes taking without the slightest sense of betrayal, is repeatedly understood in terms of genitivity.[17] To which we may respond that desire is infinite, permeating all things everywhere—as soul has care of all things: desire to give and care, perhaps, for the sake of the good, rather than to take and have.

Socrates concludes the dialogue with a speech, knowing that speeches are contaminated by genitivity. The search for truth and goodness in the form of dialogue and dialectic may be resistant to genitivity. Socrates' own words and beliefs are not. He leads us back to the good, first in terms of *sōphrosunē*, temperance and moderation. Goodness is temperance in the soul (507a), moderation in pleasure, perhaps, and property. Or perhaps pleasure and property are never in moderation. We may recall erotic madness and Socrates' blasphemy in *Phaedrus*. Madness in good things, in divine ways, is goodness. Madness in earthly things, owned and possessed things, is not. Even so, Socrates speaks here in the genitive. "[E]ither we must refute this argument and prove that happiness does not come to the happy through the possession of justice and temperance, nor does misery come through the possession of wickedness, or, if my argument is true, we must consider the consequences" (507cd). In the genitive, resisting a capitalist view of possession. The best way to live is not saving and being saved, not having and being had, owning and possessing. How can we best live the life that is to be ours where such a life is never in the genitive? (512bc)

Socrates concludes with a fine story that most will "consider fiction," *mimēsis*, but which is "fact," "the actual truth" (523a): a story from old indistinguishable from a dream, another phantasm of property. "Now in the days of Cronus there was this law about mankind, . . . that the man who has led a godly and righteous life departs after death to the Isles of the Blessed and there lives in all happiness exempt from ill, but the godless and unrighteous man departs to the prison of vengeance and punishment which they call Tartarus" (523ac). In response to complaints that "the wrong people were going to both places," Zeus strips humanity of foreknowledge of their deaths, strips them naked; "and the judge must be naked too and dead" (523ad), stripped of all worldly possessions and property. Given the rewards and punishment that are their due, the only genitive worth owning, receiving what cannot be had or taken but that insists on the better: "it is proper for everyone who suffers a punishment rightly inflicted by another that he should either be improved and benefited thereby or become a warning to the rest, in order that they may be afraid when they see him suffering what he does and may become better men" (525bc). Giving up all possessions: "I renounce the honors sought by most men, and pursuing the truth I shall really endeavor both to live and, when death comes, to die, as good a man as I possibly can be" (526de). This story may be a bit fantastic, yet it contains an enduring truth: "[T]his alone stands steadfast, that we should be more on our guard against doing than suffering wrong, and that before all things a man should study not to seem but to be good, whether in private or in public life. . . . This is the best way of life—to live and die in the pursuit of righteousness and all other virtues" (527be). To live and die for the sake of the good without possessing the finest things of worldly life, including wealth, honor, and glory. Perhaps without having goods at all.

This seems so plainly resistant to owning, having, and possessing goods of any kind that I will pursue it for the rest of my discussion, noting that Socrates speaks of living and dying in pursuit of, not having, wisdom, virtue, and justice. Elsewhere, he denies every advantage they may offer, denies that wisdom and virtue can be owned—in *Theaetetus* and *Meno*, for example—and suggests that true justice comes before the city of pigs, before any owning and possessing, including the possession of justice itself and of life and death.

What if we were to read *Phaedo* as suggesting that the impossibility of death is that it both destroys and insists on the genitive: *my* life and *my* death, *my* past, present, and future? Having what cannot be had. What if the preoccupation with death were always in the genitive where the good and abundance in the earth marked the end of the genitive? The deaths, the disasters, that are never mine, or yours, or others', mourning without genitivity.

# CHAPTER 3

## Sovereign Properties

the object of man's desire, is not to enjoy once only, and for one instant of time; but to assure for ever, the way of his future desire....
...I put for a general inclination of all mankind, a perpetual and restless desire of power after power, that ceaseth only in death. (Hobbes, *L*, 85)

Not far from the city of pigs, in proximity with Callicles' dream of tyranny, in the genitive, the state of nature re-emerges in another, famous dream of property:

Nature hath given to every one a right to all; ... to do what he would, and against whom he thought fit, and to possess, use, and enjoy all what he would, or could get. (Hobbes, *DCV*, 9)

A time of war, where every man is enemy to every man.... In such condition, there is no place for industry; because the fruit thereof is uncertain: and consequently no culture of the earth; ... and the life of man, solitary, poor, nasty, brutish, and short. (Hobbes, *L*, 113)

Hobbes dreams a dream of property, ownership, and desire—to own, to stockpile and consume without limit; of boundless genitivity. The rock upon which property stands is the genitive of desire, tightly linked with power: to assure the way of one's future desire forever. This limitless desire to own securely engenders the state, setting infinite limits on the infinite. "Where there is no common Power, there is no Law: where no Law, no Injustice, Force, and Fraud.... It is consequent also to the same condition, that there be no Propriety, no Dominion, no *Mine* and *Thine* distinct; but only that to be every man's that he can get; and for so long, as he can keep it" (p. 188); for as long as he can perform what is required to have. Economy here circulates in the genitive, *mine* and *thine*, as the *mimēsis* of a desire

43

without limit.[1] Desire's betrayal is its insistence on imposing limits where there can be no limits.

One might imagine from Hobbes that property in European life and thought, joined with law and other requisites of the social contract, rest upon Callicles' insistence—and admiration—that the highest life for human beings is to be powerful enough not just to satisfy every desire, but to expand them beyond limit and still be strong enough to fulfill them: "to grow to the greatest extent and not check them, . . . to satisfy every appetite with what it craves" (Plato, *Gorgias*, 492a).[2] Not only, as Hobbes says, do human beings find themselves beset by limitless desires, but as Callicles says, they most admire those who can let their desires increase to infinity and still fulfill them.

This staging of history as one of coveting has its most effective political history and economy from Locke through Kant and Hegel, producing the familiar resistance we know of in the nineteenth century in Marx and Engels. A genitive description, all proper names. This political history and economy represents the themes of the next two chapters. In the rest of this chapter I hope to evoke the betrayal of genitivity in the interstices of that economy and that history.

The predominant interstice of restricted economy, passed over lightly in the last chapter, is the division of labor, which, once implemented, institutes economy, exchange, and trade. And one might imagine that although Socrates defines justice in *Republic* as the ecology, the unison, within the internal economy|ecology of the soul as well as the external economy|ecology (ethicoeconomoecology, ecolonomy, or economology) of the state,[3] he does not have markets, trade, or exchange in mind, does not equate justice and virtue with acquisition, wealth, and circulation. To the contrary, if a genitive is essential to the ecology of justice, it is that which is properly one's own, which cannot be exchanged, consumed, or accumulated.[4]

The arrival of industrial economy, in a world of expanding markets and worldwide trade, produced a different sense of acquisition, possession, and the division of labor. One might say that economy and economics took the place of ecology and ecosophical ethics, that what could be owned and accumulated became the touchstone of the good rather than what, still in the genitive, could neither be owned nor accumulated. A choice between economy and ecology no doubt present in all cultures including Greece, but giving rise, in Plato and later in the Middle Ages, to the possibility that ecolonomy might reign without accumulation and consumption—giving without having. Beginning with what we call the modern period, the rise of world trade, colonialism, slavery, and industrialization, economy rather than ecology defined the division of labor—if we insist on such a division. In Adam Smith: "This division of labour, from which so many advantages are derived, . . . is the necessary, though very slow and gradual, consequence of a certain propensity in human nature which has in view no such extensive utility; the propensity to truck, barter, and exchange one thing for another" (Smith, *WN*, 25). He suggests an ecological possibility in the genitive, that trucking, bartering, and exchanging are more primordial than owning. Perhaps a capitalist view. Perhaps a view that resists accumulation and consumption, expressing general economy. We may understand capitalism as exchange without possession, circulation without acquisition. "When the division of labour has been once thoroughly established, it is but a very small part of a man's wants which the produce of his own labour can supply. . . . Every man thus lives by exchanging, or becomes in some measure a merchant, and the society itself grows to be what is properly a commercial society" (p. 37). The division of labor takes over life in the genitive. Everyone lives by exchanging, by circulating more than having.

Smith's words open onto the possibility that exchange might be more fundamental than accumulation and consumption, together with the division of labor, understanding the latter as the production of identity and kind—as *mimēsis*, presented on the stage of life and being, expressed in endless circulation. Exchange, trade, and the division of labor are linked with general economy, giving beyond having. Abundance is circulation without the privilege Locke and Smith insist on assigning to labor, in the genitive.

> The property which every man has in his own labour, as it is the original foundation of all other property, so it is the most sacred and inviolable. The patrimony of a poor man lies in the strength and dexterity of his hands; and to hinder him from employing this strength and dexterity in what manner he thinks proper without injury to his neighbour, is a plain violation of this most sacred property. (Smith, *WN*, 138)

Insist on capitalizing under the repressions of modern economy, evoking the possibility of exchange, trade, and labor without dividing property, without enclosing the land. "As soon as the land of any country has all become private property, the landlords, like all other men, love to reap where they never sowed, and demand a rent even for its natural produce" (p. 67).

If labor creates value, and exchange creates the division of labor and property, then economy is accumulation and consumption in the midst of circulation and exchange. But if circulation and exchange are excessive, exceed acquisition and enclosure as the genitive exceeds possession, then capitalist economy, every large-scale economy, exceeds the restrictions that define it, betrays general economy—which I understand to evoke the possibility of ecolonomy, without having, without enclosure. Division of labor becomes the multiplication of identities, resisting the insistence that something is what it is, that people and things are what they are. What it is and what they are exceed enclosure and accumulation. That is general economy's division of labor. As exposure and proximity. General ethicoeconomoecology. Perhaps capitalist economy.

I imagine a very different possibility here of political economy than understood by Smith and Hobbes, though, I would say, indirectly present within their views. An example:

> The experience of all ages and nations, I believe, demonstrates that the work done by slaves, though it appears to cost only their maintenance, is in the end the dearest of any. A person who can acquire no property, can have no other interest but to eat as much, and to labour as little as possible. Whatever work he does beyond what is sufficient to purchase his own maintenance, can be squeezed out of him by violence only, and not by any interest of his own. (Smith, *WN*, 387)

Unless one owns property, unless one can accumulate, one will labor as little as possible—as if to labor, to live, were to acquire. What if we lived and labored to give? What if the problem for the slave is that slavery is acquisitive? Within a political economy of having slaves, owning human beings, how can one give if one cannot have?

In genitive economies giving without having presupposes the possibility of having. Freedom and justice are evoked as giving beyond (the risk and hope of) having. Instituting the state. When Smith speaks of justice, he has property in mind. "Commerce and manufactures can seldom flourish long in any state which does not enjoy a regular administration of justice, in which the people do not feel themselves secure in the possession of their property, in which the faith of contracts is not supported by law, and in which the authority of the state is not supposed to be regularly employed in enforcing the payment of debts from all those who are able to pay" (p. 910). The state exists for accumulation. This seems a striking prospect, foreshadowing Marx and Engels, the production of political economy. The division of labor, capitalist economy, is political, presented as instituting the modern state and its administration of justice to enforce genitivity. The confidence we insist on for commerce and manufacture is that we will be able to keep what is our own. An alternative possibility is an economy in which we have confidence that we will be able to sell, to circulate all sorts of goods more widely, to reach further, to give more to more buyers—who may need neither to accumulate nor consume. In a capitalist economy, evoking general economy, sellers sell and buyers buy, sometimes with no further goal, without intending to have.[5] What of giving without having, beyond restricted economy ruled by use and consumption?

What, one may ask, is ecology in this capitalist economy? I imagine ecology as the flourishing of things without an overarching teleology; as circulation—the exposure and proximity of creatures and things—without fixing, accumulating, or consuming goods; without genitivity.

I interrupt to cross the channel to the chains that bind possession and genitivity.

> Man is born free, and everywhere he is in chains. He who believes himself the master of others does not escape being more of a slave than they. (Rousseau, *SC*, 141)

> Each member of the community gives himself to it at the instant of its constitution, just as he actually is, himself and all his forces, including all the goods in his possession. . . .
> . . . Every man by nature has a right to everything he needs; however, the positive act whereby he becomes a proprietor of some goods excludes him from all the rest. (p. 151)

In another place, I might explore the inequality that occupies the heart of the social contract. In another, I might examine how possession becomes property. Here I am more concerned with the gifts each member of the community makes to it of all that member's goods and possessions. Every person *by nature* has a right to possess and have whatever that person needs. For what?, one might ask, evoking the possibility not only that that person might live, but live well; or that that person might have enough to care for others: family, children, parents, neighbors, and still others, stretching who knows how far? Everything we need might be everything around us; everything we desire might be more.

The social contract emerges from a gift in which every person bestows everything to the community, an absolute and unqualified gift beyond possessing and having. One might say that belonging-together demands this unqualified gift, except that we may question the possessiveness that surrounds Rousseau's account, question whether belonging together is having and owning.

In the state of nature one is surrounded by goods that one may take up as one needs and wishes, living together with things and goods and other living creatures. Such living together is surely ethical except where we take possession and genitivity for granted, as Rousseau does, especially propriety, excluding the goods of some proprietors from all other would-be proprietors. Being and belonging together here are having and taking. Rousseau insists that the condition of togetherness, at least for human beings, presupposes an unqualified gift of all possessions and goods, of whatever one has. I imagine the possibility that he has a more remarkable giving in mind, without having, taking, or possessing. To be or become or participate with others is to give and be given—not to or from the state or community or anything definite or powerful, but giving without possession or authority for either donor or recipient. I imagine being together as giving without having or giver or receiver: giving as ethical being, resisting genitivity.

I understand Rousseau to verge upon the two economieslecologies that define property and genitivity, general and restricted economology, perhaps general ecology and restricted economy. Restricted economy is given under the social contract, exclusive proprietary rights to some goods and things, perhaps some persons or human beings rather than others, bounded by social powers and political forces; haunted by general economy, by giving beyond limit, beyond having and owning, beyond taking the goods one needs—again, for what? For whatever one desires, and desire has no limits. But here we may understand desire in relation to giving rather than taking, so that the limitlessness of desire is not for accumulating and consuming but for expending and giving, desiring not to have but to—who knows what? My desire, perhaps your desire, desire in general, presupposes both taking and having and a giving beyond having and taking. Both. Sometimes known to us as love, possessive, demanding, erotic, rapturous, ecstatic love. I postpone love to another place.[6]

I return from giving to seizing and enclosing. Rousseau writes of enclosure well after the enclosure of the land—or earth—taking it for granted at the point I call it into question.

> In general, the following rules must obtain in order to authorize the right of the first occupant on any land. First, this land may not already be occupied by anyone. Second, no one may occupy more than the amount needed to subsist. Third, one is to take possession of it not by an empty ceremony, but by working and cultivating it—the only sign of property that ought, in the absence of legal titles, to be respected by others. (Rousseau, *SC*, 152)

He goes on to question where the right to enclose property in the earth might end, knowing that taking and desiring to take have no limits. "In fact, by according to need and work the right of the first occupant, is it not extended as far as it can go? Is it possible to avoid setting limits to this right? Will setting one's foot on a piece of common land be sufficient to claim it at once as one's own?" (p. 152). He takes enclosure and genitivity of the earth for granted without considering the possibility that these are ethical and political conditions—or ethicoeconomoecological—and that owning and having by nature—if anything is by nature—give rise to questions of limits, produce conflicts of exclusion, but giving does not. We may think of the right of first occupant not as a seizing and taking but as a giving and responding.

I am here, Levinas says, face to face with my neighbors. On this land I find neighbors, others, with whom I bear a relationship of giving and responding, resisting possessing. I have needs and desires; others give to me. Others have needs and desires; I give to them. The abundance of the earth is giving. This is not to deny the possibility that there will not be enough for some, for any. Abundance is not a measure, not much or little, but giving in the midst of multiplicity, diversity, and heterogeneity, beyond limits, desiring beyond limits to respond, to give. To live, or live well, we must be given goods in sufficient measure, and must give to others. Yet living, and living well, come from desiring, and there is never enough to have or own to fulfill desires. Giving exceeds all possibilities of conflict, does not belong to the sphere of having. Yet Rousseau speaks the language of acquisition. "What is remarkable about this alienation is that, in accepting the goods of private individuals, the community is far from despoiling them; rather, in so doing, it merely assures them of legitimate possession, changing usurpation into a true right, and enjoyment into proprietary ownership. . . . This paradox is easily explained by the distinction between the rights of the sovereign and those of the proprietor" (p. 152). The paradox of a giving beyond measure that is not a loss is explained by a distinction between sovereign power and owning. Something distinct from having lies at the heart of the social contract, not as it has been instituted in historical societies—where having and ruling always go together—but in the nature of having itself—giving beyond having; and in the nature of authority—power *(le pouvoir)* beyond Power *(« le » pouvoir)* in Foucault's words (Foucault, *HS*, 92–97); authorization beyond authority, as Derrida suggests (Derrida, *FL*, 57–63). Giving and calling beyond having and ruling. General beyond restricted economology. Inseparably beyond.

Something of this echoes in Rousseau's words describing the social contract as what human beings give to the community, interpreted as a giving beyond price, giving what one does not have to others. We can hear something similar linking Rousseau's words in *The Social Contract* with the words beginning his *Discourse on the Origin of Inequality*.

> [I]nstead of destroying natural equality, the fundamental compact, on the contrary, substitutes a moral and legitimate equality to whatever physical inequality nature may have been able to impose upon men, and that, however, unequal in force or intelligence they may be, men all become equal by convention and by right. (Rousseau, *SC*, 153)

> The first person who, having enclosed a plot of land, took it into his head to say this is mine and found people simple enough to believe him,

was the true founder of civil society. What crimes, wars, murders, what miseries and horrors would the human race have been spared, had some-one pulled up the stakes or filled in the ditch and cried out to his fellow men: "Do not listen to this impostor. You are lost if you forget that the fruits of the earth belong to all and the earth to no one!" But it is quite likely that by then things had already reached the point where they could no longer continue as they were. (Rousseau, *DOI*, 60)

It was already too late, is always too late, to abolish the right to own and have, because that right has always been instituted in the belonging to-gether of human beings in and with the things of the earth, present in the hand that grasps and takes in the name of desire and need, that labors to provide. Yet in that belonging and withness is a recognition—betrayal—that enclosure and possessing are not belonging and withness, that giving without having and requesting without authority are the (impossible) con-ditions of the possibility of taking and owning. Inequality and property under law are tightly linked; having is injustice.

> From the cultivation of land, there necessarily followed the division of land; and from property once recognized, the first rules of justice. . . . (p. 66)

> Such was, or should have been, the origin of society and laws, which gave new fetters to the weak and new forces to the rich, irretrievably destroyed natural liberty, established forever the law of property and of inequality, changed adroit usurpation into an irrevocable right, and for the profit of a few ambitious men henceforth subjected the entire human race to labor, servitude and misery. (p. 70)

Property is the origin of inequality; owning, having, and accumulating is domination and exclusion. Yet society is not based on property but on giving what cannot be had, gifts that cannot be given away.

> [S]ince the right of property is merely the result of convention and human institution, every man can dispose of what he possesses as he sees fit. But it is not the same for the essential gifts of nature such as life and liberty, which everyone is allowed to enjoy, and of which it is at least doubtful that one has the right to divest himself. In giving up the one he degrades his being; in giving up the other he annihilates that being insofar as he can. (Rousseau, *DOI*, 74)

Rousseau is read as designating properties, rights, or claims that can-not be alienated, cannot be sold or given away. Goods and properties can be alienated; life and liberty cannot. I am exploring another reading, another possibility, that goods are both owned, possessed, in the genitive, and beyond the genitive, beyond possession. Life and liberty are gifts that call for giving to others. That my life and liberty might be mine alone—in the genitive—is impossible. So I am called, required, to give them to others insofar as they are given to me. Suggesting that I might claim them for myself and deny them to others. Familiar enough if I am wealthy or powerful. Familiar betrayal and injustice.

Why not other goods as well? I have goods that I can accumulate against others, beyond any use I may make of them. I can accumulate power and authority as well. The laws of society may allow and encourage such acquisition—and typically do. But betrayed in the idea of such an accumulation is a giving that is neither having nor alienating, that was never mine to own so can never be mine to sell or give away. A giving that is not giving away. Not only life and liberty, body and soul, but all the goods that I live among, the things and creatures in the abundance of the earth, I cannot sell them because I never owned them, though I lived among them, and sometimes to live had to expend them. But the primary ethical relation is giving rather than having, giving to them as well as other people, not just giving under the social contract, selling and buying. Living is giving and its betrayal.

Alienation is a giving that is a taking, a grasping, on the other side. And perhaps we must seize and take some goods to live. Or perhaps we may never take to have but always give beyond having or receiving the goods we need to live and desire for our happiness. For living and desiring are giving rather than taking, take to give again. Among the animals and things of the earth. And even for human beings. Taking is not hoarding but giving beyond.

We return to the *oikos*, to household management, distinguishing state management and public economy under the general will from private households and economy under private will. "It follows from all I have just put forward that one has good reason to distinguish public from private economy and that, since the state has nothing in common with the family except the obligation their respective leaders bear to render each of them happy, the same rules of conduct could not be suitable to both" (Rousseau, *DPE*, 113). The general will, public, political economy is absolutely different from private economy, giving from taking.

> I. The first and most important maxim of legitimate or popular government, that is to say, of a government that has the good of the populace for its object, is therefore, as I have said, to follow the general will in all things. But to follow the general will one must know it, and, above all, properly distinguish it from the private will, beginning with oneself. . . . How is it possible that they obey and no one commands, that they serve and have no master, and yet are actually more free because,

under what appears to be subjection, no one loses any of his liberty except
what can be harmful to the liberty of another? These wonders are the work
of the law. It is to the law alone that men owe justice and liberty. (p. 116)

Here the general will is something known, possessed and had, under law,
instituted in state authority, exceeding every possible authority. "The second essential rule of public economy is no less important than the first. Do
you want the general will to be accomplished? Make all private wills be in
conformity with it. And since virtue is merely this conformity of the private
to the general will, in a word, make virtue reign" (p. 119). Whose virtue,
whose authority, is in charge, under whose reign? Perhaps the greatest
inequality comes from this insistence on equality under the general will—
insistence, we might say, on property and genitivity, on instituted proprieties of the general will. "Certainly the right to property is the most sacred
of all the citizens' rights, and more important in certain respects than
liberty itself" (p. 127); "the foundation of the social compact is property,
together with its first condition that each person should be maintained in
the peaceful enjoyment of what belongs to him" (p. 132). Political economy
is the public solution to inequality in property—no solution at all. The
general will in the genitive is domination and oppression—in Rousseau's
other words, slavery and chains, miseries and horrors.

Yet on the other side, the general will offers no authority or accumulation. No one loses anything under the general will because it gives nothing to have. It is not the determinate will of the state, community, or
populace, not even that of France or the human world. The scale of human
society is incongruous with the household; economy becomes political
economy beyond the borders of the state. Similarly, the scale of the earth
is incongruous with the home: ecology becomes the earth's ecology, dwelling in the earth.

Impossible. Giving without having, ecology beyond economy, general
economy without restricted economy, living without owning. All impossible, yet interrupting the unbroken reign of property and the authorities
that betray it.

I conclude this discussion with some supplementary observations suggesting that there is nothing natural or universal, nothing to be taken for
granted in genitivity. What modern philosophy calls most my own, Dewey
suggests, is not owned at all, dispossessing genitivity and decentering the
subject—not to deny the existence of selves, persons, and subjects, or of
ownership, but their necessity and universality.

> To say in a significant way, "*I* think, believe, desire, instead of barely
> *it* is thought, believed, desired," is to accept and affirm a responsibility and

to put forth a claim. It does not mean that the self is the source or author of the thought and affection nor its exclusive seat. . . .

. . . There is nothing in nature that *belongs* absolutely and exclusively to anything else; belonging is always a matter of reference and distributive assignment, justified in any particular case as far as it works out well. (Dewey, *EN*, 232–34)

It is tempting to read these words as about experience, or knowledge, or rights, about what is said to belong absolutely to human beings as legal or ethical or epistemological subjects. And so we should. But Dewey is making a more sweeping claim about genitivity. Being is not *as such* having or owning; nor is it neutral *as such*; it is never *as such*, always requiring supplementation in context and contingency. So with genitivity, always something more and less than owning, having, and possessing. "No unprejudiced observer will lightly deny the existence of an original tendency to assimilate objects and events to the self, to make them part of the 'me.' We may even admit that the 'me' cannot exist without the 'mine.' . . . only a callous imagination fancies that the institution of private property as it exists A.D. 1921 is the sole or the indispensable means of its realization" (Dewey, *HNC*, 116–17).

Foucault says something similar in relation to the author's proper name, clearly if silently in the genitive.

We can conclude that, unlike a proper name, which moves from the interior of a discourse to the real person outside who produced it, the name of the author remains at the contours of texts—separating one from the other, defining their form, and characterizing their mode of existence. . . . The author's name is not a function of a man's civil status, nor is it fictional; it is situated in the breach, among the discontinuities, which gives rise to new groups of discourse and their singular mode of existence. (Foucault, *WA?*, 123)

The genitive is situated in the breach, establishing modes of existence far beyond the relations of individual human beings to their surroundings. It establishes what is taken to be the destiny of both. To which we may respond to Foucault's question, "What matter who's speaking?" (p. 138) with others: "What matter who possesses and what is possessed?"; "What matter in the genitive?"; "What is the matter with genitivity?": all dispossessions of genitivity; all betrayal and *mimēsis*.

What if nothing belonged to anything or anyone except proximately and contingently, not even to the earth? What of living and being by dispossessing genitivity, disallowing authority, betraying genitivity, genitality, and authority?

# CHAPTER 4

## Destined Properties

92. Property, whose original is from the right a man has to use any of the inferior creatures, for the subsistence and comfort of his life, is for the benefit and sole advantage of the proprietor, so that he may even destroy the thing that he has property in by his use of it, where need requires: But government being for the preservation of every man's right and property, by preserving him from the violence or injury of others, is for the good of the governed. (Locke, *TT*, 1, Ch. 2, 209)

44. A person has as his substantive and the right of putting his will into any and every thing and thereby making it his, because it has no such end in itself and derives its destiny and soul from his will. This is the absolute right of appropriation which man has over all "things." (Hegel, *PR*, 41)

A few more dreams and I am through with dreams, if not with spectters, famous genealogical fantasies of the advent of property. First Locke, beginning with something I have so far largely neglected, where in his Essay he speaks of the "quiet and sure possession of truths" (Locke, *E*, 1, ch. 1, 31).[1] We have, we own, knowledge and truth, as if they were something to hold, possess, to stockpile ready to use. Together with his famous words on property, Locke establishes that we hope to have, to possess as our very own, that which makes us human, whether it be other human beings, creatures and things, understanding and truth, perhaps independence and freedom. We hope to own as property that which can never be owned, that which both makes property possible and also makes it impossible. I continue to postpone this thought of the betrayal of property.[2]

Locke's explicit views on property may be decisive in defining humanity's genitive relation to themselves and other creatures and things, thereby to other people. I mean European or Western humanity in the first instance, but through colonialism and economic development becoming humanity's views in general.[3] The origin of property, Locke says, is the right to use any inferior creatures—Aristotle's view in modern dress—because human beings are proprietors to themselves, own themselves and thereby others, must own themselves to be human and free. Other things and creatures are inferior, thereby available to human beings for use in any way whatever, for the benefit and sole advantage of the owner, to the point of their destruction if the owner chooses. Government—closer to Plato's view—is for the sake of the governed. Here, explicitly stated, is the view of owning as compared with governing that has come to dominate modern societies. In the name of democracy, government is for the sake of the governed, supporting the right of the governed to use, even destroy, every thing other than human beings, to the advantage of the owner.

To which we might respond—Locke does not overlook this possibility—that owning may be more like governing than taking (though rulers and ruled frequently confuse the two), for the sake of what is owned; that property may not be seizing, possessing, taking, but caring for, bearing responsibility for, that which is owned, thereby for the sake of the good.

When God gives dominion over the earth to Adam—lord of all things— "he means nothing to be granted here but property" (Locke, *TT*, 1, ch. 4, 156). The issue here for Locke is monarchy, whether all things are a ruler's private property. "That by this grant God gave him not private dominion over the inferior creatures, but right in common with all mankind; so neither was he monarch, upon the account of the property here given him" (p. 157). Authority, sovereignty, and rule all pertain to property, public or personal. And what, we may ask, of the possibility of being together without possession? For example, distinguishing private property, individually possessed, and public property, owned by the community or state, still possessed, from a relation to things and creatures and other human beings without possession, owning, or having? As may have existed in relation to the land among nomadic people until recently. As existed widely in the United States in the last century: unowned land to be claimed as property by fencing it off. Property arrives with the props essential to it: fences and plows. From land given in abundance.

> The earth, and all that is therein, is given to men for the support and comfort of their being. And though all the fruits it naturally produces, and beasts it feeds, belong to mankind in common, as they are produced by the spontaneous hand of nature; . . . yet being given for the use of men, there must of necessity be a means to appropriate them some way or other, before they can be of any use, or at all beneficial to any particular man. The fruit, or venison, which nourishes the wild Indian, who knows no enclosure, and is still a tenant in common, must be his, and so his, i.e. a part of him, that another can no longer have any right to it, before it can do him any good for the support of his life. (Locke, *TT*, 2, ch. 5, 286)

The double key to Locke's view of property is that the world belongs to human beings in common. Not to beasts or plants or wild lands themselves. Humanity is the sole proprietor, in common and in general. Commanded to subdue. "God commanded, and his wants forced him to labour. That was his property which could not be taken from him wherever he had fixed it. And hence subduing or cultivating the earth, and having dominion, we see are joined together. . . . And the condition of human life, which requires labour and materials to work on, necessarily introduces private possessions" (p. 292). Individuals must claim some of this goodness for themselves by taking and enclosing it. Even the Indian, the forager, must take to live—according to Locke—from the pool in common. Locke does not consider the possibility that one might take—or receive—what one needs to live without owning or enclosing, gathering what one finds good supposing that others will find goodness elsewhere. Yet he takes for granted that there will be enough, that the goodness of things provides enough so that taking by one or a group does not deprive others. "Nor was this appropriation of any parcel of land, by improving it, any prejudice to any other man, since there was still enough, and as good left; and more than the yet unprovided could use. So that, in effect, there was never the less left for others because of his enclosure for himself. For he that leaves as much as another can make use of, does as good as take nothing at all" (p. 291).

This is a quantitative understanding of abundance: there is so much and enough that taking and enclosing does not diminish the quantity needed by others, who find as good left for themselves. One might respond that such abundance is no longer available on the surface of the earth, if it ever was, indeed that at the time of which Locke writes, among foraging and gathering peoples, there was never enough for all, and that intricate webs of social relationships were required to provide for all who lived off the land. More of this later.

Here I hope to distinguish this measured view of abundance as plenty, linked with and understood as wealth, from abundance as giving, not as less or more, dearth or plenty, but as providing, allowing, emergence beyond measure, where neither giving, receiving, nor responding is measurable or determinate, where to receive is to bear responsibility. In the earth, in receiving, echoes a call, an obligation. Property is responsibility. Having is betrayal.

For Locke, property arrives before political power and authority, perhaps before arrival. "Political power, then, I take to be a right of making laws and penalties of death, and consequently all less penalties for the regulating and preserving of property" (TT, ch. 1, 268). The state of nature is a state of possession, property having already arrived: "a state of perfect freedom to order their actions, and dispose of their possessions and persons, as they think fit, within the bounds of the law of nature; without asking leave, or depending upon the will of any other man" (2, ch. 2, 269). It is a state of private possession, where human beings may act as they think fit toward their possessions. Famously, however, not quite so. It is a state of equality and liberty (p. 269) given as responsibility.

> But though this be a state of liberty, yet it is not a state of licence: though man in that state have an uncontrollable liberty to dispose of his person or possessions, yet he has not liberty to destroy himself, or so much as any creature in his possession, but where some nobler use than its bare preservation calls for it. . . . For men being all the workmanship of one omnipotent and infinitely wise Maker; . . . ought he, as much as he can, to preserve the rest of mankind, and may not, unless it be to do justice to an offender, take away or impair the life, or what tends to the preservation of life, the liberty, health, limb, or goods of another. (p. 270)

All things and creatures are the workmanship of God—as Descartes says, machines made by God, beyond human knowledge, bearing infinite responsibility. Locke approaches the possibility that to own is to be in debt, that property belongs to human beings in service beyond themselves, for the sake of God or the good or things themselves, beyond measure. Liberty in property—still in the state of nature—is not license, according to Locke: is given in relation to the good, comes in debt. By no means to be disposed of as the owner sees fit, or for the owner's sake alone. Locke approaches a possibility largely unknown to contemporary capitalism—especially of this moment, where greed and acquisitiveness seem to coincide—that may be at the heart of capital itself. Capital is not owned as property, neither public nor private, to be disposed of according to its owners, but incurs a debt beyond measure, promised to circulation. I raise the specter of general economy within restricted economy, haunted by the ghost of the good.

I insist that this promise beyond measure is beyond church or state, that neither the king nor parliament nor officers of church and state can determine exchanges beyond propriety. That is the issue in relation to giving beyond having: in the state of human need and authority, we must have to live, to live well, to be free; in the giving beyond any need and authority, freedom is giving without having. In neither case is owning license to harm or destroy. In neither case does one have without responsibility and care— or without betrayal.

I will not pursue Locke's limitation of this debt to humanity, his understanding that the state of nature is a state of human equality—not including other creatures and natural things—in which the right and duty and necessity to preserve oneself imposes an obligation to preserve the rest of mankind. Why not understand the responsibility toward oneself and other human beings to reach out toward all God's creatures? Locke's humanism is qualified, does not extend as far as I would insist it must. Most of all, it remains qualified by the doubling inherent at its heart. The things that are owned are owned by God, speak of God, express a responsibility beyond disposal and exchange. That which human beings own imposes a double responsibility, between human beings in relation to each other and their possessions; and between human beings and the things they own, divine things. Property is an ethical matter. Doubled in betrayal.

Yet this is not what Locke says when he addresses the advent of property. I come to the view of property that has had the greatest effect on the earth as we know it.

> Though the earth, and all inferior creatures, be common to all men, yet every man has a property in his own person: this no body has any right to but himself. The labour of his body, and the work of his hands, we may say, are properly his. Whatsoever then he removes out of the state that nature hath provided, and left it in, he hath mixed his labour with, and joined to it something that is his own, and thereby makes it his property.... For this labour being the unquestionable property of the labourer, no man but he can have a right to what that is once joined to, at least where there is enough, and as good, left in common for others. (TT, ch. 5, 287)

Several things here are worth noting, extended repetitions of my reading of Locke

First is that the earth and its creatures and things belong to human beings in common, no longer, apparently, belonging to God. I have questioned whether this gift is given in debt and responsibility, as Locke himself says, promised to something beyond the owner. The uncontrollable liberty to dispose is promised to a nobler use or something further, exceeds disposal and personal desire. Property is owned for the sake of something else, something otherwise, perhaps nothing at all, nothing possessed. Property exceeds the liberty of the owner, puts the owner in debt. If owned in common, the insistent demand from properties owned is our collective responsibility toward them, ourselves, and the earth.

I have questioned whether this primordial relation of humanity to the earth—all other creatures and things demarcated as inferior—is one of ownership and possession, rather than collective beings touching the earth together, creatures and things in proximity.

Second, the primordial relation of human being to self is one of property and possession. No one has a right to anyone's body but that person. No one has a right to enslave another human being. I interrupt to note that slavery surrounded Locke, that the British colonies engaged in slave trade during his lifetime.[4] I return to question the assumption of possession, as if the enslavement of human beings, taking possession of their bodies, might be resisted only by insisting on their possession of themselves. We have our bodies, have property rights to our bodies, that no one else may override. In this way, we may claim that slavery is wrong, claiming to possess what cannot be possessed. Many writers deeply indebted to Locke doubt that individuals have property rights in themselves, their qualities, and their bodies.[5]

What if we resisted slavery by resisting all property rights to self and others, understanding all claims to property as insisting on possessing what cannot be possessed, as betrayals. To be is to be in proximity, touching, responding, called to responsibility. To be for the self, and others, is to be responsible to oneself and others. Exposure, proximity, responsibility, generosity. Levinas's terms.[6] Across possessed things, the face, the ethical—perhaps all things in the earth, which we designate as property—generosity reaches toward the face, resists possession. Perhaps resistance to possession, to property, is the mark of things in the earth. As property. The betrayal of property.

Third, the right of property in one's body extends from body to labor through the hands. The labor of a man's hands determines what is properly his. (I keep the masculine gender of property here to mark its betrayals, though I mean to resist it throughout.) At the beginning, the advent, of humanity in the world—albeit it a dream, filled with ghosts—something is properly mine or yours. Propriety never arrives, is always there. In the flesh and the hands.[7]

I would think of a relation to the earth—giving, caring, cherishing—that neither begins nor ends in taking and having, not even in exposure, proximity, and responsibility. I would think neither of possessing things as mine, not yours, nor of possessing things in common, but of giving without a genitive, betraying the genitive. To own, possess, to claim as mine not yours, perhaps even mine and yours, is to affirm a responsibility. Property arrives in debt, given beyond ownership and propriety. Even in common. Nomadic peoples do not own the land or sky or earth, may live wonderfully with land and sky—though some own cattle and implements for their work.

I would pursue the thought of buying and selling what we do not own, in debt beyond the use of the user, for the sake of something beyond user and things. We use and exchange them for the sake of a responsibility, in debt. I think of debt here as exposure and proximity, linked with betrayal, not as property and possession. If the earth is not humanity's property, humanity is not the property of the earth.

I turn here to another dream of the earth as human property, perhaps the ultimate dream in the genitive. Early in his *Philosophy of Right*, where

Hegel expresses the idea of freedom as right, he speaks of property, reenacting the dreams we have already dreamed, with the peculiar force of the dialectical register, its characteristic extremity. "Every stage in the development of the Idea of freedom has its own special right, since it is the embodiment of freedom in one of its proper specific forms" (Hegel, *PR*, 34); "A person must translate his freedom into an external sphere in order to exist as Idea" (p. 40). We may consider here a number of things: (1) Hegel shares Kant's view that the purpose of the universe is human freedom; (2) this freedom begins with the curse, the primordial alienation of Spirit from nature; (3) the primordial form of the relation of Spirit to things is appropriation, property; (4) things exist to be owned by human beings; (5) human beings exist to own; and finally, (6) humanity and the earth have a destiny, an end. A person has the right and obligation to put his will into an external thing and make it his; it derives its destiny and soul from his will. The absolute arrives in the genitive. Spirit "thus discovers this world in the living present to be its own property" (Hegel, *PM*, 802). Rochelle insists—if she insists—that she has no destiny, and wonders at the fate of human beings and other things.

If we suspend the absoluteness of the absolute and the dialectical form of the dialectic—to many a distinctly non-Hegelian gesture—then the remarkable appeal we may find in Hegel—I speak for myself—is the profusion of differences as the movement of time and history, refusing to be *merely* differences and *merely* reconciliations, but always more, refusing every *only*.

> Logic shows that the subjective which is to be subjective only, the finite which would be finite only, the infinite which would be infinite only, and so on, have no truth, but contradict themselves and pass into their opposites. (Hegel, *EL*, 355)

> Of the Absolute it must be said that it is essentially a result, that only at the end is it what it is in every truth; and just in that consists its nature, which is to be actual, subject, or self-becoming, self-development. (Hegel, *PM*, 81–82)

The absolute, only absolute at the end, as result, passes away from itself. I have called this remarkable relation to less and more, alienation and sublation, *lownliness: onlyness, loneliness, and ownliness*;[8] the triad of loneliness—man alone before death; onlyness—only man; and owning, having. Here I am concerned especially with the last, understanding the movement of the dialectic from the onlyness and loneliness of spirit's alienation as expressed by Hegel in the genitive, insisting on owning and having. If the absolute refuses every only, the dialectic is its endless betrayal—

revealing and overcoming onlyness everywhere by having. In the spirit of lownliness.

Not for a moment does Hegel explore the possibility that spirit might give up its alienation, might cease to be lonely in the onlyness of otherness, not by having and taking but by giving, not by owning but exposed in proximity with the things in the earth together. I would consider the possibility that lownliness calls for giving, relinquishing, generosity, not taking and having as one's own but releasing spirit's demand to own to generosity to things and kinds in the earth. I would explore the possibility of giving up alienation in the exposure of things to each other. Spirit comes to know that it is not alone, that others are with it not as property but in and with it, constituting its identity among them in virtue of their heterogeneity. That in part is what one may say of giving. Spirit discovers that it is not alone, touches others in exposure and proximity, in endless betrayal.

For Hegel it belongs to the nature of spirit to discover that what it took to be other is its own property, not its neighbor; spirit insists on overcoming its lownliness by mastery.[9] Mastery, overcoming, and possessing are inextricably linked in Hegel, expressing human freedom as taking and having. "In relation to external things, the rational aspect is that I possess property" (Hegel, *PR*, 44); "Since property is the *embodiment* of personality, my inward idea and will that something is to be mine is not enough to make it my property; to secure this end occupancy is requisite. The embodiment which my willing thereby attains involves its recognizability by others" (p. 45). Recognized as mine, not yours, mine not others'. Without a doubt human beings externalize their wills in things as property and hold that property as their own, exclusive of others.

I interrupt to note that this understanding follows from an extreme reading of Kant on freedom as property in relation to things and other creatures in the earth—already an extreme reading of Locke. For following Hobbes's trajectory, Kant moves from desire to property as freedom, the ultimate purpose of the world. Man is the final purpose of creation as free owner of all things.[10] The first condition of humanity on the way to freedom is the right to accumulate without limit. The presence of desire in freedom gives rise to Right, not as a relation of person to thing, given from the thing, but of person to person toward the thing, where the latter has no status except as object of desire. Right is an intricate relation of person to person, human to human, as if untouched by anything nonhuman. Desire needs no recognition except the desire of another human. "The concept of Right, . . . has to do, *first*, only with the external and indeed practical relation of one person to another, insofar as their actions as facts, can have (direct or indirect) influence on each other[,] . . . insofar as choice is regarded merely as *free*, and whether the action of one can be united with the freedom of the other in accordance with a universal law" (Kant, MM, 56). What it needs is the ability to own without gripping. "[S]omething *external* would be mine only if I may assume that I could be wronged by another's use of a thing even *though I am not in possession of it*"; "possession of an object *without holding it*" (p. 68). Having without holding, if that is possible. Property exceeds the grasp of the hands, the reach of labor. Law of human to human reaches out to have and hold beyond every limit except those determined by law itself.

Put another way, property beyond possession, right of law beyond holding, follows a single reading of the trajectory from God to humanity as understood by Locke, Kant, and Hegel—shall we think of it as uniquely Judeo-Christian? Everything is given in the world to humanity as property, in the genitive, to have and own, rather than in care and love, to cherish and foster. Human freedom is freedom to have and control beyond grasping. "[T]he concept to which the concept of a right is directly applied is not that of *holding*, which is an empirical way of thinking of possession, but rather the concept of *having*, in which abstraction is made from all spatial and temporal conditions and the object is thought of only as *under my control*" (Kant, *MM,* 74–75). To have from afar, in another place. "It is not because I occupy a place on the earth with my body that this place is something external that is mine. . . . It is mine if I still possess it even though I have left it for another place; only then is my external right involved" (p. 75): absentee landowners charging rent to tenants without having to put their labor into the land; European regimes colonizing remote corners of the world despite aboriginal dwellers who do not know how to own because they do not possess by right.[11]

Such right is from the first linked with genealogy, genitivity, and genitality: having other people as possessions. "I cannot call an object in *space* (a corporeal thing) mine unless, *even though I am not in physical possession of it*, I can still assert that I am actually in some other (hence not physical) possession of it. . . . I cannot call a *wife*, a *child*, a *servant*, or, in general, another person mine because I am now in charge of them as members of my household . . . but only if, . . . I can still say that I possess them merely by my will" (Kant, *MM,* 70). Genitivity insists on genitality. The will to have is erotic desire. The will to possess is the desire to enjoy human beings and things in the home. Others respond by evoking the crime of treating human beings as things—*reification*. And what is so bad about being a wonderful thing that shares the earth with other things and creatures, except for the proper destiny assigned to things?

I hold this ecological thought in abeyance, emphasizing genitivity in Kant within the walls of household management, traditional ecolonomy.

### On Rights to Persons Akin to Rights to Things

This Right is that of possession of an external object *as a thing* and use of it *as a person*. What is mine or yours in terms of this Right is what is mine or yours *domestically,* . . . called a *household.* . . . Acquisition of this status, and within it, therefore takes place . . . by principle. (Kant, *MM,* 95)

In terms of the object, acquisition in accordance with this principle is of three kinds: A *man* acquires a *wife*; a *couple* acquires *children*; and a *family* acquires *servants.* (p. 98)

With some honesty, Kant acknowledges that sex is appropriation and use of another's body. If anything can be appropriated and used. *"Sexual union* is the reciprocal use that one human being makes of the sexual organs and capacities of another. This is either a *natural* use (by which procreation of a being of the same kind is possible) or an *unnatural* use, and unnatural use takes place either with a person of the same sex or with an animal of a non-human species" (p. 96). In the context of such an expansion of use and appropriation, it seems immaterial to distinguish natural from unnatural uses or reciprocal from coercive uses, expropriation from appropriation. I would hope to think instead of love as disappropriation, as giving what we cannot have.

Kant, however, demands that love and sex be made right under law, that thereby human beings turn themselves properly into possessed things.

For the natural use that one sex makes of the other's sexual organs is *enjoyment,* for which one gives itself up to the other. In this act a human being makes himself into a thing, which conflicts with the Right of humanity in his own person. There is only one condition under which this is possible: that while one person is acquired by the other *as if it were a thing,* the one who is acquired acquires the other in turn; for in this way each reclaims itself and restores its personality. (pp. 96–97)

Erotic desire is desire to own and to be owned, to be turned into a thing so long as the other is also a thing. Suspending the abjection and hatred of the flesh inherent in this much too Christian a view, I would recall the possibility of love in things that expresses their expressivity, that they are to be cherished and cherish each other. I have been holding this line of thought in abeyance. Kant remains with persons owned as things. "From this duty there must necessarily also arise the right of parents to *manage* and develop the child" (p. 99); "From a child's personality it also follows that the right of parents is not just a right to a thing, since a child can never be considered as the property of his parents . . . It is, instead, a right to a person *akin to a right to a thing*" (p. 100). Persons and things are present in the genitive in the nature of freedom itself—always the owner's freedom. More of that shortly, the owner's freedom to have.

I return from this extended interruption in the name of freedom as property to Hegel's view of property as destiny. Things are there for us as property, a relation among human beings. Human freedom is the destiny of things in the earth to be owned—instead, as I have been wondering, of being exposed to things in proximity.

For Hegel, the externalization of will in things, as the embodiment and expression of freedom, takes place repeatedly in the genitive, indeed, the genitive of the genitive, the *mimēsis* of *mimēsis*. Things as property, in the genitive, are marked *as things to be owned* under law, in relation to human wills, in the plural. Being property, under law, is in the genitive of the genitive, as if being something were nothing at all without contract rights under law. "Contract brings into existence the property whose external side, its side as an existent, is no longer a mere 'thing' but contains the moment of a will (and consequently the will of a second person also)" (Hegel, PR 57–58). Things are taken over, in the destiny of their natures, into relations among human wills. Human freedom is the right or power to take and the fulfillment of freedom's destiny and promise. Yet while human freedom may be the destiny of human beings, it is incredible that it should be the destiny of wolves and fields, as if they were nothing whatever except in genitive relations inscribed between human beings. In a movement clearly present in Marx and Engels, and in all post-Marxist Marxisms—political economies indebted to Marx, even political economy itself—things are marked for human beings as property, seized under contract.[12]

Ethics takes this relation for granted, in the double genitive. "The right of individuals to be subjectively destined to freedom is fulfilled when they belong to an actual ethical order, . . . and it is in an ethical order that they are actually in possession of their own essence or their own inner universality" (p. 109). Rights and duties between human individuals coalesce in the reciprocation of ethical freedom, presupposing a relation without reciprocity: human beings taking possession of things as property, a relation among human beings, not between human beings and things. In the genitive. And in the genital. Household management becomes surrender and domination, with the economy of capitalism the model. The unequal distribution of the goods of the earth becomes the destiny of things in the family and nation. The genitality of economology. Cascading down the lines of human demarcation.

165. The difference in the physical characteristics of the two sexes has a rational basis and consequently acquires an intellectual and ethical significance. . . .

> Thus one sex is mind in its self-diremption into explicit personal self-subsistence and the knowledge and volition of free universality. . . . The other sex is mind maintaining itself in unity as knowledge . . . in the form of concrete individuality and feeling. In relation to externality, the former is powerful and active, the latter passive and subjective. It follows that man has his actual substantive life in the state, in learning, and so forth. . . . Woman, on the other hand, has her substantive destiny in the family, and to be imbued with family piety is her ethical frame of mind. (p. 114)

> 169. The family, as person, has its real external existence in property; and it is only when this property takes the form of capital that it becomes the embodiment of the substantial personality of the family. (p. 116)

> 202. The classes are specifically determined in accordance with the concept as *(a)* the *substantial* or immediate [or agricultural] class; *(b)* the reflecting or *formal* [or business] class; and finally, *(c)* the *universal* class [the class of civil servants]. (p. 131)

One might understand Marx's claim to turn Hegel on his head at this point of hierarchical distribution. The destiny of human beings and things is to become unequal in the structure of family and class, under capitalism, in the genitive. Marx refuses the destiny but not the genitive, especially not the genitive in which the free human individual takes possession of the thing through labor.[13]

It is time to bring these dreams of destiny to closure with Engels's dream of the family. I postpone this moment to the next chapter to consider one of the few extreme resistances to genitivity to be found in European history, perhaps in the history of humanity itself. For to the understanding that property is destiny, Proudhon replies—receiving Marx's scorn—that slavery is murder and property is theft (Proudhon, *WP?*, 13), linked through the genitive. Owning, possessing, and having are theft and murder, inequality, despotism, and injustice. If slavery—owning human beings—is murder; if property—owning things that others may not own—is theft; then what of owning and having in general? Owning animals: is that not murder? Having children, insisting that they do one's will: is that not theft? Having wives, insisting that they provide children and hospitality in the home: is that not murder and theft? Having the right to control the future and the past as author, provider, originator, historical figure: is that not theft and murder, stealing the past and future, murdering the event—if these can be stolen and killed? Proudhon evokes the possibility that genitivity is injustice, returning us to Anaximander in a modern register:

every imaginable argument made on behalf of property, no matter what it may be, always and necessarily leads to equality, that is, to the negation of property. (p. 33)

> To sum up, liberty is an absolute right because it is to man what impenetrability is to matter, a sine qua non of existence; equality is an absolute right because without equality there is no society; security is an absolute right because in the eyes of every man his own liberty and life as precious as another's. These three rights are absolute, that is, susceptible of neither increase nor diminution because every member of society receives as much as he gives. . . .
> But property . . . is a right outside of society. . . . (p. 42)

Proudhon adopts two stances on property, one I call the *enlightenment* view that property presupposes equality but promotes inequality. Liberty and equality are absolute rights of social life. I call it *enlightenment* in virtue of the language of equality and liberty that frame it, evoking *The Declaration of the Rights of Man*. French Enlightenment thought expresses in a modern register what Anaximander understood in Greek: the inescapable contradiction between being—life and liberty—and having. In the extreme, this contradiction pertains directly to Locke's and Marx's views of the genitivity of labor. Although Marx reviles Proudhon for his ignorance of the proper science of political economy, Proudhon's much more extreme challenge to Marx and Engels was his rejection of property and use-value altogether, resisting genitivity more profoundly than Marx imagined, understanding anarchism as the dispossession of genitivity. Labor does not found but abolishes property: "in the order of justice, labour *destroys* property" (Prodhoun, *WP?*, 81).

This leads to Proudhon's second stance on property, interrupting genitivity and all scientific foundations of political economy. It is more radical and more fundamental, approaching the possibility that property is genitivity and genitivity is to be abolished. Property and genitivity are impossible. Proudhon's arguments are entertaining—quite a bit of *mimēsis*. The point is something more. The impossibility of property opens up the possibility of dispossessing genitivity in the extreme. I list Proudhon's arguments before evoking this betrayal:

> Property is physically and mathematically impossible. . . .
> First proposition: *Property is impossible because it demands something from nothing.* . . .
> Second proposition: *Property is impossible because wherever it exists, production costs more than it is worth.* . . .
> Third proposition: *Property is impossible because with a given capital production is proportional to labour, not to property.* . . .

>　　Fourth proposition: *Property is impossible because it is homicide.* . . .
>　　Fifth proposition: *Property is impossible because with it society de-*
>*vours itself.* . . .
>　　Sixth proposition: *Property is impossible because it is the mother of*
>*tyranny.* . . .
>　　Seventh proposition: *Property is impossible because, in consuming*
>*what it receives, it loses it, because in saving it nullifies it, and because*
>*in using it as capital it turns it against production.* . . .
>　　Eighth proposition: *Property is impossible because its power of ac-*
>*cumulation is infinite, while it is exercised only over finite quantities.* . . .
>　　Ninth proposition: *Property is impossible because it is powerless*
>*against property.* . . .
>　　Tenth proposition: *Property is impossible because it is the negation*
>*of equality.* (*WP?,* 118–68)

The impossibility of property exceeds its injustice. And perhaps we may, with Marx, mock the scientificity of Proudhon's claims—as I would reject, if not mock, the scientificity of Marx's claims.

With Marx, I would say that economic, social, and political practices influence the very possibility of representational practices, discourses of truth and knowledge, human life itself and the surface of the earth. All betrayals. With Proudhon, I would consider the possibility that the appropriations that define these representational practices emerge from the enlightenment sense of destiny expressed in Hegel, still present in force in Marx, that humans exist to labor and own—collectively if not individually—and that nonhumans exist to be labored upon and to be owned. Here the impossibility of property, of genitivity, exceeds the injustices of owning—slavery and property—with respect to equality and liberty. The impossibility of genitivity exceeds the contradictions between accumulation and circulation necessary to human social life.

We may take the impossibility of property in Proudhon's words as betraying something beyond accumulation and consumption, beyond increase: general economy, beyond measure. "In other words, property is not equal to property: it is a negation, a delusion, NOTHING" (*WP?,* 168–69).[14] Betraying genitivity, dispossessing possession. Genitivity is the right to claim something and someone against others—persons and things—beyond right itself. Genitivity turns nothing into something: mine forever, impossible to hold or have. Genitivity, property, is having, possessing, what cannot be possessed or had. The impossibility of having is that there is nothing to be had without infinite responsibility or care, without impossible justice, without endless giving, without exposure and proximity. Without exposure to other things and people, as neighbors, there is nothing to have. Without being in proximity, vulnerable to things and people, we can be nothing in relation to them. The endless betrayals of genitivity emerge from the unboundedness of responsibility in exposure and proximity. Yet it profoundly betrays that responsibility itself.

What could be more impossible? What more common in the fabric of human life? What is our hope but anarchy as interruption, dispossessing every possession, unauthorizing every authority?[15] What else could be human, or anything else, in giving from the good? Giving without the trace of destiny, pervaded by the desire for liberty beyond communism and property (p. 212). To this question—what else?—I now turn, from destiny to other possibilities, to the genitivity of Engels and Marx.

# CHAPTER 5

## Family Properties

In each historical epoch, property has developed differently and under a set of entirely different social relations. Thus to define bourgeois
property is nothing else than to give an exposition of all the social relations of bourgeois production. (Marx, *PP*, 129–30)

The overthrow of mother right was the *world-historic defeat of the
female sex*. The man seized the reins in the house also; the woman was
degraded, enthralled, the slave of the man's lust, a mere instrument for
breeding children. (Engels, *OFPPS*, 198)

I come to my final dream of the advent of property, sharing the genealogical feature of the dreams of which I have spoken, the link of property
with the props of property—blood, sex, kin, class, food, desire, and power;
said to be ethics itself: accumulation, consumption, domination, exclusion.
I imagine that when I speak of dreams you may think of ghosts, after
Descartes. Hamlet's ghost, perhaps, Hamlet's dream. Derrida writes of dreams
and ghosts, Marx's specters and ghosts in abundance, far too many phan-
tasms arriving on the scene without departing, insisting on exorcism. Including that enigmatic table standing on its head and feet at the same time.
I postpone the return of the table for a while. Together with *Capital*.

I begin with the advent of property in that other specter's writing after
the death of Marx. As if, perhaps, this arrival of property, this naming of its
arrival, could appear only after Marx himself had become a ghost. In his
name. I am speaking of Engels's *The Origin of the Family, Private Property
and the State*. Family, property, and authority—the origin as potboiler:
blood, sex, wealth, desire, and power. Genitivity as the origin, retold as
genealogy. "According to the materialist conception, the determining factor
in history is, in the last resort, the production and reproduction of immediate life. But this itself is of a twofold character. On the one hand, the
production of the means of subsistence, of food, clothing and shelter and

71

the tools requisite therefore; on the other, the production of human beings themselves, the propagation of the species" (Engels, *OFPPS*, 155–56). The production of property and of human beings. The genitality of genitivity.

In the materialist view of history, the family, private property, and the state arrive, successively linked together. Each constitutes an event, an advent, an explosive arrival. "The old society based on sex groups bursts asunder in the collision of the newly-developed social classes; in its place a new society appears, . . . in which the family system is entirely dominated by the property system, and in which the class antagonisms and class struggles, which make up the content of all hitherto *written* history, now freely develop" (p. 156). Arriving as written history, *mimēsis*, from a state Engels describes as sexual promiscuity and *gynecocracy*, the rule of women, dominance and descent along the maternal line; passing over to monogamy, the ownership of women by men, "where the woman belongs exclusively to one man" (p. 159). At the beginning was property, first children, then women—still sex, gender, blood, linked with genitivity. Women, children, and things, owned and possessed. Polyandry is "the common possession of a woman by a number of men"; "among undeveloped peoples forms of marriage existed in which a group of men possessed a group of women in common" (p. 163). I hold undeveloped peoples in abeyance. For the moment, I note that in Engels's account of the arrival of the family, private property, and the state, these arrive from bonds of kinship and blood intimately linked with ownership and possession. Children, women, and wealth are the originary conditions of human life, as property. Primitive life rests on mother right—to children and possessions as property. Civilized life rests on father right—to women, children, and wealth; on slavery and animal domestication, to which we will come momentarily.[1]

The props of property arrive under the curse.[2] Vestiges of Hegel. "[I]t becomes apparent that animal societies have, to be sure, a certain value in drawing conclusions regarding human societies—but only in a negative sense. . . . The animal family and primitive society are incompatible things" (Engels, *OFPPS*, 179). Like Hegel and Heidegger, Engels does not know enough, and does not want to know, about the ways in which animal social life resembles human societies. He does, however, insist on knowing the social history of women and children as property, insists on knowing who belongs to whom. "In all forms of the group family, it is uncertain who the father of a child is, but it is certain who the mother is. . . . Descent is traceable only on the *maternal* side" (p. 185).[3]

The domestication of animals, the institution of slavery, and the subordination of women under monogamy all have the same origin: the establishment of (private) property, life in the genitive.

Here the domestication of animals and breeding of herds had developed a hitherto unsuspected source of wealth and created entirely new social relationships. . . . on the threshold of authenticated history we find that everywhere the herds are already the separate property of the family chiefs, in exactly the same way as were the artistic products of barbarism, metal utensils, articles of luxury and, finally, human cattle—the slaves. For now slavery also was invented. (p. 195)

The domestication of animals and institution of slavery created wealth, with extreme consequences for women. I hold cattle in abeyance. "According to the division of labour then prevailing in the family, the procuring of food and the implements necessary thereto, and therefore, also, the ownership of the latter, fell to the man; . . . according to the custom of society at that time, the man was also the owner of the new sources of food stuffs—the cattle—and later, of the new instrument of labour—the slaves" (p. 196). Genealogy is descent of property along lines of blood, sex, kin, desire, and power. All developments of the social division of labor. Described by Engels as "one of the most decisive [revolutions] ever experienced by mankind" (p. 197); one of the most eventful of events; the *parousia* of *parousia*s as a transformation in the props of property, heralded in blood. The advent of patriarchy and patrilinearity. The genealogy of genealogy. Together with the arrival of philosophy in Greek.[4] I add philosophy and writing to the props of property, repeatedly inscribed on the bodies of human property, especially women and children. Property exists to be passed on from the father to his sons, of which he must be certain. Monogamy closes the circle of property tightly around its props. "It is based on the supremacy of the man; its express aim is the begetting of children of undisputed paternity, this paternity being required in order that these children may in due time inherit their father's wealth as his natural heirs" (pp. 201–2).[5]

It is time to consider the event in which communism made its name, the advent, *parousia*, of the new. Sex again in the genitive. What Aristotle calls *oikos*, household management, in a different register. Economic sex linked with parental ecology.

Since monogamy arose from economic causes, will it disappear when these causes disappear?

. . . Prostitution disappears; monogamy, instead of declining, finally becomes a reality—for the men as well.

. . . With the passage of the means of production into common property, the individual family ceases to be the economic unit of society. Private housekeeping is transformed into a social industry. The care and education of the children becomes a public matter. Society takes care of all children equally. (pp. 212–13)

Messianic ghosts, as Derrida says. Of a world without property? Or of a world with public, collective property? But not public, collective sex. Still insisting on property's props. Marriage based on property—no longer capitalist property—still fulfills the ethical life. "Thus, full freedom in marriage can become generally operative only when the abolition of capitalist production, and of the property relations created by it, has removed all those secondary economic considerations which still exert so powerful an influence on the choice of a partner. Then, no other motive remains than mutual affection" (p. 218).[6]

The materialist view of history gives to it a twofold character: property in things and in human beings. If humanity's relation to itself and everything else rests in property, in owning or possessing, in being owned or possessed—common, public, or private—then the abolition of capitalism, together with the property relations proper to it, will not entail the abolition of property in things, women, or children. Are my children, is my lover, is the love I receive truly *mine*?[7] Sex is not the way to freedom but another of the dreams that haunt wealth and power. As Foucault says, emphasizing *"regulatory controls: a biopolitics of population"* (Foucault, *HS*, 139), for which "sexual freedom" is a technique. Yet he intimates that "a different economy of bodies and pleasures" (p. 159) might be possible while ridiculing the belief "that our 'liberation' is in the balance" (p. 159).

Engels and Foucault express something of the same posture toward the future in relation to power and sex, perhaps the only stance possible for genealogy:

> Thus, what we can conjecture at present about the regulation of sex relationships after the impending effacement of capitalist production is, in the main, of a negative character, limited mostly to what will vanish. But what will be added? That will be settled after a new generation has grown up. . . . Once such people appear, they will not care a rap about what we today think they should do. They will establish their own practice and their own public opinion, conformable therewith, on the practice of each individual—and that's the end of it. (Engels, *OFPPS*, 219)
>
> it remains to be discovered. (Foucault, *OPJ*, 28)

We will not get rid of God until we get rid of property, Until we abolish the genitive. If that were possible. Until we abolish the genitivity of sex. As if that were possible.

Engels captures something of this insistence on the genitality of the genitive—are my children, my lover, truly *mine*?—when he considers the role of capitalism as the great equalizer, still within the horizon of property.

By transforming all things into commodities, it dissolved all ancient traditional relations, and for inherited customs and historical rights it substituted purchase and sale, "free" contract. . . .

But the closing of contracts presupposes people who can freely dispose of their persons, actions, and possessions, and who meet each other
on equal terms. To create such "free" and "equal" people was one of the
chief tasks of capitalist production. (Engels, *OFPPS*, 216)

People are free and equal as property, were not free and equal until the
arrival of commodities. The question arises whether freedom and equality
can be conditions of anything but commodities in circulation and exchange.
A truly exhilarating thought, almost schizophrenic.[8] Human freedom arrives not in resistance to circulation and exchange, to commodification, but
in increasing the velocity to the point where, perhaps, genitive relations
can no longer hold, whether of wealth, or women, or family, or works. I
postpone this consideration for a while, with the possibility that the props
of civilization and development regulate property for men. Perhaps before
and after the revolution.[9]

Engels's final concern in *The Origin of the Family* is with the advent
of the state, with the creation of "an armed 'public power' at the service of
these authorities and, therefore, also available against the people" (p. 239).
The development of surplus property threatened the knowledge and control
of producers over their property. Again, *their* property.

The appearance of private property in herds of cattle and articles of luxury
led to exchange between individuals, to the transformation of products
into *commodities*. Here lies the root of the entire revolution that followed.
When the producers no longer directly consumed their product, but let it
go out of their hands in the course of exchange, they lost control over it.
They no longer knew what became of it, and the possibility arose that the
product might some day be turned against the producers, used as a means
of exploiting and oppressing them. Hence, no society can for any length
of time remain master of its own production and continue to control the
social effects of its process of production, unless it abolishes exchange
between individuals. (p. 242)

Words reminiscent of Socrates' remarks in *Phaedrus*, the *mimēsis* of *mimēsis*.[10] I continue to hold cattle in abeyance. Written words cannot be owned.
They wander, get into undesirable hands, and do not know their fathers
*(patros)*. Socrates speaks of writing, philosophy, *mimēsis*, along lines of
inheritance and descent, as property. Beware of property as *mimēsis*, or the
*mimēsis* of property, or *mimēsis* as property: all betrayals. The link expresses the demand to own what cannot be owned, to possess what cannot

be possessed, to genitivize and genitalize the genitive. As philosophy. Philosophy arrives—most say, with Plato—bound to patrilinear descent, patriarchy, and property. Philosophy, writing, *mimēsis*; the props of property, accumulation and consumption.[11]

We will not get rid of God until we get rid of grammar, or *mimēsis*, or property, or food—if these can be abolished, or alienated, as if owned. Owning God or language or *mimēsis* or genitivity itself, the genitivization of the genitive—I say, betraying the genitive. Engels does not suggest that we abolish property but exchange between individuals. The producer owns the product of his labor, without question one might say. Still master. Still the ruler-owner-master of nature, under the curse. The father owns what he has made with his own hands—never paws, fangs, hooves, or claws. Perhaps with other parts of his body. Perhaps kidnapping women. Or engendering children. Keeping them present for his use.

We are led to another dream, or fable, of the social division of labor: *mimēsis* of the genitive, repeating its genitalization. First, the *"first great social division of labor"* (Engels, *OFPPS*, 280): the domestication of cattle, surplus production, creating exchange—"in short, cattle assumed the function of money" (p. 280). From surplus production to surplus labor, then to slavery, human cattle, always with women in mind. "All the surplus now resulting from production fell to the man; the woman shared in consuming it, but she had no share in owning it" (p. 281). We may extend Engels's striking link between the domestication of animals—cattle—and the need for human cattle—slaves—to women, whose domestication may have preceded the domestication of cattle and certainly followed: "The emancipation of women becomes possible only when women are enabled to take part in production on a large, social scale, and when domestic duties require their attention only to a minor degree" (p. 282). Emancipation is possible only by engaging in socially productive work, on a large, social scale. Some emancipation! Many—perhaps especially women—would regard this as more of the rat race. The male rat race. Perhaps not even human. Rats and cattle. Perhaps the emancipation of women will be possible only with the emancipation of cows.[12]

Engels describes *three great social divisions of labor*: *"the second great division of labour* took place, handicrafts separated from agriculture. . . . The division of production into two great branches, agriculture and handicrafts, gave rise to production for exchange, the production of commodities; and with it came trade" (*OFPPS*, 283); and the third: "Civilization . . . created a class that took no part in production, but engaged exclusively in exchanging products—*the merchants*" (pp. 284-85). Producing money, "the commodity of commodities" (p. 285), the indispensable prop of property, that which makes property possible in its absence. Another dream. Another *mimēsis*. Tightly linked with slavery. "Besides wealth in commodities and

slaves, besides money wealth, wealth in the form of land came into being"
(p. 286): private property in the name of the father.

Finally the state arrives, the result of the fourth great division "of
society into classes" (p. 288). Reaching fruition at the moment that the
entire edifice collapses, the advent, arrival, of another humanity, another
property, with strange and phantom props. As if property might wander
without a name. "The producer parts with his product in the course of
exchange; he no longer knows what becomes of it.... Commodities now
pass not only from hand to hand, but also from market to market. The
producers have lost control of the aggregate production of the conditions
of their own life, and the merchants have not acquired it. Products and
production become the playthings of chance" (pp. 292–93). Still insisting
on the genitive, a producer who insists that he keep and own and consume
what is his without confronting strange and spectral powers. Hand to hand.
A totally restricted economy, surrounded by ghosts. I think of general
economy without totality, of *Phaedrus* and *mimēsis*. I wonder what is so
bad about becoming a plaything of chance. As if we were ever anything but.

All this talk of consumption leads to another interruption, returning
to cattle. One might say that humanity became humanity—in the economic register—with the ownership of cattle. And humanity became humanity—in the ecological register—with the ownership of women. Again
betraying the great "truth" of freedom, that one of the tasks of capitalist
production was to create *free and equal* people to facilitate exploitation.
"Now, it was not long before the great 'truth' was discovered that man, too,
may be a commodity; that human power may be exchanged and utilized by
converting man into a slave" (p. 293). Freedom is a construction of capitalist economy, tightly linked on one side with commodities, slavery, and
the exploitation of women, on the other with the domestication of animals
and their transformation into money. I would recall that slavery utilized the
tools of animal domestication, the first true form of exploitation, if there
was a first. A reminder that Engels may have forgotten.

> The human "invention" of domesticating wild animals predates the
> adoption of agriculture, having begun some 2,000 years earlier when hu-
> mans and dogs first hunted together. What distinguished the Neolithic
> Revolution was the sheer number of new animals domesticated—for now
> joining the dog were sheep, goats, pigs, cattle, horses, among others....
> (Jacoby, *SN*, 90)

> Slaves and domesticated animals exist in relationships of domination,
> requiring a master as much as a servant....
> The drive for control is so essential—and so similar, whether the
> object of control is a slave or a domestic animal—as to overwhelm most
> distinctions between humans and animals. (p. 92)

> Virtually all of the practices cited [toward domestic animals] . . . were ones
> that humans also applied regularly to human slaves. (p. 92)

Or if not the first then the last. Endless exploitation. Resisting Engels's
ghosts. And every destiny. If we can resist destiny. "The time which has
passed away since civilization began is but a fragment of the past duration
of man's existence; and but a fragment of the ages yet to come. . . . *It will
be a revival, in a higher form, of the liberty, equality and fraternity of the
ancient gentes*" (Engels, *OFPPS*, 295–96; quoted from Morgan, *AS*, 552). As
if nothing new might be our destiny, as if there might be a destiny, final or
otherwise.

It is time to consider a departure from the intimate link of families and
things with genitivity and property—together with its props—to another
intimacy—if it be other—with the commodity and the fetishism—the desire—that defines it, perhaps another genitivity, or genitality, perhaps another slavery. I would turn from Engels to Marx, from the origin of the
family to the fetishism of the commodity, the institution of capital, interrupted at the very beginning by a ghostly figure of acquisition, Shylock,
who replaces Hamlet's father's ghost in Marx's writing. The Marx who admires Hamlet despises Jews. The Jewish Marx despises capitalist Jews, despises people who suffered repeatedly under historical oppression in Europe's
rise to world dominance through capitalism. What irony! And another, that
those who would read Marx against the genitive, the genitivity that others
insist on in reading Marx, do not read Marx against his Jewishness—or
rather, his anti-Semitic anti-Jewishness, in the genitive. The Jewish question. The question of the *revenant*, the wandering Jew.

A ghostly interruption. Preceded by another interruption in the name
of the impossibility of property that founds accumulation. Preceded by an
act of homicide perpetrated upon Proudhon, in the name of science.

> I showed, among other things, how little he has penetrated into the secret
> of scientific dialectics and how . . . he shares the illusions of speculative
> philosophy . . . how instead of conceiving them as *the theoretical expres-
> sion of historical relations of production, corresponding to a particular
> stage of development in material production*, he transforms them by his
> twaddle into *eternal ideas* existing prior to all reality. . . . (Marx, *MS*, 167)

Twaddle in the interest of science, as if science preceded the institution of
property, at least *bourgeois* property: property which is always present and
never the same, developing differently under different social and material
conditions. Proudhon is assassinated by Marx as *unscientific*, recalling Hegel's
homicide against Schelling.

What has this to do with property? Perhaps everything in the genitive, Proudhon's and Marx's genitive, *science's* genitive. The proper way to understand, to know, the genitive of truth; science's, reason's genitive relations to truth. Proudhon insists on having the science of political economy, as does Marx, who denies that Proudhon has grasped it securely. The debate is in the genitive, and Proudhon—that unscientific, twaddling utopian—does not own or possess the truth of property. As does Marx.

What is this truth that Marx insists on having? That property develops differently under different social relations and in each historical epoch. Property is never the same but always present. As Foucault says of the subject. The nonuniversal universal, emerging in Hegel but given critical expression in Marx. Property is the non|universal (universal), based on the more fundamental non|universal, *material conditions of production*, which are also different under different social relations and in each historical epoch. I pause to note the remarkable difference in the genitive between different social relations and different historical epochs. Also to note the non|universality of genitivity.

Just how mobile are productive relations? How mobile is the development of property and genitivity? One might say that genitivity is always changing, fluid, responsive to the social—and perhaps surrounding, climatic and geographical—conditions. Historical epochs suggest something much less fluid, the genitive relation of the components of an epoch to its concomitants. Each epoch unfolds in particular property relations, owns and has authority and force over them. And, moreover, over the genitive relation of historical movements, epochs succeeding epochs according to the genitivity of material forces.

I am led to a reading of Marx—within this interruption—that addresses the genitivity of science explicitly, seeking in Marx what he says is missing in Proudhon, strange to say perhaps missing in Marx himself—understandably, because its invisibility is the condition of its visibility, its absence the condition of its presence. Profoundly connected with genitivity.

> What political economy does not see is not a pre-existing object which it could have seen but did not see—but an object which it produced itself in its operation of knowledge and which did not pre-exist it: precisely the production itself, which is identical with the object. What political economy does not see is what it *does*: its production of a new answer without a question, and simultaneously the production of a new latent question contained by default in this new answer. (Althusser & Balibar, *RC*, 24)

> It is therefore a question of producing, in the precise sense of the word, which seems to signify making manifest what is latent, but which really

means transforming . . . something which in a sense *already exists*. This production, in the double sense which gives the production operation the necessary form of a circle, is the *production of a knowledge*. To conceive Marx's philosophy in its specificity is therefore to conceive the essence of the very movement with which the knowledge of it is produced, or to conceive knowledge as *production*. (p. 34)

Althusser speaks of the production of knowledge and discourse from knowledge and discourse. I speak of the production of genitivity from genitivity. Having knowledge, truth, and science reverberates with prior having, perhaps the very first having, owning, and possessing that is life itself among things, perhaps that of things among things, having the wherewithal to be a thing—genitively and properly; the properties of being something.

Althusser also speaks of the condition of the possibility of a science as invisibility. I speak of it as impossibility. The condition of the possibility of a science—of truth—is its impossibility. The condition of the possibility of property is its impossibility. Returning us to Proudhon, who says just that. Property is impossible, yet it is everywhere and said to be absolutely necessary, inescapable. Like truth and justice. Perhaps justice and truth and property are impossible, nowhere, but this impossibility gives rise to the possibility of truth and justice and property everywhere; or, put another way, to the insistence that we resist untruth and injustice and appropriation—and they are everywhere—knowing that they are the inescapable conditions of ethical life. An insistence I call *betrayal*.

Property, then, and genitivity are different in every epoch and under different social relations—perhaps everywhere. Yet property and genitivity are always present, if not in the form of capitalist ownership. This is crucial for Marx. Capitalist property is produced by capitalist production from the property given by individual labor.

> The capitalist mode of appropriation, which springs from the capitalist mode of production, produces capitalist private property. This is the first negation of individual private property, as founded on the labour of its proprietor. But capitalist production begets, with the inexorability of a natural process, its own negation. This is the negation of the negation. It does not re-establish private property, but it does indeed establish individual property on the basis of the achievements of the capitalist era: namely, co-operation and the possession in common of the land and of the means of production produced by labour itself. (Marx, *C*, 1, 929)

Marx takes for granted that capitalist property—commodification and fetishization—emerge from use-value, property based on personal labor, and that the proprietor effectively seizes the property of the producer for himself. Marx takes property for granted, for without it he cannot speak of appropriation and expropriation. Without property, without labor producing ownership, without the laborer possessing the right to the products of his labor, no right can accrue to the proprietor. Expropriation presupposes appropriation. Seizing presupposes having.

We may now understand the crime of which Proudhon must be accused, not only the twaddle of unscientificity—a crime in the genitive—but the greater crime against genitivity itself. Property is impossible, capitalist and labor property. The laborer must own his labor in the first place, must have rights to both his labor and its products, in order to sell them, to convert them and himself into commodities. And what if property were impossible? What if no one owned anything in the genitive, neither individually, personally, nor in common? Suppose things were available to be used, or not, without the least right to them—knowing that every right becomes excessive. Genitivity is excessivity, especially excess authority. Human beings and animals and plants are alive and seek the goodness that may be provided for their lives. Things exist and require other things for their being—I do not say endurance, for some exist by self-destruction, or exist momentarily. Even so, they cannot be except in proximity with other things, sometimes using them for themselves, always benefiting others. Let us say, without genitivity, without owning or having, without rights. Property, owning, having, as the unequal right to something—the key word is *right*—is impossible, I do not say *unjust* but *impossible*. But of course, it is unjust.

One may say that Marx resists this impossibility. Indeed, his entire analysis of commodities and fetishes presupposes the inescapability of genitivity, of the unboundedness of the desires that attach to objects as possessions. Marx's theory is in the genitive, both in its scientificity and in its insistence on propriety. The ghost of genitivity haunts Marx in the conditions he insists on giving to material production—the owner and haver of all giving and assigning. Necessity in political economy is genitivity.

I do not insist on abolishing genitivity, as if we might live without having, but insist on the betrayal of living by having. Put another way, the circle of genitivity is doubled; genitivity presupposes genitivity, having and possessing. And in this inescapable circle, genitivity and property are impossible, and that impossibility is the condition of both the possibility of owning and having and their betrayal. We must betray, must live against, the genitive in a life that cannot take place without having. We must pursue giving without having although life cannot be lived without taking.

I end this interruption within an interruption to return to the interruption that was named but not begun. Another genitive that cannot be given away: Marx's Jewishness, Marx the Jew who hated Jews, hated them as proprietors in a world in which they were persecuted and oppressed, hated them as if they were capitalist powers in a world in which they were deprived of power. What could justify such hateful irony? Or put another way, how are we to read such a confusion on Marx's part from within Althusser's understanding that the question is always of what is produced, and why, made visible from within an invisibility? What invisibility?

First the visible: "What is the Jew's foundation in our world? Material necessity, private advantage. What is the object of the Jew's worship in this world? Usury. What is his worldly God? Money. Very well then; emancipation from usury and money, that is, from practical, real Judaism, would constitute the emancipation of our time" (Marx, *WWJ*, 37). Jews are usurers; Judaism is usury. Yet this terrible view of Jewish life and history is by no means the worst. "The Jews of Poland are the smeariest of all races. *(Neue Rheinische Zeitung*, April 19, 1849)" (p. vii); "The organization of society so as to abolish the preconditions of usury, and hence its possibility, would render the Jew impossible. His religious conviction would dissolve like a stale miasma under the pressure of the real life of the community" (p. 37). One wonders at such words of hate. "Money is the zealous one God of Israel, beside which no other God may stand. Money degrades all the gods of mankind and turns them into commodities.... Money is the essence of man's life and work, which have become alienated from him: this alien monster rules him and he worships it" (pp. v-vi). Jewish life and religion rest on money, the monster that rules humanity.

Why such hatred, to the point of self-revulsion, against the truth of historical antisemitism throughout Europe? Because some Jews were capitalists, able to survive in moneyed circles at the dispensation of greater powers? Very few and with little state power. How could Marx understand the force of capitalism to be linked with Jews and Jewish religious practices, both persecuted throughout European history? How could he imagine that Jewish history was a history of rich exploiting poor?

In reverse, and invisibly, perhaps Marx hated capitalism and its exploitations because they reminded him of his Jewishness, ghosts of a genitivity that he did not choose. Of Jews holding onto their chosenness in the face of persecution, insisting on their divine genitivity, on the divinity of genitivity. Cosmopolitanism always meant anti-Semitism, but it suggests escape from genitivity. Always in the name of Christianity, another genitive.

I end this interruption, allowing us to return to capitalism and the commodity, holding them up in the genitive.

> A use-value, or useful article, therefore, has value only because abstract human labour is objectified or materialized in it. (Marx, *C*, 1, 129)

> Commodities come into the world in the shape of use-values or material goods, such as iron, linen, corn, etc. This is their plain, homely, natural form. However, they are only commodities because they have a dual nature, because they are at the same time objects of utility and bearers of value. (p. 138)

I have noted the table that begins as a use-value, in the genitive, belonging to the laborer-producer, which in a mysterious way turns itself upside down to belong to no one as a commodity and, thereafter, to the capitalist, who produces nothing.[13]

> It is absolutely clear that by his activity, man changes the forms of the materials of nature in such a way as to make them useful to him. The form of wood, for instance, is altered if a table is made out of it. Nevertheless the table continues to be wood, an ordinary, sensuous thing. But as soon as it emerges as a commodity, it changes into a thing which transcends sensuousness. It not only stands with its feet on the ground, but, in relation to all other commodities, it stands on its head, and evolves out of its wooden brain grotesque ideas, far more wonderful than if it were to begin dancing of its own free will. (pp. 163–64)

> The mysterious character of the commodity-form consists therefore simply in the fact that the commodity reflects the social characteristics of men's own labour as objective characteristics of the products of labour themselves, as the socio-natural properties of these things. . . . It is nothing but the definite social relation between men themselves that assumes here, for them, the fantastic form of a relation between things. . . . I call this the fetishism which attaches itself to the products of labour, as soon as they are produced as commodities, and is therefore inseparable from the production of commodities. (pp. 164–65)

The thing, the table, remains physical and natural wood yet undergoes a mysterious transformation into a commodity, becoming a fetish through the production of purely social relations that attach to things and transform them into commodities. All in the genitive—one may say, with property in mind, the genitive of genitivity. All in the possessiveness of desire—one may say, with Callicles in mind, the desire of desire, to own. The (real and true) thing is what it (really and truly) is, in the genitive, belonging to the producer who gives the form to the thing—an enduring Aristotelian image. In virtue of exchange, however, prevailing social relations convert the thing that belongs to the producer into a mysterious commodity that circulates in exchange relations, taking on the fantastic form of a relation between things. Things mysteriously possess the exchange value given to them through social relations; desires are transformed by social relations in a mysterious way from true and useful desire to phantasmatic specters, from what we truly need to have to what we hope to have beyond any bounds—circulating beyond regulation. Genitivity is a mysterious, fetishistic, social relation linked with desire in a fantastic, fetishistic, excessive relation, exceeding every condition that would institute it, including labor and material production. Fetishism is the betrayal, the phantasmatic, phantasmagoric specter of desire in things, desire for things in the genitive, the genitality of genitivity, beyond having, owning, and taking. The fetish gives things to desire beyond having. The fetish gives the thing and its value as whatever desire takes them to be—exceeding every limit, breaking the bonds of the identity of things in the genitive. The fetish of the commodity expresses the impossibility of owning the thing forever. Or at all. Property is impossible. Desire is unfulfillable.

On this reading, fetishism is the symptom of genitivity itself as desire, production, and excess, not just capitalist production; betrays the excessiveness of having, owning, and possessing as desire. In a world of excessive desire—by no means just human desire, by no means just human having—things are never just things, but exceed themselves in desire as desire exceeds itself in every place and thing in the name of the fetish. Commodities are fetishes, circulate in an excessive, mysterious way, take on lives of their own. Owning, having, and possessing take on unexpected and mysterious lives of their own wherever they are, in the household or in the factory, becoming surprisingly mobile. The commodity visibly expresses this invisible life of things—let us say, in them in virtue of the extravagance that surrounds them, social and natural. Commodities express the excessiveness of things themselves in their proximity with other things, living and not. The supreme fetish is to hope to grasp securely against the mobility of things. Property is the supreme fetish, genitivity without giving. As Hobbes says, the desire to have forever.

We return to the household, to economology, where the mysterious fetishism of the thing is linked with other genitives beyond the labor that gives it use-value, linked with the props of property; accumulation, consumption, domination, and exclusion. All excessive, fetishistic. The fetish of the commodity is preceded by other fetishes, by other mysterious—or not so mysterious, but excessive, authoritarian—institutional and productive structures for the implementation of desire beyond desire. In the home. Women and children in the home, together with things for life and pleasure, circulate from one home to another.

If women, children, and animals were among the first social products to be exchanged and circulated, with the things gathered around them, would it be plausible to distinguish use-value from exchange-value? Or might the exchange of women, children, and animals betray that the fetishistic excess of the commodity belongs to every genitive, every thing of value, of use or exchange? Let us consider the possibility that value and genitivity are inseparable: we value what we have, we hope to have what we value; we desire what we value, we hope to have what we desire. Genitivity is intimately linked with genitality, joining the props of property; accumulation, consumption, domination, and exclusion. Resistance to genitivity is resistance to exclusion, to what is had by some and not by others. Resistance to genitivity is living and acting for the sake of the good, giving beyond having, beyond grasping and possessing. Including—or especially—women, children, and animals, but also things in general, things made, things found, things that have not yet been and may never be found.

The household is the place where we may hope to live with the things and creatures we have gathered. What might a household be but a gathering? And what are commodities and exchange economies but the mobility of things that cannot be gathered? Capitalism introduces a strange and difficult thought in the context of the history of the household, the *oikos*, linked with *ethicoeconomoecology*, now *economology* or *ecolonomy*[14]— where the compression betrays the dominations and oppressions that have haunted gathering in the household—especially women, children, slaves, animals, and implements—under the categories that mark the kinds that human beings—historically, men—have appropriated in the satisfactions of their lives. *Economology|ecolonomics*, inscribed as the props of property.

Who controls the kinds of creatures and things that are needed for a rich and satisfying human life? Who has them under control, in the genitive? If they must be controlled, against the possibility of a giving and circulating, reevoked under capitalism as the commodity, in which producers and things move beyond having and accumulating.

I find this possibility explicitly denied in Marx, not, however, without betrayal. For the commodity appears in a doubled form—doubly doubled, betraying itself. I go to the very beginning of *Capital*, right after the preface.

> The commodity is, first of all, an external object, a thing which through its qualities satisfies human wants of whatever kind. (Marx, *C*, 1, 125)

> The usefulness of a thing makes it a use-value. . . . It is therefore the physical body of the commodity itself . . . which is the use-value or useful thing. This property of a commodity is independent of the amount of labour required to appropriate its useful qualities. . . . Use-values are only realized in use or in consumption. They constitute the material content of wealth, whatever its social form may be. (p. 126)

> Exchange-value appears first of all as the quantitative relation, the proportion, in which use-values of one kind exchange for use-values of another kind. This relation changes constantly with time and place. (p. 126)

A commodity plays the double role of use- and exchange-value, where we may take the first to mark the *oikos*, the household, where goods are used and consumed. Marx takes for granted that in the first place—if there is a place and any can be first—a thing, a commodity, has a use-value. He does not imagine either of two alternatives: first, that the great profusion of things may have no use, cannot be owned, do not belong to human beings. Use-value is appropriation; commodities—standing outside us—satisfy human wants; creatures and things are for human use, to satisfy human desires. And what if creatures and things and commodities circulate in their own ways in the abundance of the earth, without regard to human wants and needs? What if value were always appropriating, seizing, grabbing, taking for human use what does not belong to human beings?

Second, with the household in mind, where things are used in proximity, that the exteriority of the commodity reflects not a fall from true and authentic value, but freedom from genitivity against the insistence that everything in nature and the world belongs to human beings—historically to men. What if use-value bore within itself the fall into genitivity, into having, away from giving and abundance? And what—as strange as this may seem to imagine in the context of Marx and Engels—if exchange-value were a certain liberation, if commodities were not the confinement of useful things but the possibility of their emancipation? Held up, of course, by the demand to use and accumulate and devour that goes along with genitivity in the home, where human beings consume useful things—together with useful women, children, and animals. What if the contradictions of capitalism did not belong to the commodity but to insistence on use, accumulation and profit, rather than on circulation and exchange? What if the exchange of women were oppressive not in the circulation—which might well belong to women—but in their accumulation in the household? The household, the place of use, dominates our understanding of political economy, is where we think human beings may hope to live rich and satisfying lives by using other creatures and things. What if we were to link economics with ecology at this point of utility and satisfaction, breaking the bonds of genitivity? The household is where women and children and animals and things have been appropriated in the name of utility. Now liberated beyond utility. Instead of *my* satisfaction, sometimes *our* satisfaction, in the genitive—meaning a satisfaction that can be measured, that takes place in a certain place, the household, what if desire and joy were in circulation beyond place and measure together with things and creatures, always ecstatic, outside themselves—that is, outside any having, any place or relation? Desire and joy are beyond limit, touching down here and there long enough for life—and no more. We must avoid Callicles' confusion of the unboundedness of desire with acquisition and genitivity. We must give ourselves over to joy and desire for life, as Nietzsche says, beyond the genitive.

To do so would entail immense consequences for the labor theory of property, that the measure of value is "the quantity of . . . the labour, contained in the article" (Marx, *C*, 128–29). As if desire and joy must be measured, along with value: utility or labor. Marx disregards the possibility that things and labor have no measure, that economics takes measure for granted—traditionally defined by utility—where capitalism creates desire yet opens desire onto itself beyond measure. Anything whatever may be valued. Not just labor. Anything whatever may give joy. Not just what Marx or society or the proprietor or the worker say. The truth of capitalism is that anything may be joyful, worthy of desire, even desire itself, beyond any measure. Economics insists on measuring the unmeasurable in exchange and circulation. I insist on circulation beyond accumulation and measure. Ecolonomics promotes exchangei beyond measure.

Marx insists on the grip of the household on the thing—every thing. The destiny of things is not to circulate beyond measure in the earth and its abundance, but to be consumed usefully in the home. Let us resist the dominations of the home as we resist the dominations of the market. Provisionally—within a doubled sense of its betrayal—let us resist accumulation, including the accumulation of labor power in the commodity.

Now we may reconsider Marx's early examples—not just the topsy-turvy table, standing on its head, the one Derrida brings again on stage, but the one Derrida ignores, that does not arrive so dramatically but in plain and homely form for use in the home: a linen coat. "Let us take two commodities, such as a coat and 10 yards of linen. . . . The coat is a use-value that satisfies a particular need" (Marx, *C*, 1, 132). In a strangely Aristotelian register, linking matter and form within the household, privileging form. "If we subtract the total amount of useful labour of different kinds which is contained in the coat, the linen, etc., a material substratum is always left. This substratum is furnished by nature without human intervention. When man engages in production, he can only proceed as nature does herself, i.e., he can only change the form of the materials" (p. 133). One might say, lacking excess. Marx rejects—and betrays—the possibility that the value of things is unmeasurable—in nature if not in circulation and exchange; that what is given by nature is immeasurable abundance. Economics insists on form and measure, insists on being the science of measuring the unmeasurable. Commodities presuppose the impossibility of economics, but not perhaps the impossibility of ecology, or of economology—resistance to every measure of joy and satisfaction, especially derived from the home.

"Everyone knows, if nothing else, that commodities have a common value-form which contrasts in the most striking manner with the motley natural forms of their use-values. I refer to the money-form" (p. 139). What people know is that commodities circulate beyond any use that can be found for them, that uses are found for the most useless things, that money allows for trade among motley things it is joyful to have and to give away. Marx insists on depositing value in the bank, accumulating it against a rainy day. "In the production of the coat, human labour-power, in the shape of tailoring, has in actual fact been expended. Human labour has therefore been accumulated in the coat. From this point of view, the coat is a 'bearer of value,' although this property never shows through, even when the coat is at its most threadbare" (p. 143). Why not say instead that for all the labor expended, for all the visible forms that might impose value on the linen, transforming it into a coat, the threadbare coat circulates beyond value, beyond money, where given away, picked up, used and abused, whatever? As Spinoza says, no one knows what bodies can do. No one knows what commodities can do, what they are for, what they are worth. In their material abundance.

This is what the fetish says in the language of desire. For the mystical character of commodities does not originate in their use-value, or go back to any use-value—that is, to the household. The fetish—and there are plenty in the household, perhaps everything in the household is a fetish— escapes the restrictions insisted on in the household, in the name of use-value or any value, any utility, beyond any attempt to accumulate desire into property. Desire in things is not accumulable, inaccumulable, is disappropriation and expropriation, beyond appropriation.

Oddly—phantasmatically—enough, this is what the wooden table knows with its wooden brain, knows upside-down, while Marx the right-side, upside human with his human body and bloody brain does not. The table knows that every corporeal thing including humans and human bodies are fetishes, beyond any accounting, any economy—the ecolonomy of the fetish. This is not what Marx says, for he hopes to exorcise the specter of the fetish. "The veil is not removed from the countenance of the social life-process, i.e. the process of material production, until it is becomes production by freely associated men, and stands under their conscious and planned control" (p. 173). He hopes to strip off the veils that make the commodity phantasmatic, as if desire might be made pure, held in place by conscious regulation and a settled plan,[15] as if we might hope to solve the mystery of the fetish.

What if the truth of genitivity were genitality—I mean, the excessive-ness of desire? What if it were impossible, and undesirable, to eliminate the fetish? What if the fetish expressed the abundance in value itself, in every genitive? What if human beings could not master the fetish because they cannot master things, cannot master material production, because they do not and will never know what bodies can do—human and otherwise? What if mastery betrayed genitivity—as *mimēsis*?

> Commodities cannot go to market and perform exchanges in their own right. We must, therefore, have recourse to their guardians, who are the possessors of commodities. Commodities are things, and therefore lack the power to resist man. If they are unwilling, he can use force; in other words, he can take possession of them. In order that these objects may enter into relation with each other as commodities, their guardians must . . . recognize each other as owners of private property. . . . Here the persons exist for one another merely as representatives and hence owners, of commodities. . . . The characters who appear on the economic stage are merely personifications of economic relations. . . . (Marx, *C,* 178–79)

Marx says it is plain that commodities need human beings to perform exchanges.[16] I would say it is anything but plain in the phantasmagoria of the fetish—the dramaturgy of economic relations. The *mimēsis* of the fetish betrays Marx's claim that things are docile against humanity and that the only relevant will—or desire—belongs to human beings. One never owns desire, and the genitivity of freedom of the will—shades of Kant and Hegel—is the mysterious and fantastic fetishism of the subject, the representational melodrama of personification. Marx insists that the economic subject is nothing but an owner of commodities. We might respond that the economic person represents the fetishism of unbounded circulation and exchange, where money is the fetish of all fetishes, the *mimēsis* of *mimēsis*.

> Money is the absolutely alienable commodity, because it is all other commodities divested of their shape, the product of their universal alienation. . . . Since every commodity disappears when it becomes money it is impossible to tell from the money itself how it got into the hands of its possessor, or what article has been changed into it. (p. 205)
>
> The complete metamorphosis of a commodity, in its simplest form, implies four *dénouements* and three *dramatis personae*. (p. 206)

Foucault elaborates this view of money as representativity: "money is that which permits wealth to be represented. Without such signs, wealth would remain immobile, useless, and as it were silent" (Foucault, *OT,* 177). Money is the *mimēsis* of wealth;[17] commodities are the *mimēsis* of things, their representativity. The name of this expressivity of things is fetishism.

The circulation of commodities expresses generosity, betrays abundance. "The whole system of exchanges, the whole costly creation of values, is referred back to the unbalanced, radical, and primitive exchange established

between the advances made by the landowner and the generosity of nature"
(Foucault, *OT,* 195); "The creation of value is therefore not a means of
satisfying a greater number of needs; it is the sacrifice of a certain quantity
of goods in order to exchange others" (p. 192). Marx describes the creation
of value—fetishism, commodification, *mimēsis*—as alienation, Foucault as
sacrifice, I as betrayal. The creation of value—perhaps not just capitalist,
exchange-value, but human value, value itself—involves a loss, a reduction
of desire, betraying hierarchy and domination.

I end my discussion here of Marx with a spectacular reemergence of
genitality in genitivity, a hateful reinstitution of the genital desires that
haunt money and exchange everywhere—one might say in every household, here the anti-Semitic material essence of Christianity. For in the
chapter on the transformation of money into capital we encounter Marx's
view of Jews in an extreme figure of dismemberment: the fetish of the
member as hatred of Jews, as if that hatred were what drove Marx's critique
of capitalism, commodification, and fetishism. In relation to the capacity of
value to exceed any determinations but its own, Marx is overcome by two
remarkable figures. "By virtue of being value, it has acquired the occult
ability to add value to itself. It brings forth living offspring, or at least lays
golden eggs" (Marx, *C*, 1, 255). We might understand these words to express
the possibility that for the first time in human history desire might not be
channeled and controlled, but in a phantasmatic way might pursue whatever and wherever it craved, not in the service of the proprietor, or noble,
or philosopher, but free beyond limits to pursue and give value. Value and
desire under capitalism become capable of spontaneous generation. I keep
this economy of desire's spontaneity in abeyance for later chapters.

Marx, however, recoils in a terrible, heinous figure: "The capitalist
knows that all commodities, however tattered they may look, or however
badly they may smell, are in faith and in truth money, are by nature circumcised Jews, and what is more, a wonderful means for making still more
money out of money" (p. 256). Watch out for commodities—they are secret
Jews, surreptitiously marked as Jews—on their genitals. Watch out for Jews
who pass themselves off as good Christians. Tattered and smelly Jews. Marx
links commodities and Jews in an extreme mimetic figure, each making the
other more revolting. Hatred of Jews—anti-Semitism—as hatred of capitalism. Anticapitalism as anti-Semitism, hatred of what looks and acts strange
and different, insisting on nobility at the expense of Jews.

What if Marx's insistence on use-value were anti-Semitism? What if
Marx's insistence on communism were another oppression, another imposition of arbitrary desires? What if Marx's hatred of prostitution was linked
with fear of circumcision?

Father knows best. Someone knows and insists on the best. For his children.

In a less anti-Semitic world—if such a world may come to be—we might take this link between exchange and life and sexual bodies to suggest, still *mimēsis*, that no matter how mean and trivial, no matter how oppressed and broken, all people and things have value, can live joyfully, in an economy in which things circulate free from the régime of the Father, or the State, or the Church. All things are given from the good, are beautiful in the eyes of God. Anything may be desirable, may be valuable under capitalism. In ecolonomics. In economology.

Repeating words I have expressed elsewhere, here in the register of genitivity. Giving without having; cherishment, sacrifice, and plenishment.

> Everything matters, everything is precious, infinitely, inexhaustibly, heterogeneously, every individual thing and every kind. Everything in the earth is precious, in its ways, known and unknown, in the kinds in which it participates. . . . To cherish, love, revere the goodness of things is to let them pursue the good for themselves without hoping to own, or possess, or master them, in the genitive.[18]

# CHAPTER 6

## Enclosed Properties

An ethic, ecologically, is a limitation on freedom of action in the struggle for existence. . . .

There is as yet no ethic dealing with man's relation to land and to the animals and plants which grow upon it. Land, like Odysseus' slave-girls, is still property. (Leopold, *LE*, 217–20)

Before human beings took their destiny to lie in owning things, before the destiny of things in the earth was given over to genitivity, before the destiny of humanity was enacted through the control of women and children, human beings and their forebears lived in and on the earth, among other creatures and things. They lived and worked and died together, without accumulation. I would like to think of human life before the social contract—if human beings lived human lives before society, before genitivity—as one of productive relations among human beings, other creatures, and things, relations of commingling, understanding, joy and suffering, instrumentality, and much more. I would imagine life on the earth as participation in the richness of things beyond any demarcations, any social institutions, filled with joy and sorrow, celebration and mourning, struggles to live, to know, to leave marks upon the earth. All pointing beyond themselves, to past and future, to other places, to other creatures and things, elsewhere and otherwise in the earth, perhaps to the gods.

I would like to think of these relations without the genitive. If that were possible. To think that no one owned or possessed any creature, thing, or person; creatures and things commingling in life and death. Lions do not own antelope even when they chase and kill them, even when they seize and devour them. The antelope may be caught and eaten, but it is not there *for* the lion, not owned by the lion. The lion's life, and the antelope's life and death, commingle and cohabit, come together, not always to the benefit of either. If in the genitive, it is without accumulation, exclusion, or alienation. Provoking Callicles' question for the earth today: *can human beings live in and on the earth without the endless expanse of accumulation and consumption?* Which is by no means to restrict circulation and participation.[1]

For much of human life this question has taken the form of how human beings are to live on the land, questions of territory and enclosure—which practically speaking represent the conditions of the earth that seem to exist free from genitivity—land, sea, air, and sky. No one can own these; no one can own the earth. Yet land can be enclosed and claimed to belong to one person or group rather than others. Even where no fences divide tracts of land, people and animals fight over territory, battle to control access to goods useful to them and under their protection. Shall we regard these struggles as under the rule of genitivity? Shall we regard the land and its enclosure as a passage to genitivity from something else—land, sea, sky, and air as common to all, perhaps including other people, creatures, and things?

*Can human beings flourish in and on the earth without enclosure, without genitivity?* We have considered Plato's exploration of the possibility that the most complete human life is without possession, that the ills of human life arrive with genitivity. Owning pigs and cattle, leading to acquisition and war; struggles to accumulate the most important things—women, children, animals, and food—and the least—money and gold; unbounded efforts to consume.

*Can human beings, can men, live peacefully in the earth without genitivity?* Can they live peacefully in any other way? Must I know and be secure in what is *mine* in order to live well? Must I know what is *mine* in order to protect it?

Stirner follows Hegel's sense of proprietary destiny in things to an extreme, perhaps too extreme for Hegel, for whom property in things passes over into ethics and law, into collectivity. Not for Stirner.[2]

> The communists affirm that "the earth belongs rightfully to him who tills it, and its products to those who bring them out." I think it belongs to him who knows how to take it, or who does not let it be taken from him, does not let himself be deprived of it. (Stirner, *EO*, 171)

> What then is *my* property? Nothing but what is in my *power*! To what property am I entitled? To every property to which I—*empower* myself. I give myself the right of property in taking property to myself, or giving myself the proprietor's *power*, full power, empowerment. (p. 227)

Stirner remains lawless—pre-lawful, if you will—resting human freedom on might. That may be less important to questions of genitivity than his insistence on appropriation as the human mark. Empowerment is appropriation, expropriation, reappropriation. Human life is seizing, taking, coveting, without veil or mask. Callicles again, colored in modern hues of freedom and right. The right of human beings to take and the destiny of things to be taken. Everyone and everything must own or be owned, where owning is taking from others. Rochelle knows nothing of taking.

The ethics of humanity, in its glorious freedom, is theft—or worse: the ethics ascribed to animals under Darwinian demographics—not individual animals but animals in groups. *Take what you can, whenever you can, from whomever you can.* Unto death, without fail, at least for animals like deer that overrun their range, that outstrip the capacity of their environment to sustain them. Given the opportunity, deer and rabbits multiply to the point of exhaustion, destroying both their kind and other kinds in their environment. Given the opportunity—or seizing it—human beings take what they can to the point of exhaustion, destroying themselves and other kinds.

We come to the subject of this chapter, land, enclosure, and the earth. Locke writes of the commons—the land, the earth—as if there might be still enough and as good left after some seize land for themselves. Stirner holds the opposite: there is never enough left; the powerful must take and hold what they can. Enclosure is seizing common property for oneself, ownership is taking from others. The commons—those conditions of life that cannot be taken—can be understood instead as what is available, guaranteed to anyone or everyone, given to all instead of taken. Especially not taken away.

If we were like rabbits and deer—perhaps far worse—multiplying where we could, seizing and taking what we had the power to take and hold no matter the consequences for ourselves, our children, other human beings, creatures, and things, then perhaps some thoughtful members of our species might ask us to think again of the consequences for ourselves and others. And perhaps some might think about appropriation and acquisition, about living ecologically in the earth. Still, one might say, in the genitive. And far worse than deer or rabbits—certainly than lions and wolves, who seldom expand beyond their limits. Stirner's insistence on the inseparable link between humanity and genitivity promotes an accumulation, consumption, and wastefulness beyond the reach of other species. Freedom is accumulation beyond consumption. Theft unto death.

Some claim that those who utilize the commons together will always strive to maximize their accumulation at the expense of others, destroying the commons, depredating the land.[3] Humans are far worse than deer and rabbits, not to say wolves and lions, who do not accumulate even when they breed and consume too much. Yet in times of plenty, human beings accumulate but do not overbreed, suggesting that this argument may not carry the day. Many communities share a common resource by guaranteeing access to all, resisting exclusive and oppressive appropriation. More of this later.

We may consider reappropriating genitivity from its link with enclosure. Land, sea, air, and sky are present and available, but at least until very recently, only land could be enclosed. Join this enclosure with the insistence on destiny as appropriation, that everything that can be owned be owned, that everything that can be enclosed be enclosed: exclusive rights to land, sea, air, and sky; to wombs, sperm, and reproduction. The progress of humanity toward its freedom is expressed by enclosing everything and everyone. I do not exempt human beings. Slavery exists. Far more important, however, human beings live everywhere under the enclosure of property rights among themselves. Rights to property over land, sea, air, and sky, as well as to animals, plants, and things, are rights exclusively between human beings as if the others—land, sea, air, and sky; animals, plants, and things—do not count in legal terms, are for human beings to seize and claim. Only human beings are free, free to own; everything else is to be owned. Yet exclusive rights of some human beings to the earth, to possibilities of life and joy, always divide this freedom again, into those who freely own and those who do not. Property, as Proudhon says, is impossible because it presupposes that all are free but only some may freely own. Genitivity is theft, not of things alone—terrible enough—but of freedom itself in the name of freedom.

The destiny of human beings is owning, proprietorship, over everything that can be possessed and owned. The destiny of the earth is genitivity, linked with genitality. Reproductive property rights are necessary to any destiny. So for their destiny, human beings must own rights to future human beings, to their progeny and to the women who make progeny possible; joined with requisite erotic rights. The most pressing struggle in life is over property rights to children and erotic rights in women, throughout the world. The political economy of sex.

But I am ahead of myself, though only briefly. The enclosure of land, I believe, is accompanied—and preceded by—the enclosure of women, children, and animals. The accumulation and consumption of things and money cannot be separated from the accumulation and consumption of animals and people. I hold this crucial link between genitivity and genitality in abeyance, postponing genealogy for a while.

Here I am concerned with enclosure, with the link between humanity and genitivity, throughout human history, which becomes in modern terms the link between freedom and having. Freedom, some say, is the capacity to act voluntarily in accordance with one's desires with respect to other people and the creatures and things of the earth. All sorts of questions have been raised about the voluntary capacities of individual human beings who are profoundly historical and social creatures. All sorts of other questions have been raised about human desires, their limits and requirements. Such questions frequently suggest that something other than individual human beings should set limits to their choices and desires.

I would instead consider a different approach to this question, insisting that it is not for anyone to restrict any other person's, creature's, or thing's desires and freedoms, that no one knows the good for another better than that other, even where that other does not know, and may not have, a good for itself.[4] I suggest an approach that insists on desire and freedom but resists genitivity. "Freedom, too, has come to be so closely tied to individualism that it is difficult for us to conceptualize that there might be another way to experience our freedom that is not tied to property rights and an inflated sense of the self. There is also a danger that under consumer capitalism, the idea of freedom itself has been reduced to the concept of choice. . . . Choice is another kind of enclosure" (Schleuning, *THTH*, 29). Freedom in modern society is genitivity—seizing, taking, and holding, as one chooses. What if freedom were giving—again, as one chooses? Choice would not be linked with enclosure if it, like property and land, were not bound to a genitive of exclusion.

*To think of human lives and relations to other human beings and things, resisting exclusion. An ethic, a life, of inclusion.*[5] Giving without taking, beyond having. Not without betrayal.

Living in the land together with the other creatures and things of the earth. What might be more human? What might be human beyond humanism or anthropocentrism?

> If we are to remain true to the highest values of the land—life, liberty, and the pursuit of happiness—we need to radically restructure the economic and political institutions that sustain them. We need to guarantee the right to survival for every member of our society, to ensure access to the resources necessary for survival, and to expand democratic rights to include economic equality. We need to empower ourselves to participate more completely in the political arena. We need to reassess our personal relationships with one another, and cultivate a social environment of mutual respect, and we need to care for our environment and ensure the future life, liberty, and happiness of children and grandchildren. (Schleuning, *THTH*, 208)

Whose sacrifices and which desires? What betrayals? Schleuning does not say, does not consider the possibility that *the highest values of the land*, like economic freedom, might serve social hierarchy and exclusion, that radical restructuring always benefits some more than others. I postpone these considerations for a while. I return to desire against the best-meant efforts to control it. I insist on the fetish, on the topsy-turvy, anarchic nature of desire, resisting every enclosure.

> The dominant symbolic order in contemporary society is built on a Stirner-like radical individualism and an ethic based on personal wants and desires. Desire is expressed in a variety of ways and ownership takes many forms but both desire and ownership are always grounded in the individual. (p. 20)

> Capitalism transsubstantiates images of women into habits of consumer behavior through stimulation of the impulse to fetishize objects and the manipulation of ideas of power and control. (p. 21)

Shades of Marx, fetishism as phantasmagoric desire, out of control. I insist on desire's *mimēsis*. "Things. Objects. Belongings. Possessions. Goods. What lies at the heart of the human relationship with the material world? . . . People not only 'own' things, they use things to communicate a wide range of information to others" (p. 104). People communicate with others and themselves through things, put desire in things and mark that putting—giving—on things and themselves. Property is fetishism as *mimēsis*, has always been fetishism together with *mimēsis*. Back to the dream of a beginning without beginning or end.

> One of the simplest meanings of ownership in early societies was the belief that the human personality could be projected onto an object, a place, or another person. Ownership was seen as a powerful extension of self into the material world. . . .
> A further refinement in the human/material world relationship was the creation of fetishes—objects that were concrete manifestations imbued with personal power and under the control of the person creating the fetish. The fetish is a power object: it is not merely representative. (p. 105)

I would like to read this understanding against genitivity but not against desire in things. Instead of taking the fetish in tribal societies as power over things, the desire to master, let us think instead of desire and power *embodied, expressed, in 'things*, the power of things and creatures that may pass over to human beings: fetishistic objects as sites of human longing and struggles to live, individually and collectively. Here owning and having represent attempts to control the powerful things and creatures and spirits of the world. Having is the control of powers in creatures and things, insisting that they can be mastered and enclosed. The fetish expresses what cannot be mastered, be it the commodity that circulates beyond mastery or the artifact imbued with spirit powers. Giving and circulating take place without genitivity. Including things, objects, belongings, possessions, and goods.

Do we want to respond to the presentation of women as erotic objects by restricting desire and imagination? To men: don't lust after women! Or may we hope instead to pursue the fetish through the anarchic possibilities of *mimēsis* to open possibilities of desire beyond genitivity, disrupting the exploitation of women? Schleuning responds with a double gesture. "[H]owever natural, or close to the 'real thing' the fetish comes, it is still only a simulacrum, a substitute. It leaves the consumer of the fetish unfulfilled, without the ability to bring closure to the desire" (Schleuning, *THTH*, 159). I resist this closure with another gesture, doubling the doubling. What if the fetish were the thing, the only thing; what if reality were the fetish, so that neither *mimēsis* nor desire could be brought to closure? What if the limitlessness of having and exchanging reflected the impossibility of closure, betrayed the limitlessness of desire? Could we respond with another movement beyond limit, beyond the closure of desire, or *mimēsis*, or accumulation?

I understand the enclosure of land, animals, and women as domination in the name of freedom—the proprietor's freedom—the walling in of territory, people, creatures, and things in the genitive as someone's freedom rather than another's, mine not yours, ours not theirs. Leading to the genitivity of kin and kind expressed as genealogy. Freedom as genealogy, in kin and kind.

But I have not dwelt enough in the land. Nor have I circulated enough with women, animals, and slaves, enclosed in the name of freedom. I hold these in abeyance to dwell further in land, sea, air, and sky without enclosure. We live and dwell in abundance in the earth, in a giving from the good, calling us to endless responses beyond enclosure. For the sake of the good—which is nothing; for no person's or thing's sake, not even our own. In the earth beyond genitivity. We take hold of things to live, in the genitive. And we must let them go, give them up, interrupt accumulation and consumption, open every enclosure. I understand this interruption as giving, understand giving as *mimēsis*, inseparable from expression, from exposure and proximity, betraying the endless impossibility of having and holding securely, of enclosure.

But I have not dwelt enough in the land. Or the mountain. Reminding ourselves of the gestures in which every reflective creature lives in the earth. *Mimēsis* again. In the land.

> A deep chesty bawl echoes from rimrock to rimrock, rolls down the mountain, and fades into the far blackness of the night. It is an outburst of wild defiant sorrow, and of contempt for all the adversities of the world.

> Every living thing (and perhaps many a dead thing as well) pays heed to
> that call. To the deer it is a reminder of the way of all flesh, to the pine
> a forecast of midnight scuffles and of blood upon the snow, . . . Yet behind
> these obvious and immediate hopes and fears there lies a deeper meaning,
> known only to the mountain itself. (Leopold, *TLM*, 129)

The deer provide the double gesture, the *mimēsis* of the mountain. Leopold's
famous figure is thinking like a mountain. As if a mountain could think, or
be, or own, in the genitive, without *mimēsis*.

The double gesture: "just as a deer herd lives in mortal fear of its
wolves, so does a mountain live in mortal fear of its deer. . . . A range pulled
down by too many deer may fail of replacement in as many decades" (p.
132); "Game management is the art of making land produce sustained
annual crops of wild game for recreational use" (Leopold, *GM*, 3). The
mountain lives in fear of deer, the prairie of rabbits, who multiply and
destroy themselves and their surroundings. Not as if the destruction were
unnatural or improper, yet still destruction. Game management gives some
of us the opportunity to shoot deer as a sport, gaining pleasure while saving
the mountain—or sparing it abuse. As if we human beings might know the
good for the mountain better than the deer or the mountain itself.

Leopold expresses the vulnerable skin of the mountain as it touches
and is touched by deer and wolves, as the mountain expresses in the beauty
and fragility of its trees and flowers its expressive vulnerability to deer. I
would say, so that there is no confusion, that the deer are vulnerable in
their skins to the mountain, that they share life productively and destructively, are exposed to each other in these and different ways. Always expressively. Nature's *mimēsis* gives rise to an ethic—Leopold's famous *land
ethic*—in endless movement, vulnerable to instability. Most of all, however,
betraying genitivity. We need an ethic that will limit freedom of action over
land for the collective good. We need to abandon land as property and
regard it ethically.

I wonder if such an ethic would confine freedom or might enrich,
enhance, and expand it, especially if property is theft, if owning is exclusion. Whose property and whose freedom?, one might ask, in an ethical
voice. "All ethics so far evolved rest upon a single premise: that the individual is a member of a community of interdependent parts. . . . The land
ethic simply enlarges the boundaries of the community to include soils,
waters, plants, and animals, or collectively, the land" (Leopold, *GM*, 219–
20). I wonder at the evolution of a land ethic, an ethic in the earth, responsive to the earth's abundance, how it might limit freedom of action without
betrayal. At stake are our understanding of freedom and the earth, and the

practices associated with them. I hold freedom in abeyance, though it constantly returns. A fundamental concern of this book is freedom without genitivity—that is, freely giving without having.

I return from these interruptions to land, as if we had ever left it, as if our feet were not always on the ground. "Land, then, is not merely soil; it is a foundation of energy flowing through a circuit of soils, plants, and animals. Food chains are the living channels which conduct energy upward; death and decay return it to the soil" (p. 231). Abundance in the earth itself, land, sky, air, and water, together with the creatures and things that compose the abundance. An ethic of abundance: "It is inconceivable to me that an ethical relation to land can exist without love, respect, and admiration for land, and a high regard for its value. By value, I of course mean something far broader than mere economic value; I mean value in the philosophical sense" (p. 239). Well, perhaps not in the philosophical sense, given that philosophers have insisted on property and the destiny of things to be owned, including earth and sky.

Cherish the land. Cherish abundance in the earth. I stay with the land and its *mimēsis*, enclosure and disclosure. I insist on resistance to genitivity, to the enclosure of land, the domestication of animals and plants, and the institution of the social contract. Perhaps a different contract, a natural contract in the earth. Perhaps no contract, no rights at all, resisting the right to enclose, domesticate, rule, and own. Giving beyond having. Living without fearing wilderness as demanding enclosure.

I turn to the fear of wilderness at a time when many claim to love it, when many choose to live as close as they can get to it, when some fear its encroachment and others yearn to possess it. The luxury, one might say, of cherishing wild things and wilderness without fear or deprivation. I trace this trajectory into the heart of Greek-Judeo-Christianity. "The sense of being lost, displaced, and homeless is pervasive in contemporary culture. The yearning to belong somewhere, to have a home, to be in a safe place, is a deep and moving pursuit" (Brueggemann, *L*, 1); "Land is a central, if not *the central theme* of biblical faith. Biblical faith is a pursuit of historical belonging that includes a sense of destiny derived from such belonging" (p. 3). To be safe, to have a place, a home, to be destined to arrive in safety—all are defined in the genitive. Coupled with a figure that haunts the history of Judeo-Christianity. "The land for which Israel yearns and which it remembers is never unclaimed space but is always *a place with Yahweh*, a place well filled with memories of life with him and promise from him and vows to him. It is land that provides the central assurance to Israel of its historicality" (pp. 5–6). Humanness as identity and transcendence, destiny and freedom, is linked with owning the land through divine gift. Giving becomes having. Being in place with God is owning one's land, always in fear that it will be taken away. Haunted by terrible memories of wilderness. "Israel is a landless people . . . on the way to a promised place" (p. 6); "the wilderness period . . . is a route on the way to the land, but it is also a sentence of death" (pp. 7–8). Filled with betrayal. "To be placed in the wilderness is to be cast into the land of the enemy—cosmic, natural, historical—without any of the props or resources that give life order and meaning. . . . Not only is nothing growing, but nothing can grow. It is land without promise, without hope, where no newness can come" (p. 29). Without humanity. "In the history of Western thought, nature has repeatedly been viewed as a wilderness in the worst sense, full of dangers and evils as well as lacking the symmetry, order, and therefore beauty of the domesticated landscape created by civilization. . . . Nature without the proper action of human beings is not divinely ordered" (Botkin, *DH*, 85–86).

Brueggemann wonderfully expresses the insistence on owning that lies within the biblical desire for land, the yearning for home, the demand for safety.[6] "In the midst of wondrous manna, Israel is tempted to hoard. In the midst of stridency and death, there is an assertion of weakness which is blessed. The two together announce the possibility and limits of hope for wilderness. And Israel always wants less than or more than. But characteristically there is enough, but not too little and not too much (Ex. 16:18)" (Brueggemann, *L*, 40). Too little, too much, or enough are calibrated genitives in relation to giving in abundance. Manna is given and arrives in abundance—without measure and without having. Being alone, abandoned, in the wilderness—where, perhaps, we continue to wander—leads to thoughts of safety as having, falling away from generosity and God. "Being in the wilderness is enough. Being there alone, abandoned, is unbearable. Inevitably the issue of God's presence is raised as a desperate question" (p. 40); "Israel is not abandoned in wilderness. But it has no glory to manage or administer. It has only goodness, covenantal generosity, expressed as water, quail, manna" (p. 42). Gifts and giving, generosity, but gifts that cannot be had or held, that betray, awaiting—perhaps forever—having and holding. Life under God is precarious and inscrutable—wandering—in the midst of plenty. Brueggemann's narrative reaches from land to giving through the dangers and temptations of coveting, from wilderness to giving through the gift. "Finally Israel comes to the land. The Exodus is about to be completed. The promise is about to be fulfilled. Landless sojourning is about to end. . . . Nothing is more radical than this, that the sojourner becomes a possessor. . . . Land entry requires of Israel that it cease to be what it had been in the wilderness and become what it had never been before. Land makes that demand" (p. 45). Land enclosure means giving up being in the wilderness, remembering generosity, wandering without having, in giving, a generosity that may give nothing but memories of betrayal, mourning, responsibility, and vulnerability. In this narrative, God is closest, giving is most present, when human beings take and receive the least. When human beings have and hold, God's giving from the earth recedes so far as to threaten the covenant, threaten any social contract beyond what can be taken and held.

Including land. Israel comes to own land with its obligations and transformations. And destructions. For Israel almost destroys itself in owning the land. In destroying the giftedness of the land, in taking land as something it can manage and own, Israel gives away what is abundant in the land, betrays the generosity of God.

I continue in Brueggemann's radiant language, though I yearn for more secular expression. "You did not build . . . ; you did not fill . . . ; you did not hew . . . ; you did not plant" (p. 48); "Israel lives under gift, not gift anticipated, but gift given. That is its new consciousness, and nothing is more radical, especially to landed, empowered people, than to discover they are creatures of gift" (p. 51). Creatures of abundance, giving; called by giving to responsibility, in exposure and proximity. But the danger, the risk, is that the giving becomes a gift, that the radicality of living in the wilderness, on the journey, becomes something to have and hold. Owning in the genitive transforms the giving into having, the earth into property. Owning and having betray forgetting. "Israel's central temptation is to forget and so cease to be an historical people. . . . Settled into an eternally guaranteed situation, one scarcely knows that one is indeed addressed by the voice in history who gives gifts and makes claims. And if one is not addressed, then one does not need to answer" (p. 54).

I would pursue this suggestion in its extremity, from temptation to actuality. In and upon the land, human beings take things and possess them. Genitivity is beyond temptation, is forgetting and betraying—forgetting God, of course, and history, forgetting giving, betraying the abundance of things in the earth. "The central temptation of the land is coveting. . . . The central question at the boundary is this: Can Israel live in the land without being seduced by the gods, without the temptation of coveting having its way? Can Israel live in the land with all the precarious trust of landlessness?" (p. 59). The central question of life in the earth, at the boundaries between wandering and home, life and death, earth and sky, body and spirit, finite and infinite, is whether humanity can live in the earth in the trust of its abundance without being seduced to covet and without insisting on taking, in the genitive. With Nietzsche in mind I think of the seduction not as pagan but as monotheistic. Pagan gods can never be mine, can never insist on the genitive. My one and only God may give beyond having, but I am sure the gift is given to me. Or Israel. Given as the son, beyond betrayal.

Within Brueggemann's tracing of landlessness is the double gesture that it must not become yet cannot avoid becoming taking. "The central learning about the land motif . . . is that grasping for home leads to homelessness and risking homelessness yields the gift of home . . . . Jesus' embrace of homelessness (crucifixion) is finally the awesome, amazing gift of home (resurrection)" (pp. 189–90). The giving of home—which is nothing, nothing that can be had or owned—becomes the greatest gift of all. Brueggemann comes to the boundary of dispossession and stops. Having remains the goal of desire. No matter how offensive. "There is only trust in the promise of a land of rest and joy. But surely such a gift is a scandal!" (p. 196).

I would consider a different possibility, deeply betrayed in Brueggemann's account of Israel's journey, not so openly betrayed in the resurrection, even in a theology of the cross, of homelessness. I postpone much of my discussion of giving and taking to a later chapter, in relation to Derrida's *The Gift of Death*, more than anything else on this subject, of the God whose giving beyond having is always received as a taking and grasping, of the scandal and paradox of an infinite generosity that becomes finite as having and owning.

Here I wish to consider giving in abundance beyond any gifts. In relation to land, the earth, and home we—not just humans, not just living things, all things that are, as Spinoza says—are given abundance, given in infinite ways and kinds, given in desire, *conatus*. Betrayed. Giving becomes having, becomes the gift. Desire yearns to hold and take the gift—of life, of pleasure, of joy, even of giving away to others so that they may receive pleasure and joy. But at the heart of every gift, consumed, accumulated, or given away, is a giving beyond them all. At the heart of every relation to the land, destroying it, enclosing it, or relinquishing it, is betrayed an abundance that belongs to no one, to no thing or kind. It is an abundance of giving, of being with and on the earth, an arrival that cannot be restricted or confined, possibilities of generation and transformation that cannot be possessed.

# CHAPTER 7

## Domestic Properties

Those peoples who have been classified as aboriginal, as foragers, face an obstacle uniquely applied to that classificatory status—the claim that they, alone among the peoples of the earth, have no institutions of tenure in land. (Wilmsen, *WAH*, ix)

The origins of property rights in the United States are rooted in racial domination. . . . It was not the concept of race alone that operated to oppress Blacks and Indians; rather, it was the *interaction* between conceptions of race and property that played a critical role. . . . (Harris, *WP*, 1716)

The people of Israel related to themselves as a people and to their God in terms of land—a land they sometimes inhabited and owned, more frequently yearned for as they wandered in exile. The promised land is a land of riches. Having property in land to call one's own lies in the historical memories of the Judeo-Christian tradition: to be human, to be worthy, to be chosen, to be divine creatures in the grace of God, is to belong to and to have land.

This is a generous way to approach the disenfranchisement in land and rights that has haunted European society throughout its history, especially during colonization and the expansion of trade, including the enslavement of peoples regarded as less than human—where less than human means, among other things, unable to possess and manage land. So judged by those who coveted the land, who took for granted that they would own and keep it as it deserved to be kept. Perhaps in the eyes of God—our god, not theirs; for their gods were no more worthy than they to give propriety to ownership in land.

We arrive at two questions in extremity, still avoiding precipitous conclusion, yet bearing the full weight of the discussion here. The first question, following from Wilmsen's suggestion that aboriginal peoples, foragers and hunter-gatherers, were deemed too primitive under law to possess

property in land, is this: *could the idea of property from the first, in Eu-*
*ropean history especially but in other histories as well, have been evoked*
*within a double exclusion, one the exclusion in property itself: what is*
*mine is not yours, what is ours is not theirs; the second, property itself as*
*exclusion, excluding certain peoples—not Western, civilized, autonomous,*
*sedentary, or chosen—from the possibility of owning and having land,*
*from the proper destiny of humanity?* Here property belongs to traditions
that evolve toward the nation-state, or at least toward political systems in
which some kinds of people are systematically excluded from power. Here
law operates to determine who, which people, may own.

> [T]he operational dichotomy perceived to exist between forager and hus-
> bandman relations to land lies in European intellectual history in con-
> junction with the colonial experience as interpreted through that
> intellectual lens. That is, the dichotomy was constructed in European
> minds to serve European needs. (Wilmsen, *WAH*, x)

> Thus, in defining the acts of possession that make up a claim to
> property, the law not only rewards the author of the "text"; it also puts an
> imprimatur on a particular symbolic system and on the audience that uses
> this system. (Rose, *POP*, 85)

My second question concerns property itself, whether it is intelligible
apart from systems of social control and political power. Here the anthropological reply to the historical disenfranchisement of aboriginal peoples is
worth close consideration. Three examples:

> On every continent where Europeans encountered peoples whose
> economies were perceived to be exclusively—or even substantially—based
> on foraging, the same rationale was invoked to disenfranchise their land.
> Overlooked was the fact that all such peoples were actively engaged politi-
> cally with a host of others through complex social and material exchange
> networks. (Wilmsen, *WAH*, 2–3)

> My argument is that "things" (objects, ritual, land, prerogatives, duties)
> have meaning—that is, significance or social value—for the Pintupi largely
> as an expression of autonomy and what I have elsewhere defined as "re-
> latedness" or shared identity. (Myers, *BTHC*, 15)

> Property law in tribal society defines not so much rights of persons
> over things, as obligations owed between persons in respect of things.
> (Gluckman, *PLRTS*, 46)

The second question, then, is this: *does property in all societies serve to*
*demarcate relationships between human beings in contradistinction to*

*relations of humans toward everything else—land, territory, animals, and things; sometimes toward other human beings such as women and children?*

Let us take seriously this claim that property law—in tribal, aboriginal, or any society—defines rights among persons, where the overruling consideration is, who is a person and who is not?, that is, who can own and who or what can be owned? Under slavery, at least certain kinds of slavery, some persons can both own and be owned. After slavery, this distinction hardens, and some earthly creatures can own but cannot be owned, while all other things and creatures can be owned but cannot own. That is, according to law, for we know that the situation is different in practice, in the interstices and byways of social and political life. Women in many countries are seized, taken to places out of reach of the law, treated as property. And when this practice comes to light, frequently the law punishes them more than those who possessed them.

I would pursue the double exclusion at the heart of property in relation to aboriginal peoples especially, and women.[1] I insist on the unequal way in which rights institute domination, in which those who claim rights insist on taking. I would consider a very different kind of example, perhaps more to the point, preceded by a brief allusion to Stirner, who expresses the German views of his time in a doubled genitive gesture toward aboriginality.

> The history of the world, whose shaping properly belongs altogether to the Caucasian race, seems until now to have run through two Caucasian ages, in the first of which we had to work out and work off our innate *Negroidity*; this was followed in the second by *Mongoloidity* (Chineseness), which must likewise be terribly made an end of. Negroidity represents *antiquity*, the time of dependence on *things* (on cocks' eating, birds' flight, on sneezing, on thunder and lightning, on the rustling of sacred trees, and so forth); Mongoloidity the time of dependence on thoughts, the *Christian* time. (Stirner, *EO*, 62–63)

Not only is Negroidity almost certainly aboriginality, with the least cover over contempt for aboriginal practices in Africa and Australia as pre-human—that is, not human—but even this pre-human, nonhuman way of life is appropriated by White European Caucasian Man, who owns the only proper shaping of the history of the world. The World, not Europe. All other races, other kinds of human beings, are properly Caucasian, to be taken over and appropriated to the civilized manners of Europeans. To those who can properly own.

That is the issue of this chapter, the ideas and practices instituted by Caucasian human beings to justify expropriating the things of non-Caucasians, as if they could not own or possess things properly, as if they were too close to things and animals to be human, too dependent on things.

Aboriginal peoples, hunter-gatherers, foragers, do not know how to own, to have, are subhuman dregs, sediment at the bottom of the barrel (Wilmsen, *WAH*, vii–viii). If we are to think of the earth or society as a barrel, or container, rather than circulating in abundance.

The grim and likely consequence is that it might be impossible to rise from the bottom, that racism or industrialism or something similar might work to keep aboriginal peoples incapable of possession even as they might decide, free and human, to give up their aboriginality. Aboriginality sticks to the skin like a leech. I am speaking of blackness. I have been leading up to this interruption in the name of whiteness. Rochelle interrupts—however silently—to remind us that the world is made up of white and black and colored stones, present in abundance. She marks the point of this interruption, that abundance is never good enough for those who insist on owning. And what they insist on owning is whatever distinguishes them from the others, what marks abundance with poverty—always claimed to be more than abundance. As if acquisition were more than generosity. Rather than less. Or something else.

Harris describes property rights as entwined with race throughout United States history: race and property; race as property. The entire history of the United States, beginning with indigenous peoples who were regarded as lacking a civilized sense of property, through slavery to the present, linked race and property to the advantage of whites. Yet even this sweeping claim is but an opening onto a more striking possibility: whiteness itself as property—a valued, precious property worthy of legal protection. Blackness and other forms of non-whiteness did not deserve such protection.

> [T]he law has established and protected an actual property interest in whiteness itself, which shares the critical characteristics of property and accords with the many and varied theoretical descriptions of property. (Harris, *WP*, 1724)

> Whiteness is not simply and solely a legally recognized property interest. It is simultaneously an aspect of self-identity and of personhood, and its relation to the law of property is complex. . . . According whiteness actual legal status converted an aspect of identity into an external object of property, moving whiteness from privileged identity to a vested interest. (p. 1725)

To understand whiteness and its alleged correlates, high culture and civilization, as property is to understand them as valued possessions, vested interests. Privileged identity, accumulated possessions, more powerful political, industrial, and social institutions, claims to superiority of mind and body, to the epitome of human fulfillment, are not enough for whites under white law. That which confers privilege and superiority must be claimed to be possessed and owned.

Harris argues that "whiteness fits the broad historical concept of property described by classical theorists" (p. 1726); even more, however, it represents the expansion of property rights in the modern era to include the wealth distributed by government and the security in goods sold by corporations—an expansion Reich understands as property. "The valuables dispensed by government take many forms, but they all share one characteristic. They are steadily taking the place of traditional forms of wealth—forms which are held as private property" (Reich, *NP,* 179); "Property is a legal institution the essence of which is the creation and protection of certain private rights in wealth of any kind" (p. 180). Harris continues:

> Property in this broader sense encompassed jobs, entitlements, occupational licenses, contracts, subsidies, and indeed a whole host of intangibles that are the product of labor, time, and creativity, such as intellectual property, business goodwill, and enhanced earning potential from graduate degrees. (Harris, *WP,* 1728)

> Reich's argument that property is not a natural right but a construction by society resonates in current theories of property that describe the allocation of property rights as a series of choices.
> ... This theory does not suggest that all value or all expectations give rise to property, but those expectations in tangible or intangible things that are valued and protected by the law are property. (p. 1729)

This is the other side of property rights, the side Reich does not consider in detail. He claims that property rights protect the individual against the state.[2] Indeed they do—for some, under some conditions. Under certain tyrannical conditions, where property rights exist and are protected against arbitrary state power, owning property is security against the state. Sovereignty and property, where they do not coincide, can open independent spaces of individual authority. For people with standing, one might say. Not for Jews in Nazi Germany, whose property was seized together with their bodies and lives. Even so, many bought their way to freedom. And not for non-whites in the United States today, who do not possess the supporting conditions that enable different spheres of freedom to coexist.

I am for the moment concerned with the darker side of the expansion of property rights, present in the idea of property. For where Harris and Reich understand a growing movement from property in things to rights to whatever might be valuable in human life—at least, whatever might be accumulated, consumed, or exchanged—I have suggested that the origins of this broad association of values with what can be accumulated or gathered lie far back in the recesses of time and human history. Whatever human beings may have and hold is good for life and well-being, is good as genitivity, in the holding and having, in the assembling and gathering. Including knowledge and truth, at least to those for whom these are valued, to be assembled in certain places. Also including marks of value, inscribed upon human bodies, that can be said to be had or owned by some rather than others, that carry social and economic weight. Whiteness for example.

Maleness and heterosexuality are other examples. Even for men who seek surgical intervention to transform themselves into women, the truth is that being male is an economic value, and that one might well protest—and sue—if one were subjected to a change in gender from male to female against one's will, that one had been deprived of property. Similarly, the assumption that homosexuality is a disease for which it would be good to find a cure entails that if a cure were known, deprivation would be the denial of a property right; and if one were made or even regarded as a homosexual against one's will, that again could be interpreted in property terms.

The extreme, evident in Harris's discussion, is that human and even, perhaps, nonhuman identity—identity in general—is inseparable at a deep and pervasive level from having, owning, and possessing, from genitivity. To be something or someone is to have the properties or qualities that make one that something or someone. Nietzsche's denial that anyone or anything can give human beings their qualities may be understood to deny the genitive, the investment in those qualities that can be understood as rights in property.

The point is the way in which a law that claims neutrality serves the interests of unequal privilege: "In creating property 'rights,' the law draws boundaries and enforces or reorders existing regimes of power. . . . In this sense, . . . property rights and interests are not 'natural,' but are 'creation[s]' of law.' In a society structured on racial subordination, white privilege became an expectation and, . . . whiteness became the quintessential property for personhood" (Harris, *WP*, 1730). I postpone discussion of the complex links between personhood and property to chapter 9, beyond the legal concept of the person. Here I am interested in the ways in which everything said or thought to be of human importance is understood in terms of genitivity—having, accumulating, giving, consuming. One must have, or give, or consume whatever one needs to live well.[3] Living well is having, owning, accumulating, gathering. Above all, if living in a systematically unequal society means that being white, or being male, or being heterosexual is better than being something else, then each of these is better when the essential, defining property is had, possessed by some and not others: whiteness, maleness, heterosexness. We have always had the answer, I believe, to Derrida's question: how can I (or we) learn to live finally? Deferring finality to infinity, we answer that we do not need to learn, but need to have. Living is accumulating, consuming, exchanging, sometimes giving. In terms of property.

Including whiteness—and, I have insisted repeatedly, maleness and other privileged forms of humanity. "Within the worlds of de jure and de facto segregation, whiteness has value, whiteness is valued, and whiteness is expected to be valued in law. . . . The existing state of affairs is considered neutral and fair, however unequal and unjust it is in substance" (pp. 1777–78). Harris's discussion of property rights leads her to a striking argument in favor of affirmative action. "If affirmative action is viewed through the prism of distributive justice, the claim of white innocence no longer seems so compelling, because a distributive justice framework does not focus primarily on guilt and innocence, but rather on entitlement and fairness. Thus, distributive justice as a matter of equal protection requires that individuals receive that share of the benefits they would have secured in the absence of racism" (p. 1783). If whiteness has been protected under law, then harm has been done to non-whites who have been deprived of life and property. This applies to whites and non-whites today who might never have participated in racial discrimination on either side—if that is thinkable. The principle required is equal right to property: "[A]ffirmative action calls for *equalizing treatment* by redistributing power and resources in order to rectify inequities and to achieve real equality" (p. 1788).

Harris resists the historical appropriation of the goods of non-whites as illegal seizure of property. In the name of property, of genitivity, let us restore equality. Such a program presupposes that we understand life and goodness as having and owning. A more radical way to understand affirmative action—ineffective perhaps under current property law—might be that life, living well, living ethically, are not having or accumulating goods or things or human qualities, in the genitive. Privilege accumulates where there must not, even cannot, be accumulation. Freedom, for example, and happiness cannot be accumulated or had, cannot be consumed, though they can be taken away and perhaps given. Similarly, knowledge and truth cannot be accumulated or had, but can be given. Teaching is giving what one does not have, what no one has, to those who also will not have it.

Learn to read and read well; read whatever you want as well as you can; learn from reading, and listening, and watching; help others to learn. With the least accumulation or, for that matter, consumption. Without genitivity.

Learn to live and live well; live in the ways you desire as well as you can, as well as you may hope to; live from life and experience; help others—

friends and children—to live. With the least accumulation and consumption. Betraying genitivity.

I return from Harris, who gives us something to remember as we move on, to seizures of aboriginal land and property, noting that she employs the master's tools to rebuild the master's house. Insisting on genitivity. I wish to consider the possibility that property as a tool of mastery, the predominant and inescapable tool of control, may be resisted much more forcibly. Instead of seeking equality in property against every inequality, let us seek equality in living without genitivity. I postpone such generosity to later chapters.

I conclude this chapter with another example of the ways in which the law has served property against life and justice. Another way in which property law works against those whose goods are coveted. Another way in which having becomes seizing and its justification. I return to the link between sovereignty and property in relation to land and territory. "If the United States had viewed its treaty commitments with American Indian nations seriously, it would have attempted to renegotiate the treaties with its treaty partners. . . . More often, however, the United States simply abrogated the treaties. The federal government has a long and appalling history of breaking treaties with Indian nations whenever it was convenient for the United States to do so" (Singer, *SP*, 1–2). Native American nations had to be deprived of both political sovereignty and economic rights to property if their land was to be seized. The United States Supreme Court exercised one against the other wherever it suited non-Indians' right of possession. "In recent years, the Supreme Court has manipulated the public/private distinction as it applies to tribes in a way that has given tribal governments the worst of both worlds. When tribes would benefit from being classified as property holders, the courts often treat them as sovereigns" (p. 6); "the Court has become more and more sympathetic in recent years to the argument that it is improper for Indian nations to exercise sovereign authority over non-Indians" (p. 4). This worst of both worlds lies, I believe, at the heart of property itself. Which is not to deny that property rights have sometimes protected individuals against state power—but always some individuals protected, given standing under that state, while other individuals, especially, groups and kinds of individuals, were deprived of standing and property under the same laws.

I return to the injustices with which we began, denying some kinds of people the right to own in virtue of their kind, this time Canadian.

> in 1971, an Appeals Court judge boldly asserted with respect to the Nishga Indians that "[they] were undoubtedly at the time of settlement a very primitive people with few of the institutions of civilized society." As a

result of such thinking, the commonly held notion in the late 1960s and early 1970s was that aboriginal peoples had no aboriginal rights in law. (Asch, *NC*, 118)

Governments (both federal and provincial) do not accept that aboriginal rights are related to "special" political rights such as the right to self-government with senior legislative responsibilities. (p. 120)

Sovereignty and property rights are played off against each other repeatedly to the detriment of indigenous peoples. To which we have seen the anthropologist's reply that indigenous peoples knew how to own and to implement political self-determination. Sovereignty and property in territory and land are not the same, but every human tribe has known how to own, possess, and have. "It is my view, therefore, that the meaning aboriginal peoples attach to the notion of aboriginal rights is closely analogous to the idea of the right of colonial peoples to political self-determination. It is a right that is said to continue even when the indigenous nations come under the sovereignty of a new colonial regime" (p. 128).

In the context of a legal system in which property rights are identical with autonomy and self-determination, what can the anthropologist do but represent beleaguered people as capable of owning and having as they are capable of knowing and learning. In this context, again determined by the conqueror, who insists on defining the terms under which the conquered may bring their case, people are to be regarded as not so primitive only if they can engage in recognizable property and political claims under both tribal and national legal and political systems—a tremendous obligation, one might say.

But something else has also to be said, that such an obligation obscures the possibility of another relation to land and territory than that recognized by European industrial institutions; that global development in property—the expansion of capitalist economy—operates under a double mandate, mandating everywhere both the economy itself, if one is to be modern, civilized, to have the goods that make life worthwhile today, for anyone, anywhere; and the legal rights and privileges that constitute the intelligibility of having goods in the modern world. Everything, Marx said, is turned into a commodity—accumulated, exchanged, consumed, laden with manufactured desire. Bad enough, perhaps. But on top of this, in the very flesh of commodities and the yearning of desire, whatever one might require to live well one must have. The essence of living well in the human world is what one has, in the genitive: if not animals, then things; if not things, then community; if not community, then sovereignty; if not sovereignty then freedom, truth, and goodness. Or whiteness. Law accumulates the accumulation, as does desire. At least, modern and postmodern, Western and post-Western, law and desire and life and goodness accumulate as property, in genitivity.

This recognition allows us to understand the seizure of aboriginal lands as something beyond greed for what others have and owned, as betraying possibilities of life otherwise, other than owning and having. I do not say that aboriginal peoples, including hunter-gatherers, have lived without having and owning. To the contrary. But the possibility of doing so is very close to the lives they lived. We take for granted that they—all of them—would choose to accumulate more if they could, if they had the resources. Or that they accumulate authority in tribal elders, accumulate wisdom in old men and women. We assume that they accumulated what they could. I would consider the possibility that where these people accumulated authority and things, they understood other possibilities, because they lived without accumulating very much, very many goods. And truly, it is hard for human beings to live without accumulating wisdom. Even so, accumulating wisdom fixes it in place, destroys its living soul.

One answer to the question of how we are to live well is to have whatever we need, whatever it takes. To have. To accumulate and consume. Rochelle interrupts to remind us that she has very little, perhaps nothing at all. But she flourishes where she lies among the others.

The ethical question is of flourishing without grasping, giving without having, circulating without accumulating.

# CHAPTER 8

## Gender Properties

In what ways have relationships between women and men been structured by access to, control over and transmission of property? To what extent and in what respects do women themselves or their offspring constitute property? (Hirschon, *WPWP*, 1)

Men have the power of owning. Historically, this power has been absolute; denied to some men by other men in times of slavery and other persecution, but in the main upheld by armed force and law. In many parts of the world, the male right to own women and all that issues from them (children and labor) is still absolute, and no human rights considerations seem to apply to captive populations of women. (Dworkin, *P*, 19)

The questions addressed to genitivity by the good concern the possibility of flourishing without having, of living without accumulating, perhaps of giving without gifts. Yet accumulation and consumption are everywhere, though the forms, discourses, and laws of consumption and accumulation differ from culture to culture. In the preceding chapter, I explored aboriginal relations to land as possessions both for indigenous peoples and for colonists who seized their land in the name of a higher law. Here I turn to aboriginal and other property relations involving women and children, further pursuing the dialectic of genitivity opened up by Engels in relation to the family, the props of property: blood, sex, kin, class, food, desire, and power.

It is time for me to organize this discussion of aboriginal property relations into several related questions, insisting that from the first and throughout these have been inseparable, indeed that the most important questions concern their inseparability. Beginning with aboriginal properties, leading toward property in general, genitivity—if there be such—we may consider the following:

1. To what extent are human relations among themselves and to other creatures and things to be understood in terms of property: owning, possessing, having?

2. To what extent have such property relations been instituted in practices of seizing the goods and transforming the lives of other peoples, members of the same or different social groups?

3. To what extent have the identities of individual human beings or social groups been constituted by property relations—in particular: (1) by their possessions and the practices associated with them; and (2) by being either owners or owned?

4. Concluding with the central questions of this project: to what extent are the understandings and practices whereby human beings relate to the world and among themselves fundamentally genitive, having to do with who has what, and how whatever and whoever exists is to be understood and given status—ethical, political, legal, epistemological—in terms of what it—perhaps he or she or they—has, and who or what has it; to what extent human understandings of their lives and experiences—the only ones human beings will ever know—are organized around taking, receiving, and having, accumulating and consuming, rather than giving, expending, and circulating; and finally, is it possible to imagine human prosperity as giving, resisting genitivity?

If these are questions to which we are led in considering genitivity, questions to take seriously if not perhaps to answer, then for the moment we may consider the related set of questions evoked by Engels concerning the genealogy of genitivity, to which I return in a more contemporary venue, concerning the kin and family relations that turn around property, understood in terms of the preceding questions. Not land, one might say, but women and children. Genitivity as genealogy and genitality: blood, sex, women, kin, and reproduction. Inseparable from animals, human and animal blood and other secretions and excretions. Aristotle got it from Hesiod, perhaps, and the rest of us may have gotten it from Aristotle. But perhaps it goes without saying. The life of (a) man requires first and foremost a house, a woman, and an ox. Men require and must have a place, a woman, and domestic animals.

In Irigaray's words—an interruption:

> If traditionally, and as a mother, woman represents *place* for man, such a limit means that she becomes *a thing*, with some possibility of change from one historical period to another. She finds herself delineated as a thing. Moreover, the maternal-feminine also serves as an *envelope*, a *container*, the starting point from which man limits his things. . . .

... She would have to re-envelop herself with herself, and do so at least twice: as a woman and as a mother. Which would presuppose a change in the whole economy of space-time. (Irigaray, *ESD*, 10–11)

Man demands a place, *his* place, insists on having a house, a domicile, together with women and animals—whatever is required for his prosperity. He controls the economy of living and being, of being as having, the earth itself. He insists on having in such a way that women, animals, and the things required for his prosperities are deprived of their place(s) because they represent places for men. And what is even more striking, this insistence on having goods—persons and things—pervades a world in which most men neither are prosperous nor have much. Still they insist on having, insist that they are what they are in virtue of having. He who has a place is a man. She who lacks a place is a thing.

This understanding again evokes the haunting question of this project, expressed in terms of having and owning, returning repeatedly to Hegel and the destiny of humans and nonhumans. For Irigaray takes for granted, at least here, that to lack a place is to be a thing; at least, that the violence done to women in virtue of being there for men is not to be there for themselves, thereby to be things. Human beings must be there for themselves, risking the thought we find ourselves repeatedly caught within, that human beings prosper where we possess ourselves. Being there is having one's own being. Compared with being here, giving beyond genitivity.

Irigaray would certainly deny this. For one thing, she insists—if not loudly or vociferously enough for me—that nature must be rethought in relation to kinds.[1] "*Genre is confused with species*. Genre becomes the human race *[le genre humain]*, human nature, etc., as defined within patriarchal culture. This genre corresponds to a people of men which rejects, consciously or unconsciously, the possibility of an other genre: the female" (Irigaray, *NSR*, 201). The human kind turns out to be the masculine kind, insisting on having the truth and nature of the other kind, of accumulating it in kinship for the future. The heterogeneity of kinds is subordinated to the imperative of acquisition and reproduction. One might say that Irigaray acknowledges the Hobbesian sense of infinite desire as implicit within the practices of humanism: the desire to have forever a place with houses, women, and animals, the goods requisite for prosperity. Even where we cannot have these things, they represent the objects of desire. Desire for Hobbes is desire by men—but perhaps not by women or other human beings or animals and other creatures and things—to accumulate and consume forever. To accumulate others as if they were things—if we take for granted the goodness of the desire to accumulate things. For things are also others, other things, as other creatures are other living beings, as women and members of other cultures are other human beings. If we must not accumulate the one, perhaps we must not accumulate the others.

For another thing, Irigaray denies that being there is having, insists that *there* (or *here*) is mobile, transitory, ecstatic, that place is a boundary figure: endless circulation, movement, crossings.

> The angel is that which unceasingly *passes through the envelope(s)* or *container(s)*, goes from one side to the other, reworking every deadline, changing every decision, thwarting all repetition. Angels destroy the monstrous, that which hampers the possibility of a new age; they come to herald the arrival of a new birth, a new morning. (Irigaray, *ESD*, 15)
>
> They represent and tell of another incarnation, another parousia of the body. (p. 16)

Angels accumulate nothing, own and have nothing, do not understand their being, their task, to be accumulation but circulation, passage. They give us, in their movements, the possibility of new births, new meanings, new mornings, a new age, in their speed, their transgressions, their giving, the endless arrival of what cannot be had. "A new morning of and for the world? A remaking of immanence and transcendence, notably through this *threshold* which has never been examined as such: the female sex. The threshold that gives access to the *mucous*. Beyond classical oppositions of love and hate, liquid and ice—a threshold that is always *half-open*. The threshold of the *lips*, which are strangers to dichotomy and oppositions" (p. 18). Giving interrupts having—half-giving, half-having: thresholds of betrayal, of desire and love, love for and care of the other, always between, resisting the fixing of borders and the accumulation of goods.[2] Betraying blood, mucus, and other abject seepages and flows.

If giving interrupts having, it must do so in the transgression of the boundaries of humanity and nature, especially every insistence on absolute differences between human and thing in memory of other such differences between man and woman, human and animal, modern and aboriginal. What is at stake in genitivity is always who shall have it, and who shall not, together with who may have and who or what may be had. Somehow, those who have more always find a justification for their having, a justification that holds down those who do not have as much and who might be able to seize it by force if they did not accept the justification, if they did not believe that they do not deserve it because they belong to the kind that is owned rather than owns. Wolves and sheep some say. Men and women others say. Civilized and primitive others have said.

I return to the questions with which this chapter began: how are differential relationships between men and women organized around genitivity, including differences in what men and women are permitted to own and in what may be owned or treated as property? Is it possible that differential property rights—some are richer than others, permitted to accumulate more goods, more of what life requires—always contain within the differentia, the economic disparities organized around genitivity, the suggestion that those who have fulfill the destiny of humanity, while those who have less, or who do not have well, fail their destiny not only in not having what they require, but evoking the destiny that theirs is not to have but to be had, to be exchanged? As one might say of most known societies, those who have wealth and power have women, where, in general, women do not have power and wealth.

Shall we ask what women require for prosperity? It would not seem quite as important to Aristotle—or, for that matter, to most men. Engels imagines, on little evidence, that women's needs and rights were more respected before men got their hands on cattle, when women more completely controlled the reproductive cycle. Put another way, then, men must have children as well as other possessions. Human life—men or women—is a life in which goods are had, including other human beings as well as things.

One of the questions evoked by Hesiod is what women and children must have in order to live well. Another is whether men must have women and children. So we come back to the questions at the head of this chapter. To what extent do women get to have what they need? And to what extent do men have and own and exchange women for the satisfaction of their needs? Whose needs, again? One would imagine that society has insisted throughout that men have women for the good of both men and women—not to forget the children. The destiny of what is owned is fulfilled in being had, women, children, or things.

Dworkin describes the self as one who takes, who owns, who insists on having. The human self as owner—an image of humanity haunted by Callicles. As if we could not escape. "The power of owning comes from the power of self defined as one who takes. Here the taking is elevated in significance: he takes, he keeps; once he has had, it is his. This relationship between the self that takes and ownership is precisely mirrored, for instance, in the relationship between rape and marriage. . . . Marriage meant the taking was to extend in time, to be not only use of but lifelong possession of, or ownership" (Dworkin, *P*, 19–20). Shall we imagine that such an image of the male self as owner, taker, is present only in industrial societies, postcapitalist societies? Or does it express accumulation everywhere, where some (men) accumulate more than others, accumulating goods together with women and children? Sometimes too much accumulation provokes battle or hospitality; but even hospitality is giving to take, to mark one's greatness—in goods, women, and children.

Dworkin insists that this taking belongs to men not women, that the self that insists on having is male:

> The power of money is a distinctly male power. Money speaks, but it speaks with a male voice. In the hands of women, money stays literal; count it out, it buys what it is worth or less. In the hands of men, money buys women, sex, status, dignity, esteem, recognition, loyalty, all manner of possibility. . . . [I]t brings with it qualities, achievements, honor, respect. On every economic level, the meaning of money is significantly different for men than for women. (p. 20)

This would have to be true, indeed, in every culture in which women were exchanged for goods, in which, for example, men offered dowries to pay off the women's families for their investment. I leave aside whether this turns women into things. I think it important that where slavery was practiced systematically, human slaves were never regarded as things even where they were treated like things. And where animal domestication is practiced systematically, animals are not things even where they are treated like things. Or worse.

I have insisted repeatedly that this question of the genitive relations between human beings and things is central for this project, beyond human social relationships. For the moment, in an indigenous social context, I remain with men and women, at least for a while, though the things around us—Rochelle reminds us—continue to break in upon and through the restrictions. For the desire to have and own women—exceeding sex and reproduction—leads to the boundary between human and thing, as if the desire to control that border remained central to humanity and its humanism. Owning and having are bound inseparably to the curse in which humanity transfigures nature as if owing things no debt, thereby justifying the possession of other human beings.

"Male sexual power is the substance of culture. It resonates everywhere" (Dworkin, *P*, 23).[3] This culture, perhaps any culture in which women are exchanged—humanity itself—forms itself under the curse in which human beings separate themselves from nature absolutely so that some may lord it over others. The danger is that resistance to oppression will remain within the curse, under the absolute separation of some human beings from others. "Through most of patriarchal history, . . . women have been chattel property. Chattel property in the main, is movable property—cattle, wives, concubines, offspring, slaves, beasts of burden, domesticated animals. . . . Chattel property for the most part is animate and sensate, but it is perceived and valued as commodity. To be chattel, even when human, is to be valued and used as property, as thing" (pp. 101–2).

The chapter in which Dworkin speaks of women as property—along with animals and slaves—is entitled "Objects," evoking two possibilities. One is that treating anything as a thing, as property, brings it under the yoke of oppressors: animals, land, forests, all things in the earth. This is the line of thought pursued by this project. Owning is oppression, for anything in the earth. The other is that treating human beings as things, as property, must be resisted, but not things themselves. Perhaps animals and other sensate creatures should not be treated as things, but things are things.

Surely this is a distinction we do not want to abandon, between living and other things. They should be treated differently, they should belong differently to human worlds. But perhaps neither should be treated as property, as something to be accumulated and sold at will. Perhaps nothing should be accumulated even where we cannot live except by having and consuming some things, even using and consuming other human beings. We cannot live without treating other human beings as means, without treating other beings as means. But never, perhaps, means alone. Never something to be had, accumulated, consumed, expended, or exchanged without responsibility or care.

Dworkin may not be immune to the curse in relation to things, but she recognizes it explicitly in relation to women. "The inevitable and intrinsic cruelty involved in turning a person into an object should be apparent, but since this constricting, this undermining, this devaluing, is normative, no particular cruelty is recognized in it. Instead, there is only normal and natural cruelty—by the normal and natural masochism of the female. . . . The object is allowed to desire if she desires to be an object: to be formed; especially to be used" (p. 109). I mean the invisibility of the curse, the denial at its heart. We are human because we are free from the curse of nature—which curses us with abjection. There is only normal and natural accursedness, only normal and natural abjection, only normal and natural desire. Some desire to be owned; some desire to be things; some desire to be sexual objects, objects of desire. Desire desires to be desire under the curse, under restriction. At least for objects and things, and for humans who accept themselves as things. "The object, the woman, goes out into the world formed as men have formed her to be used as men wish to use her. She is then a provocation. The object provokes its use. It provokes its use because of its form, determined by the one who is provoked. . . . When the object complains about the use to which she is put, she is told, simply and firmly, not to provoke" (p. 111). As if it were possible for women or children or animals or natural things, small and large, not to provoke, not to betray, as if the curse were not a curse, as if desire contained under the curse did not exceed every containment. The way in which humans are said to be turned into things, commodities, marks the impossibility of fixing the borders

of desire. The fetish returns desire to the object, undermining every appropriation, every upright gesture. "[E]very fetish, expressed on whatever level,
manifests the power of the erect penis, especially its power in determining
the sensibility of the male himself, his ethical as well as his sexual
nature. . . . On the cultural level the fetish is expanded into myth, religion,
idea, aesthetics, all necessarily and intrinsically male-supremacist. The
uniting theme is the hatred expressed toward women" (p. 127).

This is a harsh account. And many women, for their own reasons, have
resisted Dworkin's reading. Women are not so passive, incompetent, dominated by persuasion or force. Women may choose to be sexual objects if
they choose—though as MacKinnon suggests, under conditions of systematic social inequality, it may be impossible to choose:

> To women I want to say: what do you really want? Do you feel that
> you have the conditions under which you can ask yourself that question?
> If you feel that you are going to be raped when you say no, how do you
> know that you really want sex when you say yes? (MacKinnon, *FU*, p. 83)

> All women live in sexual objectification the way fish live in
> water. . . . The question is, what can life as a woman mean, what can sex
> mean, to targeted survivors in a rape culture? (MacKinnon, *S*, 149)

I want to expand this question without diminishing its force: what can life
for other creatures mean in a culture that knows them only to own them?
What can being be for things in the earth where being is being had?

This returns us to the role of women in culture, under the curse, as
extreme betrayals of the reach of property, where the role of women as
something to be owned and exchanged remains ambiguous. This ambiguity
is the point of Dworkin's and MacKinnon's accounts. Women are treated
like possessions where even the men who possess and own them and the
women themselves would deny that they are property.

> The society we know, our own culture, is based upon the exchange
> of women. Without the exchange of women, we are told, we would fall
> back into the anarchy (?) of the natural world, the randomness (?) of the
> animal kingdom. The passage into the social order, into the symbolic
> order, into order as such, is assured by the fact that men, or groups of
> men, circulate women among themselves, according to a rule known as
> the incest taboo. (Irigaray, *WM*, 170; her question marks)

> The symbolic order, without which there can be no meaning, no language,
> no society, depends on it. But what does women being exchanged mean
> if not that they are dominated? (Wittig, *SM*, 31–32)

The exchange of women does not necessarily imply that women are objectified, in the modern sense, since objects in the primitive world are imbued with highly personal qualities. But it does imply a distinction between gift and giver. If women are the gifts, then it is men who are the exchange partners. And it is the partners, not the presents, upon whom reciprocal exchange confers its quasi-mystical power of social linkage. (Rubin, *TW*, 174)

The inequality in which women are gifts and men are givers institutes a system in which women do not benefit. And the ambiguity of owning what cannot be owned—women and children; freedom and truth—exposes the insistence on genitivity. For society must take for granted that men can have women and children. Society insists on its reproduction, and its reproduction comes through having women and children.

The exchange of women calls for a political economy of sex and gender. "The needs of sexuality and procreation must be satisfied as much as the need to eat, . . . [but] these needs are hardly ever satisfied in any 'natural' form, . . . . Hunger is hunger, but what counts as food is culturally determined and obtained. Every society has some form of organized economic activity. Sex is sex, but what counts as sex is equally culturally determined and obtained" (Rubin, *TW*, 165). Production and reproduction, certainly, but the political economy of sex and gender far exceeds reproduction, exceeds the exchange of women. "The organization of sex and gender once had functions other than itself—it organized society. Now, it only organizes and reproduces itself. . . . One of the most conspicuous features of kinship is that it has been systematically stripped of its functions—political, economic, educational, and organizational. It has been reduced to its barest bones—*sex and gender*" (p. 199). I postpone this political economy for a while, noting that it depends on the ambiguity of sexual property and genitivity.

I return to Hirschon's question, at the head of this chapter, to resist another ambiguity, evoked in the last chapter, taking Western rights to property for granted, to women, children, and things. Other societies have very different understandings and practices of human relations to land and objects—very different, yet with remarkable similarities, not least the restricted access of women to having and controlling things, including things they have made.

On the one hand, then: "Property for us is based on the idea of 'private ownership' which confers on the individual the right to use and to disposal. . . . But what we take for granted—the idea of an individual actor having defined rights *vis-à-vis* others, and the notion of property as consisting in objects or things—is far from universal" (Hirschon, *PPGR*, 2). On the other, returning to the question of women as things:

> Women in Highlands New Guinea society are often equated with
> wealth, they are exchanged on marriage between patrilineal clans, and in
> some places the product of their labour is appropriated by men. Are they
> therefore to be seen as property? . . . In these societies, the notion of the
> person does not involve the manipulation of 'things' nor does the concept
> of wealth involve 'objects' in the western sense. . . . Women and things are
> exchanged as inalienable gifts, but not as disposable property. (p. 3)

What, one might ask, are the stakes involved in recognizing that women
are frequently deprived of property, frequently exchanged for things, frequently exchanged for other women? Crucial differences between societies
concerning the treatment of things, artifacts, and women? Crucial differences in the rights of individuals—rather than groups—to have and dispose
of animals, things, and children? These are immensely important, though
it is worth repeating some of the conclusions of the preceding chapter, that
differences may be employed to justify oppression as well as to foster respect. The treatment of land and objects by aboriginal peoples was the basis
for denying them rights to own them. And although their social relations
to land were different from Western relations—more modulated and complex—still they were enough like Western relations that we might think of
them as property relations.

We are confronted by two explicit principles: owning and having remain
the fundamental human relations to the world, to nonhuman things, in
many ways to relationships among human beings; and denying human beings rights to own amounts to severe deprivation in modern society. To avoid
this deprivation, we may insist that even hunter-gatherers, who do not own
property, relate to the world around them in property terms, modulated
along complex kinship relationships. "In prestate societies, kinship is the
idiom of social interaction, organizing economic, political, and ceremonial,
as well as sexual, activity. . . . The exchange of goods and services, production
and distribution, hostility and solidarity, ritual and ceremony, all take place
within the organizational structure of kinship" (Rubin, *TW,* 169).

We arrive at two possibilities: first, that we might deny that aboriginal
or any other relations to land and things need be recognizably like our own
to have standing, insist that law recognize its raison d'être, to control the
borders of social acceptability, repudiating its authority. This insistence
would amount to repudiating the demand that the goods of life be owned
and had under a system of social and legal rights in order to be recognized
under law. It might also amount to repudiating kinship as another system
of social organization, based on its unequal denial of the rights of women.

Second, we may be led to the more radical possibility that we might
repudiate in understanding and in law the notion that human life and

satisfaction turn on having and owning, exploring possibilities of relations to things and human beings other than having—including the genitivity of kinship. This is a difficult line of thought to pursue. We might still recognize goods and commodities, without acquisition or expenditure. In the language of rights, the right to have might be profoundly qualified by responsibilities; the right to accumulation might be profoundly qualified by consumption and exchange requirements; one might accumulate to invest, one might seek profit to reinvest.

All this sounds draconian and regimented. I believe it is because we have inherited a fundamentally negative language of rights: the right of the individual or group not to be impeded in its practices. Instead, we may think of rights as relations to land and things analogous to relationships of people to other people, especially in family and neighborhood: as responsibilities and obligations, as gifts and giving. What we are exposed to in our proximity is what we owe to and what we give to: humans, other creatures, things. We are with them not to have or take them, or to have or take from them, but to give to them, to bear responsibilities toward them, to care for them. Women, who traditionally bear the burden of caring for children, men, and animals, elicit the possibility of another ethical practice, not women caring for men and others, but human beings and other things cherishing others in their proximity. Not always fostering and nurturing, building up at the expense of others; not always at the expense of some, justifying their sacrifice. To the contrary. More than anything else, perhaps, resisting the thought that some kinds of creatures and human beings— women and animals—bear the burden of sacrifice for human prosperity, bear the burden of their destiny to be sacrificed, to be owned and had.

We return, then, to issues of women owning and being owned, traced along two trajectories. First, property as the fundamental relation of human beings to their surroundings, thinking of human life as requiring resources for its practices and satisfactions; second, recognizing the immense variations in property relations:

> Property as the social construction of resources is an integral aspect of both domestic-group organisation and of forces in the wider sphere of social life (economic, political, legal, ideological). (Hirschon, *PPGR*, 5)

> What is culturally and materially construed as "property" shows great variation: privately-owned coconut trees and usufruct rights to land (East Africa); trucks, pigs, and shell valuables (New Guinea); orchards, houses and reputation (Turkey); bridewealth cattle, rights to urban housing and employment (South Africa); capital, market-tradition positions and arcane knowledge (Accra). (p. 7)

From an anthropological perspective, resources managed in social networks of kinship and exchange vary widely from place to place—still within the general framework of property. Things are there for human beings, resources for their lives, as things are resources for other living creatures. The questions then arise: *only* resources, *only* for their lives? Ecologically speaking, many living things are *for others*. Ethically speaking, I would say, even more: human beings enable the possibility of lives of giving.

Under the first heading, women as property owners, there is widespread variation. Even so, in many places, women have a subordinate right to property.

> Before the twentieth century, China was a society in which women had virtually no property rights and where women's labour, fertility and person constituted a form of property, itself exchanged in a number of transactions and chiefly in marriage. (Croll, *EWP*, 44)

> In rural China [studies] suggest that marriage is still conceived as a contract negotiated between members of the older generation, and financial transactions continue to validate the transfer of rights over women. (p. 49)

> In societies where "kin corporations" (i.e., descent groups) are strong, and where women as "sisters" (or descent group members) have full rights, then women are relatively equal to men. (Caplan, *CD*, 23)

We may be thankful that in different places, under differing social systems, women are not always deprived of property. We may be thankful also that in different places, under differing social systems, women are not always treated as or regarded as property. Moreover, where some women are treated as property, other women benefit.

> It would seem that in India the rapid inflation of dowries in modern times has led to a situation in which brides are more controlled by than controllers of property. . . . However, if the institution of dowry diminishes the social power of brides and even endangers their lives, it strengthens the hand of the mother-in-law. . . . In this sphere, as in so many others, property divides women among themselves. (Sharma, *DNI*, 73)

Indeed, the question of women in relation to property becomes the question of property itself.

> How can we conceive of women being "deprived" of "rights" over the disposal of property when such rights appear not to have been allocated them in the first place? More crucially, what do we mean by "property"? (Strathern, *SO*, 161–62)

> Embedded in our notion of "property" is that of "rights" exercised over others or at the expense of others. . . . Such a western concept of property entails a radical disjunction—property relations are represented not as a type of social relations but as relationships between people and things. The disjunction between people and things can also be merged with that between subject and object. As subjects people manipulate things: they may even cast others into the role of things insofar as they can hold rights in relation to these others. (p. 162)

At issue is the relation between human beings and other creatures and things, subjects and objects. Different destinies are at stake—the curse again—in the landscape of owning and having. "It is the western dichotomy between subject and object which often informs the anthropological desire to make women the proper subjects for analysis, to treat them in our accounts as actors in their own right. We are terrified of rendering them as mere 'objects of analysis' because this diminishes our own humanity" (pp. 162–63). Are women commodities when treated as things, if they are passed around, exchanged for wealth? The answer, surely, is yes and no. Any answer must be yes and no. Even under slavery. Domesticated animals are not treated as things exactly, but as animals, to be owned, used, treated by their owners as property. But living, sentient property. Always threatened by abuse. Women exchanged for wealth are still women, human beings. Sometimes threatened by abuse, always subordinated within social authority. In the context of the social authority of some—almost always elders, sometimes both men and women—others possess graduated and recognizable authority, sometimes lack authority, in relation to other people and things.

We need to develop a political economy of sex and gender, far exceeding acquisition, accumulation, and exchange. Exchange for what and under what circumstances? Accumulation when and where?

> There is an economics and a politics to sex/gender systems which is obscured by the concept of "exchange of women." For instance, a system in which women are exchangeable only for one another has different effects on women than one in which there is a commodity equivalent for women. (Rubin, *TW*, 204)

> Is the woman traded for a woman, or is there an equivalent? Is this equivalent only for women, or can it be turned into something else? If it can be turned into something else, is it turned into political power or wealth? On the other hand, can bridewealth be obtained only in marital exchange, or can it be obtained from elsewhere? Can women be accumulated through amassing wealth? Can wealth be accumulated by disposing of women? Is a marriage system part of a system of stratification?
>
> These last questions point to another task for a political economy of sex. (p. 207)

We have returned to Rubin's suggestion that such a political economy, in its microtechniques and micropolitics, might expose human social life in vivid detail. Yet this detail, this political economy, obscures the assumptions that we know what are things and what are not, that we know how to treat things as property, and that no matter how far we undertake to break down the distinctions between human beings and animals or things—in concentration camps, for example—the distinctions remain. In both cases, we take for granted that we know how to dispose of things as property and that human beings are not things. Even so, we do not know how to treat things as we might, as they should be treated, in all ways—for we do not and cannot know what bodies can do; and we do not take human beings—or for that matter, animals—to be things, but we may treat them disrespectfully, harmfully, wrongfully, as if we did not grant them respect or care as human beings, animals, or things.

We return to the curse from the possibility that we do not treat animals as things when we abuse them, but *abuse them as animals*. It is because of their capacity to suffer, because of their strength and beauty, that we insist on torturing them. "Why so much hatred if animals are only things?" (Ferry, *NEO*, 44); "since we are more or less covertly aware that in truth animals are not entirely things that as luck would have it they suffer, the tortures we inflict remain interesting" (p. 47). Interesting because they are animals and not things.[4]

This is the curse with a vengeance. I insist on evoking it here. For the likelihood is that where women are treated like property it is *because they are women*, human beings not things. They are to be owned and controlled as reproductive agents in their full humanity. Anything less and tribal history would be at risk. Slavery remains the implicit human condition despite claims to the contrary, if what we mean is that social and economic conditions establish that some human beings—especially women and children—are exchanged and valued in relation to things.[5] But under capitalism, in effect, every human being is valued and exchanged, measured in relation to things, frequently with respect to body parts as well as work. And again, it is human—and animal—bodies that are valuable, that are to be owned as property. Human beings and animals are treated as property, as *mine* or *ours*; human life turns on the genitive, on having and owning human beings and animals. Not just things. And not as if things. The greatest thing by far is to have another human being as one's own, neither regarded as a thing or treated as a means, but *my own as a person*. Always in conflict with human freedom. Always in conflict, I say, with the abundance in the earth of that which is not there for me to have.

I am here in debt, responsible in virtue of having been given my place in the world, which I betray in insisting on having. "What do we mean when we refer to a cash income or to exchange valuables as 'property'? Are these wealth items 'objects' in the western sense? . . . Highlands valuables, including money, are not always treated as objects in the western sense, and are not to be understood as 'property' if property entails objectification" (Strathern, *SO*, 164). The modern, industrial view is that only persons can exchange their labor for things, that persons cannot be owned. The wider view, I believe, is that human beings seek to own and exchange whatever makes them human, especially including other human beings as persons. Tribal societies may know much more complex relations of genitivity than permitted under Western law.

Some of these may be described in terms of gifts: "A gift is nothing more than the social form of a thing or a worker in much the same way that a commodity is a social form of a thing or worker. But a gift is different from a commodity in that whereas a commodity exchange establishes a relation between the objects of a transaction, gift exchange establishes a relationship between the subjects. . . . 'gifts are inalienable whereas commodities are not'" (Gregory, *ECPPNG*, 404). Here relationships between human beings and relations of human beings to things become even more complexly entwined, if possible, as if we do not know and may never know what bodies—human and otherwise—can do. "If a thing exchanged may stand for an aspect of a person, it follows that when people are exchanged they may at that point stand not just for themselves but for aspects of personal substance or social identity located at another level. . . . Their symbolic referent is not a thing in the sense of an object, but aspects of personhood" (Strathern, *SO*, 165).

Here things are not "just things" and human beings possess mobile identities. Property pervades the social world, under the curse, so that it is always too late to escape life in the genitive. Memory and inheritance are always in the genitive, divided by gender and species. For women are exchanged and men are not. "Where the producer is a clan and the produced are people, the inalienable gifts are people. . . . Women as gifts are the inalienable property of the clan that produced them" (Gregory, *ECPPNG*, 641). In the genitive but not perhaps as property: "Falsity lies not in the equation between women and wealth, but in the implicit equation between wealth of this kind and 'property' as we understand the term" (Strathern, *SO*, 166). I respond that if it is always too late to escape genitivity, it is always too early, always necessary, to betray genitivity as itself betraying possibilities otherwise.

I conclude this chapter by turning to the final paper in the Hirschon collection, emphasizing the construction of identities—human especially, but also otherwise—embedded in the ideas and practices of (private) property. I have repeatedly endorsed Engels's claim that modern capitalism created (the idea of) free individuals who possess the right to alienate their labor. "Capitalism . . . thus requires the assertion of an *individual's* rights as against all other individuals. It requires, that is, the separation of property out of social relations. . . . The right of some individuals to own property entails the corresponding propertylessness of some other individuals" (White-head, *WMKP*, 179). Whitehead takes us back to the fetish form of the com-modity in which things are separated from their social relations—their producers—and, I would add, relations to other things so that some may own property and others not. In many societies, we have seen, people and things are intricately embedded in complex networks of kinship, social relations involving obligations, status, and social markings. One cannot opt out of such relationships, for example, by disowning or selling objects, animals, labor, or land. They constitute the social identities of people and things. In other words, industrial, capitalist societies depend on multiple separations, alienations: people from things; individuals from social rela-tions; commodities from the conditions of their production; and so forth.

Separation lies at the heart of genitivity, with profound implications for women.

> [A] woman's capacity to "own" things depends on the extent to which she is legally and actually separable from other people (as does a man's). Put very crudely, the issue raised is the extent to which forms of conjugal, familial and kinship relations allow her an independent existence so that she can assert rights as an individual against individuals. . . . Conjugal, familial and kinship systems appear often to operate so as to construct women as a subordinate gender, such that by virtue of carrying kinship (or familial or conjugal) status women are less free to act as full subjects in relation to things, and sometimes people. This I would argue is the gen-eral form of their relation to property. (Whitehead, *WMKP,* 189–90)

In its starkest form, this argument suggests that kinship and other tradi-tional relationships situate women—and others—so that they are effec-tively deprived of property because the latter depends on a separability incompatible with such relationships. One conclusion is that only in a modern society, with its multiple forms of separation and alienation, can women be given equal rights to ownership with men. The alternative I am exploring is of human social lives where none can own or possess, in which separation is impossible for both men and women, yet in which networks of relationships do not become so tightly coiled as to enforce systems of domination.

It is time to consider separation as the defining condition of person or self in relation to genitivity: the self that exists in the mode of acquiring and having, said thereby to be free. It is time to explore the possibility that property is an absolute condition of free persons and autonomy, even where we insist that it marks a stage to be overcome. Overcome, after private property—by what? Certainly not public property. And certainly not women as property. First women as full subjects, free individuals, sole proprietors of themselves, then what? More freedom as having? That women as well as men may have? Or abolishing genitivity? Not just private property, but property as such, giving up the association of having with human identity, giving up destiny as genitivity.

# CHAPTER 9

## Free Properties

What makes a man human is freedom from dependence on the will of others. (Macpherson, *PTPI*, 263)

My freedom becomes complete only when it is my—*might*; but by this I cease to be a merely free man, and become an own man. (Stirner, *EO*, 151)

My power is *my* property
My power *gives* me property.
My power *am* I myself, and through it am I my property. (p. 166)

If the individual is to survive in a collective society, he must have protection against its ruthless pressures. There must be sanctuaries or enclaves where no majority can reach. To shelter the solitary human spirit does not merely make possible the fulfillment of individuals; it also gives society the power to change, to grow, and to regenerate, and hence to endure. These were the objects which property sought to achieve, and can no longer achieve. . . . We must create a new property. (Reich, *NP*, 787)

Callicles is alive and well in industrial societies, at least in genuinely liberal societies—if there be such. The human life is one of infinite desire, to accumulate and own, and freedom is this fulfillment, accumulation and acquisition, the more the better. Human freedom is freedom from dependence on the will of others, realized in owning and having. "Inequality of property is just so long as it is a necessary feature of an institutional structure that fosters, indeed maximizes, human freedom" (Chapman, *JFP*, 317). Freedom is the highest good; its corollary is accumulation. In a genuinely liberal society—if there be such—freedom means unequal property.

Several components of this claim may be identified:

1. freedom as individual autonomy;
2. freedom as fulfillment of desire;

133

3. will and desire as infinite, immeasurable;
4. will and desire as owning, accumulating.

Throughout the history of ethical life, freedom as individual autonomy of action has competed with other notions of freedom, particularly those related to a higher good or purpose: divine commandments, social harmony, virtuous conduct, and so forth. Socrates' arguments in *Gorgias* that our actions are for the sake of the good, and that it is better to suffer than to commit injustice, express a desire for goodness and freedom that is higher than the fulfillment of any individual desire. The greatest freedom is not found in ordinary goods and practices, but in relation to beauty, truth, and the good. These are frequently understood as higher goods and practices. I understand them as infinite beyond owning and accumulating, beyond fulfillment.

Freedom is not to be found in fulfillment because infinite desire cannot be fulfilled. Owning, having, and possessing halt the movements of freedom and desire, limit and restrict them to goods and things, to what can be stored and accumulated. Even unbounded accumulation is a limitation on desire; even desire can be desired—greedily or ascetically, excessively in either case. Fetishization and fascination flaunt desire's excessiveness on every hand. Freedom may, then, in its excessive relation to desire and will, reach beyond having and owning to giving otherwise, beyond fulfillment, beyond containment.

What is *wrong*—if that is the word—with Callicles' insistence on infinite desire is not the excessiveness of desire and freedom, but the suggestion that they may contain each other in the tyrant's satisfaction, that infinite desire may be matched in scale by infinite power to have and enjoy. If each is excessive then the two together, in their coexistence, match nothing, provide neither scale or measure. This is the trouble with the suggestion that infinite freedom and infinite desire might be fulfilled by infinite grasping or having. To the contrary, as Nietzsche suggests, infinite desire might be not to have or enjoy. The excessiveness of desire points in various directions: to have, master, and control; to submit, subordinate, give in; to cringe abjectly. Subjection and abjection belong to unbounded freedom and desire. If the will is free, it is free to deny itself. Which is not the same as denying its freedom, for self-denial may reach infinite (dis)proportions.

This, I believe, is where the equivalence between freedom and property breaks down—one might say, caught too deeply in the quagmires of equality. For equality is given as another measure—if an impossible measure—that has no meaning in relation to an immeasurable will. "There is virtually nothing in the world that cannot become active property" (Minogue, *CPCS*, 14). There is nothing, in or out of the world, that cannot be desired beyond containment, including goods and things—sometimes to destroy them rather than to accumulate them—but also desires themselves, representations, expressions, and figurations: intangibly intangible properties, perhaps not properties at all, including giving, giving up, throwing away, and out, and up—introjection, extrojection, abjection. Abjection belongs to the will—as Céline and Dostoevsky insist—in a way that makes the notion of property redundant. And, for that matter, makes capitalism and industrialism redundant. If anything whatever may become property because it is desired or willed, then so may what may be described as *anti*-property, disappropriation, disowning—if willed excessively. And what is to limit the will except by tyranny—despotic or democratic tyranny: I mean the despotism of equality? "We have seen that one solution to the practical problem of unequal powers of enjoyment of property . . . is the principle of equalizing the goods of this world. . . . Instead of equalizing property, one might destroy its correlate, the will" (p. 15).

The crucial assumptions, one might say of the modern social world, are that an infinite will, a will that cannot be contained, is grasping, based on individual accumulation and consumption of goods. We have seen in past chapters that accumulation and consumption have frequently been social, kin-based, genealogical, more than individual. Freedom for women as women, or certain families and groups linked by class and color, frequently lies in group possession of goods and wealth available to women as women more than to individual women.

The other assumption is in question here, whether the infinite will might fulfill itself in grasping, accumulating goods for self-realization and recognition by others. I postpone self-realization to the next chapter, returning there to Stirner and others. Here I hope to dispossess the genitive organized around the individual who possesses goods and things. For the question of equalizing goods arises only after taking for granted the inequality inherent in restricting freedom's unlimited desire to grasping, having, taking, and owning. If these are freedom, if these are every individual person's desire, every group's and family's desire—always human—then perhaps each is regulated by the presence of others. I would go back to the founding equation: long before we insist on equating goods we insist on equating infinite will with owning and having.

Let us imagine as strong a resistance as possible to restricting the will, repudiating as tyranny those who would take our goods and well-being from us, but also repudiating those who would insist that our happiness, well-being, and joy lie in accumulation and consumption, repudiating all who insist that happiness and joy lie in the genitive: mine or ours. If my infinite happiness lies in your infinite happiness, then they do not conflict—except around goods and things. Infinite freedom and infinite desire allow both for infinite accumulation, having, possessing, owning, and for infinite giving, dispossessing, disowning; not giving goods to other individuals to accumulate and have, even to enjoy, but giving, dispossessing, disowning so that desires and things may circulate as widely as possible without restriction. Anyone may desire and enjoy certain things—the air, the sky, the earth; goodness, knowledge, beauty, truth—that cannot be accumulated, cannot be bought and sold, cannot be had or given away, but may be received as a gift. Perhaps these are not things at all. The issue, perhaps, is whether freedom can be restricted to things, to their acquisition, accumulation, consumption, and expenditure; whether restriction is compatible with infinite freedom and infinite desire.

Here the possibility that some institution—or oneself—might restrict freedom in the name of something higher is to be resisted. No positive freedom to replace negative freedom; no *freedom to* higher than *freedom from*. But negative freedom is damaged beyond repair if it is restricted to individuals and individual goods. Freedom from restriction is freedom from the will of others and from institutional control—the greatest dangers by far; but also from insidious restrictions that follow from understanding will and freedom as possessions, things to have, to hold against being taken away by others. Tyrannies do not just take goods from some to give to others—though that is common—but also repress other goods and wills, frequently in the name of the truth of desire and freedom.

Capitalism releases and forms desire beyond any prior limits, only to bring it under monetary form, restricting it to goods and things. What if we were to imagine desire permeated by fascination and fetishization—mobile, fluid, changeable, beyond containment, beyond monetary form? Accumulation is one of the possibilities of desire—Hobbes's desire, to own and have forever. But others desire to give, to know, to stand on the back of the world, to live with the gods, or something entirely otherwise. In the proximity of others—other human beings, but also every other creature and thing: others in the earth—is my freedom, not to have but to give as I have been given to—given in proximity. I give as neighbor in virtue of my neighbors, who I can never say I have—as they never can say they have me. Instead we touch, in proximity, exposed to each other, free beyond having or grasping. I remain individual—in proximity, vulnerable to others, but a vulnerability beyond measure.

Think of what it might mean to live an ethical life in which every condition were beyond measure—contrasted with two quite different relations and conditions. First, the identity of freedom and having: "The right to private property is an indisputably valid, absolute principle of ethics. . . . [N]othing will suffice but . . . the establishment of a contractual society based on the recognition of the absoluteness of private property rights" (Hoppe, *EEPP*, xi); "The average person believes that each individual has unlimited rights to *all* property over and against all other individuals, and, further, they have extremely limited responsibilities to others" (Schleuning, *THTH*, 183–84). Indisputable despite incessant controversy; absolute despite incessant qualifications. The extremity betrays the poverty of the will to have. Second, the demands of others understood as restricting our desires, rather than evoking a desire in us toward them beyond restriction: infinite responsibility, infinite responsiveness; erotic intimacy beyond measure. Rochelle laughs at how human beings insist that contingency is absolute, smiles at the genitivity of philosophy.

One may imagine the identity of freedom and having as expressing two different relations: the first that having provides protection against others; the second that having expresses the will itself. The first is certainly true where despotic institutional powers are mobilized against weaker individuals. Individuals require protection against the state even where some individuals profit from the practices of the state. Yet it is anything but clear that such protection is liberty itself. To the contrary, individuals may be protected yet fulfil few of their desires. As for the second, that the will itself is expressed in having: the will is limited to having even for wills that express themselves beyond having, in giving or caring.

For the moment, let us put the immeasurability and excess of desire and will aside, understanding that the infinite will to have, accumulate, and possess is a harsh restriction on immeasurability. If excessive, beyond measure, desire cannot be limited to having and consuming. Even so, the question remains as to whether limiting having and accumulating can be justified—though all today who believe in property believe in such a justification. This is the question of whether, once having limited will and desire to property, society can limit property itself, or whether in the name of liberty, absolute rights to property must be sustained. In the context of human life, individual or social, (infinite and excessive) desire must be limited. For the moment, then, I remain within the limits of rights to property.

At the head of this chapter, MacPherson and Reich associate freedom with property, liberty with having, in the genitive. We may add other celebrations of freedom's genitivity, including Chapman's, with a difference. "Liberty and property form an indissoluble unity in society and politics. If one aspires to preserve the liberal philosophy of life, the irremediable damage that liberty and property inflict on human equality must be accepted. And we must cling to justice tempered by equity" (Baechler, *LPE*, 287). Baechler and Chapman identify the conflict facing liberty of property as a conflict with equality. Reich identifies the demand for property as the need for an enclave of private life against the encroachment of the state. However difficult it may be to defend the borders of the private world against the encroachments of the public sphere in a world in which everything appears to have become public, however contaminated it may be to ignore the liberties wrested from women and children in the domestic sphere, still there is something important here. Not so much Reich's famous articulation of a "new property" involving claims to social support, but something closer to Proudhon's sense that everyone has a right to have what they need to live against competing claims of others, that others cannot have a right to seize what one needs to live. Limitation is inherent in property.[1]

Against this is the line of thought derived from Hegel leading to Stirner: infinite freedom is infinite genitivity, unrestricted owning. I am myself in virtue of my ownness. Infinite freedom, infinite ownness, infinite owning, infinite might. I postpone the *I—der Einzige*—that owns and owns itself to the next chapter. Here I pursue another line of thought that does not become infinite so quickly, that arises in the earth's abundance with qualifications and responsibilities, yet leads—in Baechler and Chapman as examples—to Stirner-like infinite accumulation.

We have seen that Locke, who is the founder of this view of property, limits property from the first. There must be enough and as good left in common for others. The liberty to own and disown is not absolute but for the sake of something nobler. Locke does not turn freedom to have, any freedom, into a liberty to abuse or destroy either the possession or others in the act of possession. Locke speaks of both the uncontrollable liberty to dispose of one's possessions, including oneself, and of a responsibility to oneself and things inherent in nature and its belongings. He approaches a freedom of responsibility, a liberty of proximity. He approaches such a liberty, yet is read to defend the absolute limits of the individual owner's will against the wills of others.

I do not read him so, and have said as much. I understand him to insist on the rights of the owner to own and dispose not against one's neighbors—ordinary people like oneself, struggling to enjoy life—but against the tyrannical powers of greater forces, institutional, aristocratic, and state. "The defense of private property was almost entirely a defense of its abuses— an attempt to defend not individual property but arbitrary private power over other human beings" (Reich, *NP*, 773). Yet the qualifications Locke suggests seem impossible to sustain in a world riddled by competing powers. One rests on the distinction between one's neighbor and one's enemy, in whose proximity one may find oneself indebted as well as fearful. The neighbor is someone who deserves my care. I would add that no creature in the earth fails to know this responsibility. Living in the earth is living in debt toward some others even where still others are prey to destroy. Proximity and intimacy call for something other than accumulation and disposal, other than possession itself, defined as follows:

Full ownership is the concatenation of all the ... elements, in whatever way they may be defined. . . .

1) *The right (claim) to possess*—that is, to exclusive physical control of the thing.

2) *The right (liberty) to use*—that is, to personal enjoyment of the benefits of the thing. . . .

3) *The right (power) to manage*—that is, to decide how and by whom a thing shall be used.

4) *The right (claim) to the income*—that is, to the benefits derived from foregoing personal use of a thing, and allowing others to use it.

5) *The right (liberty) to consume or destroy*—that is, to annihilate the thing.

6) *The right (liberty) to modify*—that is, to effect changes less extensive than annihilation.

7) *The right (power) to alienate*—that is, to carry out *inter vivos* transfers by exchange or gift, and to abandon ownership.

8) *The right (power) to transmit*—that is, to devise or bequeath the thing.

9) *The right (claim) to security*—that is, to immunity from expropriation.

10) *The absence of term*—that is, the indeterminate length of one's ownership rights.

11) *The prohibition of harmful use*—that is, one's duty to forbear from using the thing in ways harmful to oneself or others.

12) *Liability to execution*—that is, liability to having the thing taken away as payment for a debt.

13) *Residuary rules*—that is, the rules governing the reversion to another, if any, of ownership rights which have expired or been abandoned.

Many varieties of ownership, and thus of property rights, do not each the level of full ownership. (Becker, *MBPR*, 190–91)

I would say that no variety of ownership reaches full ownership as described here, because owning can be neither unqualified nor implemented with impunity. The qualification, whatever it may be, is ethical as well as political. It involves relations between the owner and what is owned as well as with other human beings and living things. Insistence on having as the identifying mark of humanity institutes endless struggles over property, propriety, and proper names constituting human history and the individuals and groups whose genitive traces demarcate it— rulers, historians, authors, artists, scientists, ordinary men and women. It includes every relation between human beings and the creatures and things that make up their worlds—as I said, ethical and political. I do not understand how the right to liberty can become a right to alienate, harm, or destroy, either in the nature of what is owned or in relation to other people who may lack some of the resources for a rich and satisfying life.

The second qualification concerns the nobler use, the higher purpose—in my terms, given from the good. All deeds, life and being themselves, are for the sake of the good—which I interpret not as setting a standard, defining a measure, instituting a goal, but in terms of the infinite yearning beyond measures, goals, and norms that is desire itself, excessive beyond owning, possessing, and consuming. The desire to have is immeasurable, but it is not the only immeasurable desire, nor is it desire itself—if there be such—for in the having is a desire to consume and expend; in the desire to acquire is desire beyond accumulation. To desire to have forever is to give what one has to one's heirs, or others, to the posterity and the multiplicity in which moves forever.

The question to which we come, evoked above, cannot persuasively emerge in Stirner, who expresses something at the limits of owning and having.[2] But it can be evoked in relation to Locke, on my reading, and in relation to such a complex view of property as Becker's, where "full ownership" appears to be as violent an imposition as tyranny or despotism. Human beings need to live, and well, in their persons. And they must have the resources so to live. Perhaps the difficulty in owning and having is not owning and having themselves, at least in relation to the person—personal property—but accumulating beyond personal needs, expending beyond personal desires, having beyond what one can use. As Locke says repeatedly, one owns that in which one has mixed one's labor, making it available for use.

> As much as any one can make use of to any advantage of life before it spoils, so much he may by his labour fix a property in: whatever is beyond this, is more than his share, and belongs to others. Nothing was made by God for man to spoil or destroy. (Locke, *TT*, 290)

> Whatsoever he tilled and reaped, laid up and made use of, before it spoiled, that was his peculiar right; whatsoever he enclosed, and could feed, and make use of, the cattle and product was also his. But if either the grass of his inclosure rotted on the ground, or the fruit of his planting perished without gathering, and laying up, this part of the earth, notwithstanding his inclosure, was still to be looked on as waste, and might be the possession of any other. (p. 295)

It is tempting to emphasize the spoilage and waste, understanding Locke to encourage accumulation without squander. What one can use—great wealth, great expenditures, great industry—one may own. Yet he speaks of the everyday, personal life as one of use and enjoyment, as do most who address owning and having. Where goods are enjoyed, that domain of life in which human beings hope to live well by owning, where their liberty requires that they be secure in person and property, is the private sphere, what others call household management. "The greatest part of things really useful to the life of man, . . . are generally things of short duration; such as, if they are not consumed by use, will decay and perish of themselves: . . . He that gathered a hundred bushels of acorns or apples, had thereby a property in them, they were his goods as soon as gathered. He was only to look, that he used them before they spoiled, else he took more than his share, and robbed others" (p. 299). Wasting and spoiling may be associated with great accumulation in the double sense that what one accumulates is taken from others, more than one's share, and that accumulating and hoarding, investing and building, are beyond one's personal use. In the extreme, modern technology as stockpiling and standing in reserve may be understood to characterize the industrial world against a personal sense of use that does leave good enough behind, that does not stockpile.

My interest is not to defend or assail Locke but to consider some of his qualifications in relation to the absolute right to property, not as inherent in personality—postponing that to the next chapter—but as liberty itself, understood as freedom to enjoy. The alternative is that the private sphere is that of use and enjoyment, that it bounds the right to have. Perhaps we all have a right to have what we need to live and live well—in the private sphere. Perhaps no one has a right to take from another what that other needs for private use and enjoyment—with the qualification that private use and enjoyment typically mean having women, children, and animals, sometimes slaves, I turn to a somewhat different question. This is whether the private sphere can be distinguished from the public, whether personal enjoyment can be bounded ethically against the infinite will, whether we can defend a sphere of sustainable enjoyment—as almost all environmental writers insist we can—against unrestricted global development, accumulation, and consumption.[3]

I hope to explore the possibility of a sphere of life in which human beings are surrounded by things and creatures and human beings that provide for their enjoyments—but perhaps none of them possessions or properties or means to life, perhaps not as individuals owning and having things; in which human beings are surrounded by things and creatures and other human beings for which they care, which they care about—but perhaps none of them properties, owned or had, in the genitive; in which human beings experience and pursue their freedom in relation to things and creatures and other human beings—by caring for them, without owning or having them, or being owned or had, concerned for flourishing and well-being. Giving life and support to oneself and others, responsive to

them and others. This is unlikely to be a private sphere of life and enjoyment, separated from others, liberty cut off from the wills of others. It is
more likely to be a sphere of life and enjoyment enabling individuals to
resist public institutional forces that would bind the desires and wills of
individual persons. It cannot be restricted to the one or the other. It must
nevertheless be restricted, belongs to restricted economy.

One of the strongest defenses of a personal sphere of property can be
found in Radin's discussion of the relation between personhood and property. It is worth close attention, in part because it represents an admirable
line of thought, yet one I would refrain from following.

> [T]o achieve proper self-development—to be a *person*—an individual needs
> some control over resources in the external environment. The necessary
> assurances of control take the form of property rights. (Radin, *RP*, 35)

> Most people possess certain objects they feel are almost part of them-
> selves. These objects are closely bound up with personhood because they
> are part of the way we constitute ourselves as continuing personal entities
> in the world. (p. 36)

Her solution to the expansion of genitivity in the modern world, stretched
beyond all limits, is to reinstitute (reasonable) limits. "[P]erhaps we could
recognize that some categories of property rights do justifiably become
bound up with persons and then ought not be prima facie subject to rear-
rangement by market forces, while at the same time recognizing that other
categories of property rights do not, or do not justifiably" (p. 197).

Several important notions are present here. One is that people are
bound up with things in ways that constitute them as persons, human
beings. This is so profound a truth, so irresistible, that I would radicalize
it drastically. Things are bound up with people in today's world in ways that
constitute them as things—the fundamental truth of all environmental
principles. The world is made up of human beings, other creatures, and
things in ways that define the limits and identities and boundaries of each
and all, in complex, entangled relations of constitution and reciprocity.
People and things are exposed to each other in profound, identificatory
ways. Thus, a second notion, that human personal development and liberty
must take the form of property rights, is immediately controversial and
questionable.

Radin presents genitivity as composing the sphere of personality and
personal development. More perhaps than liberty, self-development requires
other people and things in mutually supportive, constitutive relations. One
may sacrifice some liberties for self-development, but one cannot develop

without the support of others. The question is, having things, or giving them, giving to them? Having other people, or sustaining their development, thereby sustaining one's own? Nurture, care, generosity toward others, receiving their generosity toward oneself, may be more fundamental to personal self-development than any possession or acquisition. Mother and father care for their children, thereby constituting themselves and their small world. The gardener, framer, or carpenter who works with land and wood care for what they make and what they make from it, thereby caring for themselves. No doubt without land and seeds and wood, they would not be able to develop in this understanding of care and love. But these need to be available, not to be owned or had. They need to be abundant, given forth to be cared for; they do not need to be *mine* or *ours*.

Radin's third notion is that self-development requires a sphere of propriety—that is, *proper* development and *proper* possessions. The propriety of life requires the proprieties of property. "If there is a traditional understanding that a well-developed person must invest herself to some extent in external objects, there is no less a traditional understanding that one should not invest oneself *in the wrong way* or *to too great an extent* in external objects" (Radin, *RP*, 38). This traditional understanding is that human beings must *invest* themselves in owning and having things, but must do so *properly*. Yet—to take two of her most persuasive examples— wearing a wedding ring that becomes part of one's life, marking and displaying the bond that defines that life with others—turns neither them nor it into something owned or had, but may be understood as the debt one bears to care for the ring, cherishing it as one cherishes one's parents, spouse, and children. Similarly, the bond of people to their dwellings is evoked much more in how they care for where they live than in how they may dispose of it as theirs. The genitivity is borne in responsibility and debt, not having or owning, perhaps not even as *mine*, but giving to the dwelling more than one receives from it, as we perhaps might hope to give back to God more than God has given us. If that were possible. If abundance allowed for more.

I do not think Radin appreciates this kind of generosity.

[A]n object is closely related to one's personhood if its loss causes pain that cannot be relieved by the object's replacement." (RP, 37)

Once we admit that a person can be bound up with an external 'thing' in some constitutive sense, we can argue that by virtue of this connection the person should be accorded broad liberty with respect to control over that 'thing.' But here liberty follows from property for personhood; personhood is the basic concept, not liberty. (p. 37)

In part the issue is liberty, the link between one's sense of self and person and the liberty to control. I have responded that the sense of person and thing may be as much or more a responsibility to tend and foster. The ties that bind people among themselves and to other creatures and things are taken much too readily to be havings and takings rather than givings and carings.

I hope to pursue the possibility that in the desire and care that bind human beings with others neither personal property nor proper personality may be found. Unlimited desire and will exceed and demolish both the propriety and the property, shatter the borders and limits of personality and world. Not a *we* cut off from other *wes*, but kinds of human beings among other human kinds and other nonhuman kinds: a wealth, a plenitude, of relations, constitutions, and givings. Reducing these to property reduces personality and desire to shadows of their vibrant and excessive possibilities. The liberty embodied in propriety and property is a restricted liberty hardly worth preserving in relation to the abundance of desire and things.

If the question is one of liberty, and we think of persons as the embodiment of liberty, then the wealth of embodied relations to material creatures and things in the world is both requisite for liberty and necessary to its impediments. If we ask, in this context, what human beings need for self development—equivalent with asking how to live—the answer is both simple and impossible. Live among the other creatures and things of the earth; live in their abundance, drawing from them, giving generously to them, caring for them, hoping to be cared for. Whatever this means. Owning and having other people and things is but the shadow of an answer, so dark a shadow as perhaps not to betray generosity or giving.

Something of this betrayal can be found in Radin's account of market inalienability—a notion much closer to gifts and giving than having and taking—articulated within the absolute distinction between persons and commodities at a point where that distinction breaks down. "If the person/thing distinction is to be treated as a bright line that divides the commodifiable from the inalienable, we must know exactly which items are part of the person and which not. . . . If the person/thing distinction is not a sharp divide, neither is inalienability/alienability" (Radin, *MI*, 1896-97). We cannot divide persons from things metaphysically, subjects from objects, but we must do so legally and properly.

> My central hypothesis is that market-inalienability is grounded in noncommodification of things important to personhood. In an ideal world markets would not necessarily be abolished, but market-inalienability would protect all things important to personhood. . . . In the nonideal world we

do live in, market-inalienability must be judged against a background of unequal power. In that world it may sometimes be better to commodify incompletely than not to commodify at all." (Radin, *MI*, 1903)

In the world we live in, the boundaries between commodities and noncommodities—things and persons—cannot be sustained. I would say that everything is inalienable, persons and things, to be cherished as what or who they are; yet we must exchange to live: trade, exchange, consume, and nurture. So the question becomes how to live among priceless things and people, while exchanging things—sometimes people—with love and respect for what and who they are, dissolving the borders that cut off human beings from the world, resisting the curse. Radin insists on giving but cannot resist the curse.

> To conceive of something personal as fungible also assumes that persons cannot freely give of themselves to others. At best they can bestow commodities. At worst—in universal commodification—the gift is conceived of as a bargain. . . . A better view of personhood should conceive of gifts not as disguised sales, but rather as expressions of the interrelationship between the self and others. To relinquish something to someone else by gift is to give of yourself. Such a gift takes place within a personal relationship with the recipient, or else it creates one. (p. 1907)

Commodification is alienation because it takes the conditions of exchange to represent all worth and value. Radin adds personal worth, still within equivalence and measure.[4]

What if giving were of oneself and things to others within the infinite worth of self and others: other selves, other things, other creatures, all infinitely worthy, infinitely beautiful, infinitely desirable, infinitely desirous? Such a gift, such cherishment, takes place within inexhaustible relations with others, marking, betraying, their excessiveness. In such ways, property and propriety fail to express the excessiveness of giving and desire; fail to express the boundlessness of liberty; fail to express the abundance of the earth; fail to betray betrayal.

I conclude this chapter with another attempt to bound the boundlessness of the abundance of things in the name of liberty. If absolute liberty does not justify absolute propriety over things and creatures, even other human beings, then perhaps we may follow liberty—renaming it *autonomy*—to its limits in relation to propriety. Autonomy here is not an infinite will striving for infinite acts—havings, takings, or givings—but is bounded from the first. "[T]he autonomy principle, is that every one ought to act so as to respect each person's equal right to decide for himself what his own good is, how to pursue it. . . . [E]ach person has an equal right to decide upon his own good and how to pursue it while respecting others' autonomy" (Grunebaum, *PO*, 143). It might be difficult to explain why this is an autonomy principle rather than respect by those who have goods of their own for the goods of others—living for the sake of the good. It may be arbitrary to restrict autonomy and goods to human beings; pursuing one's own good, insisting on one's autonomy and that of others, may not be taking but giving, however impossibly, giving in abundance. More of that later.

Autonomous ownership establishes a sphere of property rights to labor and its fruits entirely within each individual's sphere of decision making. Land and resources, however, remain communal, fostering autonomy through collective access and rights to use and allocation. "The autonomous ownership rules for land and resources resemble communal ownership in that each individual must have the right to participate in decisions about how land and resources are used as well as the right to a share of the income produced by land and resource utilization" (Grunebaum, *PO*, 2). Autonomy here is not infinite will or excessive desire but is limited by other wills and desires. Infinite autonomy becomes a maximal principle—if it can.

I do not think it can, and I think that Grunebaum's configuration presupposes that liberty and abundance can be contained. Yet there is something admirable about how he undertakes that containment—so admirable that I would pursue his suggestions without the theory, within a different understanding of human relations to the world. I think that each human being—but also, each creature and thing—must be allowed to pursue that being's own good; that such goods and desires for them are not restricted to human beings; that goodness is love and respect for the goods and desires of others; that liberty is freedom to choose for oneself.[5] Grunebaum suggests dividing goods and things into those into which human labor has been given and those that make up the resources, the abundance of things in the earth, as if once taken up by human beings, things may no longer serve as resources, have been irrevocably withdrawn from abundance and care. I would insist that they remain precious even where made and used by human beings, that labor confers no special status on owning and having—and may promote giving and releasing. The person who cares for the bobcat kitten takes on a responsibility for returning it to the wild, does not acquire a creature to own. The care fosters its return to the earth's abundance—which on my view it never left. I would not insist that whatever human beings labored upon became theirs to have and dispose of, but would insist that human beings, among others, deserve the means of life and enjoyment against greater state and institutional powers especially, but also against arbitrary encroachment by others, be they other human beings or wild animals. Fences make good neighbors, just not too high and not too thick. And I would insist even more that even those goods that one made one's own should be one's own but for a while, that they were taken from the abundance of things to be returned.

The point is that autonomy and abundance do not accommodate the genitive. Genitivity is restriction, perhaps inescapable restrictions for the flourishing of human and other beings. But flourishing is intimately entwined with general economy, with abundance and unrestricted autonomy—not having as much as possible, perhaps having nothing but sharing everything, perhaps not as collective having but intimacy and proximity. Intimacy, proximity, and exposure betray genitivity, interrupt the closure of desire around having and taking, interrupt the *I* that insists that only it—*He*—can flourish. Yet I remain convinced that we may learn something from Grunebaum and others about how to undertake flourishing among the goods of the earth in an economy of exchange and circulation. I postpone this something to the final chapters.[6]

# CHAPTER 10

## Self Possession

I secure my freedom with regard to the world in the degree that I make the world my own. (Stirner, *EO*, 149–50)

Because Dasein has *in each case mineness [Jemeinigkeit]*, one must always use a *personal* pronoun when one addresses it: "I am," "you are." (Heidegger, *BT*, 67–68)

At the extremes of individuation, the essential characteristic of identity is that it is one's own. In my separation from others, in private and "alone with myself," deprived of others, this self with which I am alone is conceived on the logic of private property: it is my own unique possession, exclusively mine. (Wikse, *AP*, 1)

The angel's sin was a sin of ownership: *stetit in se*, as Saint Augustine says. Ownership, of course, is nothing but self-love or pride . . . (passage from Fénelon: 1651–1715; quoted in Nancy, *SL*, 94)

I confess to fascination with Stirner and his obsession with genitivity. Obsessed with his obsession, fascinated by his fascination, his fetishism toward the fetish of having and owning. Not so much with his egoism, his fixation with himself, but with his endless subjection of the ego—the *I*, the self, the unique one—to genitivity. A subjection to the authority of the genitive I understand as the abjection of the subject who throws itself down into genitivity, insists on having everything, having beyond any possibility of having, having and owning what cannot be had or owned. Instituting another abjection. *I subject/abject myself to myself and to what I may have.* I insist on having, possessing myself, insist on genitivity as myself. As Wikse says.

Stirner's glorious writing[1] expresses consummate genitivity—if there be such a consummation—bringing to a certain fulfillment what had been expressed by Hegel as the double destiny of spirit in the world toward genitivity: of human beings to own, of all other creatures and things to be owned. The height of humanity is having—alliterative expression of the curse of forgetting another alliterative possibility, the glory of giving, the generosity of the gods, ghosts of gifts beyond genitivity. Giving beyond having. Refusing the height.

Stirner insists on height, dismisses liberalism and humanism—including socialism and communism—in terms that have been associated with anarchism[2] for instituting the state at the height where *I* should rule.[3] He knows something of the soul of the state that only anarchists seem to know, something of its supreme genitivity: the heart of sovereignty in the genitive, insisting on belonging together; the authority of philosophy as love or truth or goodness, insisting on fitting together. "What is called a state is a tissue and plexus of dependence and adherence; it is a *belonging together [Zusammengehörigkeit]*, a holding together, in which those who are placed together fit themselves to each other, or, in short, mutually depend on each other: it is the *order* of this *dependence [Abhängigkeit]*" (*EO*, 198).[4]

Stirner institutes the ego, the unique one, at a height where there can be no height, filled with irony perhaps insufficient to undermine the possibility of another edifice, built on property seized from others.

> "Does not the spirit thirst for freedom?"—Alas, not my spirit alone, my body too thirsts for it hourly. . . . How do you mean to come to the enjoyment of those foods and beds? Evidently not otherwise than in making them your property!
>
> If you think it over rightly, you do not want the freedom to have all these fine things, for with this freedom you still do not have them; you want really to have them, to call them *yours* and possess them as *your property*. . . .
> . . . You should not only be a "freeman," you should be an "owner *[Einer]*" too. (pp. 141–42)

Stirner does not imagine that freedom cannot be possessed or had, that freedom and liberty are not something to own, returning us to the struggle to remember and to act for the sake of the good—which is nothing at all. I do not mean to dismiss Stirner's voice, with its striking insistence on a genitivity beyond having, a having that cannot be possessed.

He speaks repeatedly of having what freedom makes impossible, of an ownness that seems to be something when it is nothing.

> What a difference between freedom and ownness! One can get *rid* of a great many things, one yet does not get rid of all; one becomes free from much, not from everything. . . . Ownness, on the contrary, is my whole

being and existence, it is I myself. I am free from what I am *rid* of, owner of what I have in my *power* or what I *control*. *My own* I am at all times and under all circumstances, if I know how to have myself and do not throw myself away on others. (*EO*, 143)

As if my insistence on genitivity accomplished what could not be accomplished. "My power is *my* property. My power *gives* me property. My power *am* I myself, and through it am I my property" (p. 166). As if we might have and possess what is around us, take possession of what others have in their grip, knowing that the stakes always concern authority. Stirner resists the authority of ghosts and spooks, the insistence on law, but does not resist his own authority.

> Property in the civic sense means *sacred* property, such that I must *respect* your property. "Respect for property!" Hence the politicians would like to have every one possess his little bit of property, and they have in part brought about an incredible parcellation by this effort. Each must have his bone on which he may find something to bite.
> The position of affairs is different in the egoistic sense. I do not step shyly back from your property, but look upon it always as *my* property, to which I need to "respect" nothing. Pray do the like with what you call my property! (p. 220)

Too many ghosts and spooks, Marx tells us, too little sense of material forces. I say too many authorities, ghosts and spooks or commodities and labor. Stirner does not accomplish the seizure of property, does not achieve genitivity, but shows that these cannot be accomplished, that authority undermines itself. As I said, abjection. The return to the ego and its own, to the unique one and its property, is a return from nowhere to nowhere in the circulation and abundance of material forces. To the nothing and nowhere that is law, which cannot institute genitivity.

> Private property lives by grace of the *law*. . . . It is *mine* not through *me* but through the—*law*. Nevertheless . . . So long as I assert myself as holder, I am the proprietor of the thing; if it gets away from me again, no matter by what power, as through my recognition of a title of others to the thing—the property is extinct. Thus property and possession coincide. It is not a right lying outside my might that legitimizes me, but solely my might: if I no longer have this, the thing vanishes away from me. (Stirner, *EO*, 223)

In a certain way, Stirner gives Marx's answer to the question I brought back to Marx, no doubt for quite different reasons. If property is the right of some under law to take from others, under the authority of the church or state or society, then shall we abolish property—not just mine or the state's in the name of another power, but property itself? "What I produce, flour, linen, or iron and coal, which I laboriously win from the earth, is *my* work that I want to realize value from. But then I may long complain that I am not paid for my work according to its value: the payer will not listen to me, and the state likewise will maintain an apathetic attitude so long as it does think it must 'appease' me that *I* may not break out with my dreaded might" (*EO*, 226). Most today would probably remain unconvinced by Stirner's dreaded might—or mine—except for the few who control the ghosts of collective property: the church, the state, corporate management, the law. Some are always much more in command of the institutions that regulate property, against which the egoistic individual bears no weight at all, even at a point of utmost resistance. Which is not to repudiate resistance, but to insist on its dispersion, to repudiate its genitivity.[5] Yet what kind of human life is possible if we cannot have or own the means, the determining conditions, of our identities? Stirner's answer is that except for myself all other conditions belong to others, do not belong to me. My response is that all conditions escape me, including myself, but that does not mean that they belong to others. Power, resistance, language, *mimēsis* all cannot be possessed, but wander in endless betrayal.

I do not mean to repudiate Stirner's egoism, which contains something of great value, echoing Nietzsche: "But I would rather be referred to men's selfishness than to their 'kindnesses *[Liebesdienste]*,' their mercy, pity, etc. The former demands *reciprocity* (as thou to me, so I to thee), does nothing 'gratis,' and may be won and—*bought*. But with what shall I obtain the kindness? it is a matter of chance whether I am at the time having to do with a 'loving' person" (Stirner *EO*, 275). Loving kindness is another genitive, is linked with state and social authority. It is not so much whether I can count on kindness, on receiving the care I may need or desire, but that genitivity cannot escape the curse. "As we do not see our equals in the tree, the beast, so the presupposition that others are *our equals* springs from a hypocrisy. No one is *my equal*, but I regard him, equally with all other beings, as my property. . . . an *object* in which I take an interest or else do not" (pp. 275–76). Others are nothing but *objects* to me, as if I were not myself an object, even to myself. Abjection again. Insisting on having what must be mine. As if I might have it, must have what cannot be had. "I am *owner* of my might, and I am so when I know myself as *unique*. In the *unique one* the owner himself returns into his creative nothing, of which he is born. Every higher essence above me, be it God, be it man, weakens the feeling of my uniqueness, and pales only before the sun of this consciousness. . . . All things are nothing to me" (p. 324). All things are nothing to me but myself. Only through owning—possessing and having—

am I a self. We have seen this in Heidegger and Nietzsche. Even in Marx, where we would least expect it.

I interrupt to read Marx reading Stirner. I begin before Stirner occupies the stage:

> The first premise of all human history is, of course, the existence of living human individuals. Thus the first fact to be established is the physical organisation of these individuals and their consequent relation to the rest of nature. . . . Men can be distinguished from animals by consciousness, by religion or anything else you like. They themselves begin to distinguish themselves from animals as soon as they begin to *produce* their means of subsistence. (Marx, *GI*, 31)

Marx is scathing toward Stirner for his spooks and ghosts. More of that in a moment. Yet Marx begins his critique at the same questionable point that is Stirner's center of gravity. The absolute foundation of history and production lies in living human individuals, who produce their means of subsistence and thereby distinguish themselves from animals, insisting on the curse. How do they do so? By possessing the means to produce what they need to live. Stirner—Marx calls him *Saint Max*—does not develop a theory of material production. And we may agree with Marx that he juxtaposes another ghost—the ego—against all those spooks that would demand allegiance from the one. No allegiance, power, or authority without materiality.

> The way in which men produce their means of subsistence depends first of all on the nature of their means of subsistence they actually find in existence and have to reproduce.
>
> This mode of reproduction must not be considered simply as being the reproduction of the physical existence of the individuals. Rather it is a definite form of activity of these individuals, a definite form of expressing their life, a definite *mode of life* on their part. As individuals express their life, so they are. What they are, therefore, coincides with their production, with *what* they produce and with *how* they produce. Hence what individuals are depends on the material conditions of their production. (Marx, *GI*, 31–32)

Saint Max is ghostly in his abstraction: I and my own. Saint Ma(r)x insists on *definite* forms of production and reproduction, *definite modes of life*. In a preceding chapter I considered the possibility that what is meant by the determining forces of production and reproduction is the continuing interplay of material conditions and their representations. Modes of life are mobile, contingent, and specific in their materiality and expressiveness. Moreover, it is not individuals alone that live and express, that represent and reproduce, but social institutions and agencies. Human beings are embedded as both individuals and groups in contingent and changing material institutions and systems of representation. All these wander, and all are gripped repeatedly by genitive insistences that we know their owners, their fathers. Otherwise they will escape us. If not God then Mammon. Or Me. Or the State, the Church, or God. Who owns the definite mode of life that is owned by human individuals or that owns them? Perhaps no one owns what wanders. Perhaps Saints Ma(r)x insist too much on genitivity, on the genitives of science and a science of genitivity, leave out too much of genitality and genealogy, not to mention ghosts of ghosts. A brief interruption inside this interruption, returning to *Specters of Marx*, to where I omitted certain discussions of the two Saints.

What is in question is the disappearance of the ghost.

> It is an art or technique of *making disappear....*
> The spectral effect corresponds, then, according to Marx, to a position of the ghost, a *dialectical* position of the ghostly body as body proper.... The living body, the "mine," "my property," *returns* by annulling or taking back into it the phantomatic projection, the ideal prostheses.... up to the point where Marx, and not Stirner, determines the ultimate moment to be a ghost, the body proper of the I, the mine, my property. (Derrida, *SM*, 128–29)

The disappearance of the *I* in the genitive from the stage of life and property. The subjection of property to what cannot be a ghost—of which Saint(s) Ma(r)x write thousands of words, words on words, *mimēsis* of *mimēsis*. First Derrida on Marx on Stirner: "I take them back into my own corporeality and *announce* I alone am corporeal. And now I take the world as it is for me, as *my* world, as my property" (p. 130); then on Marx: "Marx denounces a surplus of hallucination and a capitalization of the ghost: what is really destroyed are merely the representations in their form as representation *(Vorstellung)*" (p. 130). The ghost—no matter how corporeal—insists on representation, on *mimēsis* and betrayal. Insists on the *mimēsis* of the commodity, or the ghost, or the ego, or the historical individual, that which cannot be brought before us without *mimēsis*. Perhaps without speculation. "Stirner's exemplary fault, for which he must be judged, judged for the example, would be the vice of modern speculation. Speculation always speculates on some specter, it speculates in the mirror of what it produces, on the spectacle that it gives itself and that it gives itself to see" (p. 146). Always with authority. And with genitivity, as if authority insists on genitivity. So the point is to have or own the ghost without ghostliness, to represent without representation. Still *mimēsis*. Still Derrida reading Marx reading Stirner. "These ghosts that are commodities transform human producers into ghosts. And this whole theatrical process . . . sets off the effect of a mysterious mirror: if the latter does not return the right reflection, if, then, it phantomalizes, that is first of all because it naturalizes" (p. 156).

> What is one to think . . . of the stinging irony with which Marx treated Stirner when the latter dared to speak of a becoming-ghost *of* man himself, and *for himself?* . . .
>
> . . . To say that the same thing, the wooden table for example, *comes on stage* as commodity *after* having been but an ordinary thing in its use-value is to grant an origin to the ghostly moment. Its use-value, Marx seems to imply, was intact. It was what it was, use-value, identical to itself. . . . But whence comes this certainty concerning . . . a use-value purified of everything that makes for exchange-value and the commodity-form? (p. 159)

I have spoken of the use-value purified of everything fetishistic, purified of *mimesis*. Here I would think instead of the genitivity of the historical human individual, with whom everything begins and ends. For both Saint(s) Ma(r)x.[6]

I am sure that I cannot live, certainly cannot live well, without goods and resources for enjoyment, without secure borders of self, without friends and lovers, neighbors and companions, among whom I make my way—our ways. Throughout, however, I have resisted taking these proximities as havings and possessions, as takings, without qualification, insisting that we question the assumptions at the heart of genitivity. To live, we must find goods and resources, friends and lovers, neighbors and companions, impinging on ourselves; but perhaps we need not possess or have, certainly need not take any of these for ourselves, from others. Might I live, circulate in the earth, care for myself and others, without possessions? Might I resist the encroachment of civil and corporate powers without having fixed borders of private life and property? Without having things and creatures of my own? Without having an identity I call my own? Without genitivity?

I confessed to fascination with Stirner, to obsession with his obsession with genitivity—the genitivity of one's own as oneself. Not, perhaps, genitivity in general, genitivities of community and humanity. Even so, perhaps the genitivity of genitivities for human beings shows itself in Stirner, humanity's ownership of whatever makes humanity human. Humanism as genitivity, insisting that human beings have what counts in the earth, from rationality to finality to sociality to iterability. Of which Derrida says that "[t]hese possibilities or necessities, without which there would be no language, *are themselves not only human*" (Derrida, *EW*, 284), do not belong to human beings. The conditions of life without which there would be no language, no humanity, no enjoyment, no freedom, and so forth, do not exist in the genitive, are given in abundance beyond genitivity. More of this later.[7]

If I am obsessed with Stirner, I am captivated by Wikse, whose preoccupation with genitivity exceeds any I know, including Stirner's, if not so extravagantly, if not so far as I would hope to go. Beyond Stirner's because his egoism, as exuberant and prodigal as it may be, represents but one of many forms of self possession upon which Wikse fastens his gaze—the self as private property, alienated and alienable. "The ideas of being 'true to oneself,' of being one's own person, of being a self-actualized individual each refer us to the assumption that what is essential about the self is its separation from others: that it is 'ownness' or 'mineness' which defines the experience of self. When it is extended into a philosophy of existence this idiocy is what we call 'authenticity'" (Wikse, *AP*, 1).[8] He understands the idea of genitivity, the self as owner, as a "modern phenomenon" (p. 1). "The philosophy of authenticity, its roots in the beginnings of industrial and entrepreneurial capitalism in the modern West, extends the logic of commodity production and fetishism to embrace even the self as one's own possession. . . . The idea of authenticity is rooted in the conception of 'possessive individualism' which grew . . . from Hobbes to Locke" (pp. 1–2). And to the present, even in those who would most directly resist it, at least resist its commodification. I allude to Marx and Engels, who never imagine abolishing genitivity, because it is essential that my labor be mine, and to Radin, for whom proper self-development—to be a *person*—requires that one have the resources one needs.

Like Stirner, in a different register, Wikse expresses the pervasiveness of genitivity—in modernity or in general, perhaps leaving that question undecided. The (modern) phenomenon of genitivity is that the self, the person, the *I*, exists for and to itself as owning and having, and as owned and had. Everything is in the genitive, belongs to someone, including the self. In psychological terms. "The struggle for sanity today has to do with whether you are yourself or another's" (*AP*, 4).

Something needs to be said, if by way of interruption, of the possibility of a modern self without genitivity. The first two volumes of the Deleuze and Guattari collaboration, *Anti-Oedipus* and *A Thousand Plateaus*, are subtitled *Capitalism and Schizophrenia*. This places them in the space of Wikse's self that can exist only in the form of genitivity. The possessive self belongs to capitalist rationality, one might say, in the genitive. Schizophrenia disrupts both the rationality and the genitivity. In the name of desire. "Everywhere *it* is machines—real ones, not figurative ones: machines driving other machines, machines being driven by other machines, with all the necessary couplings and connections" (Deleuze & Guattari, *A-O*, 1). Desiring-machines—humanity and nature—disrupt the boundaries of self and world, resist the reduction of desire, interrupt genitivity. Rochelle laughs— if she laughs—a little schizophrenically.

"There is no such thing as either man or nature now, only a process that produces the one within the other and couples the machines together. Producing-machines, desiring-machines everywhere, schizophrenic machines, all of species life: the self and the non-self, inside and outside, no longer have any meaning whatsoever" (p. 2). Nor does genitivity, in capitalism or schizophrenia. The possessive self dissolves into producing and recording machines.

> What the schizophrenic experiences, both as an individual and as a member of the human species, is not at all any one specific aspect of nature, but nature as a process of production. . . . Everything is production: *production of productions*, of actions and of passions; *productions of recording processes*, of distributions and of co-ordinates that serve as points of reference; *productions of consumptions*, of sensual pleasures, of anxieties, and of pain. (pp. 3–4)

The schizophrenic experiences in the productiveness and expressiveness of things a loss of the self that owns, the genitive self, experiences the self as a producing and desiring machine, in a full body in the earth. "What is specifically capitalist here is the role of money and the use of capital as a full body to constitute the recording or inscribing surface. But some kind of full body, that of the earth or the despot, a recording surface, an apparent objective movement, a fetishistic, perverted, bewitched world are characteristic of all types of society as a constant of social reproduction" (p. 11). The body without organs, the full body of the earth, cannot be owned or had, expresses the surplus that falls back on all social production, the impossibility, expropriation, disappropriation, disowning that betrays all owning and having.

> The body without organs now falls back on *(se rabat sur)* desiring-production, attracts it, and appropriates it for its own. . . . The body without organs, the unproductive, the unconsumable, serves as a surface for the recording of the entire process of production of desire, so that desiring-machines seem to emanate from it in the apparent objective movement that establishes a relationship [of owning, having] between the machines and the body without organs. . . . But the essential thing is the establishment of an enchanted recording or inscribing surface that arrogates to itself all the productive forces and all the organs of production. . . . (pp. 11–12)

The essential thing is the betrayal, production falling back onto itself, genitively, in desire. We return to the fetish of the commodity, understood beyond capitalism, perhaps as schizophrenia, linking desiring and recording machines as enchanted surfaces that arrogate—insist on owning—production. Genitivity is produced phantasmagorically as (re)production, in processes of production that cannot be owned but are recorded as if in the genitive. If we seek a way to represent, express, a modern, industrial, capitalist life of human beings without genitivity, Deleuze and Guattari both express it and insist that it is expressed everywhere in modern capitalism and modern schizophrenia.

I return to Wikse, allowing this interruption to speak both of the modern form of genitivity as self and of genitivity itself, falling back upon its destiny and necessity. This is not to disdain Wikse's insistence on the pervasiveness of genitivity even among those who would be exemplars of dispossession. I return to this insistence through the words that close his discussion, words of salvation through dispossession.

> I have written this book in the conviction that idiocy is the preparation of our future "objectivity," in Nietzsche's sense, and in Marx's sense as well. When Marx noted that private property had made us so stupid that we could conceive of no meaning apart from possession or having, he added: "Human nature had to be reduced to this absolute poverty so that it could give birth to its inner wealth." This is the pathos and the poetry of the self as private property. (Wikse, *AP*, 157)

I continue to wonder, as I have done throughout, at this conviction of a new birth, at the sense of a destiny that must bring about its own salvation.

The pathos and poetry of the self as property is something else altogether, something profoundly otherwise. Not so much the self and its pathos; we have seen too much of that. The pathos of the self is its genitivity, wanting to have what it cannot have, wanting to own what cannot be owned. The poetry is another matter, for even in the genitive poetry cannot be owned.[9] The crux of giving is that it circulate, give again. Here, however, there is nothing about the poverty that gives forth abundance. To the contrary, as Deleuze and Guattari suggest, it is the exuberance and extravagance of (the full body of) the earth that is giving. The threat—impossible to fulfill—is to reduce the giving to the point where having triumphs, where the desire—itself beyond fulfillment—to have and own, genitivity itself, insists on nothing but having.

Among the magical qualities of Wikse's reading of the modern self as proprietor—much more, I believe, than consumer—in an industrial world in which individual proprietors matter little, is his reading of self and ownership everywhere words matter.

> [N. O.] Brown understands how deeply the notions of person and private ownership are historically associated in the Western tradition: "Free

persons ... are those who own their own persons. It is because we own our persons that we are entitled to appropriate things that, through labor, become part of our personality or personalty. ... Hobbes says a person is either his own or another's. This dilemma is escaped only by those willing to discard personality." (Brown, *Love's Body*, 146; quoted by Wikse, *AP*, 4–5)

We live in a world in which, more and more, no one owns anything, and whatever private ownership still exists is separated from political control. (p. 5)

In a world in which less and less is owned by individual human beings, in which fewer and fewer human beings possess what they desire, personality has become identified with having ourselves through our own labor. We have seen the crucial premise before, that a person is either his own or another's, that everything including myself must be owned, must either be mine or another's.

The strength of Wikse's reading lies in how many of the notions that define humanity in the twentieth century are pervaded by genitivity. For example, *behavior* as having:

The constitution of human identity as a property relationship of the self to self is the logic of behavior. (p. 16)

Our word *behave* was formed in the late fifteenth century from the word *be-* (an intensive, originally meaning "about," more figuratively in the sense of "thorough"), and *have* (verb) in order to express a qualified sense of having, particularly in the reflexive: "to have or bear oneself." (p. 28)

To have oneself as one's best and closest friend and companion, to be oneself and no other, to observe oneself in the mirror of idiocy is the madness of modernity and the logic of behavior. (p. 18)

In Nietzsche's words, "the feeling of guilt, of personal obligation, had its origin, as we saw, in the oldest and most primitive personal relationship, that between buyer and seller, creditor and debtor. ..." (Nietzsche, *GM*, 506); read by Wikse as the sacrifice to create oneself, constituted as the gift: "To locate giving within the self, to *become* a gift, is to take the principle of archaic community within the self. ... The modern burden of guilt is, from this perspective, the internalization of the archaic legacy of indebtedness as a relationship with oneself. ... Guilt, the price which we pay for the internalization of man, is the price of solitude; but at least we are out of debt" (Wikse, *AP*, 24).

The modern world is characterized by genitivity, and we do not know what it means to give, to give up having. Wikse turns to Nietzsche, posing the challenge of genitivity more acutely: "To choose oneself, to become one's own, one must reparent oneself. For Nietzsche, the fundamental question in politics is: Who are my parents, my ancestors? Nietzsche's answer is: I am" (p. 151); "To become your own ancestor, your own heir, to love yourself, to cease to be your own contemporary, is to become your own danger; it is a catastrophe, an idiocy, the wretchedness of those who can *only* give" (p. 155).

The question of what it is to inherit, to be an heir—perhaps a question we cannot evade if we are human, if we are anything, if we belong to history—is a question of genitivity. From whom do we inherit, and what? What becomes our property, and what property do we acquire? If these are the questions for us rather than others, for example: How may we live without being burdened by goods? How shall we live without having and taking when we have been given without the possibility of return? How may we be heirs of Marx, or Kierkegaard, or Hegel, or Stirner? These are questions with which we began, Derrida's allusions to ghosts, ghosts we disdain, ghosts we cannot evade, ghosts we are ourselves. Ghosts of having, having ghosts; ghosts of giving, beyond having. As if we might inherit without genitivity, without receiving, taking, and having. As if inheriting were having rather than giving. Without a doubt, if we are heirs, we will have to give to others, other heirs, alive or dead. Something of abundance in the earth.

We begin our approach to giving in abundance from four corners of the earth: *ecstasy, squander, generosity, sustenance*. Are they good enough for those who hope to inherit? In the next four chapters, we may hope to see.

# CHAPTER 11

## *E c s t a s y*

I believe that this much is true, that the gods are our keepers, and we men are one of their possessions. (Plato, *Phaedo*, 62b)

The difference is, then, whether feelings are imparted to me or only aroused. Those which are aroused are my own, egoistic . . . ; but those which are imparted to me I receive, with open arms. . . . and am *possessed* by them. (Stirner, *EO*, 61)

*Extasis* is that condition of basic dissociation, privacy, and social isolation wherein meaning, value, and truth come to be located within the individual. (Wikse, *AP*, 49)

Syncope: an absence of the self. (Clément, *S*, 1)

I leave the world and then I return to it. I die, but I do not die. I am placed between the two, between life and death, exactly in the between-the-two, refusing one and the other. And that is how I dupe not only death but the difficult exercise of *the end of life*. (p. 261)

The "soul" escapes outside herself, opening up a crack in the cave so that she may penetrate herself once more. The walls of her prison are broken, the distinction between inside/outside transgressed. (Irigaray, *M*, 192)

From different vantagepoints, Wikse and Stirner share revulsion toward ecstasy, being possessed by another, be it person, creature, thing, or god. A revulsion inherent in the opposition that expresses the curse of humanity—in the genitive: humanity's curse—more truthfully and deeply than any other. I am either my own property or I am the property of another, possessed. Either self possession or possession by others.

Possessed by ghosts, Stirner insists, who would exorcise the spirits that possess us: "Yes, the whole world is haunted! Only *is* haunted? Indeed, it itself 'walks,' it is uncanny through and through, it is the wandering seeming-body *[Scheinleib]* of a spirit, it is a spook" (Stirner, *EO*, 36). To be possessed is to be haunted by spooks, not one's own person; and the greatest thing by far, the only thing, is to be one's own person, to know oneself as the highest being. Perhaps another spook. "You are yourself a higher being than you are, and surpass yourself. . . . Every higher essence, such as truth, mankind, and so on, is an essence *over* us" (p. 36). Truth, humanity, god, spirit are all *over* us where we must resist anything over, anything higher, that is not *ourselves*. The truth of genitivity is that everything is either owner or owned, master or slave, and the highest achievement is to belong to no one but oneself, owner and owned together, resolving the dialectic of propriety.

Who could doubt Stirner's truth, that to be haunted, to be possessed by others, even the highest and best, is to be enslaved? "Is it perchance only people possessed by the devil that meet us, or do we as often come upon people *possessed* in the contrary way, possessed by 'the good,' by virtue, morality, the law, or some 'principle' or other?" (p. 44). With these oppositions in dialectical movement—owning or being owned; possessed by self or other—anything other than self possession is slavery, whatever may be the virtues of the master. The master-slave dialectic is the key to property.[1]

Wikse, who does not share this dialectic and would not participate in it—insists on its idiocy—in resistance slips into its grasp. *Extasis*, being outside oneself, possessed by others—if we take this opposition for granted— is dislocation, experienced as loss. "*Extasis* is that condition of basic dissociation, privacy, and social isolation wherein meaning, value, and truth come to be located within the individual" (*AP*, 49). Yet the Greek experience of ecstasy—contemplation or vision—need not be understood as withdrawal. Ecstasy belongs to the gods and to their surrogates, priests and priestesses. The worldliness of which he speaks is structured by opposition. Either we are in relation with others, mediated in our being by others, or we mediate our identities inwardly.

Heidegger responds that *ekstasis* interrupts these relations, mediates nothing. Being possessed is not, need not be, an expression of genitivity but its interruption. If *Dasein* insists on having its place, on its genitivity and mineness, *Dasein* must also come to know its *ek*, its being away from itself as historicality. History's *ekstasis* is resistance to its lownliness, to its genitivity;[2] to the lowly self, seeking to make the world its property, struggling to overcome every separation. History's destiny is the overcoming of its lownliness, fulfilled in owning and having. Heidegger responds that if *Dasein*'s relation to itself is ownness, mineness, genitivity, history's *ekstasis* puts *Dasein* outside itself, away from its place. The *ekstases* of history, past, present, and future, resist the gathering of being. Gathering is always outside itself. To which Levinas and Derrida respond that within the ungathering, Heidegger favors gathering, assembling, order, jointure, thereby resisting the *ek*, the *par*, of *parousia*.

*Ekstasis* betrays the hold of genitivity, resists owning and having, without being owned or had. We need not turn to philosophy or any other academic discipline to see the incessant impulse to escape from possession to something else, giving oneself over to ecstasy, rapture, or syncope, to being possessed. By drugs—alcohol, cannabis, coca, opium, in myriad trans-migrations. By gods—tongues, dreams, raptures, enchantments, in myriad transcendences. By images, sounds, tastes, smells. By arts—of image, sound, and movement. By erotic, corporeal, affective experiences and disorders. By deities, demons, spirits, ghosts, *revenants*, specters, genies, gods, and demi-gods. By *mimēsis* betrayed.

One might conclude that within the opposition of owning or being owned that marks the history of human life, human beings have insisted throughout on contradictory genitives: freedom as the right to own and not be owned, together with endless experiences of dispossession, freely throw-ing themselves away upon experiences and practices that put them outside themselves. So long as it is free, one might say; so long as it is intentional, as I may choose it for myself. With the contradiction that the quality of ecstatic experiences, of being outside oneself, is to have been chosen and not to choose.

What if we understood ecstasy's *ekstasis* not to belong to the structure of humanity's destiny—as do Stirner and Wikse, taking that structure for granted even where calling it into question—but as betraying destiny and thereby humanity itself, as breaking the irresistible hold of humanism on humanity in the form of genitivity? As interrupting every genitivity, every form of *mine, yours,* and *ours,* including *Dasein's mineness* and Stirner's *ownness.* Disowning self and earth. Giving up the binary of master and slave. What if we understood the endless ways in which human beings have chewed, drunk, inhaled, injected this or that, dreamed, deprived themselves of this or that, as putting themselves away from themselves and what they might possess and own?

I turn to the possibility of ecstasy as disowning, a disowning of self that is not surrender, a surrender that is not enslavement, a caring that is not subordination, despite a history of surrenders, enslavements, and sub-ordinations typically experienced by women.

> The romantic and clinical scenario has usually, in our society, been allotted to woman: it is she who sinks down, dress spreading out like a flower, fainting, before a public that hurries forward; arms reach out, carry the unresisting body . . . people slap her, make her sniff salts. When she

comes back, her first words will be, 'Where am I?' And because she has come to, 'come back,' no one thinks to ask where she has been. The real question would be, rather, 'Where was I?' But no, when one returns from syncope it is the real world that suddenly looks strange. (Clément, *S*, 1)

Clément evokes the possibility that this strangeness—allotted, assigned, perhaps best known to women—might be something to remember, though it can never be held in check, possessed or owned; something to recall that cannot be grasped. Syncope, rapture, ecstasy as marks of resistance rather than submission, despite echoes of being possessed by another, being forced to submit. Being possessed not as being taken over, subordinated, forced into subjection, but as disowning, giving up the insistence on having and owning. Taking a cue from feminism, women's resistance, without taking anything to have.

Being possessed as *ekstasis*, out of place, understood as interrupting self possession, is foreign to Wikse's identification of *extasis* with the inward self out of the world of others: *ekstasis* as resistance to the boundaries of the self, to the binary of owning and having; syncope as absence, disowning the self as something to have. "Physical time never stops. That may be, but syncope seems to accomplish a miraculous suspension.... Where does the subject go who later comes to, 'comes back'? Where am I in syncope?" (Clément, *S*, 5). Perhaps no *I*, no *where*, no *when*. Giving up time—if that were possible—as giving rather than having in time.

Some explicit ways of disowning:

> Our first circle will be that of *tremors*, of impacts and falls.... So it is with the cough.... Paroxysmal, like a fit, it brings on coughing that doctors call syncopal, during which one gets ringing of the ears, vertigo, and loss of consciousness....
>
> The sneeze, which is nothing, is less perceptible; yet it shakes us and closes our eyes for the space of an instant so brief that we have already returned from it....
>
> Then there is laughter, but only as long as it is in bursts, unrelenting, an insatiable fire, until consciousness is extinguished. (Clément, *S*, 8)

I would understand laughter as Dionysian, after Nietzsche, the disruption of the demand to have, to master, disowning the boundaries that define self and world as properties. The paroxysm is the loss that loses nothing, from which one always returns. "But the advantage of syncope is precisely that one always returns from it.... I'm speaking for Europe. We place ourselves in the *before* death, in the *after* death. The real crossing is forgotten" (p. 15). Interruptions, embracing extreme and contaminated figures, betrayals of betrayal.

Screams, tears, tremors, uncontrolled excretion, foaming at the mouth: with epilepsy, syncope joins in. One could say that a wicked genie had gathered all the imaginable symptoms together in this strange ailment. (p. 9)

Epilepsy, which was sacred, was recognizable by the fall it brought on: the body on the floor, foaming, convulsed, was the prey of a god. The second circle begins here, the circle of the fainting fit.

There are innumerable scenes where the overwhelmed consciousness disappears in order to let the god speak. (p. 11)

All these ways—moments, techniques—in which the self, the *I*, gives itself up as *myself* to recover itself as other, to enter a relation with others by giving up itself, thereby a relation to the world, nature and the earth. All ways—we hope—that do not insist that syncope, rapture, ecstasy be another privileged form of being, in relation to self and other, but the depriviledging of privilege as loss, yet not a loss of what should be owned, must be possessed. "We are in the third circle, the circle of ecstasy. . . . There one is, *outside oneself*, etymologically" (p. 12). Outside oneself, *ekstatic*, is away from owning and having without being anywhere else. Otherwise, perhaps, elsewhere. Disowned, unhad, unhinged without being mad—though that is not far away.

Nor are love and death:

The fourth circle is also the last, coming closest to death. The phenomenon, though familiar, looks so much like it that it is sometimes called the "little death"—but also "seventh heaven," for example. *Orgasm*, like music and ecstasy, seems indescribable; there are few words to depict it, always the same ones: explosion, eruption, earthquake, ascent, rending, bursting, vertigo, and the stars . . . .

Human jouissance requires that one lose one's head; that is the foundation. . . .

The ideal death in the East prolongs the highest ecstasy, of which it is the desired completion. (pp. 14–15)

The ideal death as the loss from which one returns? How trite! one might say: a catastrophic loss from which one is sure to recover. Another betrayal of disaster and death, the death that is not a death. Another effort to deceive death. I die but do not die. Perhaps I do not die at all, but find a way to live that is not owning life. Perhaps we have not listened carefully, for rapture offers no guarantees. The return is not the point, the point is loss, the point is love, giving oneself over, away, to an other. "Joyfully, between laughing and crying, between ecstasy and agony. Joyfully, between the pleasure of orgasm and the happy sadness that follows" (p. 21); "so similar to death that it is also called 'apparent death'; it resembles its model so closely that there is a risk of never recovering from it" (p. 1). A strange risk, perhaps, as if to lose oneself were to die. Consider instead another risk. That one might lose oneself to live, might give oneself and everything else away to love; refusing ecstasy as having something, anything, as owning and possessing. "It would be too easy to interpret syncope as a lapse, a failed act; in short, it would be premature to put it in the huge cupboard of products of the unconscious" (p. 19). To put it, have it, define it, own it, in relation to the unconscious, or god, or religion, or poetry, or anything else. Rather than disowning, interrupting, betraying.

Let us consider another striking image of ecstasy, enflamed with desire. "The 'soul' escapes outside herself" (Irigaray, *M*, 192); "Thus 'God' has created the soul to flare and flame in her desire" (p. 197). The quotation marks around *soul* and *God* do not become quotation marks—figures of hesitation—around *she* and *her*. The soul is female, feminine: *l'âme. Her* desire is *jouissance*. One might say, corporeal desire without insistence on having the body. "But if the Word was made flesh in this way, and to this extent, it can only have been to make me (become) God in my jouissance" (p. 200). Elsewhere expressed as out of place. "Woman is neither open nor closed. She is indefinite, in-finite, *form is never complete in her*" (Irigaray, *VF*, 229). Yet remaining in the genitive; woman taking possession of herself.[3] "Woman is still the place, the whole of the place in which she cannot take possession of herself as such" (p. 227); "Woman remains this nothing at all, or this all at nothing. . . . She must continue to hold the places she constitutes for the subject, a place to which no eternal value can be assigned lest the subject remain paralyzed forever by the irreplaceableness of his cathected investments" (p. 227). I would understand fluidity, volume without contours, as ecstatic, living without having, possessing, or owning; understand maternity as enclosing without closure, as touching without grasping, caressing intimately without coveting. The nothing at all that resists enclosure. "The/a woman cannot be collected into *one* volume, for in that way she risks surrendering her own jouissance, which demands that she remain open to nothing utterable but which assures that her edges not close, her lips not be sewn shut" (p. 240).

I return to Clément to turn toward another outside place. "Bataille is turning up often? . . . He has patrolled the pathways of syncope without respite, drawn up his own list of 'supreme processes' through which ecstasy is attained—laughter, drunkenness, eroticism, meditation, sacrifice, poetry" (Clément, *S*, 13). Bataille—by no means a woman, by no means sinking down in a faint with her dress spreading like a flower—incessantly patrols the pathways of syncope. With a difference. For Bataille understands *ekstasis* in economic terms, links it with expenditure and possession. An ecstatic economy, one might say, another name for general economy. Bataille presents an extreme refusal to let the boundaries of human life become fixed, to the point where even dispossession evokes possession. "Contemplating night, I see nothing, love nothing. I remain immobile, frozen, absorbed in IT. . . . In IT, I communicate with the 'unknown' opposed to the *ipse* which I am; I become *ipse*, unknown to myself, two terms merge in a single wrenching, barely differing from a void—not nevertheless differing from it more than does the world of a thousand colors" (Bataille, *IE*, 124–25). He offers a virile grasping of what cannot be grasped, puts himself in possession of a giving over to be possessed, abandonment to ecstasy. He suggests that he enters into possession of things in ways that do not make them property. "But whereas ecstasy before the void is always fleeting, furtive, and has only little concern to 'persevere in being,' the felicity in which I was immersed wished only to last" (p. 113). Still reserved against the passage of time, the obtrusiveness of discourse, the losses and contaminations of every moment and state of life.

I am especially interested in how ecstasy becomes economy, how Bataille links ecstasy with expenditure, with consumption beyond life itself.

> Human activity is not entirely reducible to processes of production and conservation, and consumption must be divided into two distinct parts. The first, reducible part is represented by the use of the minimum necessary for the conservation of life and the continuation of individuals' productive activity in a given society. . . . The second part is represented by so-called unproductive expenditures: luxury, mourning, war, cults, the construction of sumptuary monuments, games, spectacles, arts, perverse sexual activity . . . repressed activities which, at least in primitive circumstances have no end beyond themselves. (Bataille, *NE*, 118)

Production and accumulation do not exhaust human activity and life. And production includes its own disruption: unproductive production; productive unproduction. If consumption need not be bound to utility and productivity, but interrupts them with its unproductivity, then unproductivity is the interruption, betrays production. Consumption repeatedly falls back upon itself as expenditure without reserve.[4] As *glory*. "Made complete through degradation, glory, appearing in a sometimes sinister and sometimes brilliant form, has never ceased to dominate social existence: it is impossible to attempt to do anything without it when it is dependent on the blind practice of personal or social loss" (pp. 128–29).

*Glory* is the name of an unproductive expenditure that cannot be made useful, cannot be reduced to utility, as if it were different from, opposed to, utility. I follow something of Levinas's notion that glory is not different, not other, not opposed, but otherwise. As Bataille almost says. It is impossible to do anything without it. Including the most useful things. It is impossible to belong to restricted economy, impossible to limit and have in place, to restrict by having and owning, without something otherwise that the limits limit, betray, thereby exposing their unlimits.

The general economy of abundance and ecstasy, beyond genitivity, evokes another interruption filled with exuberance, another ecstasy. Three linked corporeal intrusions, two engaged with property.[5] I restrict myself here to Lyotard's *Libidinal Economy*, understanding it ecstatically as an expression of general economy. "There is no need to begin with transgression, we must go immediately to the very limits of cruelty, perform the dissection of polymorphous perversion, spread out the immense membrane of the libidinal 'body'" (Lyotard, *LE*, 2). Transgressive in more than two respects, no doubt, but two are worth remarking. One is that pain and cruelty are defining conditions of desire's economy: cross every regulated border, turn every enjoyment into suffering, enjoy suffering as if it were enjoyment.

Leading back to the second, if we ever left it: the theatricality of desire—desire's *mimēsis*, inseparable from *mimēsis*'s desire. "It is certainly not a libidinal theatre then, no density, intensities running here and there, setting up, escaping, without ever being imprisoned in the volume of the stage/auditorium. Theatricality and representation, far from having to be taken as libidinal givens, *a fortiori* metaphysical, result from a certain labour on the labyrinthine and Moebian band" (p. 3). It is not a theater of desire without the effort given to staging, without theatricality and representation, desire reaching beyond itself. Lyotard understands something of the way desire and theatricality relate to each other and to law.

> Our danger, we libidinal economists, lies in building a new morality with this consolation, of proclaiming and broadcasting that the libidinal band *is good*, that the circulation of affects *is joyful*, that the anonymity and the incompossibility of figures *are great and free*. . . . But it is not an ethics, this or another, that is required. . . . *One cannot assume a position* on the twisted, shock-ridden, electrified labyrinthine band. (p. 11)

In general or libidinal economy there is no choice. Choice takes place in restricted economy. The link between general and restricted economy is not that one gives way to an other, or supports the other, but that general economy interrupts restricted economy and restricted economy interrupts general economy. The barriers constructed to hold desire in check break down before desire itself and its theatricality, especially before the excessiveness of the desire to hold, to own. General economy, the event, excess, beyond, *au-delà*, otherwise, heterogeneous, whatever, knows nothing of effectiveness or utility, except in interruption and betrayal.

Betraying Marx. "We must come to take Marx as if he were a writer, an author full of affects, take his text as a madness and not as a theory, we must succeed in pushing aside his theoretical barrier and stroking his beard without contempt and without devotion, . . . Marx must be introduced, the big fat Marx, and also the little Marx of the Epicurean and Lutheran studies, this entire continent, into the atlas of libidinal cartography" (Lyotard, *LE*, 95). And little girl Marx, sealing the restricted economy with desire.

> The young innocent Little Girl Marx says: you see, I am in love with love, this must stop, this industrial and industrious crap, this is what makes me anxious, I want the return to the (in)organic body; and it has been taken over by the great bearded scholar so that he may establish the thesis that *it cannot stop*, and so that he may . . . perform the obstetrics of capital; and so that he may give, *to her*, this *total body* he requires, this child, . . . of the proletariat, of socialism. But alas, he does not give her this child. (p. 98)

Marx and Marxism present themselves to their heirs from within a libidinal economy where the desire to have an economy of life reaches beyond that economy, where the desire to have and own, even desire itself, is always beyond itself. As desire. In the word of Sade. *Jouissance*.[6] "And let's finally acknowledge this *jouissance*, which is similar, Little Girl Marx was clear on this point, in every way to that of prostitution" (pp. 111–12); *"Jouissance is unbearable"* (p. 113). Another staging of the prostitute and the capitalist, just a bit different from the more family-oriented one we heard before, because after all, this is libidinal economy: the communist, the capitalist, and the prostitute; "his whole critique draws its impetus from the following denial: *no, you cannot make me come.* . . . In the immense and vicious circuit of capitalist exchanges, whether of commodities or 'services,' it appears that *all the modalities of jouissance* are possible and that none is ostracized" (p. 139).

Coming—the word is irresistible here—to the subject that has been with us throughout on this libidinal stage: "If mimesis gives you a hard-on, gentlemen, who are we to object? This is rather what interests us. Capital is also mimetic, commodities producing commodities, that is to say, being exchanged for commodities, the same commuted into the same according to an immanent standard" (p. 249). And ending on a Zarathustrean note. "We invent nothing, that's it, yes, yes, yes, yes" (p. 262). Yes, yes, yes. And laugh.[7] No need to set examples, to criticize, to resist, to act. Intensity, intensity, intensity. The full bodies of the earth, perhaps. The bodies without organs of signs.

I am considering general economy as ecstasy, and ecstasy as *mimēsis*, where *mimēsis* is the interruption and the staging, the staging and inter-

ruption as interruption and staging. Dispossessing possession, making propriety improper. Insisting that possession always presupposes a dispposses-
sion beyond having, an impropriety beyond propriety, desire beyond itself;
as *mimēsis*. A giving beyond having where having is always beyond itself,
thereby giving. Not giving gifts—though that cannot be avoided, and any-
way why avoid it? Gifts are necessary to live. But giving gifts takes place in
an economy otherwise, where the giving and the abundance are not more
than less, have nothing to do with measure. Giving interrupts having, returns us to volatility. In this way *ekstasis*, ecstasy, is not a dispossession of
self as if it were a possession, but a giving that interrupts the havings,
desire interrupting, disrupting, adjourning, betraying itself—as property.

CHAPTER 12

## *S q u a n d e r*

Everywhere everything is ordered to stand by, to be immediately on hand, indeed to stand there just so that it may be on call for a further ordering. We call it the standing-reserve. (Heidegger, *QT*, 298; *QTOE*, 17)

The sublime refinement involved in this respect for the other is also a way of "eating well," in the sense of "good eating" but also "eating the Good" *[le Bien manger]*. The Good can also be eaten. And it, the good, must be eaten and eaten well. (Derrida, *EW*, 283)

To eat is to appropriate by destruction; it is at the same time to be filled up with a certain being. (Sartre, *BN*, 614)

I insist on the fact that there is generally no growth but only a luxurious squandering of energy in every form! The history of life on earth is mainly the effect of a wild exuberance; the dominant event is the development of luxury, the production of increasingly burdensome forms of life. (Bataille, *AS*, 1, 33)

What does one do—if anything—with property, with what one owns or has, with what is ours? We hold it, reserve it for our use, stock it up, insist that it is mine, not yours, ours, not theirs. Or consume it, waste it, use it up. In every case, we insist on having something, on the need and right to acquire and have, to the point of ruin. As I have been arguing throughout, the Subject, Man, is defined by having, where having is grasping, holding, accumulating, reserving, but also using and consuming and expending to have something else, something better, something more appropriately mine. Mineness is the condition of humanity, of the human self, of *Dasein*, whatever language is spoken, as if the human language said the same thing everywhere and always. Even Derrida, in a moment of profound critique, identifies the absolute condition of responsibility in relation to genitivity:

171

"Under the heading of *Jemeinigkeit*, beyond or behind the subjective 'self' or person, there is for Heidegger a singularity, an irreplaceability of that which remains nonsubstitutable in the structure of *Dasein*. This amounts to an irreducible singularity or solitude in *Mitsein* . . . but it is not that of the individual" (Derrida, *EW*, 271). The self, or person, or individual, or subject—whatever, whoever—is identified, at least in Heidegger, in terms of a singularity—irreplaceability, nonsubstitutivity, irreducibility, perhaps nondeconstructibility—defined in genitive terms. Derrida understands this as a repetition of the unrepeatable that defines responsibility, that makes it possible, the disowning beyond owning.[1] The genitivity of mineness is the disappropriation beyond all appropriation, including that of the subject. Put another way, perhaps, beyond owning and having is squandering, as Bataille says: an ethics of disowning, disappropriating, of giving without having.

This ethics of disowning and generosity is the burden of these final chapters, exploring the meaning and possibility of resisting genitivity, without assuming that it can be abolished—or that it cannot. Attempting to think of giving without having, even if we cannot give without genitivity, cannot give except from ourselves. In the last chapter evoked as ecstasy, being possessed rather than possessing, without enslavement. Turning here to the resistances to genitivity gathered under the heading of squander. Against, or alongside, or within—dislocating, disrupting, interrupting, betraying—accumulation, stockpiling, reserving, consuming, using and using up, Bataille suggests that we think of squandering, consuming or wasting without utility. Against, or alongside, or exceeding use, utility, instrumentality, is the purposeless energy of the earth. Filled with squander as well as ecstasy.

These are crucial notions, not perhaps because they describe the joys of wastefulness, the exhilaration of ecstasy—though they are worth remembering. Such exhilarations serve here as better than other joys, other enthusiasms—serve as the better. As such, they are oppositional and binary, suggest that calculation is worse than extravagance and waste—where *worse* belongs to utility. Yet we may understand ecstasy and exuberance, as in the last chapter, not to institute another hierarchy, another binary within which we must choose, but as articulating something more primordial or excessive or originary—or none of these—than any binary. Still, however, something rather than nothing; or if nothing, something positive rather than negative, bewaring of another binary. Ecstasy, extravagance, and exuberance express an affirmation, a joy, an exhilaration at being responsive. Perhaps the most important insistence of Nietzsche: learn to laugh; learn to say *yes!*; learn to squander.

> Ten times a day must you laugh and be cheerful; else you will be disturbed at night by your stomach, this father of gloom. (Nietzsche, *Z*, part 1, 2)

Why sacrifice? I squander what is given to me, I—a squanderer with a thousand hands; how could I call that sacrificing? (part 4, 1)

*laughing lions must come!* (part 4, 11)

Amen! And praise and honor and wisdom and thanks and glory and strength be to our god, from everlasting to everlasting!
But the ass brayed: Yea-Yuh. (part 4, 17)

This crown of him who laughs, this rose-wreath crown: to you, my brothers, I throw this crown! Laughter have I pronounced holy; you higher men, *learn* to laugh! (part 4, 13)

Learn to laugh. Learn to say yea! The lesson Zarathustra would teach—if any—the lesson learned by those who come after Nietzsche and Zarathustra is to say *yes* rather than *no*, in the voice of the ass, unafraid to be an ass. Squandering sacrifice in laughter, in braying "Yea!"

I have spoken of the "yes, yes," of the "come" or of the affirmation that is not addressed first of all to a subject. . . . Such a vigil leads us to recognize the processes of differance, trace, iterability, ex-appropriation, and so on. These are at work everywhere, which is to say, well beyond humanity. (Derrida, *EW*, 274)

The experience of an "affirmation," of a "yes" or of an "en-gage" [this is the word I use . . . to describe *Zusage*, that acquiescing to language, to the mark, that the most primordial question implies], that "yes, yes" that answers before even being able to formulate a question, that is responsible without autonomy. . . . (p. 261)

To be able to say *yes, yes* when life insists on saying *no*; to squander exuberantly in pain; to affirm what cannot be affirmed yet must; to say *yes!*, to laugh extravagantly in the face of betrayal:[2] all impossible, all impossible to avoid, the impossibility and necessity of responsibility. I hold responsibility at bay for a while to look more closely at squandering exuberantly, at wasting with laughter, without utility. If that is the alternative. If there is an alternative to squander, an alternative of squander, as if one might choose to squander rather than to hoard, as if we were speaking of alternatives rather than something else, something otherwise.

In the violence of every critique, in the treachery of every betrayal, we find a *yes*, an intimate proximity. Here I am—that is, there you are. Here I am before you; there you are before me. In joy or sorrow, in every *no*, there is—*es gibt*, is giving, is given—a *yes*. Not a *yes* instead of a *no*, but a *yes* as *exposition*, the touch of touch, the laughter of betrayal. Even the *no*, even the violence and disaster, take for granted a *yes* present in being here to answer, being present to respond, in the expressiveness of things. This touching, corporeality, this circulation among the things and creatures of the earth, is an affirmation beyond affirmation, a *yes!* beyond any *yes* that would resist *no*, a call beyond the binarity of *yes and no.*

As perhaps Plato insists more than any other philosopher, has always insisted, and has always been misunderstood. For at the moments at which Socrates insists that he does not know, insists that the greatest sin by far is to claim to know when one doesn't know, that the greatest virtue by far is to be refuted; at the moment at which it appears that we must conclude that knowledge is impossible and skepticism is right, that we must give up the search for truth, he insists that giving up is worse. In the face of death, we must guard against misology and misanthropy: hatred of humanity and truth. Whatever we do is for the sake of the good *even where faced with disaster*—perhaps especially then. Giving cannot be giving up even where we cannot have or possess the good, cannot have what we have been given, where giving is betrayal.[3] Such a giving is more like squander, more exuberant, than it is like hoarding or reserving. The *yes, yes!* of *Zusage*, of responsibility, of giving, is the promise without fulfillment that resists the demand to own, defies coveting, betrays betrayal.

All this is the curse. The *yes, yes!* is linked intimately with the curse, together with squander, exuberance, and eroticism. Not to mention ecstasy and rapture. Squander, giving, exuberance, extravagance all express the curse, betray betrayal, bear the weight of disaster—and joy—instituting other disasters, other betrayals. These *other disasters and betrayals* are *ek-static*, away from themselves, beyond disaster toward a hope, a *yes!*, in betrayal, as the curse. By no means is this to pretend that disaster is not disaster, that the curse does not ruin, that betrayal does not do terrible harm. But that harm is still the affirmation, the exhilaration, of life and being—beyond neutrality. The *yes, yes!* beyond neutrality is the touch of every thing, the joy of exposure and proximity. I am speaking of *cherishment* first and *plenishment* last. I postpone these to consider squander and sacrifice, recalling Zarathustra's insistence that squander is not sacrifice.

I am interrupted by Rochelle to remind us—silently as always, a silence that betrays infinity—of the beauty of stones. The *yes, yes!* of life, the laughter of lions and jackasses, is the astonishing wonder of the earth, in abundance, toward a beauty beyond mediocrity and ugliness.[4] Not a beauty and goodness that we can hold onto in its separation and everlastingness, but the beauty and goodness in the changing expressiveness of things, good or bad, radiant or ugly, abundance beyond neutrality; the splendor and vitality of living things, exceeded by the abundance of all things, not gathered together in their harmony but abundant beyond any gathering. This beauty, known as nature itself, being itself, beyond neutrality, may also be known, betrayed, as squander. I return from this interruption to squander.

Bataille insists on the luxurious squandering of energy without growth as if we might have one without the other. "Beyond our immediate ends, man's activity in fact pursues the useless and infinite fulfillment of the universe" (Bataille, *AS*, 1, 21). As if the infinite circulation of creatures and things led either to fulfillment or to uselessness. And what, I ask, of the infinite fulfillment of the absence of fulfillment, the infinite desire not to have, the uselessness of utility, and the reverse? I would deny the binarity, the alternation, of utility and uselessness, of having and squandering. I would insist that we do not choose to squander rather than to possess, but that possessing and owning are another useless squandering of possibilities.

Squander becomes problematic at the point where Bataille links it with sacrifice, where it becomes violence under the curse. "Servile use has made a *thing* (an *object*) of that which, in a deep sense is of the same nature as the *subject*, is in a relation of intimate participation with the subject. It is not necessary that the sacrifice actually destroy the animal or plant of which man had to make a *thing* for his use. They must at least be destroyed as things, that is, *insofar as they have become things*" (pp. 55–56). Things—people, animals, and other living creatures insofar as they have become things—must be destroyed as things, as if things were for human beings to destroy. As if using things made them servile, degraded them, while destroying them in sacrifice made them sacred once more.

I am reminded of Derrida's insistence on sacrificing sacrifice.[5] I insist on betraying betrayal. Derrida alludes to the sacrificial structure of the discourses that would resist the genitivity of the subject: sacrificing animals to the gift of language; sacrificing other human beings under the curse; excluding, destroying, all justified as sacrifice. We must sacrifice to live. Including squander as sacrifice: killing and eating—it is said—to live, to live well, to live for the sake of the good.

Derrida insists that the discourses that would most profoundly criticize humanism, that resist the binarity of calculation, reinstate another binary within sacrifice itself, as if those who are sacrificed are nothing more than instruments to something higher. Another domination in the name of sacrifice. What we eat, or squander; the death of the animal—always The Animal—as that which enable Man—The Human—to Be Human. Squander represents a powerful figure of abundance, deeply joined with sacrifice. As if abundance required us to squander, and as if squander could be justified. As if we could justify sacrificing sacrifice. Sacrificing sacrifice is not the solution to genitivity but betrays every solution.

Squander, consumption, eating, ingestion, introjection: everywhere everything is ordered to stand by, to be immediately on hand, to be eaten, including, Derrida says, The Good. What is *mine, my own*, is appropriated by ingestion. "The virile strength of the adult male, the father, husband, or brother . . . belongs to the schema that dominates the concept of subject. The subject does not want just to master and possess nature actively. In our cultures, he accepts sacrifice and eats flesh" (Derrida, *EW*, 280). The (male, virile) subject wants more than to master and possess the things and creatures of the earth, but insists on sacrificing them to the schema of subjectivity, makes them flesh and eats them, through "the orifices (of orality, but also of the ear, the eye—and all the 'senses' in general)" (p. 281).

> The "Thou shalt not kill" . . . has never been understood within the Judeo-Christian tradition, nor apparently by Levinas, as a "Thou shalt not put to death the living in general." It has become meaningful in religious cultures for which carnivorous sacrifice is essential, as being-flesh. (p. 279)

> Do we have a responsibility toward the living in general? The answer is still "no." . . . (p. 278)

I insist on the cut whereby living things become flesh,[6] the way in which consumption and squander are related on the one side with responsibility and goodness and the call from the good, on the other with the ways in which sacrifice transforms the infinite heterogeneity of the other kind into something available for use and consumption. We have seen that the figure with which one turns animal bodies into meat is a figure under which kinds of human beings are gathered for exploitation and abuse.[7] "[A] structure of overlapping but absent referents links violence against women and animals. . . . Just as dead bodies are absent from our language about meat, in descriptions of cultural violence women are also often the absent referent" (Adams, *SPM*, 42–43). Under the heading of the absent referent— representation, language, *mimēsis*, betrayal—violence against women is linked with violence against animals. Living animals are expressed as meat; living women are expressed as bodies for use; living things are expressed as (dead) things for consumption and squander; creatures and things of the earth are sacrificed to possession and use. Genitivity, sacrifice, responsibility, and expression are intimately linked.

We again are led to the possibility that the key to dispossession, to having, to sacrificing sacrifice, lies in *mimēsis*—not a *mimēsis* of human language, not the *mimēsis* of absent referents, not a *mimēsis* to be stripped of all excessiveness beyond the claims of language to possess the truth of things, but the expressiveness within which we and others are thrown into the world, among others, in debt. As *thrownness (Geworfenheit)* as *mimēsis* as exposure as responsibility as betrayal. *As.* As Derrida says: "if one re-inscribes language in a network of possibilities that do not merely encompass it but mark it irreducibly from the inside, everything changes. I am thinking in particular of the mark in general, of the trace, of iterability, of differance. These possibilities or necessities, without which there would be no language, *are themselves not only human*" (*EW*, 284–85). *Mimēsis*, betrayal, exposure exceed humanity as betrayal, exceed humanity's genitivity.

It is with this genitivity that I return to the institution of sacrifice as eating flesh: sacrificing animals; sacrificing all things and creatures on and in the earth to human purposes, to the authority of heads of households and heads of state. Consumption suggests squander, opposed to stockpiling and accumulation, a figure of disowning and expropriation. Sacrifice suggests destruction, expulsion, loss, a figure opposed to holding in reserve. Yet in the production and calculation of the subject, that subject takes hold of himself—until very recently, and still, *him*self not *her*—by building or by unbuilding, by taking or by squandering, by production or by reproduction. Sacrifice becomes the figure of stockpiling for the subject who either stocks up the things of the world for his use or sacrifices them to his greater glory—still taking hold of and insisting on his authority. The curse remains the curse. Sacrifice repeats abjection. In the name of genitivity.

For the point of this difficult reversal is to possess oneself, to appropriate for oneself the highest possibilities of human life, to know what one must have in order to live well. *Il faut bien manger* is the insistence that living is living well, that human beings have a right to live well, and that that right is the right to enjoy—by taking for oneself what one needs for enjoyment, sacrificing others; or that if we are not to sacrifice others to ourselves, we must sacrifice ourselves and our egos to others, thereby gaining possession of our true selves. Sacrifice is the name of The Good—but not the good—under whose mark all creatures and things of the earth come under the rule of The Human. "The question is no longer one of knowing if it is 'good' to eat the other or if the other is 'good' to eat, nor of knowing which other. One eats him regardless and lets oneself be eaten by him" (Derrida, *EW*, 281–82).

On the one hand, consumption is learning to take and grasp and give, becoming hospitality: "'One must eat well *[il faut bien manger]*'" does not mean above all taking in and grasping in itself, but *learning* and *giving* to eat, learning-to-give-the-other-to-eat. . . . It is a rule offering infinite hospitality" (pp. 282–83). On the other, squander, giving away, becomes taking. "We need to give away, lose or destroy. But the gift would be senseless (and so we would never decide to give) if it did not take on the meaning of an acquisition. Hence *giving* must become *acquiring a power*" (Bataille, *AS*, 1,

69); "The exemplary virtue of the potlatch is given in this possibility for man to grasp what eludes him, to combine the limitless movements of the universe with the limit that belongs to him" (p. 70). This movement, whereby the hospitality that would release the grip of having and owning becomes another taking, remains the circular movement of general and restricted economy. Which is by no means to repudiate the *yes, yes!* of general economy, of giving from the good, of economies of practice for the sake of the good. Every disappropriation, every disowning, becomes something to have, possess, and own. As sacrifice and squander. In betrayal. Perhaps because we cannot escape the right to have and enjoy what is needed for life. We cannot live without having, even if the highest living, the very best living, under God or The Good, is giving away everything we have.

This is perhaps to say that giving is not giving gifts, not giving anything at all; that general economy is nothing, that acting for the sake of the good cannot be acting in the genitive—*my* acts, *my* goals, *my* accomplishments: can accomplish nothing. But it is not to deny that giving gives, that it makes a difference—an affirmative difference—by interruption and betrayal. This is the crux of giving and having, expressed in betrayal. All the ways in which giving falls into the world become having, are grasped by those who want to give under rules of genitivity. And why not? The practice of giving becomes a way of life, and it is time to emphasize that the very best, the most open, the most caring and creative way is something we want to have for ourself if we are to practice it, must have or possess as the practice, as the way. Genitivity is the form of every life, in relation to itself and to others: having what it needs to live, even if what it needs is to give, if it struggles to give. Giving gifts is in the genitive. Even so, this recognition is an ethical revelation: disclosure and betrayal. It is what I hope to express in these final chapters on disowning and giving. Always within the betrayal that every disappropriation is a reappropriation, that the very best is the worst, that giving is having.

This is to say that we cannot avoid sacrifice, but it must be resisted. It haunts the finest giving as destruction, demanding justification, as if destruction could be justified, as if we could possess a justification for violence. And what if we could not? Still we might hope to live as well as we could, avoiding violence as much and as frequently as we could, sometimes failing, sometimes insisting that violence is best. Always betraying, disclosing, a peace beyond violence. Still we might hope to live without insisting that it is right to have and own and eat and stockpile the things and creatures of the earth, including other human beings. We cannot live without betrayal, where betrayal betrays that it is never right.

We have been led from owning and having to squandering and consuming in search of giving beyond having. And we have repeatedly found the giving to fall back down into taking and having. Giving passes into gifts, betrays itself; to receive gifts—if not giving—is to take and have even where squandered and consumed, where thrown away. Thrownness is being thrown among gifts, down into abjection and subjection, under authority; and also, inseparably, being thrown beyond any having, any gifts, beyond genitivity. "Starting at 'birth,' and possibly even prior to it, being-thrown re-appropriates itself or rather ex-appropriates itself in forms that are not yet those of the *subject* or the *project*. The question 'who' then becomes 'Who (is) thrown?' . . . The other resists all subjectivation" (Derrida, *EW*, 270–71). We are thrown into general and restricted economy. All the figures of general economy are restricted where they are thrown, betrayed; restricted economy is inseparable from general economy, reveals it in every betrayal.

# CHAPTER 13

## *Generosity*

For whose sake do you care about God's and the other commandments? You surely do not suppose that this is done merely out of complaisance toward God? No, you are doing it—*for your own sake* again.—Here too, therefore, *you* are the main thing, and each must say to himself, *I* am everything to myself and I do everything *on my account.* (Stirner, *EO*, 147)

Possession is preeminently the form in which the other becomes the same, by becoming mine. (Levinas, *TI*, 46)

It is in generosity that the world possessed by me—the world open to enjoyment—is apperceived from a point of view independent of the egoist position. (p. 75)

From the beginning of philosophy, perhaps of life itself, is the prominence of self. *Know thyself!* In the genitive. Having—not giving—oneself. Stirner understands the question of life itself to be *for what or whose sake* do I act, am I here? He answers, if not for my own sake, then for some other thing or person's sake. Why them rather than myself? Even knowing, believing, that one is possessed by the gods, still one turns to oneself—one might say, from oneself, for oneself. The task of philosophy, of life itself, has to begin somewhere, and every beginning, other than that of the gaze with which *I* look upon things, the touch with which *I* make myself at home among things, the knowledge with which *I* take possession of things—every other place with which *I* might begin—nature, earth, things, other people, the gods—may be said to convince me of its truthfulness only insofar as *I* can take possession of it. If it is true, *I* must believe it for myself—*for myself* even if it is commanded by greater authorities than I.[1] A world that is not *my possession* remains alien, out of reach, beyond the grasp with which *I* make it *my own.* Levinas responds, it is in generosity that the world opens up, in giving that I find myself, I am given to myself from others.

181

Heidegger insists on the genitivity of being. "Said plainly, thinking is the thinking of Being. The genitive says something twofold. Thinking is of Being inasmuch as thinking, coming to pass from Being, belongs to Being. At the same time thinking is of Being insofar as thinking, belonging to Being, listens to Being" (Heidegger, *LH*, 196). In German, thinking of Being belongs to being, marks its genitivity as, perhaps, might be avoided in English, where thinking may listen to being, care for being, resist its own, humanity's, and being's genitivity. As Levinas says, in French, the other summons me, calls for me, begs for me; gives to me, requires generosity.[2] In Heidegger's German, it all belongs to Being in the genitive. *We* belong to being; being there, being thrown, is genitivity; the being of being is genitivity.[3]

Levinas insists that European—perhaps Christian—history, including Heidegger, has been one of sedentary rather than nomadic, wandering, foraging peoples, hoping to own and build. Possession is the condition of humanity belonging to and dwelling in the earth.[4] Standing and building upright. Coveting, hoping to own and have. Possession, having, genitivity is the form in which an other becomes other for me, by becoming mine: my friend. I dwell in the earth with lovers and friends. That is what Levinas says. Not *mine, my friend,* from which I receive good things. But offering generosity toward a neighbor who is not mine. In generosity, my world ceases to be possessed, passes from genitivity to giving.

The opening section of *Totality and Infinity*, after the preface, is *"The Same and Other,"* reminding us, perhaps, of *The Ego and Its Own*. The opening words are "'The true life is absent.' But we are in the world," (Levinas, *TI*, 33), reminding us, perhaps, of Stirner's opening words, in the section *"All Things Are Nothing to Me,"* "What is not supposed to be my concern! First and foremost the good cause, then God's cause. . . . Only *my* cause is never to be my concern" (Stirner, *EO*, 5). At least, I am so reminded. I take Levinas to begin with the question of *myself: what is my concern?* Answered by Stirner, we have seen, entirely in the genitive. "My concern is . . . solely what is *mine.* . . . Nothing is more to me than myself!" (p. 7). Levinas's answer begins in this place from which phenomenology begins, from which many believe that philosophy begins, and life itself. What is my concern except that which is mine, that which gives me my enjoyment, that which I must face as *my own death* or may know as *my truth?* We are in the world among these concerns, and I must feed on them, must take and possess them, to be myself. All questions of life and death and being come down to what it means for me, what I can make my own. As if we must always begin with myself and what is mine. As if we must begin.

Levinas responds with something else entirely:

I can "feed" on these realities and to a very great extent satisfy myself, as though I had simply been lacking them. Their *alterity* is thereby reabsorbed into my own identity as a thinker or a possessor. The metaphysical desire tends toward *something else entirely*, toward the *absolutely other*. (*TI*, 33)

... it appears as a movement going forth from a world that is familiar ... toward an alien outside-of-oneself [*hors-de-soi*], toward a yonder." (*TI*, 33)

He calls it *metaphysics* here, retrieving the term from Nietzsche and Heidegger. Elsewhere he calls it *ethics*, as I would, *another ethics*: revaluation beyond valuation, perhaps; generosity beyond genitivity. Within the movement of the self, the ego, within the genitivity of the *I*—which it—*I, myself*—must enjoy to be, to live well, is a desire beyond enjoyment, beyond need and want and lack: away from self to outside-self, away from having and possessing to giving.

If *I* begin with the genitive, with *I, myself, my own*, then where *I* find *myself*, have always found *myself*, is in the home, where *I* dwell. Dwelling is where *I* have what *I* need to live and enjoy life, where *I* find what *I* need to have, where *I* live life itself, *for myself*. In private, we might say, not in public where great acts are performed—or acts of terror and domination. But even a tyrant returns to the home to enjoy life to the fullest. Dwelling is the place of genitivity for the *I, myself, my own*, where *I* have the goodness of things. The place, Levinas insists, of welcome, hospitality, and generosity. In my house, my tent, together with my women and children. In the abundance of the earth. Dwelling in the genitive.

I must have been in relation with something I do not live from. This event is the relation with the Other who welcomes me in the Home, the discreet presence of the Feminine. But in order that I be able to free myself from the very possession that the welcome of the Home establishes, in order that I be able to see things in themselves, that is, represent them to myself, refuse both enjoyment and possession, I must know how *to give* what I possess. (Levinas, *TI*, 171)

We are not alive to suffer, to suffer when we might not, to suffer because others suffer, to suffer in renunciation. Desire for goodness, for the sake of the good, is not self-renunciation. Still in the genitive. For your sake rather than mine. For the other. It is for the sake of the good, which is nothing at all except responsivity, the call, the desire, the recognition, of a giving beyond genitivity, beyond welcome, hospitality, and generosity. First, however, we live in generosity, give what we possess. In dwelling, in the home, where we live to be ourselves, to enjoy the fruits of life. Gifts and welcome are present in intimacy and its promise without coveting and taking. But they can be overwhelmed by coveting and by deprivation. "[H]unger and fear can prevail over every human resistance and every freedom! There is no question of doubting this human misery, this dominion the things and the wicked exercise over man, this animality. But to be a man is to know that this is so. Freedom consists in knowing that freedom is in peril. . . . the instant of inhumanity . . . [the] infinitesimal difference between man and non-man" (Levinas, *TI*, 35). Levinas insists on the genitivity of Man's Humanity. I remain within generosity.

I interpret this generosity as thrownness, not into what can be brought together—perhaps as humanity, perhaps in dwelling—but in remoteness, separation, and distance. Generosity is the relation into which we are thrown toward the alterity of others. Which I would say is anything but genitivity, anything but mine. This is not quite what Levinas says. "The alterity, the radical heterogeneity of the other, is possible only if the other is other with respect to a term whose essence is to remain at the point of departure. . . . *A term can remain absolutely at the point of departure of relationship only as I*" (p. 36). I always depart *from myself*, from the genitive. Thrownness is departing toward others beyond the genitive, either *mine* or *the other's*. Beginning—always beginning—with the *I*, identical with itself and with what is *mine*. Thinking in the genitive, perhaps thinking itself as genitive. Inescapably Cartesian. Or Kantian. "The I is identical in its very alterations. . . . The universal identity in which the heterogeneous can be embraced has the ossature of a subject, of the first person. Universal thought is an 'I think'" (p. 36).

If the "I think" precedes and accompanies the *I* as such, it is what *I* must take to be my own. *I* begin face to face—that is, against—the other, against whatever is not mine. "The *way* of the I against the 'other' of the world consists in *sojourning*, in *identifying oneself* by existing here *at home with oneself [chez soi]*" (p. 37). Even so, Levinas insists it is sojourning, not resting in place, a journey from oneself, in its genitivity, to the other. At home with oneself is where we begin. On a journey from the place where I am at home to the hospitality that makes me at home, to the welcome that makes a neutral site into a dwelling. In the genitive. "Dwelling is the very mode of *maintaining oneself*, . . . as the body that, on the earth exterior to it, holds *itself* up and *can*. . . . In a sense everything is in the site. . . . The site, a medium, afford means. Everything is here, everything belongs to me" (pp. 37–38).

Negativity begins with my own, my place, where I hope to find myself at home. "Negativity presupposes a being established, placed in a site where he is at home; it is an economic fact" (pp. 40–41). Desire goes toward something otherwise—one might say against the entire Western philosophic tradition. "The strangeness of the Other . . . is precisely accomplished as a calling into question of my spontaneity, as ethics. Western philosophy has most often been an ontology: a reduction of the other to the same by interposition of a middle and neutral term that ensures the comprehension of being" (p. 43). A tradition that converts alterity into the same, ethics into ontology, insists on gathering what cannot be gathered. "To affirm the priority of *Being* over *existents* is to already decide the essence of philosophy; it is to subordinate the relation with *someone*, who is an existent (the ethical relation), to a relation with the *Being of existents*, which, impersonal, permits the apprehension, the domination of existents (a relationship of knowing), subordinates justice to freedom" (p. 45). Levinas repeats the traditional insistence that the relation with someone is the absolute condition of ethics—someone human in the face—as if being as such must be impersonal. Levinas is no friend of animals or stones. The impersonality of being is overcome in the human face.

Levinas knows it is overcome—if that is the word—by generosity, by the welcome given to me to live and by what I give back. Possession by the other is something other than possession, perhaps beyond the (human) face. "The relationship with a being infinitely distant, that is, overflowing its idea, is such that its authority as an existent is already *invoked* in every question we could raise concerning the meaning of its Being" (p. 47). Possession with the other is dwelling, where *I* find myself thrown in the world beyond neutrality, into generosity. Intimacy, separation, and dwelling are experienced (by the ego) as welcome, hospitality. Anything but neutral.

> Recollection refers to a welcome.
> . . . And the other whose presence is discreetly an absence, with which is accomplished the primary hospitable welcome which describes the field of intimacy, is the Woman. The woman is the condition for recollection, the interiority of the Home, and inhabitation.
> . . . The Other who welcomes in intimacy is not the *you [vous]* of the face that reveals itself in a dimension of height, but precisely the *thou [tu]* of familiarity: a language without teaching, a silent language, an understanding without words, an expression in secret. (p. 155)

Hospitality, generosity, and welcome express the intimacy with which the ego would be at home in the world. "The home . . . is hospitable for its proprietor. This refers us to . . . the welcoming one par excellence, welcome in itself—the feminine being" (pp. 157–58). The home—always, I would say, I believe that Levinas says, *my* home, in the genitive, the *oikos* or dwelling in which *I* seek and find *my* enjoyment, is where *I* am welcomed by the woman—*I* who am almost certainly a man, not a woman, am welcomed in hospitality by the woman, whose generosity—one genitive after another—welcomes *me*. *I* enter the world, to make it *mine*, from a dream of generosity.

I have alluded repeatedly to the contamination of the dwelling, the site at which women have been subjected in the home. The figure of the welcoming woman (for the man, the masculine ego) is profoundly contaminated, difficult, dangerous. Intimacy is a dangerous place, not only for the man who lets down his warlike guard in love and proximity, but for those who are made to serve him and his intimacies, who are subjected to his desires. Secrecy serves to guard systems of control. Always women and children, sometimes slaves and domesticated animals. The dwelling, the *oikos*, is a site of danger, vulnerability, and betrayal.

It is important, I believe, to recognize the betrayals within this betrayal, beyond the subjection of women and animals, beyond the generosity without which humanity cannot be at home. It is important to pursue another ethics beyond the ethicality of a being that takes for granted, insists on, being welcomed and giving hospitality. Levinas articulates the journey of the ego from being thrown for itself into a world in which it finds that it cannot be for itself except insofar as it is welcomed. Generosity in this giving is not free from betrayal, does not achieve purity or goodness, but is an insistent call from within the ego's right to enjoyment. If *I* am here to enjoy life and being, it is in virtue of a hospitality given to me, something that is given but is *not mine, cannot be mine*.

This generosity, welcome, and hospitality, this place in the earth of intimacy and flesh, where I labor and produce the goods I hope to enjoy, evokes an absolute generosity, a giving beyond return, beyond welcome and hospitality, a responsibility beyond containment—but not beyond betrayal. The love between the one and the other, intimate in the proximity of life, goes far beyond having and owning toward separation and alterity—but stops, confined by familiarity. The face to face that summons me, calls for me, begs for me, the absolutely other, is infinitely beyond the generosity of the dwelling, beyond intimacy. But the latter, sites of intimacy and love, places in our lives where we live in proximity with others, gesture toward absolute responsibility, absolute vulnerability, that show themselves as betrayal.

Having and enjoying presuppose giving without having. Yet there is no place in the world, certainly not the dwelling, where one can live without having. I cannot imagine how one might express not-having except as giving, except that I think of giving in relation to the *es gibt* of being—not there but here, betraying gifts. Here I am before you, in a relation of giving—responsivity, exposure. Being there, *Dasein*, is upright, at a height, towers over animals and stones. Being here denies my height, refuses height as *my own*. Yet somehow Levinas remains at a height, as if resistance to the neutrality of being and giving demanded the superiority of humanity, sacrificing everything in the world so that human beings might be ethical subjects. "To recognize the Other is to recognize a hunger. To recognize the Other is to give. But it is to give to the master, to the lord, to him whom one approaches as 'You' *[Vous]* in a dimension of height" (p. 75). The Other must be master, must deserve mastery, must be lord in a measure of height. Rochelle remains at my feet, abundant in her qualities no matter how low she sinks. Language betrays the mark of spirit even as generosity. "To recognize the Other is therefore to come to him across the world of possessed things, but at the same time to establish, by gift, community and universality. Language . . . offers things which are mine to the Other" (p. 76).

I suggest that this interruption of genitivity as generosity and betrayal is called forth by Levinas's beginning with the genitive self, and remains in the shadow, the gift, of genitivity. *Thrownness (Geworfenheit), being thrown*, is first of all *my* finding *myself* in the world. The movement is from the genitivity of the *I* through its own desire to something otherwise. It is a doubly genitive movement, *my own journey* from possession to dispossession, beginning with the place I take to be *my own*. Alterity haunts the dwelling place of the self. I reply that once we have experienced this desire beyond want and need, beyond the yearning to have and own, then we may turn from the genitive self to others right from the start. We are thrown among others, before them, from the first, are ourselves, have ourselves in the genitive, in virtue of exposure to others, without having.

We live in genitivity; we have the right to own, to have and enjoy. Beyond genitivity, beyond having, is not not-having in the sense that one may not, must not, is called upon not to have and enjoy the things that one needs to live and live well, called upon to sacrifice oneself to something else—to suffer. If we cannot live without sacrifice—ourselves or others— we cannot understand sacrifice as the goal of life. That is what Derrida insists we must understand and live by in sacrificing sacrifice, the double movement in which we question both the recurrent insistence on sacrificing ourselves to the cause—Stirner's question—and the inescapable insistence on sacrificing others—other kinds—to human well-being.

I would not begin with ego and self; I would not begin at all. I would not understand thrownness as the being there of a (genitive) self, hoping to possess itself. I would understand being thrown as thrown into abundance, giving beyond having. In exposure and proximity. *Here before others*, exposed to them beyond genitivity. One does not begin with *myself, my own*, but finds oneself as *never oneself alone*. One does not live *Mitsein*, gathered together in being with others, but in a vulnerability mirrored in the vulnerability of others, in joys and sorrows experienced by oneself and others, exposed before others. We are thrown into the touch of others, where not death but love evokes desire beyond want and need, touch and exposure in the flesh and skin to others. Love beyond death. That is another story, another *mimēsis* and betrayal.

This story follows the double trajectory of genitivity, beginning with myself and my enjoyment toward something otherwise, absolutely other. Alterity haunts the face of my enjoyment, calls for me, begs for me, wherever I am, wherever I hope to make something my own. "A guiltless responsibility, whereby I am none the less open to an accusation of which no alibi, spatial or temporal, could clear me. . . . A responsibility stemming from a time before my freedom—before my *(moi)* beginning, before any present. A fraternity existing in extreme separation" (Levinas, *S*, 83–84). Separation before, beyond, being-with. I will speak of love rather than fraternity and friendship, holding love in abeyance together with generosity and dwelling. I concern myself here with something else, with the expressiveness of the face—excluding the faces of animals and stones; with the mortality, the death, in the face, as if joys and sorrows were not marks of the expressions of others—including animals, living creatures, and more—for who is to mark the limits of joy and sorrow?

The question others bring to me, interrupting the double genitive of myself, is where I must stop before the others. Can the face that calls me out of myself and my dwelling toward generosity, out of my own place toward others, be halted at the face? Halted at death? "My being-in-the-world or my 'place in the sun,' my being at home, have these not also been the usurpation of spaces belonging to the other man whom I have already oppressed or starved, or driven out into a third world; are they not acts of repulsing, excluding, exiling, stripping, killing?" (Levinas, *EFP*, 82). Am I not responsible for the sorrows and joys and annihilated possibilities in every place, in every face and beyond? Guiltlessly responsible perhaps, but a guiltlessness filled with debt, taking me from myself and my place in the sun to places I cannot imagine.

To these questions, calling him away from himself, Levinas responds in the name of the face. "The face is a fundamental event" (Levinas, *M*, 168). That is, The Human Face. For when asked whether there is "something about the human face which, for example, sets it apart from that of the animal," he replies: "One cannot entirely refuse the face of an animal. It is via the face that one understands, for example, a dog. Yet the priority here is not found in the animal, but in the human face. We understand the animal, the face of an animal, in accordance with *Dasein*. The phenomenon of the face is not in its purest form in the dog" (p. 169). Language remains the gift: "I think that the beginning of language is in the face. In a certain way, in its silence, it calls you. Your reaction to the face is a response. Not just a response, but a responsibility. These two words *[réponse, responsabilité]* are closely related. . . . Language is above all the fact of being addressed . . . which means the saying much more than the said" (pp. 169-70). The silence of the face—not the silent face of the animal, the leaf, the stone? Rochelle holds her silence. Not the call, the question, the *Zusage*, before every being, oneself and others, to respond to *that being, that question*, a responsivity that we know as responsibility?

To the question, "Can an animal be considered as the other that must be welcomed?," Levinas answers—with a crucial hesitation: "The human face is completely different and only afterwards do we discover the face of an animal. I don't know if a snake has a face. I can't answer that question. A more specific analysis is needed" (Levinas, *PM*, 171–72). As if reason and analysis gave us goodness, against the possibility that they answer to something beyond themselves, beyond the categories of identification. One might wonder if philosophical rationality exists to enforce the sacrificial decision that reinstitutes humanism, human ethics as the only ethics. "It is clear that, without considering animals as human beings, the ethical extends to all living beings. We do not want to make an animal suffer needlessly and so on. But the prototype of this is human ethics. Vegetarianism, for example, arises from the transference to animals of the idea of suffering. The animal suffers. It is because we, as humans, know what suffering is that we can have this obligation" (p. 172).

I would say that we have this obligation from being thrown, and that perhaps all things are thrown and we are thrown before them. The absoluteness of responsibility is its excessiveness, exceeding the terms, the borders, that Levinas faces and faces down, however hesitantly. He does not allow for the possibility that human ethics belongs to the said, thereby betraying another ethics, beyond containment, an ethics of saying.

We come to the point of the journey on which Levinas takes us, as I understand it, that the call, the face, the expressiveness of the other—which I understand as the abundance of the earth in every individual and kind—betrays every beginning, every relation, every genitive with something else, a call given from the good in the touch of others. I am led by responsivity in abundance away from myself, a responsivity expressive of others, a generosity otherwise. Which is by no means to overlook another generosity that inhabits a more intimate, familiar place, in a face that reminds us of other faces, in other places without a face. I want to consider the possibility that for human beings—and many others—responsiveness is responsibility: guiltless, excessive, whereby I am open to an accusation of which no alibi, spatial or temporal, could clear me. Of betrayal, toward every other living and non-living thing. Rochelle insists that she does not blame, but she accuses every person and thing for flourishing in her place even as she enjoys the places she inhabits, together with the other things that place them, where all dwell together. She insists on betrayal.

I insist—this is my responsibility, what I hope to give here in response to the call of things in the earth—that it is *mimēsis* that receives and offers, ambiguously and dividedly, that betrays. "The relationship between the same and the other, my welcoming of the other, is the ultimate fact, and in it the things figure not as what one builds but as what one gives" (Levinas, *TI*, 77). I pursue the possibility that this giving is betrayal, figuration is *mimē-sis*, *mimēsis* is exposure, *generosité* is *exposition*: the expressiveness of bodies in proximity, touching other bodies, touch touching touch; exposure as giving, giving way in every place to generosity. As *mimēsis*. Betrayal.

I conclude this chapter with another betrayal, turning from the generosity of the face and home to the *es gibt* of being, beyond its genitivity, beyond the face: to "let us say: *a surprising generosity of being*" (Nancy, *EF*, 120).

> It is a generosity of *ethos* more than an ethic of generosity. "Freedom" itself, in the spaciosity of being where freedom is opened rather than engulfed, proves to be generosity even *before* being freedom. . . .
> It gives freedom, or *offers* it. For the gift is never purely and simply given. . . . The generosity of being offers nothing other than existence, and the offering, as such, is kept in freedom. (Nancy, *EF*, 146)

This is a reading of the giving of being, where being, or existence, or freedom is the gift, where the *It* withdraws.[5] A saying—after Levinas—that speaks of giving in the name of being, neutralizing the face, insisting on its genitivity. We have seen that the expressiveness of the face—its nonneutrality—betrays the snake, the tree, the stone. Rochelle reminds us of her gifts. If the expressiveness of the face excludes animals and stones, the generosity of being includes them—and more. "[I]t is not obvious that the community of singularities is limited to 'man' and excludes, for example, the 'animal' (even in the case of 'man' it is not a fortiori certain that this community concerns only 'man' and not also the 'inhuman' or the 'superhuman'" (Nancy, *IC*, 28).

> Freedom *is* the withdrawal of being, but the withdrawal of being is the nothingness of this being, which is the being of freedom. This is why freedom *is not, but it frees being and frees from being*, all of which can be rewritten here as: *freedom withdraws being and gives relation*. (Nancy, *EF*, 68)

> It is freedom that gives relation by withdrawing being. It is then freedom that gives humanity, and not the inverse. But the gift that freedom gives

is never, insofar as it is the gift of *freedom*, a quality, property, or essence on the order of *"humanitas."* (p. 73)

We come to a crucial juncture for an ethics—if an ethics, or *ethos*, or anything familiar—of giving beyond having: the crossing of the exclusiveness of the face with the emptiness of freedom. Generosity betrays giving before the face or in withdrawal, gives too much and too little. "Even though freedom gives its gift under the form of a *'humanitas,'* as it has done in modern times, in fact it gives a transcendence: a gift which, as gift, transcends the giving, which does not establish itself as a giving, but which before all gives *itself* as gift, and as a gift of freedom which gives essentially and gives itself, in the withdrawal of being. . . . *Freedom gives—freedom"* (Nancy, *EF,* 73). Which is nothing. Always too much and never enough. Filled with betrayal. I insist on a giving beyond having that betrays its own betrayals.

In the name of giving I would pose the question Derrida asks of humanism in a different register: not whether Levinas and Heidegger—perhaps Nancy or Derrida himself—escape humanism, sacrifice sacrifice; but whether they escape—or betray—ontotheology. Can the generosity of being, however surprising, avoid its genitivity? "I run the risk of simply and naively reconstituting a metaphysics, in the sense in which this word designates 'the forgetting of being' and the forgetting of this forgetting. Which means the forgetting of the difference between being and beings is from the start lost from sight by metaphysics" (Nancy, *EF,* 166-67). He responds, still within the withdrawal of being: "But this difference *is not*—not even *the* 'ontico-ontological difference.' It is itself the very effacing of this difference—an effacing that has nothing to do with forgetting. . . . This retreat is the *identity of being and beings*: existence. Or more precisely: freedom" (p. 167).

Nancy would give us freedom beyond causality where causality expresses the genitivity of being. "As long as the concept of freedom remains caught in the space of causality—and of will as causality through representation—it does not permit us to think of anything other than a spontaneous causality . . . whose secret will be kept, in every case, in the principle of causality itself" (Nancy, *EF,* 99). Nancy rejects causality as the secret of being and the world; rejects the origin with its genitivity. The question is whether he rejects the secret of being as withdrawal, as having being there. Another genitivity.

The *there* of the "there is" is not a receptacle of a place arranged in order for a coming to produce itself *there*. The *there* is itself the spacing (of space-time) of the coming, because there is *all* (and totality is not the

> fastening, the completion without remainder: it is the "having there" *[y avoir]*, the taking place *[avoir lieu]*, the unlimited "coming there" *[y venir]* of the delimited thing; which means that totality is all, except totalitarian, and it is obviously a question here of freedom). (pp. 158-59)

The subject here is being thrown—in the world, of the world: thrown-*there*. The *there* is itself—*itself*—the spacing of the coming; it is the having there, the taking place. Being there is having the there of the secret (places) of being, where the greatest secret place is the totality.

I respond, with Plato (as I read him), Anaximander, and Levinas, that thrownness is not being thrown *there*, not thrown into neutral *being*, not having thereness, having what is necessary to be-*there*, but thrown *here* into the world *before* others, accused by them, responsive to them, in betrayal and debt. The causality of the good is not *of* being, but *before* being in the sense of exposure—accusation, allegation, betrayal, in debt.[6] "The word *I* means *here I am*, answering for everything and for everyone.... I exist through the other and for the other ...: I am inspired. This inspiration is the psyche.... being-in-one's-skin, having-the-other-in-one's-skin" (Levinas, *S*, 104).[7] Finite freedom is accusation, debt, exposure before the other. Never from oneself. One might say that the way in which exposure resists ontotheology turns on the multiple meanings of *before*: not the withdrawal and dividedness of being, not any being at all, but something otherwise, another causality. Assignation, obsession. For the sake of the other, given from the good.

> From the Good to me, there is assignation: a relation that survives the 'death of God.' (Levinas, *S*, 112)

> the uniqueness of the responsible ego is possible only *in* being obsessed by another, in the trauma suffered prior to any auto-identification, in an unrepresentable *before*. (p. 113)

> The responsibility for another, an unlimited responsibility which the strict book-keeping of the free and non-free does not measure, requires subjectivity as an irreplaceable hostage. This subjectivity it denudes under the ego in a passivity of persecution, repression and expulsion outside of essence, into oneself.... Without having wished it, I have to answer *(s'accuse)*. (p. 113)

Finite freedom is obligation, vulnerability, persecution, finding oneself an irreplaceable hostage to the other. If being such a hostage reminds us of the master's slave, does not appear to sacrifice sacrifice, still the *here I am* never gets reduced to *being there*. "Freedom is borne by the responsibility

it could not shoulder, an elevation and inspiration without com-
placency. . . . This describes the suffering and vulnerability of the sensible
as *the other in me*" (p. 114).

Even so, Levinas insists on the genitive. The irreplaceable responsibility, beyond all persistence in being, is *mine*. "*My* substitution—it is as *my
own* that substitution for the neighbour is produced" (p. 115); "it is I, I and
no one else, who am a hostage for the others. In substitution my being that
belongs to me and not to another is undone, and it is through this substitution that I am not 'another,' but me" (p. 116). The insistent return of the
genitive—the responsibility that must be *mine* alone, not a responsivity I
give to and share with others—marks the demand that the self before
others must have something to be here, must have finite freedom, the
wound that cannot heal. The genitive insists on having, here or there.

I return to the possibility that nature is cursed by the betrayal that
betrayal is not only human, not anywhere, any time or place, in particular,
never owned or had by anyone or anything, that nature in abundance is
betrayal. Humanity betrays this abundance multiply, and betrays the betrayal; brings abundance under the curse, insists that *mimēsis*, or language, or writing, or thinking—the expressiveness of abundance—is only
human, restricted to some and not others; yet in this limitation, in this
insistence, betrays the impossibility of excluding any from expression, from
the betrayal, betraying the abundance in its abundance; thereby betraying
that this betrayal betrays the good, the good which is nothing but betrayal,
nothing but withdrawal, nothing but responsiveness beyond any place or
limit. The good is before being as exposure, *mimēsis*, betrayal: *as*; betrays
the abundance, beyond humanity; betrays the curse, beyond subjectivity.
The good is beyond, exceeds, any secret of being, including itself.

# CHAPTER 14

## *Sustenance*

We need a nobler economics that is not afraid to discuss spirit and conscience, moral purpose and the meaning of life, an economics that aims to educate and elevate people, not merely to measure the low-grade behavior. Here it is. (Roszak, Introduction to Schumacher, *SB*, 10)

According to the Sigalovada Sutta a householder should accumulate wealth as a bee collects nectar from a flower. The bee harms neither the fragrance nor the beauty of the flower, but gathers nectar to turn it into sweet honey. (de Silva, *HWMSD*, 22)

Just as our own life is precious to us, so is the life of another precious to it. Therefore reverence must be cultivated towards all forms of life. (p. 23)

I undertake what I and many other people think is called for by human beings who hope to live ethically in relation to the earth—sustainable local communities and practices. Right away I commit an act of violence, not to diminish the goodness of such practices, but to put goodness itself in question: "one way of practising 'respect for the environment' while fostering 'community responsibility' would be to form a committee or group to inspect neighbourhood garbage"; and while "it is refreshing to hear someone speak so openly about the surveillance, regulation and censure informing their idea of community," it is "chilling to have it spoken in the name of . . . 'radical politics' " (Jowett, *OOPN*, 26). In the name of goodness. There is such a thing, perhaps, as environmental or ecological "fascism" (a figure of "the worst"), such a thing as "fascism" of "the best and highest," where the greatest of human values, goodnesses that would free us from every evil, give rise to oppressive institutions and practices. We have seen it where an ethics of generosity becomes sacrificial oppression. In the name of the best, implementation becomes the worst. One might

say—resisting the historical roots of *fascism*, if that is an acceptable name—
that every implementation and every practice, no matter how laudatory or
emancipatory, demands authority, but that every authority exceeds the values
that initiate it, exceeds the measures that institute it, that authority becomes authoritarian, exceeds itself. The consequence is that the very best
becomes the worst, is indistinguishable from the worst in the places where
it comes to pass. Which is entirely different from saying that we cannot
pursue or achieve the best, but that we must do so within the darkness and
illumination of betrayal. To express and seek the good is to betray something, to express and show something of the world in whose light and
shadow something else is destroyed; and to betray something of the good
in the darkest places.

I postpone the light and shadow, the echoes and cacophonies of betrayal, to the final chapters. Here I would look intensely at the very best,
not so much to find the improprieties in its proprieties as the havings, the
genitivities, in the best communities in which we might hope to dwell in
the earth. I am still engaged with resistances to genitivity, explored in the
last few chapters along different lines of flight: ecstasy, squander, generosity, now sustenance and dwelling. Dwelling in the earth, touching it lightly,
remembering the contaminated history of the *oikos*, household dwelling
and coveting. Dwelling as giving back to the earth what we have been given.
Touching it lightly.

"[I]n Norwegian, there is a clearer, more value-laden word *[friluftsliv]*
that refers to the type of outdoor recreation that seeks to come to nature
on its own terms: to *touch the Earth lightly*" (Naess, *ECL*, 178), as follows:

>   (1) Respect for all life. Respect for landscape. . . .
>   (2) Outdoor education in the signs of identification. . . .
>   (3) Minimal strain upon the natural combined with maximal self-
>   reliance. . . .
>   (4) Natural lifestyle. . . .
>   (5) Time for adjustment. . . . Several weeks must pass before the *sensitiv-
>   ity* for nature is so developed that it fills the mind. (p. 179)

In small and beautiful ways. Holding tightly onto the goods of the earth:

>   I suggest that the foundations of peace cannot be laid by universal
>   prosperity, in the modern sense, because such prosperity, if attainable at
>   all, is attainable only by cultivating such drives of human nature as greed
>   and envy, which destroy intelligence, happiness, serenity, and thereby the
>   peacefulness of man. (Schumacher, *SB*, 33)

>   From an economic point of view, the central concept of wisdom is
>   permanence. We must study the economics of permanence. (p. 34)

Permanence is sustenance, living lightly on the earth to do it the least damage, to serve it well, so that it and we and the goods and creatures and things around us will endure. Except that nothing is permanent, nothing endures. Except for memories of disasters wrought in the name of permanence. Another desire to have forever.

Of course we are against greed and envy and in favor of intelligence, happiness, serenity, and peacefulness. One might ask: at what cost? The foreground questions of restricted economics are: at what expense, and with what impediments to exchange? Sustenance and permanence run the risk of presenting the greatest obstacles to exchange and circulation. Authoritarianism again. Put another way, if general economy is excessive circulation, libidinal and other uncontainable economies, then restricted economies always curb circulation and excess even where they would remove all barriers in the name of prosperity. Universal prosperity is understood as universal profitability. Profitability, like consumption, overwhelmingly restricts excess and circulation. I insist on exchange without profit, circulation without consumption, prosperity without goods. Giving beyond having, otherwise than gifts.

Before I am misunderstood, let me insist as strongly as I can that small *is* beautiful, if not permanent, that I admire Schumacher's glowing vision of restricted economies, limited in scale, gentle in measure. Treading lightly, hoping to build sustainable habitats.

> What is it that we really require from the scientists and technologists? I should answer: We need methods and equipment which are
> —cheap enough so that they are accessible to virtually everyone;
> —suitable for small-scale application; and
> —compatible with man's need for creativity.
> Out of these three characteristics is born non-violence and a relationship of man to nature which guarantees permanence. (p. 35)

Beautiful in the sense of order, proportion, and scale that somehow got out of line after the middle ages. Truly beautiful. Who could deny it? (Nor would I resist improving the environment by recycling, if I would avoid garbage police.) But perhaps not the beauty that shines upon the borders where proportion and order become tyrannies.

If I had to choose—and how could I avoid it?—I would choose small, sustainable, local practices where human beings dwell in harmony among themselves and tread lightly on the earth. If I could decide—I am not empowered to do so—I would elect peace over war, and harmony over conflict. Except that I do not have the power to choose these; except that I know many people would not choose these if they had the power; except that I love urban vitality and sprawl, if not urban squalor and congestion;

except most of all that it is crucial not to take peace and order and proportion and harmony as if they named goodness itself. If these are our choices,
they are chosen in relation to two considerations: First, to choose them is
not to choose something else, and it is imperative to know and care about
what we sacrifice for the best. Second, every system and institution of
alternatives, however laudable and good, is linked with systems of power
and authority in which some benefit and some are harmed, in which evil
is done.[1]

If I had to choose, and if I could control the choices made by others,
I would insist on living like the bee, who takes nectar from the flower and
makes honey without harm. Indeed, without bees many flowering plants
would suffer: they need bees for their propagation. Similarly, many creatures of the earth inhabit ecosystems in which they are mutually beneficial.
If this were the story of life on earth, the whole story, then we could learn
to live together, I would insist.

Except for predatory animals and their prey, and parasitic animals and
insects, who feed on other animals, use other animals for their lives and
propagation. Except for animals that propagate beyond their own survival
and their progeny if their numbers are not controlled. Sustainability and
permanence—if these are the values we admire; and how can we help but
do so?—impose destruction and pain. Not only among animals and other
living things, but among human beings. I do not mean to propose the
struggle for life among animals, insects, and microorganisms as a model for
human beings—to the contrary, perhaps. I mean to call into question
sustainability and treading lightly on the earth as values shared by the
earth, derivable from life on earth. Life on earth frequently goes wild; wildness is frequently exploitative and destructive, as well as fascinating and
exhilarating. Leopold hates the damage deer do to mountain terrain when
they are not controlled. I would insist that the most nonviolent living
creatures cannot multiply without limits and do no harm. Harm to themselves or harm to others, one might say. Calling sustainability and harm-
lessness into question.

These are difficult ethical questions in the context of property and
genitivity: of the future and the present as the future of the past; of the not-
yet and perhaps never; of the once having been and gone; of death, disaster,
and extinction. *Parousia*, the fundamental question of genitivity, is what we
may insist on regarding as *ours, mine*, and *yours*, not only in the sense of
what we must have to live, must hold in hand to enjoy and consume, but
the uncontainable question of what we must have around us to be, what is
relevant to our lives—and to everything or anything else. How do we take
up the burden of a responsibility for sustaining and treading lightly in a
universe that offers hospitality not only to us and our friends but to count-

less creatures and things that have not (yet) arrived, may never arrive, or that having once arrived are gone? Dinosaurs on the one hand, strange and terrifying machines on the other hand, weird and destructive predators on the third. How does one insist on sustainability in a world of monsters— the world we inhabit? In a world where human beings—much more destructive than deer—are the greatest monsters?

At the risk of grave injustice—I hope to give compensation—I suggest that global and local economies may suffer from the same twin faults, and that despite the terrible destructiveness and overweening authority of global economy, the former responds constructively to one such fault from within the other, where the latter, much more appealing and responsible and *ethical* in general, cannot do so. The twin faults are that these are two economies *in general*—anything but general economy, much closer to *total economy*, an overwhelming restricted economy that would seize and govern the earth, claiming to have and possess everything in and on it; and that they cannot accommodate monsters, aliens, that threaten the borders of the economy. Global capitalist economy does not recognize any borders, any monsters, with the consequence that on the one hand it would include anything whatever that can be exchanged or sold, but on the other hand does terrible harm in the name of profit. Sustainable economies insist on living close to the land, in harmony, with the consequence that what threatens the balance and order of things must be excluded: diseases, wild animals, droughts, hurricanes. In a strange and wonderful way, the global economy that destroys habitats, fells forests, burns jungles also profits from disasters and monsters. A sustainable economy must worry about what people do with their garbage. A global economy hopes to make money off garbage. Put another way, in terms of giving rather than having, in a global economy everything enters circulation and exchange, including garbage, so that nothing goes to waste. Only where we insist on profit and equivalence in trade and exchange—insist on having and controlling the measure of things—do we bring circulation to rest before waste and monsters, before that which is not profitable or profitable enough. Everything continues to circulate as if it were valuable, as if someone somewhere might desire it.

Sustainable habitats are wonderful places to dwell, but dwelling is containing. Nature, the earth, is filled with surprising, uncontainable events and monstrous creatures. Does sustainable life admire these or dread them? Who hopes to control risk by having what it takes to control them? Because I admire Wendell Berry so much for how he understands the possibilities of human life, I pause to consider his words on human scale and nature's truth:

> We can be true to nature only by being true to human nature—to our animal nature as well as to cultural patterns and restraints that keep us

from acting like animals. When humans act like animals, they become the most dangerous of animals to themselves and other humans.... Only humans squander and hoard, murder and pillage because of notions. (Berry, *HE*, 15)

Once we grant the possibility of a proper human scale, we see that we have made a radical change of assumptions and values. We realize that we are less interested in technological "breakthroughs" than in technological elegance. (p. 16)

Without a doubt, I would say—if there be anything beyond doubt—we may hope to pursue elegance rather than profit, may insist that usefulness is not the highest value. Technology can harm as well as benefit, and we may hope to nurture as well as use. The difficulty is in thinking of being true to nature and humanity as if nature were one thing with a single truth, or as if human beings were enough alike to share a human truth. If there is such a truth it is probably close to Berry's suggestion that when human beings act like animals—deer, not wolves—they are the most dangerous of animals, squandering, hoarding, destroying—less by murder than by indifference, disregard, and personal well-being. The question is whether this truth—that human beings like deer destroy the earth in pursuit of what they take to be their own good—can be offset by the notion of a proper scale, human and otherwise. Perhaps those who know this scale and its propriety will govern the others, or at least assist them in arriving at a similar recognition. One wonders who would help the deer except the wolves. I recall a different sense of squander, beyond propriety.

It is possible to imagine the human world divided into small, local communities, each treading lightly on the earth. Would all these communities together tread lightly? Or are there too many? How many human beings would have to die to make the human footprint smaller? Perhaps human beings not only disregard the harm they do, but humanity has achieved what deer and other animals cannot achieve—the ability to grow and populate the earth almost without limit.[2] At tremendous cost to other creatures and things in the earth, but most of all perhaps to other human beings. Countless human tribes and communities will be destroyed. The insects and microbes will survive.

This is a powerful argument: global populations, economies, political developments must, in virtue of their scale, reduce and destroy the variety of human life and culture on the earth. This is a compelling argument for sustainable, local communities: whatever their local conflicts, small communities allow their neighbors to flourish. Sometimes. Perhaps. The stakes are clearer than the empirical claims. Heterogeneity and multiplicity are the stakes, abundance in the earth the variety that forms of being and having in human life threaten to reduce.

This is not to overlook that heterogeneity and multiplicity are human values, and that those who can afford to pay for them frequently do so, so that the global economy invests in the monsters it is structurally organized to destroy. It is by no means obvious that small sustainable economies will be able to provide the resources to support monsters except by domesticating them.

I hope to come to terms with Berry in a different register—let me say, where I least agree with him, and I agree with him in many ways. "No good thing is destroyed by goodness; good things are destroyed by wickedness. We may identify that insight as biblical. . . . Since the start of the industrial revolution, there have been voices urging that this inheritance may be safely replaced by intelligence, information, energy, and money. No idea, I believe, could be more dangerous" (*HE*, 20). I think that things are destroyed by wickedness and by goodness. As much as I would foster and encourage goodness, I would insist that goodness cannot be separated from evil. The pathway to hell is paved with goodness.

Let me say again that if I could choose, I would choose small, sustainable, local habitats—in their places. For myself, some of the time, and for some others, though perhaps not for all. Who am I to choose for others, much less decide for all—as if anyone could? I am most at home in urban environments, captivated by urban sprawl. Moreover, some of the people who are harmed by global industrial development are most in need of some of its benefits. So that even the choice of sustainable economies is multiple: choosing the best and lightest and most caring practices; choosing to care for those who do not benefit from those practices—employing nonsustainable practices where necessary, industrial development and global exchange; refusing to choose what cannot be chosen—not choosing for others, not imposing one's choice on others, not choosing abundance, or lack of abundance, or anything that would effectively suggest that human beings have the right to choose for other human beings and other creatures and things, as if they were lords of the earth, with the right to choose to develop or to refrain from developing, to build or not to build, as if human beings bore a unique responsibility to nurture the earth, as if the earth did not exceed every responsibility.

I do not think Berry or Schumacher thinks we bear such a responsibility, yet I insist that we must keep this possibility in mind before the humblest and lightest practices. Bringing me back to Schumacher, postponing a return to Berry for a while.

Schumacher is rightly revered for proposing a serious challenge to conventional economic practice and theory, developing unorthodox, heterodox, implementable practices. That is just what is needed, I would say, as much heterodoxy as possible. Which is in some sense what capitalist economic practices offer, except for the preponderance of attempts to evoke another orthodoxy. The new world order, or the new new world order, suggest a trend to another orthodoxy in the midst of practices of exchange and trade that exceed any orthodoxy. The striking thing about the way the global market works is that profits depend on shared desire, while the technology and productivity depend on innovation. So there appears to be an inevitable movement in global development of lurching from one orthodoxy to another, while the lurches and lunges are as heterodox as possible. This frequently has disastrous consequences, and treads heavily on the earth, its creatures and things, and on human cultures—treads upon them and crushes them.

Treading lightly is, then, surely better—except for those already crushed, or left behind, who suffer deprivation so greatly that extreme economic and social measures are required, precisely the measures that entrepreneurial ventures might initiate. Huge dams weigh heavily on the earth and local communities, and far too frequently fail in their social and economic visions. But they respond to social imperatives of poverty and disempowerment. Major industrial projects tend to benefit those already well off, and harm those already harmed. But they do good as well as evil, and every practice does harm.

Which is not to refuse to choose, or to think that any choice is as good as any other, or even to choose industrial capitalism over other economies, but to insist on the excessiveness of practice and choice—in all directions. With the likely implication that we should tread lightly on the earth to avoid great harm—except when we should undertake extreme projects to remedy social and environmental harm. I understand all such decisions to fall under Anaximander's maxim that being itself is injustice, calling for endless restitution. I would pursue an economics of betrayal—*ecolonomics* again.[3]

This may be a different view of economics from any, including Schumacher's, though he addresses the problems to which I am alluding as directly as possible.

> One of the unhealthy and disruptive tendencies in virtually all the developing countries is the emergence, in an ever more accentuated form, of the "dual economy," in which there are two different patterns of living as widely separated from each other as two different worlds. (Schumacher, *SB*, 174)

> What needs to be questioned is the implicit assumption that the modern sector can be expanded to absorb virtually the entire population and that this can be done fairly quickly. (pp. 177–78)

> Development does not start with goods; it starts with people and their education, organisation, and discipline. (p. 178)

The question is how to understand such development—for example, through economics. Perhaps not even a nobler economics. Of course we hope to educate and elevate people. Of course the single factor that offers the greatest possibility of helping people—women—to resist oppression is education, female literacy. Of course social and economic practices must be suffused by practical, knowledgeable, thoughtful, and caring ventures. The question is whether these are all economics, whether there can be a nobler economics, whether the very idea of a noble economics, however thoughtful and caring, evokes an overarching ideal as global as the economics it would resist—the infinite repetition of unlimited powers and unlimited knowledge that human beings are taken to have, even recognizing their own and others' limitations; the recurrent failure to disown the genitive of having the knowledge and powers we need to live.

On the one hand, universal prosperity and the powers of technology and economics, all defined in terms of profit:

> The illusion of unlimited powers, nourished by astonishing scientific and technological achievements, has produced the concurrent illusion of having solved the problem of production. (p. 14)

> I am asking . . . *what sort of meaning the method of economics actually produces*. And the answer to this question cannot be in doubt: something is uneconomic when it fails to earn an adequate profit in terms of money. The method of economics does not, and cannot, produce any other meaning. (p. 44)

On the other hand, the nobler economics: "we must learn to think in terms of an articulated structure that can cope with a multiplicity of small-scale units. If economic thinking cannot grasp this it is useless. If it cannot get beyond its vast abstractions, . . . then let us scrap economics and start afresh" (p. 80). These passages do not insist on a nobler economics, but on scrapping economics if it does not answer to the needs of human life. As if we could, for we cannot scrap exchange and trade. Like other disciplines of similar scale, economics and history represent both the discipline and the practices, life activities, in which humanity and the world are caught up. As if any disciplines might answer to their own generic conditions; as if history or exchange or property or genitivity might lend themselves to settled answers as well as recurrent questions. History, for example, is both the academic discipline and human time itself; human life cannot avoid its historicality, cannot avoid reflecting on historicality; history presents questions of generations and inheritance that reach from one side of the world to the other. Which is by no means to ignore cultures that do not ask explicit questions of history.

All this is to suggest that if the discipline or institutional practice of economics were to be scrapped, human beings would still engage in economic activities; if the discipline or institutional practice of history were to be scrapped—or challenged—human beings would still live in and through history. The question—one question among the many—is whether the disciplinary practice can take hold of the living practices comprehensively or locally and contingently. I respond that excess inhabits every level and scale and moment of life and practice, every cranny of the earth. Environmental or ecological or economic or historical or philosophic authoritarianism is found with regard to the totality—*totalitarian*—and to the locality—*communitarian*. Perhaps the last thing we need is a nobler economics or philosophy that aims to elevate people—all people—according to a standard of height. Including prosperity and genitivity. Even the best of human qualities—intelligence, happiness, serenity, and peacefulness—will be held up as standards against which countless human beings, creatures, and things are to be sacrificed. Sacrificing sacrifice takes place against every standard, however noble, against which some (kinds of) creatures and things and people are measured as unworthy, worthy of sacrifice.

On the one hand, then, Schumacher rejects economics itself because it knows nothing but profit—his words, *money profit*. Yet life is always more than profit. "Society, or a group or individual within society, may decide to hang on to an activity or asset *for non-economic reasons*— social, aesthetic, moral, or political—but this does in no way alter its *uneconomic* character. The judgement of economics, in other words, is an extremely *fragmentary* judgement." (pp. 44–45). In the language I have criticized in Marx: "Economics, moreover, deals with goods in accordance with their market value and not in accordance with what they really are" (p. 46). Promised to infinite and excessive transformation by trade, the fetish wanders, given endless life by exchange. Things in their excessiveness and inexhaustibility take on a wandering life in circulation. Who is to deny their value to those who would pay for them, however unprofitably, however uselessly—except those who know what is noble, what is comprehensive?

What of rejecting profit but emphasizing circulation and exchange, understanding these to be where things wander in all sorts of social, aesthetic, moral, and political ways? What of understanding the fragmentariness of economics as what we may hope to foster—that is, circulate more widely— against all visions of totality?

Including Buddhism, understood as a total point of view, however laudatory: "The Buddhist point of view takes the function of work to be at least threefold: to give a man a chance to utilise and develop his faculties; to enable him to overcome his ego-centredness by joining with other people in a common task; and to bring forth the goods and services needed for a becoming existence" (p. 58). The bee takes honey from the flower without harming it. More to the point, perhaps, the bee takes pollen and turns it into honey here and there, wandering, nomadically. It is inconceivable that there might be a world of bees brought under a central authority—or a world of bee-hives brought under a central beekeeper. Beekeepers are creatures of their bees. Schumacher acknowledges something similar: "From an economist's point of view, the marvel of the Buddhist way of life is the utter rationality of its pattern—amazingly small means leading to extraordinarily satisfactory results" (pp. 60–61). I might add that from another point of view—perhaps still economic—Buddhist practices lend themselves to systems of social order in which many fail to flourish. The very best values Schumacher articulates belong to social systems of oppression and poverty: "We can say that man's management of the land must be primarily orientated towards three goals—health, beauty, and permanence. The fourth goal—the only one accepted by the experts—productivity, will then be attained almost as a by-product" (p. 119). I'm all for health and beauty; I'm not all for permanence; and I hope for prosperity for all who desire it. The earth has not stood still in its evolutionary history; why should we want it to do so now? Yet I would remember the deer and the possibility that in the name of owning the earth, human beings will destroy everything they can, harming themselves in the name of their own prosperity. I believe the answer lies in impermanence, resisting permanence, especially the permanence of domination and harm. Human possessiveness is not the only exploitation of the earth.

But of course, I have quite misrepresented Schumacher, taking one side of his economics—call it anti-economics or non-economics—much too seriously. For instead of an economics of permanence, an economics for all, Schumacher proposes the pluralization and multiplication of economies, another view of human life entirely. First locality:

> The real task may be formulated in four propositions:
> *First*, that workplaces have to be created in the areas where the people are living now, . . .
> *Second*, that these workplaces must be, on average, cheap enough so that they can be created in large numbers. . . .
> *Third*, that the production methods employed must be relatively simple. . . .
> *Fourth*, that production should be mainly from local materials and mainly for local use. (p. 186)

He calls it intermediate technology. But it answers to the dual economy without denying industrialization.

1. The "dual economy" in the developing countries will remain for the foreseeable future. . . .

3. The poor can be helped to help themselves, but only by making available to them a technology that recognises the economic boundaries and limitations of poverty—an intermediate technology.

4. Action programmes on a national and supranational basis are needed to develop intermediate technologies. . . . (pp. 200–1)

Large-scale organizations and globalization will not go away. Here, however, Schumacher passes from production, exchange, and trade to democracy, as if economics and politics cannot be separated. Five principles of organization:

> . . . *The Principle of Subsidiarity.* . . . It is an injustice and at the same time a grave evil and disturbance of right order to assign to a greater and higher association what lesser and subordinate organisations can do. . . .
> . . . *The Principle of Vindication.* . . . Good government is always government by exception. Except for exceptional cases, the subsidiary unit must be defended against reproach and upheld. . . .
> . . . *The Principle of Identification.* Each subsidiary unit or quasi-firm must have both a profit and loss account and a balance sheet. . . .
> . . . *The Principle of Motivation.* It is a trite and obvious truism that people act in accordance with their motives. All the same, for a large organisation, . . . motivation is the central problem. . . .
> . . . *The Principle of the Middle Axiom.* . . .
> . . . All real human problems arise from the *antinomy* of order and freedom. . . .
> . . . What is required is something in between, a *middle axiom*, an order from above which is yet not quite an order. (pp. 260–68)[4]

Anarchism, democracy, economics of human scale can be understood, he argues, in relation to two conditions: the excessive circulation of goods and things among human beings and throughout the earth with as little judgment as possible by others of what is good and bad; coupled with the production of organizations—corporate, entrepreneurial, institutional, and political—of intermediate size. In terms of genitivity: maximal circulation coupled with minimal consumption and accumulation (of both profit and structure). The sole justification for large-scale organization is to maximize circulation and exchange, which such organization typically impedes.

I believe that what we may hope to learn from Schumacher is less sustainability than intermediarity. But intermediarity is better understood as intermediariness—that is, velocity of circulation—than it is as a middle measure, a mean. As Buddhism suggests—again, calling for wariness at the possibility that it may lose intermediariness in its political and social world:

"The inherent ecological wisdom of Buddhism is likewise expressed in its reluctance to set anything up as a center to which everything else must refer" (Batchelor, *BER*, 181).

If Schumacher is not our champion of sustainability, but of inter-mediariness, let us turn back to Berry, in one voice championing sustain-ability, in another voice something otherwise. I postpone much of the otherwise to the next chapter. I stay here with returning and restoring, giving back. "In the recovery of culture *and* nature is the knowledge of how to farm well, how to preserve, harvest, and replenish the forests, how to make, build, and use, return and restore. In this *double* recovery, which is the recovery of our humanity, is the hope that the domestic and the wild can exist together in lasting harmony" (Berry, *HE*, 142). We have seen that Berry resists squandering and hoarding, the forms whereby human beings insist on claiming the right to accumulate and consume the fruits of the earth at any cost, with no regard to what they have been given. Taking and seizing without return, without giving back. Against this, we may under-stand harmony, balance, and mutuality as conditions of a beneficent life and practice. "If balance is the ruling principle and a stable balance the goal, then, for humans, attaining this goal requires a consciously chosen and deliberately made partnership with nature" (pp. 14–15). Understood in terms of scale—*a proper human scale*—which I have suggested is having, genitivity again. Intermediariness is perhaps not proper, but something else, more interesting and fluid, less dwelling than nomadic. Lasting har-mony suggests fostering permanence rather than celebrating abundance. The goal is not the nobler, better life—anarchists are too suspicious for that—but resistance to the institutional and organizational impediments to life itself, whatever that may be, wherever that may go.

Something similar can be heard in Berry, against propriety—against sustainability. Berry hates the way we are forced by propriety to take sides. Good anarchists hate to be pushed around by large institutions and forces that claim to have their best interests at heart. Even where they agree with them as to the best, they resist the coerciveness as the worst, including the coerciveness of the very best democracy. Wildness in the earth presents us with the earth itself as the ongoing question of being in an ethical register: what there is and how to live and be *for the sake of the good*, that is, for the sake of the earth and its abundance. "The argument over the proper relation of humanity to nature is becoming, as the sixties used to say, polarized. And the result, as before, is bad talk on both sides. At one ex-treme are those who sound as if they are entirely in favor of nature; they assume that there is no necessary disjuncture or difference between the human estate and the estate of nature, that human good is in some simple way the same as natural good" (Berry, *HE,* 137). Berry describes this as an argument over propriety, yet what he has to say resists every propriety. "At the other extreme are the nature conquerors, who have no patience with an old-fashioned outdoor farm, let alone a wilderness. These people divide all reality into two parts: human good, which they define as profit, comfort, and security; and everything else, which they understand as a stockpile of 'natural resources' or 'raw materials,' which will sooner or later be transformed into a human good" (pp. 137–38). It is essential to choose, and Berry is prepared to choose—if one must choose, if choice is relevant. Properly. "If I had to choose, I would join the nature extremists against the technology extremists, but this choice seems poor, even assuming that it is possible. I would prefer to stay in the middle, not to avoid taking sides, but because I think the middle *is* a side, as well as the real location of the problem" (p. 138).

The middle, I suggest, is intermediariness, not a place in between. I understand occupying the middle as circulation rather than dwelling. Wilderness is a figure of intermediariness without dwelling.

> 1. We live in wilderness, in which we and our works occupy a tiny space and play a tiny part. . . .
>
> 3. That we depend on what we are endangered by is a problem not solvable by "problem solving." . . .
>
> 6. To use or not to use nature is not a choice that is available to us; we can live only at the expense of other lives. Our choice has rather to do with how and how much to use. . . . There is, thus, no *practical* way that we can intend the good of the world; practice can only be local.
>
> 7. If there is no escape from the human use of nature, then human good cannot be simply synonymous with natural good. (pp. 138-39)

These assumptions express life itself, being itself, human being in the earth itself, as ethical, for the sake of the good—that is, giving beyond having. I do not think they express giving back or permanence, but local practices and local goods within the abundance, giving where one is and what one can. "What these assumptions describe, of course, is the human predicament. It is a spiritual predicament, for it requires us to be properly humble and grateful" (p. 139). Humility and gratitude on the side of preservation—remembering that conservation can be authoritarian—or an ethics of generosity resistant to every authority, especially one's own? Both movements can be heard in Berry. "[I]t is a mistake to proceed on the basis of an assured division or divisibility between nature and humanity, or wildness and domesticity. But it is also a mistake to assume that there is no difference between the natural and the human" (p. 140); a mistake to take any identities for granted—intermediariness again—including harmony and goodness. "Harmony is one phase, the good phase, of the inescapable dialogue between culture and nature. In this phase, humans consciously and conscientiously ask of their work: Is this good for us? Is this good for our place?" (p. 143). If it is something we can know, for ourselves and in our place.

He speaks of conservation, propriety, and love; I hear him speak of giving in abundance—love and care—beyond propriety and preservation. "The only thing that we have to preserve nature with is culture; the only thing we have to preserve wildness with is domesticity" (p. 143). All we have are love and care, an ethics of cherishment: caring for, caring about, caring everywhere in every place. "I would call this a loving economy . . . a particularizing love for local things, rising out of local knowledge and local allegiance" (p. 144). A local and contingent love that knows nothing of propriety, insisting on its name. "We could argue that an age that *properly* valued and cared for material things would be an age properly spiritual" (pp. 144–45); "it is not primarily the number of people inhabiting a landscape that determines the propriety of the ratio and the relation between human domesticity and wildness, but it is the way the people divide the landscape and use it" (p. 151). I would resist the propriety even of good use and spirituality. Abundance gives beyond genitivity. It is time to pursue this abundance beyond itself.

# CHAPTER 15

## *Giving*

I am assuming that the Great Economy, whatever we may name it, is indeed . . . an economy. It includes principles and patterns by which values or powers or necessities are parceled out and exchanged. But if the Great Economy comprehends humans and thus cannot be comprehended by them, then it is also not an economy in which humans can participate directly. . . . There is no human accounting for the Great Economy. (Berry, *HE*, 57)

Whatever the name, the human economy, if it is to be a good economy, must fit harmoniously within and must correspond to the Great Economy; in certain ways, it must be an analogue of the Great Economy. (p. 59)

In the vernacular, in a voice of sustenance and harmony, Berry describes two economies remarkably similar to general and restricted economy: the great and small economies, the earth's and humanity's economies. With this gesture we come to another sense of giving beyond having, after the examples we have so far considered: ecstasy, squander, generosity, and sustenance. Perhaps not another sense, an alternative or substitute for them, but *an other sense*, present in them as promise, perhaps, but also supplement, where giving exceeds each gift, uncontained and uncontainable, not something else, not another gift.

As Berry and I would insist, the great economy, the earth, is not a discrete economy, different from human or other creatures' economies, but is what makes them possible, enables them to be economies, enables human beings and other living creatures to live—I would say, makes it possible for anything to be. And there are many small economies but perhaps only one great economy, one general economy—or no number or measure of such an economy. Each kind of thing, each kind of living creature, circulates in the earth as the kind it is, circulates in general economy by belonging to the small economies in which it participates and which it helps to form. "The fowls of the air and the lilies of the field live within the Great Economy entirely by nature, whereas humans, though entirely dependent upon it, must live in it partly by artifice. The birds can live in the Great Economy only as birds, the flowers only as flowers, the humans only as humans" (p. 58).

A number of questions arise here: for example, whether the term *economy* undermines the thought and practice of general economy, restricts abundance. Another is whether the great economy evokes totality and harmony, recalling Heidegger's nostalgia for the orderliness of things. We may admire disjointure, disorder, yet yearn for jointure, hope to settle down. We may remain sedentary people, hoping to dwell more closely in the earth. This is the theme of sustenance and dwelling, considered in the last chapter. Here I hope to pursue abundance beyond dwelling.

If we decide to remain with *economy*, with *two economies*, it is to insist that what we may hope to express of giving and having cannot be expressed in one economy, general or restricted, great or small. The excess of abundance is expressed in each economy, in the multiplicities and heterogeneities of small or restricted economies, in the abundance and giving of great or general economy—but also, in the heterogeneous, excessive, and abundant relations between the different economies, in interstices where there is no measure, where we cannot choose general economy over restricted economy, where it is nothing save the interruption and abundance of each restricted economy. A *nothing* that expresses abundance and heterogeneity. In the name of genitivity and property, it expresses disowning and expropriation: giving without having, beyond having, beyond the gifts we may hope to have.

Here a fissure opens up between Berry and abundance, though I regard his two economies to express general and restricted economy as truthfully as possible—in the vernacular. This is to say that general economy is haunted by the humanity of the vernacular economy, haunted in its giving by human gifts. Which is in a certain way truthful and unavoidable, and in another way untruthful and misleading. The danger is in thinking that giving gives nothing but gifts, when every gift betrays the giving, however wonderful and joyous it is to receive, and as if giving were nothing but generosity and hospitality, giving gifts. Giving is nothing without gifts, as gifts are nothing without giving, lending themselves to exchange beyond having or possession. Every gift is promised to a circulation beyond having. Promised! The circulation is not had in the promise, not even had as a promise, but promised to a giving that may never take place, may never be had, but haunts the gift in every place it is received. Coveting is the yearning, the desire, to break the promise, to receive what was promised against the call to return it to circulation as another promise.

One expression of this difficult relation between general and restricted economy is as the endless promising to have that is endlessly given, endless giving, betrayed at every turn by coveting, by taking and receiving, insisting on grasping—in the double sense of betrayal in which the giving is both violated and revealed. Revelation is the bringing to light, displaying in the human economy, taking and possessing what cannot be owned or had. Revelation brings to having, in the genitive, always mine or ours, a giving beyond having. Revealed—betrayed—to me or us; of and from an abundance in which disclosure insists on closure, insists on boundaries that fix and enclose; where the boundaries delimit an abundance, a giving, beyond enclosure. Beyond having, beyond genitivity, belongs to genitivity and having as betrayal, in interruption. Beyond genitivity is betrayed as interruption. Giving interrupts having doubly in that it makes having possible—restricted economy—and that it cannot be contained by any property—general economy.

Berry almost says this, as clearly and radiantly as can be said in the vernacular—which is not to suggest that the vernacular fails. It may be possible to say these things only in the vernacular, some vernacular, including the vernacular of philosophy, which does not own the right to say better than any other vernacular the hidden truths of life and the good. Nor do religion or God. I postpone God and religion to remain with Berry, who speaks of the great economy as if it were the earth's economy—the Kingdom of God:

> [T]he first principle of the Kingdom of God is that it includes everything; in it, the fall of every sparrow is a significant event. We are in it whether we know it or not and whether we wish to be or not. Another principle, both ecological and traditional, is that everything in the Kingdom of God is joined both to it and to everything else that is in it; that is to say, the Kingdom of God is orderly. A third principle is that humans do not and can never know either all the creatures that the Kingdom of God contains or the whole pattern or order by which to contain them. (p. 55)

As if it were the gifts rather than the giving. We cannot count all the creatures or things, all the gifts of nature or God. We cannot know or comprehend the great economy. Perhaps, I would say, because comprehension does not pertain to it, because the great economy is not more inclusive than the small economy, the human or global economy, not because the human economy is small and nature's economy is large, one included by the other, not because the order of the whole exceeds the order of the parts, but because order and measure do not pertain to abundance. Giving is beyond measure and order. So that I disagree with what Berry says, though not perhaps with what he means: the kingdom of God is not orderly because order does not pertain to nature or God.[1] Giving gives gifts, and the gifts betray the giving. Even so, the ideal is order. And why not disorder? Why not heterogeneity, multiplicity, disarray? Why is the kingdom of God—the great economy—not order *and* disorder? Not the two together as if each helped the other to be itself, as if they belonged to each other, but something uncontainable in each? The two otherwise in betrayal.

Alterity is at stake, insisting on betrayal—perhaps something that Berry finally rejects; that environmental philosophers and ecologists reject—beyond the human or divine. Nature itself as other, alter, otherwise, heterogeneous, where order, harmony, and jointure are not ideal, do not make up the idea. Disorder too may be ideal—if anything is ideal. Disorder is sometimes better than order.

I suggested in the last chapter that proportion and order can become tyrannies—conditions, states, or properties to hold onto and to have; not intermediaries, given to endless circulation. Berry speaks of creating value, I would speak of giving gifts in abundance, to which human beings respond with values, always betrayed: "though a human economy can evaluate, distribute, use, and preserve things of value, it cannot make value. Value can originate only in the Great Economy. . . . When humans presume to originate value, they make value that is first abstract and then false, tyrannical, and destructive of real value" (Berry, *HE*, 61–62). A human, restricted economy cannot make value—perhaps with Locke and his successors in mind, including Marx and Engels, who imagine that labor produces value. And perhaps the term *value* is misleading, given its history in human economies. But whatever human beings do, whether they labor, produce, or distribute, whether they buy or sell, accumulate or consume, if these are or express values, they can do so only because of what they have been given. Being is being thrown, not as human into genitivity, but as giving, thrown as stone or sparrow or blade of grass into histories, inheritances, and movements of things.

I understand thrownness as embodied touch, skin to skin, surface to surface, reaching into the depths, touch touching touch.[2] Touch is the having and the giving, the receiving and the bestowing; but touch cannot be held or accumulated and cannot be consumed. It passes away into giving, escapes consumption and squander into exuberance and mourning. But neither mourning nor exuberance takes and holds though it must receive the gift. And give; receive the giving and respond.

Berry's wonderful lucidity is his ability to find a telling example of nature's economy beyond human economy, if not general economy. An example of giving and abundance without which human life would disappear. With a hesitation. The example is topsoil. "We cannot speak of topsoil, indeed we cannot know what it is, without acknowledging at the outset that we cannot make it. We can care for it (or not), we can even, as we say 'build' it, but we can do so only by assenting to, preserving, and perhaps collaborating in its own processes. To those processes themselves we have nothing to contribute" (p. 62). Now scientists today are attempting to make (or build) topsoil, or at least to make it better, or to make topsoil from dead soil, from something. The point is that life requires topsoil, that human life has been given topsoil, that even if we can make new topsoil out of something else, we must have been given that. Rochelle reminds us that we have been given stones as well, and that she too has been given topsoil in which to rest. Giving is the condition of being, except that human beings have forgotten giving even when they give gifts; have forgotten that giving cannot come to rest. In the most exploitive taking and hoarding there is giving, even restitution. Willy-nilly, perhaps, without the conscience and attention that human beings might otherwise give. Without responsibility and ethicality; if with responsiveness, insistence, and betrayal.

Berry returns to sustenance, resisting the possibility of other abundances in the earth, touching nevertheless upon the immeasure of abundance.

> Like the rich man of the parable, the industrialist thinks to escape the persistent obligations of the human condition by means of "much goods laid up for many years"—by means, in other words, of quantities: resources, supplies, stockpiles, funds, reserves. But this is a grossly oversimplifying dream and, thus, a dangerous one. . . . The topsoil exists as such because it is ceaselessly transforming death into life, ceaselessly supplying food and water to all that lives in it and from it. . . .
> But the industrial use of *any* "resource" implies its exhaustion. (pp. 67–68)

Nature and abundance are inexhaustible. Which is not to say that in any place there is enough topsoil or water—though the problem is less too little soil or water than how they are distributed. Sustainable practices are dwellings, sedentary, in their places. They return what they are given, and recognize the goodness of giving and gifts. But they remain sedentary, favor order and harmony and jointure. Berry knows that nature's economy bears the fruits of cacophony and disorder as well as harmony and order; that in the name of order and harmony, powerful human beings enslave others.

We return to the question of authority: under whose or what dominion are limits to be instituted? "Any little economy that sees itself as unlimited is obviously self-blinded. It does not see its real relation to the Great Economy; in fact, it does not see that there *is* a Great Economy. Instead, it calls the Great Economy 'raw material' or 'natural resources' or 'nature' and proceeds with the business of putting it 'under control.' " (p. 69) For if nature is inexhaustible, then it knows no limits. And if desire is excessive, then it is unlimited. Corresponding to two economies are two meanings of limitlessness: the very large, available as a resource; abundance, beyond use or possession. These turn repeatedly around genitivity. What we may own or have, a sphere of things to call our own; an economy beyond owning and having, including having order. "The problem seems to be that a human economy cannot prescribe the terms of its own success. . . . It is indeed possible for a human economy to be wrong— . . . but wrong absolutely and according to practical measures" (p. 71).

Here Berry's image of two economies ceases to express what I mean by general and restricted economy. Where nature, the earth, the great economy privileges order, harmony, propriety, where it gives human beings the absolute conditions of good and bad, right and wrong, where it *prescribes* to human and other beings what human economies cannot prescribe. Under that heading, in the name of what is natural, human beings have done more harm, perhaps, than under any other. Many who are driven by ethical and political concerns, who care for oppressed and disempowered human beings, domesticated animals and habitats, hope to avoid another subjection to natural order. Under the noblest headings, human beings glorify sacrifice.

What might it mean to sacrifice sacrifice, to resist its glorification under the heading of these two economies? What might it mean to disown owning, expropriate appropriation, to give rather than to have, to remember nature's abundance in resistance to every authority? What might it mean to betray betrayal in relation to the earth? Here I would consider another reading of Berry's two economies, emphasizing not nature's propriety, prescribing right and wrong, but the impropriety of every human economy: insisting on modesty, humility, and wonder before the abundance of things, not to debase human achievements but to revel in their excessiveness beyond themselves. This beyond is not outside anything or the world, but the excessiveness of every place, every economy, every order, the impropriety of every propriety. The order of human economy is exceeded in the abundance of nature—perhaps by endless orders, by endless disorders. The authority of human economy is exceeded in the lack of authority of nature—interrupted by abundance.

We return to the sense that general economy is nothing—as interruption and betrayal; that the abundance of nature prescribes nothing—incessantly disauthorizing authority and deneutralizing neutrality; that a human, restricted economy cannot prescribe the conditions of its success to itself, does not work for its own sake or for the sake of human beings or for anything else, including nature or God, and cannot justify any such kind of work; nor does something else, Nature or God or The Good, so prescribe, define the end for human economy. To the contrary, perhaps, or otherwise. Human economies work for the sake of whatever goods they can attain, in the light of responsibilities that answer to the condition that nothing represents the end of such work, that no authority justifies such work, that a restricted economy cannot justify itself and cannot be justified by anything else, and that this lack is not an absence or a defect or a failure but abundance and excess. I understand this condition as betrayal, betraying the limits of every limit as not another limit but abundance and excess, expressed as interruption; that this interruption in abundance is not a failed or diminished or broken responsibility—*impossible responsibility*—but excess, abundance, endless responsibility; not as a burden, affliction, sinfulness, or debt, but as a joyful abundance of responsiveness, care, and love in the earth for all things everywhere; exceeding every measure of fulfillment of responsibility; exceeding the immeasure of the impossibility of that fulfillment. Excess betrayed.

I cannot overemphasize this last point—I must reiterate it excessively. General economy does not mark restricted economies with failure and calamity; these are not what I mean by betrayal—though as restricted they must betray themselves and others. Betrayal carries the doubled sense of treachery and expression; and what is expressed and betrayed is abundance. Restricted economies express their achievements and their failings, the fulfillment of responsibilities and the inevitable lack of fulfillment. Injustice cries out on all sides, together with restitutions and accomplishments, if not with justice; or with finite, excessive justice interrupted on all sides, riddled through and through with injustice, betrayed incessantly by injustice—thereby exposing the possibility and goodness of justice. The impossibility of justice *is* justice; the betrayal of being by injustice *is* justice, betrays justice, betrays the injustice in justice.

We return to genitivity. Giving betrays the excessiveness in having, both too much having, too much insistence on owning, possessing, and accumulating, and the impossibility of owning, possessing, holding, having without giving, generosity, hospitality, welcome. Giving interrupts, disowns, expropriates the inheritances that we have received and hope to keep; reminding us that if they could be kept forever, we could not receive them; that the condition of receiving, having, and taking is that gifts be given, that giving is in abundance, that every gift is given to be given again, given in return, given in ways that cannot be known or held securely. Responsibility—responsivity, betrayal—is this condition and the answering: giving in touch, responding sensitively and caringly to the things around us in the abundance of the earth. We are called to answer, to respond to what is given to us, sometimes without the slightest knowledge of either the question or the answer, still in debt—the debt of being in abundance among the things and creatures and kinds of the earth. In the generosity of the earth.

Every saying, every expression, every response to this generosity is betrayal. And as frequently as we may repeat the betrayal, hope to betray the betrayal on both its sides, we are led from one side to the other. Here indeed, in Berry's two economies, I insist that we may see betrayed, revealed, expressed, what it means to belong to the earth's abundance, in as harmonious and caring a way as possible. Berry reveals cherishment to us, cherishes cherishment—if perhaps he does not know sacrifice as vividly as I would hope, if he does not come to sacrifice sacrifice because he does not betray its hatefulness or inescapability or destructiveness intensely enough. As I suggested in the previous chapter, we may not be able to care for people elsewhere in the earth if we insist on too much harmony, too much order. At whose expense? With what destruction and disorder? Who benefits from the order? Who and what?

In this difficult dialectic—if that is what it is, if anything is dialectical except in the discipline of philosophy—of betrayal and abundance, we find ourselves repeatedly turning toward the betrayals of betrayal. Pursuing this adventure further—it may be life itself, being itself—I turn from Berry back to Derrida, to reconsider economy in a different register, especially economies of sacrifice and giving; to reconsider the taking that betrays the giving, the sacrifice that betrays. In particular, the gift of death: "sacrificing oneself for another, *dying for the other*, thus perhaps giving one's life by giving oneself death, accepting the gift of death" (Derrida, *GD*, 10).

*The Gift of Death* is a reading of Jan Patočka and Kierkegaard on the arrival of responsibility. If responsibility can be said to arrive. Two Christian philosophers on the gift. Including a reading of Nietzsche on Christian *ressentiment*. I would resist too close an affinity in my reading with Patočka and Kierkegaard. I will pass over Kierkegaard almost entirely; too much has been said of his economy of sacrifice, Abraham's sacrifice, founding history itself. I will touch upon Patočka as little as possible, through the prism of Derrida's gaze. Instead, I propose to stay with Derrida, to refrain even from exploring the Christianization of responsibility. With the single remark that we must beware of the possibility that someone or something—the Catholic Church, for example—might claim to own or possess the truth of responsibility, might claim to have the right to ethics, to life itself, human and otherwise. That would be a supreme and excessive hoarding of the gift without the least memory of giving; an extreme example of the betrayal of giving into gifts without responsibility for the sake of the giving; of coveting gifts without memory of the giving that interrupts every having; of hoping to possess the secret of giving as if it were a gift, whether from God or nature or beyond or otherwise. "The genesis of responsibility that Patočka proposes . . . will be combined with a genealogy of the subject . . . as being before the other: . . . one who regards without being seen but also whose infinite goodness *gives* in an experience that amounts to a *gift of death [donner la mort]*" (Derrida, *GD*, 3). Responsibility, liberty, singularity, and infinite goodness are all *something* that is given, given to *someone*, that can be given, that can be received and taken, held in secret, even where the taking is said to be impossible—for example, the gift of death.

An aporia:

> *On the one hand,* the history of responsibility is tied to a history of religion. . . . What would responsibility be if it were motivated, conditioned, made possible by a history? . . .
>
> *On the other hand,* . . . History can be neither a decidable object nor a totality capable of being mastered, precisely because it is tied to *responsibility,* to *faith,* and to the *gift.* (pp. 5–6)

This aporia revels in the impossibilities of faith, death, and responsibility. The impossible impossibly becomes possible—no more impossible, one might say, than God becoming Man, spirit becoming matter. Faith, death, and responsibility confront impossibility impossibly, insist on possibility, insist that Christianity may know something of these impossibilities unknown to others, unknown elsewhere. Supreme arrogance perhaps.

But a prior, more difficult thought is present here, in the context of the repeated suggestion that responsibility is impossible and giving is nothing, that this nothing and impossibility open themselves to the authority and arrogance that consists in mastering nothing, in gaining authority over impossibility: the Church's authority over faith, for example. I keep returning to Christianity when I said I would hold it at bay. But it represents a metonymic figure—that is how I will hold onto it, hold it at bay—of the dilemmas of the impossible and beyond. Either the good is something that can be known, held in hand, pursued however difficult it may be to achieve it—fully genitivized; or if the good is impossible, unknowable, beyond, it cannot be pursued, cannot be promised if it can never be grasped. What is justice if it cannot be possessed? What is the good if it cannot be had? To which my repeated answer is that it is not a gift but the giving, and that no one masters or knows or can hold onto the giving, which keeps on moving. But in the motion, in the wandering, in the abundance are interruptions that betray the possibility of living for the sake of the good—which is nothing. The betrayal is that the nothing always becomes something—the double sense of betrayal. We may not be able to avoid the betrayal of holding onto, as if it were a gift, something that is no gift and cannot be held. We may not desire to avoid the betrayal. After all, we must have the means to live, must have the means to act responsibly. But perhaps we may avoid insisting on having the truth and means of having, on having the giving as if it were a gift rather than giving, on coveting and hoarding and accumulating what cannot be had. Perhaps we may betray, resist, reveal the betrayal by sacrificing sacrifice and by disowning owning, giving beyond having—which never means *without* having.

We may address this (im)possibility by bypassing responsibility and giving to consider the death in the gift of death, both in its historicality and as the mark, the repeated figure, of giving and gifts. For Patočka reminds us of the famous event in Western philosophy when Plato gives us responsibility, triumphing over mystery, as the gift of Socrates' death. Derrida's words: "The incorporation by means of which Platonic responsibility triumphs over orgiastic mystery is the movement by which the immortality of the individual soul is affirmed—it is also the death given to Socrates, . . . the death that he in a way gives himself when in the *Phaedo* he develops a whole discourse to give sense to his death and as it were to take the responsibility for it upon himself" (p. 11). This gift is given in what Derrida describes as "The famous passage of the *Phaedo* (80e) that Patočka obliquely refers to but neither analyzes nor even cites" (p. 13):

> This canonical passage is one of the most often cited, or at least evoked, in the history of philosophy. It is rarely subjected to a close reading. . . . The soul only distinguishes itself, separates itself, and assembles within itself in the experience of this *melete tou thanatou*. It is nothing other than this concern for dying as a relation to self and an assembling of self. . . . Philosophy isn't something that comes to the soul by accident, for it is nothing other than this vigil over death that watches out for death and watches over death, as if over the very life of the soul. (pp. 14–15)

The canonicity refers to the famous dialogue by Plato, to the philosophical event named with Plato's proper name, and to the event in which philosophy constitutes the individual and responsible self as obsessed with death.[3] The gift of death is enmired in genitivity, together with sacrifice. With absolute certainty. "I know on absolute grounds and in an absolutely certain manner that I will never deliver the other from his death, from the death that affects his whole being. . . . I can give the other everything except immortality, except this *dying for her* to the extent of dying in place of her and so freeing her from her own death" (Derrida, *GD*, 43). With absolute certainty concerning absolute impossibility, I know that every impossibility essential to the soul and self and its goodness belongs to an economy of sacrifice.

I cannot give the gift of death to an other because death belongs to me as my own ownmost potentiality for being. The possibility of no longer being in the world belongs to *Dasein* entirely in the genitive: *his, mine, my own.* Yet can one give the gift of life to others, perhaps to oneself, or does the gift of life, like the gift of death, arrive without giver or gift? Can one give life, can one take life, or are these givings that cannot be given or taken or held or consumed? The giving—but perhaps not the gift—of death;

the death that gives life to others and calls them from themselves? Can one give beauty, justice, or truth—or perhaps a beautiful work, a just law, a truthful claim? *We are called to act for the sake of the good, which is nothing* says, if we listen carefully, that the good cannot be given, taken, or owned, cannot be accumulated, consumed, or squandered, but gives gifts— for example, beauty, truth, and justice—which like the good are nothing but are endlessly claimed as something in the genitive, something had, possessed, or owned.

I may not have read the famous passage carefully enough, but I read it as addressing the possibility that philosophy, together with its descendants, is an obsession with death, and that Socrates questions both the obsession and the genitivity of death with his own, impending death.[4] And at an age in which I find myself obsessed more and more with death, I question the obsession. Not obsession with death, which perhaps deserves obsession, together with mourning and grief for others. Not perhaps obsession with my death, which, I would say, may not be my own, may never be mine in the genitive. I would question philosophy's obsession with death with Nietzsche who pursues a philosophy obsessed—perhaps that is no longer the word: *enthralled*—with life, beyond justice, truth, and beauty. "For all the value that the true, the truthful, the selfless may deserve, it would still be possible that a higher and more fundamental value for life might have to be ascribed to deception, selfishness, and lust. . . . Maybe!" (Nietzsche, *BGE*, #2), Perhaps to recognize that obsession with death and entrancement with life partake of desire beyond desire, betray the giving of death beyond any gifts.

Socrates does not, I believe, give the gift of death to his friends, but gives them in their fear and obsession with death the gift of life; or because that gift also cannot be given, gives them his philosophy, the memory of his life and death, and in that memory they are promised the possibility of living for the sake of the good. He gives them what cannot be given but is giving itself. He gives them gifts in memory of what is no gift, not death, not life, not being, not goodness, but the insistence that they live and die, seek truth and goodness all for the sake of something beyond these, something more obsessive than any of them, than any thing or any gift. The good, Nature's abundance. Not something. Nothing.

The obsession with death that constitutes the (Western, European) self is perhaps *Christian* more than Greek or Jewish. And perhaps the point of this obsession—that is, the obsession with the obsession that Derrida marks in reading Patočka is that it is Christian, if not Greek, falls under a proper name, in the genitive. Of a kind, I would insist. But that is another story.[5] Not the self itself, *Dasein*'s generality or genitivity, but Christianity's genitivity, the Christian self. The Judeo-Greek-Christian tradition takes the gift of life as the gift that cannot be given, the gift of death, under proper names: Abraham, Socrates, Christ. The meaning of life is death; the way to eternal, free, responsible life is death. What philosophy offers (Greek-Judeo-Christian) life is an economy of sacrifice. What we must have, in the genitive, must make our own, have as our own, to live, is to know how and what to sacrifice. "The logic of this conservative rupture resembles the *economy of a sacrifice* that keeps what it gives up" (Derrida, *GD,* 8). Keeping, holding, insisting on having what one takes as betraying what one cannot have, coveting gifts that betray giving.

This, I take it, is why Derrida dwells on Kierkegaard, not in virtue of Patočka's reading, but because Kierkegaard spells out the infinite authority of Abraham's economy of sacrifice: infinite responsibility as uncanny silence unto death. One economy of sacrifice enclosing, exchanged for, two economies. "One would thus be tempted to distinguish two economies, or one economy with two systems: *incorporation* and *repression*" (p. 21): "essentially political," based on the "axiom, namely, that history never effaces what it buries; it always keeps within itself the secret of whatever it encrypts, the secret of its secret" (p. 21): incorporation, repression, mystery, secrecy, silence. All in the genitive, holding on to what cannot be held, hoarding what must be promised to exchange if it belongs to eternal life. For the gift, the generosity beyond having and taking, always returns, sacrifices itself to take from the giving. The generosity is given in an economy of sacrifice unto death.

> Between on the one hand this denial that involves renouncing the self, this abnegation of the gift, of goodness, or of the generosity of the gift that must withdraw, hide, in fact sacrifice itself in order to give, and on the other hand the repression that would transform the gift into an economy of sacrifice, is there not a secret affinity . . . ? . . . Such is the rupture . . . between the metaphysics, ethics, and politics of the Platonic Good (that is, the "incorporated" orgiastic mystery) and the *mysterium tremendum* of Christian responsibility . . . (pp. 30–31)

Terror, death, and repentance lie in the rupture between what Patočka and, perhaps, Derrida think of as the ethics and politics of the Platonic Good— by no means what I think of as the good in Plato—and the *mysterium tremendum* of Christian responsibility, in whose name sacrifice unto death is called for. Always demanding the sacrifices of others constituting *Us*— Socrates, Christ, Saint Joan, and others: Isaac and the children of Israel, the sacrifice of Jews for Christian Europe, always it seems the sacrifice of animals; the sacrifice of those who must suffer and die in the name of someone's Good, someone's responsibility. The economy of sacrifice. Constituting Us.

Derrida never leaves the Greek-Judeo-Christianity of ethics, the gene-alogy that claims to possess responsibility—even the good—under a univer-sal name without knowing its limitations. The gift—of death—that insists on having what cannot be had, insists on halting the circulation. "The gift made to me by God as he holds me in his gaze and in his hand while remaining inaccessible to me, the terribly dissymmetrical gift of the *mysterium tremendum* only allows me to respond and only rouses me to the responsibility it gives me by making a gift of death, giving the secret of death, a new experience of death" (p. 33). However impossibly. "It is always a matter of seeing coming what one can't see coming, of giving oneself that which one can probably never give oneself . . . giving itself or reappropriating what in fact it cannot simply appropriate" (p. 40); trans-forming giving into gift, the good into goodness, instituting an economy of sacrifice forgetful of itself, betraying giving. Returning us insistently to the economy of sacrifice in which ethics has been enmired from the beginning of philosophy—if there were a beginning to philosophy or ethics or respon-sibility; if there could be an economy of sacrifice, however impossibly, if impossibility could be the condition of the possibility of goodness, if death could be the condition of the possibility of life. "What is given—and this would also represent a kind of death—is not some thing, but goodness itself, a giving goodness, the act of giving or the donation of the gift. A goodness that must not only forget itself but whose source remains inac-cessible to the donee. . . . My irreplaceability is therefore conferred, deliv-ered, 'given,' one can say, by death" (p. 41). The point, perhaps, of the economy of sacrifice is this irreplaceability, *Dasein*'s singularity, marked by death. Not by life, by giving, but taking and holding the singular gift of death. "One has to *give it to oneself by taking it upon oneself,* for it can only be mine alone, irreplaceably. That is so even if, as we just said, *death can neither be taken nor given.* But the idea of being neither taken nor given relates from or *to* the other, and that is indeed why one can give it *to oneself* only by taking it *upon oneself*" (p. 45). Assumed as death. Taken as death, my own death, the one thing that no one can take for me or from me or give to me. Supreme genitivity.

I respond that we are given life and death but do not possess singu-larity,[6] that responsibility is not taking, and that the economy of goodness and sacrifice takes what cannot be taken, cannot be given by anyone or any thing, but is giving beyond taking. Almost Christian, except for the economy. Almost Jewish and Greek, except for the economy. Sacrifice as the condi-tion of ethics, without the possibility of economy. Sacrifice as the condition of economy, inhabiting no economy. Sacrifice as general economy—which is no economy, no economy of economy, no order or logic to its economy, no secret economy, but the condition of arrival—by force if necessary, by surprise perhaps, by something other, otherwise. Plenishment is the impossible juncture of general and restricted economy, of giving and having. Ethics as betrayal, responsibility as irresponsibility, injustice in justice. "For responsibility . . . demands on the one hand an accounting, . . . and, on the other hand, uniqueness, absolute singularity, hence . . . silence, and secrecy. . . . This is ethics as an insoluble and paradoxical contradiction between responsibility *in general* and *absolute* responsibility. . . . The ethical can therefore end up making us irresponsible" (p. 61). Makes us irresponsible from responsibility.

> I cannot respond to the call, the request, the obligation, or even the love of another without sacrificing the other other, the other others. *Every other (one) is every (bit) other [tout autre est tout autre]*, every one else is completely or wholly other. . . . As a result, the concepts of responsibility, of decision, or of duty, are condemned a priori to paradox, scandal, and aporia. (p. 68)

> How would you ever justify the fact that you sacrifice all the cats in the world to the cat that you feed at home every morning for years, whereas other cats die of hunger at every instant? Not to mention other people? . . . There is no language, no reason, no generality or mediation to justify this ultimate responsibility which leads me to absolute sacrifice; . . . the sacrifice of the most imperative duty (that which binds me to the other as a singularity in general) in favor of another absolutely imperative duty binding me to every other. (pp. 70–71)

I betray the other, betray the otherwise, betray the giving in the having, betray responsibility. Every other is *other*! Worth an exclamation point. Including what is or appears not to be other, betrays itself as other. Including myself—other, stranger to myself, to genitivity. I must lose or give up myself. In the name of betrayal I must betray betrayal.

Derrida reminds us of such betrayal, interrupting the (masculine) economy of sacrifice. "Would the logic of sacrificial responsibility within the implacable universality of the law, of its law, be altered, inflected, attenuated, or displaced, if a woman were to intervene in some consequential manner?" (pp. 75–76). Women are not present in the Greek-Judeo-Christian economy of sacrifice, or present as sacrificial victim rather than as sacrificer. As if a woman were not to interpret, as if women were excluded from ethics, from the events that constitute the foundation of ethics—except as sacrifice. As if women were excluded from ethics in the name of God, as if they do not speak the tongue that "opens onto the infinite" (p. 87). In memory of the mother. "There is a secret of the mother tongue, the secret that the father's lucidity sees in, and the secret of the sacrifice of Isaac. It is indeed an economy, literally a matter of the law *(nomos)* of the home *(oikos)*, of the family and of the hearth [*foyer*: hearth, home, source]; and of the space separating or associating the fire of the family hearth and the fire of the sacrificial holocaust" (p. 88).

> The sacrifice of economy, that without which there is no free responsibility or decision . . . is indeed in this case the sacrifice of the *oikonomia*, namely of the law of the home *(oikos)*, of the hearth, of what is one's own or proper, of the private, of the love and affection of one's kin. This is the moment when Abraham gives the sign of absolute sacrifice, . . . putting to death his absolute love for what is dearest, the only son. . . . (Derrida, *GD*, 95)

In the name of the father—Agamemnon and Abraham—the economy of sacrifice interrupts the law of the *oikos*, of hearth and home, betrays what is properly one's own, *disowning genitivity*. The economy of sacrifice, entwined with the ecology of life and death—*econolonomics, economomology*—demands the sacrifice of sacrifice, of the law—any law, any restricted economy—of anything one may have or hold as one's own. One cannot have the earth, own it through economy or ecology. One cannot have death, or life, or justice, or responsibility, or beauty, truth, and the good.

To what are we brought within this denial of ethical economy? Derrida returns us to the simulacrum, betraying the economy of gifts. "This sacrificial *hubris* is what Nietzsche calls the 'stroke of genius called Christianity.' It is what takes this economy to its excess in the sacrifice of Christ for love of the debtor; it involves the same economy of sacrifice, the same sacrifice of sacrifice" (p. 114). Christianity knows the sacrifice of sacrifice and betrays it, promulgates it as betrayal.

We may be led here to a different question of sacrifice and betrayal: how we in the earth today are to recall gifts and giving without reenacting the stroke of genius called Christianity, the obsession with death called philosophy, the inescapability of these restricted economies within the circulation of general economy, the insistence on having within the giving. Derrida answers: "As often happens, the call of or for the question, and the request that echoes through it, takes us further than the response. The question, the request, and the appeal must indeed have begun, since the eve of their awakening, by receiving accreditation from the other: by being believed" (p. 115). The call of the question, from the good, takes us away from taking and having, not to another place, but interrupts having and taking in the questioning that calls itself philosophy, that interrupts philosophy, that hopes to sacrifice the economy of sacrifice by giving without hoping to escape from having. With a hope of being believed.

This is perhaps the injunction: to sacrifice sacrifice's economy, giving excessively to others—always aware of others, and more; giving something beyond to every inheritance, including *tout autre est tout autre*. And *les autres*. Betraying every law. In belief and joy.

# CHAPTER 16

## *Betraying*

In its originary iterability, a use-value is in advance promised, promised to exchange and beyond exchange. . . . This is not simply a bad thing, even if the use-value is always *at risk* of losing its soul in the commodity. (Derrida, *SM*, 162)

These possibilities or necessities . . . *are themselves not only human.* (Derrida, *EW*, 284–85)

The witness is a traitor. (Lyotard, *I*, 204)[1]

A natural thing, a human work, anything in the earth, is promised to circulation, to disowning, impossible to own or have. It promises betrayal beyond itself in every testament to itself, its identity and value. Every arrival, *parousia*, promises withdrawal, arriving as one thing and departing as another, wandering beyond genitivity. Being is promised to betrayal, as betrayal; betrayal promises to betray itself, circulates in abundance. Being arrives as (not) (beyond) having, as (for) giving, in abundance.[2] The originary promise of betrayal arrives in the genitivity of the origin, betrays the origin. *Ousia* in *parousia. Epekeina tes ousias.*

We may think of circulation in abundance beyond any fixed and definite place, beyond identity and neutrality, as general economy, where everything in the earth belongs to general and restricted economy as (not) (beyond) betrayal. General and restricted economy together are arrival and betrayal: exchange beyond exchange; circulation beyond circulation; beyond neutrality and genitivity. Circulation and exchange in abundance always betray abundance—*as not beyond.*

The promise of exchange and circulation, beyond genitivity and neutrality, is a promise performed, enacted, brought into law—restricted economy; and circulates beyond law and restricted economy, beyond any enunciation or performance. (Not) (beyond) in betrayal. The performance is essential, as is the stage, yet the performance and stage do not fix the circulation of the props. Which is to say that the promise of circulation, of wandering, is performed, inscribed, in exposure *as mimēsis*—or, more dramatically, is *betrayed as* the *mimēsis* of *of* and *as*. The call of the good. In genitivity, *as* genitivity, beyond genitivity. *As* identity, beyond identification. *As not beyond. As as*, always (not) beyond. And, moreover, in this enactment of identity, this identification, that fixes in place within the promise of exchange and circulation, lies the promise of the promise, that every promise is a promise *to*, performed within an inscription, a promise, of identification *as. As* marks the spot, the promise, of genitivity with *mimesis*, *as* betrayal; marks the promise of ethical responsibility *as* exposure with responsivity, sensitivity, expressivity. Responsibility is promised to exchange and circulation beyond identity and law, *as* expressivity, responsivity, *mimēsis*, interruption, beyond any place. *As* betrayal. And this is *not a bad thing*. Nor perhaps *a good one*. But it may be the absolute condition of good and bad. *As betrayal*. If there be such a thing as absolute betrayal. Another gesture. Another betrayal.

*Not only human*.[3] Betrayal *as not beyond* humanity, thrown beyond any border, any fixing in place, into betrayal. If we are to think from *not beyond* humanity to nature, if we are to think from *not beyond* neutrality to ethics, if we are to betray the borders that unify and divide us—whoever we are—we must circulate in betrayal *as mimēsis*, must enact and perform our identities among ourselves and the others, all expressive. We and everything in the earth are (thrown into) *mimēsis*, exposed to each other, expressive for each other, *as not beyond* ourselves, touching, responsive, promised to responsibility—in betrayal *as irresponsibility*.[4] The promise betrays neutrality *as mimēsis*. Which has something to do with beauty and art, and everything to do with the good. Given from the good *as mimēsis. As, as, as.* Betraying genitivity.

Before I undertake to betray *mimēsis as* responsibility, to portray the goodness of betrayal *as* ethics, against genitivity, I interrupt to explore ways in which Derrida intimates something similar in *Specters of Marx*: property and genitivity *as mimēsis*; which is to say, the *as* that insists on interrupting the hold of every possession, every having. This will be an extended discussion, because the wealth of figures, of insistences, the superfluity of Derrida's allusions, is extensive, and I do not pretend to exhaustiveness—if there be such a thing as exhaustiveness, or exhaustibility, within the promise of interruption that betrays *mimēsis*. It will be an extended example of betrayal, but I will keep it as short as I can, not allow it to wander too far within its promise of betrayal.[5]

I began with the props of property, to insist that property arrives on stage; Derrida speaks of the table that stands upright and upside down on the stage. Spirits, specters, cross the stage—*Hamlet*'s stage among others. Which is to insist that wherever anything arrives—Marx and Engels insist that property arrives with cattle—arrival is *mimēsis*, promised beyond itself, insisting on, performing, enacting the promise. The empty neutrality of the thing is nothing without the responses, the responsiveness, the call of that thing and the other things and persons and creatures around it, promises nothing without them. They put it into circulation *as* what it is. Without exchange and circulation, without performing and staging, there can be no promise, no meaning. Arrival is empty and meaningless except *as mimēsis*, except for the *as* of *mimēsis*, the *be* and *bet* of betrayal. Arrival is always arrival *as*, at risk; *as* something insisting on its identity, risking everything to be itself. Property, cattle, arrive in the promise that the father can hold his wealth and pass it on to his sons and beyond in perpetuity: a promise—whether it can be kept or not—that insists on being performed, allowing for the possibility of a reversal: that arrival is promising, giving, betraying; questioning, responding, responsivity, responsibility, giving—*as not beyond* genitivity. A difficult transition, each step *as mimēsis*, by way of *mimēsis*, *as* the perfidy and revelation of betrayal.

This thought is almost impossible to think in the European tradition, perhaps any tradition: that ethical responsibility is inseparable from the expressiveness of language and things—understood *as* opacity, corporeality, wandering, and betrayal. Responsibility is promised to circulation, crossing every border; promised *as* expressivity and responsivity; promised to genitivity—to having (an identity) and giving up or unhaving (interrupting that identity). All *mimēsis*.

I raise the question whether such a promise of *mimēsis*, bound to the expressiveness of language and things, binds betrayal to art, aestheticizing the demands of life upon us. *As* if these could appear except on a stage, performed; *as* if real demands could break the promise of expressivity; *as* if responsibility could be had once and for all. I insist that the promise of the good does indeed betray ethics and the demands of life—by presenting them in the promise of endless meanings in an endless future, promised to other arrivals. Betrayal betrays the sacrifices that we hope to forget; betrays them by insisting upon them, but also calls them forth, makes it impossible to forget them. Forgetting is one betrayal, remembering another, presenting betrayal itself.

Ethics in the sense of responding to the call, the demands, to which life must answer, whatever those may be, bears an infinite relation to history and practice. All are promised to a past and future, to other times and places, promised to crossings beyond fulfillment. Among those demands and promises is the need to distinguish, however hesitantly, between works in museums and criminals in prison; another is the impossibility of holding this distinction firm in societies in which resistance becomes too risky, where artists along with ordinary men and women are imprisoned, where movements of resistance and liberation institute their own regulations and confinements. In this context, ethics—living for the sake of the good—finds itself swept up in endless questions, crossings, and interruptions. These *are* ethics, instituting social formations that answer to the needs of life, recognizing the glorious and hateful promises in every answer. These *are* ethics *as* betrayal, keeping vigil over what and how what we do resists every closure. In every possible way, linked with life itself. Here, in this discussion of giving and having, linked everywhere with genitivity.

The props of property are blood, sex, kin, class, food, desire, and power—life itself, and death, *as* props. Impossible to have or hold without *mimēsis*. Except *as* performed, promised to betrayal *as not beyond*. Betraying the genitive. *As* generation, genitality, genealogy. Having under law—*mimēsis*—and giving beyond law—again *mimēsis*. The props of property, the staging of genitivity: appropriation, expropriation; owning and disowning. I understand *epekeina tes ousias as* giving beyond having in the impossibility of their separation, the props of property *as* the property *not beyond*, the impropriety beyond propriety, where genitivity is betrayal. Betraying the genitive and proper names. *Mimēsis as* genitivity and betrayal, *as* general and restricted economy.

"[T]he table begins to walk around and to put itself forward as a market value. *Coup de théâtre*, the ordinary, sensuous thing is transfigured, it becomes someone, it assumes a figure" (Derrida, *SM*, 150).[6] It promises betrayal. The genitive separates and betrays separation, falls back down into betrayal. Betrayal is falling back and down, *mimēsis*, onto others and itself.

This is by way of recapitulation—another *mimēsis*, another prop. I now extend it to the *mimēsis* of genitivity throughout *Specters of Marx*, returning to this mimetic text in another genitive iteration, promised to *mimēsis* in this reading. Almost to infinity. A few examples. Emphasizing genitivity and the earth—not only human. Betraying betrayal. *As.* Betraying the props of property in the word, the identification, the assumption of identity—*as*. Betrayal *as mimēsis*, *mimēsis as* betrayal: ethics, life, being *as* the good.

The table *as* commodity.
*Parousia as* intimacy, exposure, and proximity as well as posterity.
Given *as* mine or ours.
The table puts itself forward *as* a market value.
*As, as, as.* Property, genitivity, *as.*
Responsibility *as* responsivity *as* exposure *as* circulation *as* touch. *As mimēsis*. *As* betrayal, always betrayal *as.*
*As* calling from the good.

*Specters of Marx as* the state of the debt, the work of mourning, and the new international. *As mimēsis.*

*Specters of Marx as* heir of Marx; taking up Marx's writings *as* our property.

Derrida stages his performance, drawing the curtain onto the inescapable betrayal of Chris Hani's life and death: "A man's life, as unique as his death, will always be more than a paradigm and something other than a symbol. And this is precisely what a proper name should always name. And yet. . . . I recall that it is a **communist** as such, a **communist** as communist, whom . . . all the assassins of Chris Hani, put to death. . . ." (*SM*, xv–xvi). A man's life and being are always to be *(represented as)* more than a figure, other than a symbol, *as* unique *as* his death. Chris Hani died *as* a **communist**—always *more than* singular, *more than* common, *more than* human: betraying each, betraying each betrayal. The *as* of *always more than as mimēsis.* In this space, or interval, or something else of betrayal, in the supplementarities and traces of the *always more* than and the *not only,* marked by *as,* lie the disowning and expropriation of responsibility. Responsibility, responsivity, is always *more than* any *as,* any identification; always *as*; the identification insists on recognition, betrayal. For human beings and beyond humanity.

"*I would like to learn to live finally*" (p. xvii); "is ethics itself" (p. xviii). "Finally what" (p. xviii). *As* what? What *as*? Ethics itself *as* the wisdom of life and death, between life and death (p. xviii), always about some ghost: *never present as such* (p. xviii). Which is precisely to say, *as* I have *saying (as)* or staging: *mimēsis as* betrayal: flourishing and prospering *as* giving in betrayal—*as.* Ethics is learning to talk with ghosts, learning to respond with a ghost, *as* a ghost—*as if.* "[I]n the name of *justice* . . . to speak *of the* ghost, indeed *to the* ghost and *with* it, . . . this *non-contemporaneity with itself of the living present*" (p. xix). A non-contemporaneity with itself that goes *by the name* of *mimēsis,* that cannot appear except *as* betrayal, betraying the ghost of *mimēsis,* in the genitive. Specters, ghosts, and phantoms *as* semblances of betrayal; inheritances, memories, and generations *as mimēsis.* Always beyond *as* betrayal. Always *more than* any identity.

"There is then *some* spirit. Spirits. And *one must* reckon with them. One cannot not have to, one must not not be able to reckon with them, which are more than one: the *more than one/no more [than] one [le* plus d'un]" (p. xx). Every one betraying the others. How can there be reckoning; how can there be any spirits, fewer than one, at least one, more than one, except *as mimēsis,* except *as* staged, *as* betrayal? How can there be a promise, messianic or other, except *as* enacted and performed, everywhere betrayed?

"[O]ne does not know what it *is*, what it is presently: *It is* something that one does not know, precisely, and one does not know if precisely it *is*, if it exists, if it responds to a name and corresponds to an essence" (p. 6). Said *of* and *as* the specter—*if* it *exists*. *Of* and *as* responsibility, communism, life and death. One does not know the good—because it is *nothing*: not nothing, nothing, nothing—if nothing might be or be thought as such; but the betrayal of nothing, which is always more than nothing, not only nothing, not only anything, beyond itself *as mimēsis*. *As* responsivity, betrayed.

*As* "the furtive and ungraspable visibility of the invisible . . . that *non-sensuous sensuous* of which *Capital* speaks . . . with regard to a certain exchange-value" (p. 7); figures of *mimēsis* promised to circulation. Capital *as mimēsis*, *mimēsis as* promised (and *as* the promise, promising itself) to giving (*as* the giving itself), beyond neutrality, resistant to neutrality, the emptiness of neutrality. That is, *as* ethics, *as* responsivity. Betraying the good, for its sake. The non-sensuous sensuousness of capital and commodities, of desire. The promise in capital of love. *As* betrayal. *As* betrayed. Perhaps *as* disjointure. " 'The time is out of joint': time is *disarticulated*, dislocated, dislodged, time is run down, on the run and run down *[traqué et détraqué]*, *deranged*, both out of order and mad" (p. 18). The madness of the gods that puts writing out of place, into wandering; the wandering of *mimēsis* that betrays the father. *As if*, no matter what, we (humans) insist on order, betray betrayal to insist on order, *as if* we might avoid betraying it. *As if* we might avoid betrayal, when betrayal—avoided or faced (if either were possible)—betrays the good. *As if* this betrayal were not ethics.

Reenacting the question of this book, of genitivity, of life itself, and death, Heidegger's question (together with the question of that question, of his answer to that question): "Can it give what it doesn't have? If it gives anything at all, doesn't it give jointure away?" (Heidegger, *AF*, 43; Derrida, *SM*, 26); "Heidegger's answer: giving rests here only in presence" (p. 26); "appropriable as the same and therefore gathered together?" (p. 27). Gathered together without betrayal—*so it seems*, without the demand to betray betrayal. The double movement of giving and having, giving without having, is the betrayal of betrayal, here giving and gift and jointure and presence. The unpresence of presence is the betrayal of betrayal, betrayal itself, *as* the responsivity in which ethics arrives *as* ungathering what cannot be gathered, disowning genitivity. One cannot have the gift, receive the gift, gather the gift in presence. *Epekeina tes ousias*: giving beyond having. Giving gives what it doesn't have.

Allowing for a summary in betrayal:

Property *as* specter, ghost.

Responsibility *as* respect for alterity; alterity *as* singularity and (as) (not) (beyond) singularity. *As* figure and *as not beyond* figure. *As* and *not beyond as* genitivity and *as not beyond* genitivity: property *as not beyond* property.

Property *as* life and death, between life and death.

Genitivity *as* the promise of giving, to giving.

Genitivity *as* betrayal.

Genitivity *as* nothing; betraying nothing.

Genitivity *as* jointure, presence, having; and *as* not only having.

Some additional examples before putting genitivity into rapid circulation—*as mimēsis*, betraying *nothing*.

"When the State emits paper money at a fixed rate, its intervention is compared to 'magic' *(Magie)* that transmutes paper into gold. . . . Marx is referring to the imprint that stamps gold and prints paper money" (p. 45); transmutation, magic, the imprint that betrays.

"[W]e must take into account another essential meaning: the act that consists in swearing, taking an oath, therefore promising, deciding, taking a *responsibility*, in short, committing oneself in a performative fashion" (p. 50); to genitivity.

"[T]his anhistoric *telos* of history gives rise, very precisely *in our day*, in these days, *in our time*, to an event which Fukuyama speaks of as 'good news' " (p. 57); the event *as* news, the good *as mimēsis*.

"The specter *appears* to present itself during a visitation. One represents it to oneself, but it is not present, itself, in flesh and blood" (p. 101); the appearance and disappearance of flesh and blood, *as if* flesh and blood were not *mimēsis*, knew no *mimēsis*, yet were the essential props of property. Flesh and blood, matter, materiality, nature, and the earth all are props. Not to deny their reality, but to express it *as reality*, to stage reality *as* property's prop, to perform the genitive.

"What did he [Kojève] think he perceived there [in the United States], what did he want to perceive there? Answer: the appropriation, in abundance, of everything that responds to need or desire" (p. 72); appropriating *as* property, in the genitive, everything inherent in *as not beyond* responsibility. Having *as* the earth.

By way of a certain reading of *Specters of Marx*, of Derrida's promise (and perhaps other promises) to exchange and circulation, I propose to betray this promise—that is, to make it and show that I have made it in the fullness of its promise to giving and having, the promise in having of giving, breaking it out in the form of an iteration. I promise you a list promised to iterability *as* genitivity, betraying itself. If Derrida's inheritance from Marx concerns genitivity—and how can one be heir without property?—then this inheritance—which he claims we must all acknowledge, must be Marx's heirs, in the genitive—marks the body of the text with genitivity.

I hope to mark, with this much too long spectral list—yet it could be extended much much further—something of the reach, the circulation and giving, of genitivity and betrayal, hoping to betray betrayal itself—the sacrifice of sacrifice—for the sake of the good; betraying that betrayal betrays itself, betrays abundance, reveals the uncontainability of what it would contain; thereby allows us to resist the categories that would contain it, including the category of betrayal. *As if* it were a category or *as if* we might be sure that it is not a category, released from genitivity. The list, then, tentatively, of property and genitivity *as*, betraying betrayal; one might say beginning at the beginning, Derrida's words:

Property, genitivity—*as*:

*as* life and death (p. xvii), *as* extermination (p. xix), *as more than one/no more [than] one* [*le* plus d'un] (p. xx), *as* genealogy, begetting *(genuit)* (p. 5), *as* apparition (p. 6), *as* flesh and blood (p. 6), *as arrivant, revenant* (p. 7), *as* the visor effect, under the law (p. 7), *as* authority (p. 8), *as* the thing and its three things: mourning, generations, works (p. 9), *as parousia*, presence (p. 10), *as* ontology|hauntology (p. 10), *as* scholarship, having knowledge (p. 11), *as* reality (p. 11), *as* arresting the specter (p. 12), *as* the future (p. 13), *as* bread, apocalypse, the bread of apocalypse (p. 14), *as* history, the end of history (p. 15), *as* inheritance, the heterogeneity of inheritance (p. 16), *as* selfsameness, gathering (p. 17), *as* the disparate itself (p. 17), *as* disjointure (p. 18), *as* walking upright (p. 20), *as* more ancient than memory itself (p. 21), *as* anachrony, injustice, infinite asymmetry (p. 22), *as* calculable equality (p. 22), *as* accord, harmony (p. 23), *as* the tragic, the trace of the tragic (p. 24), *as* beyond equivocation (p. 25), *as* vengeance (p. 26), *as* favor, propriety, privilege (p. 27), *as* the absolute and unpredictable singularity of the *arrivant as justice* (p. 28), *as* the necessity of the worst (p. 29), *as* the body, a certain body (p. 30), *as* totalization (p. 30), *as* rupture, violence (p. 31), *as* promise, pledge (p. 31), *as* differance, alterity, singularity, here-now (p. 31), *as* revolution (p. 31), *as* politics, the political gesture (p. 32), *as* revolution, the permanent revolution (p. 33), *as* translation, circulation, equivalence (p. 34), *as* necessity, insistence, inescapability (p. 35), *as* resurrection, re-insurrection (p. 36), *as* future to come, teleology, eschatology (p. 37), *as* the new world order, the new world disorder (p. 37), *as* the limits of the earth and the limits of the political (p. 38), *as* the border between the present, the actual or present reality of the present, and everything that can be opposed to it: absence, non-presence, non-effectivity, inactuality, virtuality, or even the simulacrum in general, and so forth (p. 39), *as* conjuration (p. 40), *as* conspiracy (p. 40), *as* incantation (p. 41), *as* the lifeless body, cadaver (p. 41), *as* phantomalization, propriety (p. 42), *as* falsification and especially the perjury of which it is the law (p. 43), *as* malediction of malediction (p. 43), *as* the very essence of humanity (p. 44), *as* betrayal itself, perjury, abjuration, lie, and simulacrum (p. 45), *as* printing, imprinting, money (p. 45), *as* the *remainder* of money (p. 45), *as* apparition, hallucination, vision (p. 46), *as* the simulacrum to real presence (p. 47), *as* the magical exorcism (p. 47), *as* the sworn faith to conjure away the fear that makes (itself) afraid (p. 48).

Quite a list, yet I am just through the first chapter. A list of that which we may hope to hold onto, to have, in the name of resisting having. That insists on *mimēsis* to have and to hold; that promises to give to circulation in that insistence. Betraying betrayal, *as* genitivity.

I begin to skip—another *mimēsis*, another betrayal. And repeat. Still marking in order through the text, knowing that *mimēsis* knows no order. I begin to give my own and Derrida's own away. I will not exhaust the genitive in *mimēsis*:

*as* responsibility (p. 50), *as* law (p. 50), *as* witness, mourning (p. 54), *as* news, good news, *our* news, our property (p. 57), *as* democracy to come, future to come, hope, never owned (p. 59), *as* emancipatory promise, undeconstructible justice (p. 59), *as* materialism, materiality, immateriality (p. 61), *as* presence, impresence (p. 63), *as* measure, money *as* measure (p. 65), *as* contract, law, return (p. 65), *as* debt, promise to come (p. 65), *as* family, State, nation, territory, native soil or blood, language, culture in general, even humanity (p. 65), *as* gap, between, intermediary (p. 70), *as* need, labor, desire (p. 72), *as* accumulating time, stockpiling the future (p. 73), *as* debt, responsibility, rather than right (p. 73), *as* beyond labor, work (p. 75), *as* event, arrival, *parousia* (p. 79), *as* the history of the earth (p. 85), *as* capital (p. 85), *as* appropriation, exappropriation, expropriation (p. 90), *as* freedom, our freedom (p. 90), *as* servitude (p. 90), *as* being there, thrown, *Dasein*, with properties, with property (p. 90), *as* pure, purity, proper in property (pp. 95, 121), *as* not just matter, excess of matter (p. 97), *as* contract, agreement, debt (p. 96), *as* citation, iterability, *mimesis* (p. 97), *as* narcissism (p. 98), *as* the living present and future, (p. 99), *as ousia, parousia* (p. 100), *as* arrival, presence, absence (pp. 100–1), *as* frequency, oscillation, repetition (p. 101), *as* fear (p. 105), *as* love (p. 106), *as* anachrony (p. 111), *as* unpresence of presence (p. 111), *as* making oneself fear, scaring oneself (p. 114), *as* forgetting, inheriting, mourning, repeating (p. 114), *as* impossible (p. 114), *as* excess of authority (pp. 114–15), *as* excess (p. 115), *as* the juncture of public-private space (p. 116), *as* patrimony (p. 119), *as* images, fantastic panoply, on stage (p. 119), *as* presence, non-presence to self (p. 121), *as* a procession of ghosts (p. 121), *as* law of alterity (p. 123), *as* impurity in purity (p. 123), *as* discerning, knowing mine from yours (p. 124), *as* the work of mourning (p. 126), *as* disaster (p. 126), *as* incorporation, corporeality (p. 127), *as* the body proper, proper body (p. 128), *as* mine, my own, mine, mine, mine, genitivity (p. 128), *as* inherent in, from the earth (p. 132), *as* identification (p. 134), *as* specter, waiting for redemption, upsetting calculation (p. 136), *as* offspring, progeny, heirs (p. 136), *as* performance, artifice, simulacrum (p. 137), *as* representation (p. 137), *as* race, gender, kinds (p. 137), *as* collection or series of ghosts (p. 138), *as* ideology, my thesis, hypothesis, hypostasis (p. 139), *as* my feeling, my own feeling, myself (p. 139), *as* the hunt (haunt), chase, pursuit (p. 141), *as* return, fear of return (p. 141), *as* the head, in the head (p. 142), *as* reality, ghostly reality (p. 142), *as* my own ghost, ghost of my own (p. 142), *as* Marx's ten ghosts (pp. 143–46)—the supreme being, being or essence. the vanity of the world. good and evil beings. being and its realm. beings. man-god, the uncanny. man that makes himself fear, spirit of the people, everything, *AS* EVERYTHING!!, *as* proper home, name, blood (p. 145), *as* the body proper, the proper name, nation, blood, territory, and the "rights" that are founded thereon (p. 145), *as* speculation, specter, spectacle (p. 146), *as* my fear, man's own fear, making himself fear (p. 145), *as* soul of the dead (p. 147), *as* patrimony, possessed, handed down, circulated (p. 147), *as* fetish, commodity, permeated with desire (p. 148), *as* real, corporeal, use-value (p. 149), *as* invisible itself (p. 149), *as* pure and simple use-value (p. 150), *as* thing and properties (p. 150), *as* sensuous non-sensuous supersensible supernatural thing (p. 150), *as* commodity haunting thing (p. 151), *as* competition, war (p. 151), *as* inspiration of inert thing (p. 153), *as* capital contradiction, automatic autonomy (p. 153), *as* labor, doubled social relation, out of joint in time (p. 154), *as* temporality, inheritance, filiation, ghosts (p. 154), *as* exchange, social relation (p. 156), *as* nothing but social relations (p. 157), *as* if commodities could speak (p. 157), *as* fiction of speech (p. 158), *as* phantasm of commodity and social bond (p. 159), *as* loss of self, mourning (p. 159), *as* property before property, capital before capital (p. 160), *as* impure guarantee of purity (p. 160), *as* value of value in general (p. 160), *as* promised to, promise of, iterability (pp. 160, 162), *as* beginning before beginning (p. 161), *as* substitution, exchangeability, iterability, loss of singularity, singularity itself (p. 161), *as* the possibility of capital (p. 161), *as* work, put to work, iterability, giving (p. 162), *as* capital, exceeding capital (p. 163), *as* end (p. 163), *as* origin (p. 163), *as* circulation (p. 163), *as* other forms of production, other kinds (p. 164), *as* territory, place, realm (p. 165), *as* commerce, relation between things (p. 166), *as* phantasm of social relation (p. 166), *as* product, production (p. 166), *as* reappropriation, return of appropriation (p. 167), *as* return, promise, pledge (p. 167), *as* revolution, irrevolutionary, messianic, unmessianic (p. 168), *as* inhospitality, ungiving (p. 168), *as* hospitality, giving (p. 168), *as* fixing the future, counting on the future, resisting the arrival (p. 169), *as* hope, hope *as* calculation (p. 169), *as* giving, beyond calculation (p. 169), *as* virtuality, resisting opposition between presence and representation (p. 169), *as* blood (p. 169), *as* differ*a*nce (p. 170), *as* refusal of exorcism of ghosts of propriety (p. 170), *as* the political itself (p. 171), *as* outside, *out of the head* (p. 171), *as* representation *as* wandering *as* impurity *as* mim*e*sis (p. 171), *as* uncontainable, the ghost *(es spukt)* in *es gibt* (p. 172)—spooking *as* giving, *as this* (p. 172), *as* strange, stranger, strangeness, foreigner (p. 172), *as* gift (p. 172), *as revenant, arrivant* (p. 172), *as* holding fear at bay, not frightening oneself (p. 174), *as* burying the dead (p. 174), *as* mortality (p. 174), *as* doing justice to ghosts, justice to justice (p. 175), *as* the question of the ghost, questioning the ghost (p. 176), *as* rethinking the *there, as* thrown (p. 176), *as* the return of the ghost (p. 176), *as* love (p. 176).

Perhaps this was not shorter or quicker. Bringing property and genitivity on stage, promised to circulation, takes its time, takes too much time, exceeds every boundary. In the exhaustion of this list lies testimony, witness to the inexhaustibility and pervasiveness of genitivity *as mimēsis*, in betrayal; suggesting that having is betrayal; that giving is *mimēsis*; that betrayal occupies the stage on which life and death are betrayed in the name of life and death—*as* property and *as* genitivity. The *as* of *mimēsis* is the betrayal of genitivity.

All this comes from reading *Specters of Marx* (again), rereading Derrida reading Marx, inheriting from Marx, speaking again and again of inheritance *as* the return of the ghost—the double return of the double ghost, multiple returns and ghosts, promised again and again to iterability, that is, to *mimēsis*, promise *as mimēsis*, return *as mimēsis*, endless betrayal, all these repetitions of *as—as, as, as—as* the promise and the betrayal. All returns of the buried, exorcised ghost of . . . the earth, the land, of nature *as* the buried ghost of that which does not know death.[7] The return of that which insists on sacrificing sacrifice, on dehumanizing humanism, on giving beyond having, on betraying betrayal. The *mimēsis* of *mimēsis*, beyond genitivity:

*as* materialism, materiality, immateriality (pp. 61, 97, 157), *as* matter and its dematerialization (p. 152), *as* the matter *(s'agit)* of the neutrality of matter (p. 172), *as* desire (pp. 28, 62, 72, 99), *as* fear, fascination, fetish, obsession, *as* territory (pp. 65, 145, 165), *as* land, the Promised Land (p. 69), *as* nature (pp. 64, 67, 69), *as* the earth and its limits (pp. 38, 93, 98, 132, 154, 174);

*from, to, beneath, on* the earth, supplemented by: *as* promised to *mimēsis*, *as* only one|more than one [*le* plus d'un]. *As mimēsis*:

*as* flesh and blood, clothing, language, thought, being, *as* the economy of body, figure, text, wit, work, *as* pure-impure, purification, *as* metonymy, sublimation, substitution, *as* the fetish, *as* property, *as* iterability, *as* the commodity, *as* the endless return of specters, *as* the endless return of what cannot return, *as* the aporia of aporia, *as* the arrival of the event, *as* the advent of advent, *as* the body of body, bodiless body, *as* the fear of fear, *as* the death of death, *as* impure impurity, *as* the interruption of interruption, *as* the language of languages, *as* the law of law, *as* the limit of limits, *as* mourning for mourning, *as* naming names, *as* questioning questioning, *as* the repetition of repetition, *as* the representation of representation, *as* the simulacra of simulacra, *as* the specter of specters, ghost of ghosts, spirit of spirits, *as* supplementarity, the supplement of the supplement, *as* the fetish of fetish; summarizing the supplement, *as if* that were possible, *as* the *mimēsis* of *mimēsis*, *as* betraying betrayal: all, perhaps, not only human; all, perhaps, returning again and again, *as* ghosts, to sacrifice sacrifice, returning in responsibility, returning *as* responsivity *as* betrayal. *As mimēsis*. *Tout autre est tout autre, as mimēsis,* in betrayal.

In Derrida's voice. Now mine:

*as* abundance in the earth, *as* giving beyond having, *as* exposure, proximity, expression, *as* responsivity, *as* betrayal, betraying betrayal, *as* desire, *as* land, *as* nature, *as* the earth, betrayal *as* and *in* the earth—responsivity *as* giving in abundance, beyond having, always *as* having, *as mimēsis, as* beauty, loveliness, *as* love, *as* philanthropy, philogeny, philokyny: cherishment toward humanity and other kinds, in the kinds they are, *as* forgiveness, *as as as*, the *mimēsis* of *mimēsis*, responsivity in responsivity, sacrificing sacrifice, plenishment *as* betraying forgiveness.

And so we may drop the curtain on the spectral example of *Specters of Marx*. With the earth in mind *as* the ghost, always returning in the abundance without which no question of betrayal might arrive or return—*arrivant, revenant*—Derrida speaks of genitivity *as* betrayal: "One must have the ghost's hide and to do that, one must have it. To have it, one must see it, situate it, identify it. One must possess it without letting oneself be possessed by it, without being possessed of it. . . . Is not to possess a specter to be possessed by it, possessed period? To capture it, is that not to be captured by it?" (p. 132). One may hope to possess it without being possessed by it, to have it without being had, yet in the promise and the abundance, one is always possessed where one possesses, is always had where one has—*as* betrayal: that is, *as* wandering and circulation beyond having, *as* expressing, revealing, abundance beyond containment. One must have the ghost, the thing, the earth, seizing it and holding it, capturing and securing it. Always promised to giving, to further promising, to betrayal beyond having, to *mimēsis* by way of *mimēsis*.

For *mimēsis*—the expressiveness and responsiveness of things in abundance, by no means only human—is impossible to capture, unable to capture, incapable of capturing and being captured; always coveting—land, territory, the earth, humanity and its essence—hoping to have what cannot be had, to identify what exceeds identification. Responsiveness in the earth and its abundance promises giving beyond having, beyond neutrality, betraying every restriction. Responsiveness promises betrayal. *As* the fetish, in capitalism, betrays fascination. *As* thrownness, *as* betrayal, *as* desire, *mimēsis*, and giving: gifts given for the sake of the good. Exposure in abundance for the sake of the good is responsivity and betrayal *as mimēsis*, each the expressiveness, responsiveness, and promisiveness of the others, beyond containment. The joy and exuberance of (not only human) being is exposure to (other) things in abundance, beyond limit, crossing, wandering beyond containment, in betrayal.

We may come back to ecology *as* this betrayal, betraying restricted economy *as* ecology, *as* general economy—*as*, together, *ecolonomics* and *economology*. Always *as*, each *as*, a figure, of the other, understanding political economy *as* this circulation from restricted economy back to general economy and from general economy to restricted economy, one betrayal, wound, interruption after another *as* the betrayal of time.

It is time—if not time enough, never enough time—to attempt to bring together, to have the jointure of that which does not gather, cannot gather. The disparate itself: *as* beauty, *as* truth, *as mimēsis*, in betrayal. Giving—interrupting, beyond having—gifts gathered in place. In the repeated figure of *mimēsis*, *as mimēsis*; the figure *as*. In the extreme, understanding *is as as*, being *as mimēsis*, *as* representation, interruption, betrayal, interrupting identity. Yet the identity interrupted—*as* that identity, *as* other identities—must be instituted *as* that identity, some identity, in some place. The *as* of *mimēsis*, the *mimēsis* of *mimēsis*, and its *mimēsis*, are promised to circulate beyond any *mimēsis*, any identity, even the multiple, mobile, interruptions of any *mimēsis*. The promise itself is *mimēsis*, always betrayed *as*: *as* promise, *as* beauty, truth, or goodness; *as* joy, exuberance, exhilaration beyond limit: Spinoza's *laetitia*, unbounded gladness; the love, the care, that surpasses, *beatitudo*: cherishment *as* inexhaustible responsivity.

And more. For the figures around which having organizes itself *as mimēsis* are figures of owning, possessing, and having and figures of giving, circulating, exchanging, and more, always more, more betrayal, always betraying more: having and giving; giving what cannot be had but must be had to be given. Multiple figures of giving and having, of genitivity. Multiple figures of gifts—of having—and of the movements, the giving, beyond genitivity; beyond the insistence that being human, or being thrown, is always in the genitive: *mine, mine, mine,* what I must have or own *as my own* to be *myself,* or *human,* or *being there,* or *thrown.* Being thrown *as not beyond* having, *not beyond* being there, *as* into the promise *not beyond* of giving, the promise from giving.

The history of philosophy—Western philosophy, perhaps any philosophy in the genitive: *our* or *your* or *their* philosophy—is expressed *as* genitivity. The figures of that or any philosophy—in the genitive—both mark that philosophy *as ours* or *theirs*—never just *mine* or *yours,* always (not) (beyond) the genitive—and *as* something else, elsewhere, otherwise. Genitivity marks itself *as not beyond* genitivity, *as* something else, elsewhere, ecstatic. Always from the good, for the sake of the good—which is itself (nothing at all) beyond, interrupting every figure of having with giving *as* the figure itself, the figure of *mimēsis, mimēsis as betrayal.*

In this sense, the figure of *mimēsis* that marks the moment in Plato's *Republic* where philosophy cuts itself and its truth off from poetry and poetic truth, where philosophy and ethics, in their rationality, cut themselves off from something else—poetry, painting, art, aesthetics; divine inspiration and madness—this figure of *mimēsis* resists that cut, denies the cut, most of all, *betrays it—as mimēsis,* that is, *as* Plato's writing, in Plato's writing, in the act, event, exposure of writing. Writing *as* writing, *as* philosophy, *as mimēsis,* performs this gesture, insists on the promise to *mimēsis,* in *mimēsis, as mimēsis,* of what cannot possibly be contained in any gesture of containment, in any promise, in any writing. In insisting on having what cannot possibly be had—truth, beauty, the good; *as* truth, beauty, the good—*as* insistence, *as* desire, the insistence promises beyond insistence, betrays itself, betrays betrayal, betrays genitivity, for the sake of the good. Which is nothing—*not beyond* itself.

This entire project comes to a crux here in understanding being thrown *as* responsivity, *mimēsis,* always *as,* in betrayal: where the human meaning—not only human—of responsivity, of *mimēsis,* is responsibility; where being thrown, being in the world, insists on genitivity—on identity and being *as: as* identical, *as* being this or that individual or kind, marking its being and identity *as*—exposure, responsivity, *mimēsis,* betrayal.

This is to say that beauty, truth, and goodness; responsibility, duty, and obligation; community, relatedness, and love; sharing, communion, and joy; are promised to betrayal, promised *as* betrayal—are promised to themselves *as* having and *as* wandering, giving, *not beyond* having, *as* betrayed in abundance. The abundance of the earth is betrayal. The (metaphysical insistence on the) being of things is an insistence on fixing them, even, in the extreme, *as* mobile, nomadic, having them either *as* substances, identities, under the rule of the same, or *as* processes, fluxes, becomings, under the rule of the difference. Always *as* something, however mobile, and *as* something else, ecstatic, here and elsewhere. Always betrayal, betraying betrayal. This condition is being *itself*, being there and being thrown *themselves*, where even the singularities of *itself* and *themselves* express something expressive, express expression, promised *as* what they are to circulation and exchange, *as not beyond* themselves, to giving beyond genitivity. Giving betrays the insistence on having *as* that insistence and *as* genitivity.

This is to say—to express or reveal, betray—that in what is *my own*— or *yours*—in claiming something *as mine*, even *myself*, my humanity or my being or my truth or my responsibility; in claiming the boundaries of any place or thing; the claim or insistence is always promised to giving in abundance, betrayed beyond any having *as* giving. The insistence on genitivity *as* humanity or *as* being works against and betrays the insistence, divides the insistence by abundance, always *as* an insistence that marks itself *as* promise, that takes on the promise by betraying it and everything else. Not only human. Not only humans. Everywhere in the earth in its abundance.

Retracing the long trajectory of this project, returning to its beginning with art and beauty, I would say that beauty, truth, and goodness *(kallon, alētheia, agathon)* are the historical names of gifts that we may hope to have, to make our own, but that cannot be possessed. They may be given, may be received, but cannot be had or held or grasped. They may be given, are givings, in an abundance of the earth. This giving and our responding are beyond having, giving what one does not have, touching the earth beyond accumulation or consumption. I call it *responsivity*, responding to the creatures and things of the earth in the ways Derrida describes *as Zusage*, the call that precedes all questions, to which human responsibility answers. I understand responsivity, responding somehow, in the touch of flesh and skin, *as* taken for granted in all human questioning and responsibility; *as* taking for granted the expressivity and responsivity of all creatures and things. Expressivity and responsivity are inseparable. Some other names of this relation are *mimēsis* and betrayal, still others the triad of *cherishment, sacrifice, and plenishment*. All echo the call of the good, the abundance of the earth.

I arrive at three concluding gestures, mimetic betrayals—I hope miming and betraying themselves. First, the guidelines for plenishment rewritten in the exuberance of betrayal:[8]

1. We find ourselves thrown among many different kinds, mixed kinds, insisting on belonging, in the genitive, on having and owning what cannot be had or owned: kinds belonging to other kinds, by birth, by history, by

blood, by choice, by practices and expressions; buildings, sites, works, ruins, bodies, images, gestures, voices, sonorities, cacophonies, and more. This is our ethical condition, given in the abundance of the earth, exposed in betrayal. We find ourselves surrounded by many different individuals and kinds constituting who we are, as individual and human—and not only human—that we constitute in our bodies by our representations and practices. Our ethical relation to the good—not ours, not anything to be owned or had—is exposure to expressive, corporeal individuals and kinds, heterogeneous kinds to which we may belong, other kinds in our proximity to which we know we will never belong.

2. Everything matters, everything is precious, infinitely, inexhaustibly, heterogeneously, every individual thing and every kind. Everything is expressive, responsive to other individuals and kinds, and to their expressions and responses. Everything is given in the corporeal abundance of the earth in wonder and goodness, as beautiful in its ways, known and unknown, in the kinds in which it participates, beyond any having. To cherish, love, revere the goodness of things is to give to them—betray them—beyond having, to let them pursue their good, with three qualifications:

3. *(a)* They may not know or hope to have their good, though no one else can know or have it better. *(b)* Such a good—always improper, always goods in the plural—is beyond having: multiple, heterogeneous, impure, exposed to others face to face, constituted by memberships, practices, expressions, and mobilities, by inexhaustible genitivities. *(c)* The kinds of the earth, human and other, with their goods, circulate everywhere in nature heterogeneously, expressively, responsively. This heterogeneity of the good betrays genitivity, resists having what cannot be had. Genitivity works by authority, gives rise to injustice, betrays itself.

It follows that:

4. Cherishment in time betrays the impossibility of fulfilling the goods of heterogeneous things together and of a measure of fulfillment. This impossibility, sacrifice, knows no rules, demands judgment without criteria, is wounded by endless responsibilities toward the good. This responsibility and judgment bring plenishment, a certain joy enriched by sorrow, giving beyond having.

5. Among creatures who can choose their goods, they must choose and cultivate those goods for themselves, betraying genitivity. None can know the joy and suffering of another, especially another kind, none can foster the good for another, certainly not the heterogeneous goods of other kinds. None can have the good except as betrayal. The work of cherishment presupposes having what cherishment shows cannot be had, betrays itself in genitivity. Plenishment for the sake of the good serves for the most part, if not always, as giving beyond having, multiplying goods in abundance, in

expressiveness, always betrayed as having. We can never know the joy possible for another kind, but find a joy for ourselves in letting that other kind be in its joy, multiplying goodness.

6. Nothing can justify the sacrifice of any kind to the good, of any kind, women, children, animals, Jews, not even the AIDS or smallpox virus. Nothing can be owned or had to make sacrifice good. Cherishment can never in the name of kindness impose the destruction, death, or sacrifice of a kind, reducing heterogeneity, claiming to possess its secret. Such a destruction is unjust, bears with it endless responsibility for restitution. Nothing can justify the sacrifice of an individual, of many individuals. Yet sacrifice is inescapable. Nothing can justify the destruction of a kind in the march of history. Yet history is the recurrence of such catastrophes. Nothing can justify the genitivity that upholds catastrophe. Yet life is the recurrence and betrayal of genitivity.

7. In the places where we compose ourself and others in proximity, exposed face to face, we know our goods to whatever extent they are knowable and we know of, grant the goods of others, always beyond any having— know this in life, in feeling, express it as betrayal. Especially, we know the weight of our injustices in the struggle for the good. We are more effective agents, closer to heterogeneous possibilities of the good, able to undertake our endless responsibilities, face to face, in proximity with others, making things and tasks our own. The work of the good is undertaken locally, face to face, in this sense private, in this sense genitive. The work of the good disperses in the general economy of goods in circulation, in this sense public, beyond genitivity. Everything depends on the struggle between the rule of genitivity in restricted economies and the upsurge of expenditure in general economy, everywhere in nature's plenitude. Everything depends on our capacity to struggle against our own injustices more than against the injustices of others, to betray the goodness of our own genitivity. The call of the good is a responsibility for our unending injustices, responsivity betraying betrayal.

Between general and restricted economy, then:

8. Resist hoarding, accumulation, coveting, and grasping; circulate goods throughout the earth; multiply exchange and trade; increase the velocity with which commodities move; turn profit into generosity, having into giving, building into wandering; revel in the betrayals that mark genitivity with responsivity, restricted economies with general economy, goods with echoes from the good; wander in the places in which we find ourselves, open to new arrivals; celebrate the expressiveness of things, multiply responsivity.

9. Cherish the goods we have; mourn what has been lost; plenish the earth in giving beyond taking.

A second way in which I hope to express giving beyond having, giving in kinds, is not *different from*, not *not* the other ways, but as *an other* expression, another betrayal—and these are endless. In responding to the abundance in the earth, in responding to the expressiveness and responsiveness of things, we may respond with love and care and kindness to the abundant kinds of the earth, in an economic register, in terms of commodities and money. We may then think of *philanthropy* as taking place between general and restricted economy, opening beyond having, beyond humanity. We may think of philanthropy ecstatically, beyond genitivity: a love, a care, for humanity that does not stop with man's, or men's, or humanity's propriety: *as philanthropy, philogyny, philogeny, philokyny*. I have called it *ecolonomics* and *economology*. Another name for plenishment, another resistance to having in perpetuity.

In its money form, philanthropy expresses the circulation of commodities beyond the genitivity, the profit, that obstructs their circulation. If money is the commodity of commodities, expressing circulation beyond genitivity, then philanthropy is the circulation of money and goods against the possibility of profit in commodities, against the return of property, resistance to holding onto what cannot be held. Following guidelines 8 and 9, we may pursue an economy of exchange and trade beyond property, propriety, and profit, an economy of giving *as not beyond* having, certainly *as not beyond* humanity.

Between restricted and political economy, then: facilitate trade; accumulate commodities in exchange; expend and consume what you can; give everything else away; maximize the circulation of things in abundance; institute a democratic state whose economic role is to foster philanthropy, to minimize profit and maximize expenditure, giving away.

My final gesture is to explore another possibility of giving beyond having, giving beyond itself: the betrayal of forgiveness.

# CHAPTER 17

## Forgiving

Forgive us our trespasses as we forgive them that trespass against us.
(Matthew 6:12)

forgiveness is judgement which discriminates what is equitable and does
so correctly; and correct judgement is that which judges what is true.
(Aristotle, *Nicomachean Ethics*, 1143a22–24)

In the Western tradition—and others—forgiveness represents extreme
giving, beyond gifts, if we can look beyond the shadow of God. When the
Furies assail Orestes, who has committed the greatest crime a man can
commit, Athena insists on a peace *not beyond* all understanding, that cannot be given a justification—though she pretends to give one, and though
that justification appears to found civic society. As Derrida insists, reading
Montaigne and Pascal (Derrida, *FL*, 945), the foundation of authority has
no authority. I would now say that law and authority betray their own
authority.

But the subject here is not law, civil society, and political legitimacy
but goodness and its genitivity. Law, civil society, political authority, every
form of goodness and authority can have, can possess, no authority. Authority cannot be possessed, cannot be had, yet imposes itself everywhere in
excess, in betrayal. The form authority takes is by betrayal; the formal
possibility of authority lies in the *as* of its proclamation, the promise of its
implementation.

If so, then betrayal itself, as genitivity, must take the form of something profoundly otherwise to itself, betraying itself, in the endless wandering that betrays having. Extreme giving, if you will, on the way—wandering,
crossing—from general to restricted economy. Extreme, transgressive, giving in restricted economy beyond having, beyond judgment, correctness,
and measure:[1] uncontainable; that promises, expresses, reveals something

beyond itself—giving in abundance. I am speaking of the extreme giving of gifts that betrays a giving beyond gifts. I am speaking of ecstasy, squander, generosity, and sustenance as betraying another giving *not beyond* themselves, a giving beyond having in the circulation of restricted economy.

As I said *forgiveness*, a figure filled with betrayal, one might say betrayal itself. Extreme giving, *for*-giving *as not beyond*. Betraying and betrayed in becoming an instrument of God, without doubt filled with love, infinitely contained by its insistence on sin. God forgives the sinner, and we who live under God must also forgive the sinner, granting and betraying the sin, thereby betraying giving itself, which has no measure or condition, not even the mercy that returns us to genitivity.

What if the extreme giving in forgiveness—not known in English as in German to be extreme; what if the *vor* in *vor*-giveness were transgressive, betrayal, of the transgressions and betrayals to which forgiveness responds? What of an extreme forgiveness that took betrayal for granted, that betrayed betrayal and sacrificed sacrifice, but did not take sin for granted? Where transgression meant betrayal and not sin—that is, did not take the moral law for granted, by which I do not mean that it opposed that law or claimed another? I am speaking again of the endless betrayal of betrayal *as* a giving beyond having that interrupts the having—*as*.

God's forgiveness—*pardonner, Vergebung*—is extreme, perfect, utter giving. Without return, without compensation. Still in the genitive. In the shadow of such forgiveness, I offer forgiveness to the sinner without insisting on further gifts: remorse, restitution, repentance. Even so, I insist, I mark in this forgiveness the sin to be forgiven, hold the sin tightly even as I would let it pass away, touched by mercy. I let it pass away into circulation beyond any accumulation in a gesture—betrayal—that holds tightly to the sin. Above all, then, I insist on knowing and having the sin as a sin, knowing the sinner's sin in the genitive, knowing and having the act for which I offer forgiveness as a sin, a crime, a transgression. Forgiveness and transgression go together here in the assurance of sin. Holding this assurance fast, in the genitive.

The genitive betrays another possibility of transgression and forgiveness, not a better or superior or alternative possibility, a forgiveness that should be chosen instead of forgiveness in the genitive. Utter giving, giving beyond having, is not something to choose, is nothing at all, does not replace generosity, the giving of gifts. Forgiveness beyond the fixing of the transgression under law does not replace the need to enforce the law and punish the transgressor, to remember the crime, to mourn the betrayal. Forgiveness beyond does not fix betrayal in mourning and wounding, nor does it release them from this fixing. Forgiveness beyond transgression betrays the betrayal—a difficult and enigmatic possibility. Beyond, utter giving as forgiveness struggles against, betrays, the naming of the crime as a crime, understands transgression as a crime, perhaps, but also *as* a cross-ing *not beyond*—for example, beyond the law, calling the law into question; beyond the assurance of the law; beyond the justification of law by itself, in the excess of every authority. Forgiveness throws us from the authorities without which we cannot live, cannot live well, down into the possibility that those authorities have no authority, no justification, are themselves crimes, betrayals, at every border. Forgiveness is the giving at the point at which being wounded by betrayal must face the possibility that the betrayal was no betrayal, or exceeded crime and sin, at the point at which betrayal betrays too much and itself.

I briefly interrupt to consider what others have said of forgiveness—a tortured affair:

> Forgiveness to the injured does belong;
> But they ne'er pardon who have done the wrong.

> If you forgive people enough you belong to them, and they to you, whether either person likes it or not.

> He, who cannot forgive a trespass of malice to his enemy, has never yet tasted the most sublime enjoyment of love.

> To err is human, to forgive, divine.

In these perhaps most famous expressions of Christianity's understanding of forgiveness, one thing stands out repeatedly: forgiveness is linked so tightly to trespass that it can never become unconditional. So the thought behind Christian, European forgiveness is aporetic: unconditional forgive-ness insists on trespass, insists on having in the midst of unconditional giving. And perhaps that is the only alternative—in restricted economy, tightly bound to genitivity. *Our* forgiveness; *their* trespasses.

I understand this forgiveness not as extreme, utter giving, not giving beyond having, but as a giving that betrays the beyond—betrays it by an-other trespass but also, much more to the point here, reveals it. The sub-lime enjoyment of love, the love that forgives, is not bound to trespass, nor unconditional as if erasing trespass, but something else, otherwise—per-haps nothing at all. Forgiveness, the love that passes all understanding, betrays both the wound and a giving beyond joy and sorrow. Not that God alone can forgive; not that human beings who forgive serve God's law; not even that forgiveness is beyond all understanding. Forgiveness is the giving that betrays betrayal—betrays it while insisting on obliterating it—but also betrays much more, otherwise, beyond trespass and forgetting, wounding and healing, joy and sorrow, mercy and resentment. In forgiveness, by

betraying betrayal, pain and sorrow become joy beyond: Spinoza's joy—
*laetitia.*

With these words I hope to close a circle from Spinoza's doubled joy,
*gaudeo* and *laetitia*, to Derrida's yes yes! Expressed in the joy beyond all
pain that is betrayal betraying itself *as not beyond*. Joy *as not beyond* itself,
betraying itself; betrayal betraying itself as joy. To be thrown into the world
is to be thrown into joy and sorrow, into betrayal, as the joy of being
thrown, as indebted beyond all containment—still in joy, the inconceivable
and uncontainable joy of giving. The betrayal of betrayal is this joy, forgiveness the betrayal, always revealing more than the wound, forgiving beyond
mourning. Forgiveness is the revel in the revelation that is the betrayal of
being; the other side, *au-delà*, of betrayal as forgiveness. Forgiveness and
betrayal open onto promises beyond imagining, of pain and pleasure, joy
and sorrow; and this promise betrays—reveals—another joy beyond the
distress of impossible debts and obligations.

I conclude with an example of forgiveness, of unrestrained giving, joy,
and betrayal, in which, perhaps, there is no trespass, no crime or sin, no
moral transgression, no evil—perhaps no mercy; but infinite pain and sorrow betraying life itself. It is an example from Locke, who betrays its promise. I have discussed it elsewhere.[2] It seems to me to speak to life and death
more deeply than examples in which we feel ourselves exposed to evil.

> The death of a child that was the daily delight of its mother's eyes, and joy
> of her soul, rends from her heart the whole comfort of her life, and gives
> her all the torment imaginable. . . . Till time has by disuse separated the
> sense of that enjoyment and its loss, from the idea of the child returning
> to her memory, all representations, though ever so reasonable, are in vain;
> and therefore some in whom the union between these ideas is never dis-
> solved, spend their lives in mourning, and carry an incurable sorrow to
> their graves. (Locke, *E*, 532)

Locke presents this as an example of the madness that comes with the
uncontrolled association of ideas. The mother who has lost her child is
mad, and we must wait and hope for her to regain her senses, hoping that
she will not spend her life in incurable sorrow. Locke resists the accumulation of pain that is the mother's lot. Perhaps we would all wish to take
away her pain—but not to pretend that she has not been grievously wounded.
It is not wrong for her to grieve, to spend the rest of her life in grief. Not
wrong and not mad, but too much pain. Yet it is certainly wrong for her
to forget her loss.

I offer forgiveness in this place, a mother's forgiveness—not of anyone
or anything that brought about her sorrow, not even God. She need not
forgive, and is not worse for holding onto her grief. But if she forgives she

gives no gift, not even to herself, returns no gifts for the gifts she has been given and the gift taken away. Forgiveness is of no debt, insists on no trespass. If she forgives, if she returns to life and joy within a memory and mourning and grief that allow themselves to be forgiven, it is in awareness of the immeasurable betrayal that took away her child—not anyone's betrayal: the inescapable betrayal of being—and of what this betrayal betrays all the more: the rest of her life, the memory of the child she keeps alive by going on with her life. Forgiveness here is betrayal and its betrayal, the betrayal of a terrible experience, in whose shadow she must live the rest of her life, one way or another; the betrayal in that betrayal of the abundance of things—her other children, other experiences, other possibilities, life itself, always with its domesticity in mind, other betrayals.

Forgiveness here is the intermediariness—not mediation—of betrayal betraying itself, crossing between the giving of gifts that we may hope to have, must have in the genitive to live, and a giving in abundance beyond any gift, any having. Forgiveness does not erase betrayal, does not cancel or enforce it, but is betrayal as the promise of a giving and an exposure and an arrival—a giving away *as not beyond*: not beyond to God, beyond the earth, some place beyond; but the promise betrayed here in exposure. Forgiveness is the betrayal in the wounds of life betrayed, a giving without reason or justification of unbounded joy, without which daily joy and having would be impossible. From the depths of her sorrow, the mother gives— to no one in particular, to everyone including herself—the most precious gift possible, the gift that surpasses owning, genitivity, *as not beyond* having—nothing at all: the joy of being, living, in exposure, *as not beyond* any grasp, including holding onto a grief without gladness. Forgiveness is the unrestrained gladness in betrayal, the giving in and *not* beyond any having. Betrayal betrayed. The promise of being *as not beyond* itself.

# *Notes*

## General Preface to the Project

1. I recall Socrates' suggestion that knowledge, truth, and, perhaps, being itself all come as gifts from the good (Plato, *Republic*, 508–9), and his description of the indefinite dyad, which I associate with the good, "a gift of the gods" (*Philebus*, 16c): "all things . . . consist of a one and a many"; we must "come to see not merely that the one we started with is a one and an unlimited many, but also just how many it is"; must discern "the total number of forms the thing in question has intermediate between its one and its unlimited number" (16d), an intermediate number I associate with *technē*; "It is only then, when we have done that, that we may let each one of all these intermediate forms pass away into the unlimited and cease bothering about them" (16e). I understand the passing away as giving, general economy, the circulation of gifts, and understand unlimit as the good, the earth's abundance, insisting on the intermediate number, the intermediary abundance of kinds, interrupting all human and natural works. I understand the good as intermediariness, giving the possibility of measures, norms, and standards, always contingent, partial, incomplete, local, at risk, in endless circulation, resisting authority. What mediation may bring to rest, intermediariness keeps in movement. The good brings movement and rest in abundance.

I understand *rest* as a diaphoric, intermediary movement. (See my *PE*, chaps. 4 and 5, and my *GBGA*.) I understand the repeated *we*, here and elsewhere, as another such movement, betraying multiple, heterogeneous kinds. I understand *betrayal* as exposure. See n. 11.

2. I recall here several allusions to gifts and giving. One is the "gift of the gods" from *Philebus*, the movement from limit to unlimit touching intermediary numbers, intermediary movements, understood in terms of general and restricted economy (See nn. 1 and 5).

A second is Heidegger's portrayal of the "it gives" *(es gibt)* and giving of Being. "In the beginning of Western thinking, Being is thought, but not the 'It gives' as such. The latter withdraws in favor of the gift which It gives" (Heidegger, *TB*, 8). I understand these words to call attention to the giving rather than to the It or to Being, the

251

gift. I understand them to evoke Heidegger's question in his reading of the Anaximander fragment, words of giving without having: "Can [what lingers awhile] give what it doesn't have?" (Heidegger, *AF*, 43)—jointure and propriety together with property. I understand abundance in the earth as giving in memory of the good, of injustice without the slightest hope of justice, giving without having, endless circulation.

In a similar vein, my third allusion, Hyde speaks of the circulation of the gift: "a gift is a thing we do not get by our own efforts. We cannot buy it; we cannot acquire it through an act of will. It is bestowed upon us" (Hyde, *G*, ix); "The only essential is this: *the gift must always move*. There are other forms of property that stand still, that mark a boundary or resist momentum, but the gift keeps going" (p. 4). I understand the good as giving, always moving, circulating, where humanity and nature strive to slow or halt the circulation by imposing limits and exclusions. In this way the thought of the good and giving is a thought of inclusion, beyond the limits of work and *technē*, beyond possession. *Technē* works by limits, exclusions; choices, boundaries, and appropriations belong to *technē*. The thought of the good is a thought beyond the limits of *technē*, sometimes named *poiēsis*, sometimes *mimēsis*, giving in abundance, unlimiting every limit, expropriating every appropriation. I understand the circulation as general economy, after Bataille; as expression, after Spinoza; as saying, after Levinas; as exposure in proximity.

My final allusion recalls Derrida's explorations of the aporias of the gift: the impossibility of a gift without giver or return that is the condition of the possibility of ethics—given, I would say, in the name of the good.

> It must not circulate, it must not be exchanged, it must not in any case be exhausted, as a gift, by the process of exchange, by the movement of circulation of the circle in the form of return to the point of departure. (Derrida, *GT*, 7)

> For this is the impossible that seems to give itself to be thought here: These conditions of possibility of the gift . . . designate simultaneously the conditions of the impossibility of the gift. (p. 11)

He speaks of the gift as giving time and death.

> The difference between a gift and every other operation or pure and simple exchange is that the gift gives time. *There where there is gift, there is time.* (p. 41)

> The gift made to me by God as he holds me in his gaze and in his hand while remaining inaccessible to me, the terribly dissymmetrical gift of the *mysterium tremendum* . . . giv[es me] the secret of death, a new experience of death. (Derrida, *GD*, 34)

I read Derrida as examining, and resisting, the countless ways in which the good—on my view, nothing at all—becomes goodness, offers boundless rewards and possessions to human subjects, perhaps European-Christian subjects. "An event gives the gift that transforms the Good into a Goodness that is forgetful of itself into a love that renounces itself" (Derrida, *GD,* p. 40); "This occurs in particular by means of a very problematical opposition, it seems to me, between *giving* and *taking*" (Derrida, *OS,* 10–11). The giving of the good, as I understand it, knows nothing of taking, gives without return; yet time is filled with endless takings, appropriations and betrayals. I read Derrida's writing on gifts and giving to pursue these echoes of betrayal. I understand the relation between giving and gifts, general and restricted economy, as betrayal. See n. 11.

I remain with a giving from the good that is given by no subject, person, thing, or God, or given to them, that can never become goodness, but that gives responsibility for goodness everywhere. The good gives no reward, knows nothing of return, of goods and possessions, though all of time pays restitution for the giving, responding to the touch and its call. I hope to listen to the music of this call beyond the wounds of debt, resisting being's neutrality. See n. 15.

3. I think of exposure and the good in memory of Levinas, who speaks of *exposition*—exposure and expression—and of a responsibility to the other, dyadically, that endlessly grows as it is paid. See the introduction, p. 6. I hope to betray the singularity of the other in the general economy of kinds. See nn. 1, 5.

4. I think of *we* and *us* and *they* as enigmatic, intermediary figures of kinds I think of the *calling* and *giving* of the good. See nn. 1 and 2 on giving, n. 15 on calling.

5. Heidegger speaks of abundance *(Fülle)* (Heidegger, *TB,* 6; *OWA,* 34, 76); Levinas speaks of fecundity (Levinas, *TI,* 267-69): "The relation with . . . a future, irreducible to the power over possibles, we shall call fecundity" (Levinas, *TI,* 269). I speak of the inexhaustibility and immeasurability of giving in abundance.

I think of the work of the good as occupying restricted economies, goods divided from bads, binary oppositions and exclusions, setting prices. I think of the good as interrupting every restricted economy, every totality, circulating in the general economy of excess, unlimit, unmeasure. The giving of the good is the general economy of local and contingent goods that circulate everywhere in restricted economies of kinds within immeasurable exposure. It works dyadically where things touch each other in restricted economies, frequently destructively and violently; it exceeds every measure in the intimacy and responsiveness of touch. It marks the possibility of an ecology that interrupts the restrictions of economy with abundance in the earth, for the sake of the good.

Whatever comes from the good, every gift, is local, contingent: restricted economy. Yet every restriction is contingent; every limit is limited, including totality. The good gives its abundance in ideality, in heterogeneity and multiplicity, in every place, in every kind: restricted economy, local ecology. General economy interrupts limitation with abundance; locality and contingency interrupt totality. The giving interrupts the gathering of being, resists neutrality, recalls the abundance and heterogeneity of precious things that touch each other and respond as a call without fulfillment.

In this way, the good resists every binary opposition, resists every measure, not as another opposition or measure, and not as another place or thing. The good is not a good, neither good nor bad, nor good and bad, nor neuter, indifferent to good and evil. It is neither transcendent nor immanent, high nor low, inside nor outside, but interrupts the choice of either l or and neither l nor, the grip of the one or the other, the authority of "or," and "and," and "neither," and "both," of "I" and "we," all belonging to restricted economies. I speak in the name of the good of the exposure borne by every creature and thing within its limits to countless others, and the responsibilities they bear to resist the injustices of every limit by an interrupting movement. I call this movement the general economy of the good. I think of nature as the general and excessive circulation of local and contingent goods exposed to other individuals and kinds giving birth to the work they do in restricted, exchange economies.

I pursue the thought of restricted and general economies found in Bataille, *AS*. (See my *PE*, chaps. 5 and 6; my *GBGA*, chap. 7; and my *GG*, chap. 12.) I understand the crossing of restricted and general economy as the giving of the good, expressed by Plato in *Philebus* as the indefinite dyad: limit passing away into unlimit. (See nn. 1, 2, and 6.) I speak here of general economy after Spinoza as the abundance of kinds beyond possession, endless flows and streams, foldings, unfoldings, and refoldings. Always expressive. Always *mimēsis*. Giving birth to the possibility of transforming restricted economies into mobile, responsive ecologies. Giving birth in betrayal.

6. I speak of the good in memory of Plato, where the good provides no measure. I speak of the good interrupting measure rather than of instrumentality and teleology, think of inclusion rather than of hierarchy and exclusion. I speak of the good remembering excesses of desire, think of excesses of love and care, of dyads touching each other intimately in the flesh, of violence and destruction, rather than of rule and law. I speak of the good rather than of power, think of moving toward and away, of touching, rather than of causation. I speak of the good rather than of freedom, think of the call of conscience to work, to touch, rather than of movements without limit. I speak of the good rather than of being, think of truth as exposure and of exposure as touch. I speak of the good rather than of God, think of circulating in general, excessive economy, giving without ground or law. All these renunciations belong to work, to judgment, as we strive to build and control. But something in this striving summons us to know that building requires sacrifice, that judgment calls for endless vigilance, that touch demands response, that being is betrayal. I think of this something—nothing—as the good, that which calls us to and interrupts ideality, makes judgment possible. I think of the good in memory of disaster.

7. Whoever "we" are, echoes of the good.

8. Levinas speaks "Against the Philosophy of the Neuter *[Neutre]*" (Levinas, *TI*, 298), breaking with the impersonal neutrality of Being in the name of the good Irigaray speaks against nature "in the neuter" (Irigaray, *TG*, 141). My project works against neutrality in the name of abundance.

9. I have spoken of the good, after Anaximander, as betrayed by injustice, for which all works are restitutions: betrayed without measure (See nn. 11 and 14) Derrida speaks of it as justice (Derrida, *FL*). Plato speaks of it repeatedly. Again, the good is not a thing, a measure, does not divide, does not exclude, but gives all things to us, places them in circulation, exposes us to them, charges us to respond, to betray every betrayal.

10. Blanchot speaks of the step *(pas)* not *(pas)* beyond *(au-delà)* (and not a step) *(Le pas au-delà)*. I speak of *beyond* as incessantly traversing this *not*, this impossibility. The limits of limits (as) (not) (beyond), anything but absolute, impossible to have or hold. *Beyond, otherwise, excess, without*: betrayals betrayed.

11. I understand *betrayal* as *exposition*, expression together with treachery, revelation joined with perfidy, giving with disaster. I would not forget the expressiveness in betrayal, as *mimēsis*, as giving forth, giving away. Gifts betray the giving, betray the good, expose and freeze its movements: general and restricted economy. I hope to speak of betrayal on the side of its expressiveness, listening to voices from other places, mementos of abundance.

I take inspiration from Levinas's words of betrayal and the good: "The beyond being, showing itself in the said, always shows itself there enigmatically, is already betrayed" (Levinas, *OB*, 19). And from Lyotard: "[I]n witnessing, one also exterminates. The witness is a traitor" (Lyotard, *I*, 204). The good is betrayed, revealed, in exposure, given in every place that gives it birth. Exposure is disaster.

12. I understand sacrifice as betrayal, marking its exposition. Sacrifice betrays abundance as perfidy, through treachery, seduction, and duplicity, in violation; but also—another duplicity—reveals, discloses, and expresses abundance, augments it in its betrayal. In this double betrayal, itself doubly betrayed, cherishment gives itself through disaster over to plenishment. Plenishment is this giving of abundance as betrayal, betraying the giving in every gift. Having, owning, and possessing betray abundance in the earth as the (im)possibility of giving without having, where having is disaster.

13. I speak of sonance in my *RR*: the ring of representation. Levinas speaks of *la gloire de l'Infini* (Levinas, *AÊ*, 230).

14. "Kata to chreōn didonai gar auta dikēn kai tisin allēlois tēs adikias." The entire fragment from Simplicius is canonically translated as: "Into those things from which existing things have their coming into being, their passing away, too, takes place, according to what must be; for they make reparation to one another for their injustice according to the ordinance of time, as he puts it in somewhat poetical language" (Simplicius *Phys.*, 24, 18 [DK 12 B 1]; Robinson, *EGP*, 34).

15. I speak repeatedly of *the call of the good*. I hope that those who respond to this call hear multiple reverberations, for example Heidegger's *call (Ruf)* of conscience, the disclosedness of *Dasein* as constituted by state-of-mind, understanding, falling, and discourse, summoned to its ownmost Being-guilty (Heidegger, *BT*, 313–14). Yet conscience and discourse seem to me to reinstate the privilege of humanity

in the gift of language, marks of Spirit, interrupted by the good; summoning and guilt seem to me to express ethicality and the good without exposure to their betrayals. Another example is *saying* in Levinas, understood as interruption, exposure, and proximity, reinstating subjectivity. A third is the debt in memory of the injustices that Anaximander says compose the ordinance of time.

A profusion of other reverberations: I think of the call of music, echoes of wind and rain, movements of celestial spheres, the timbres of bodies touching. I think of the sounds of life; the tones of voices and instruments; songs, carols, melodies, and cries, shouts and yells; screams and bellows and roars, screeches and shrieks of animals and birds; I think of debts and obligations, of demands to act, to strive, brought by necessity to performances, to deeds, summoned for the sake of something beyond show; of events promised, heralded, greeted, or announced; of being taken to task, obligated and indebted, evoked, cited, served by decree under the law, in the name of judgment; of naming and designation, questioning and interrogation, of being asked to respond; I recall congregation and community, calls to mingle and gather, echoing the assembling of being and language in the name of *legein* (see n. 16); to augur, foretell, most of all, perhaps, to prophesy and to divine—despite the death of God. I think of calling to work, to task, to art, to labor, to master, demanding knowledge, skill, craft, *technē*, and more, always something more, *poiēsis* or beauty. I think of callers, those who call out, those who call to enter—guests, visitors, or strangers; another memory of gathering and community. Repeated calls of interruption: welcoming, giving, generosity.

The calling of the good is all of these, and more. Here it is *expression*, bodies squeezing, saying, meaning, touching, evoking responsiveness to touch, a responsiveness that is known to human beings as responsibility in the name of, for the sake of the good, where the good gives and calls but is nothing, no thing, no being; giving and calling as interruption and betrayal. As *mimēsis*.

The calling of the good is exposure and expression, corporeal movements of general and restricted economy, resisting neutrality.

16. I refer to *legein* as the gathering of being as saying in truth. With Levinas I read this gathering as betraying the good. Being in the neuter. (See my *GTGG*.) My entire project undertakes resistance to neutrality.

17. Questions that mark the course of this project through the volumes of its succession. See n. page xiii.

18. Or (as) (not) (beyond).

19. Wherever I speak of ethics or politics I hope to speak of them together as ethics | politics, or politics|ethics, circulating in intimate, diaphoric relation.

## Introduction

1. I undertake an excursus on genitivity as the mark of the origin. Like gender in English, *genre* and *Geschlecht* in French and German, the genitive is a grammatical term—said to be "grammar only"—that exceeds the limits of language—if

there be such. Language with grammar constitutes a field of demarcation and struggle over the limits of the world, obliquely marking—betraying—the abundance of the earth.

An example:

> **genitive.** *Gram.—adj.* 1. (in certain inflected languages, noting a case used primarily to indicate that a noun is a modifier of another noun, often to express possession, measure, origin, characteristic, etc. . . . ) *(RHD1)*

> 1. *Genitive case*: a grammatical form of substantives and other declinable parts of speech, chiefly used to denote that the person or thing signified by the word is related to another as source, possessor, or the like, but in different languages also employed in a variety of idiomatic usages. *(OED)*

Genitivity marks the source, ancestor, or possessor—the origin; inscribes the progenitor; defines the characteristic mark of identity. Yet once a language possesses genitivity, insists on genealogy, evokes gender, it expresses a variety of idiomatic, idiosyncratic usages betraying and exceeding its origin, exceeding every grammatical relation.

For the moment I am concerned with the origin, doubly betrayed in genitivity, insisting on neutrality—one might say, somewhat obliquely in the *Random House Dictionary*, but explicitly in the *Oxford English Dictionary*. *How profoundly is being in the earth—of humans and other creatures and things—to be understood in terms of having: possession, property, and genitivity: that is, in terms of origin, cause and determination, always struggling with neutrality, always betraying a lack of neutrality?*

Earthly things circulate throughout language in the genitive, representing the origin.

> Fries found that the possessive genitive was the most common, but that it accounted for only 40 percent of all genitives. The other 60 percent was split up among various functions. We summarize a number of these here. . . .
>     *Subjective genitive* and *genitive of origin*. . . .
>     Shakespeare's plays
>     *Objective genitive* or *object genitive*. . . .
>     Caesar's murderers
>     *Descriptive genitive* or *classifying genitive*. Fries adds the *genitive of measure* to this:
>        the room's furnishings
>        the airplane's speed . . .
>     . . . the *genitive of purpose*:
>        men's shirts
>     . . . the periphrastic form of these genitives of purpose so made with the preposition *for*, rather than *of*:
>        shirts *for* men. . . . *(MWDEU*, 475)

These examples suggest that all forms of the genitive evoke the origin in its originary meanings, present in *ousia*, as possession and property, reiterating the sense that having has been the defining characteristic of human beings and things, appearing in inflected (Indo-European) languages as the genitive.

It appears that we must not let things wander throughout the earth, but must pin them down where they belong, attached to some human being, no matter what betrayal. It appears that the question of possession—who or what may own and who or what may be owned—is to be settled grammatically, if it can be settled at all. We come to a number of questions directed toward the possibility of giving beyond having: Can language speak without genitivity, at best with local genitivity, conjoined with endless responsibility? Can humanity live without property, at best with interrupted possession, exchanging without accumulation? Can humanity receive the abundance of the earth as the giving of earthly gifts without insisting on having, owning, possessing in the genitive?

2. See my *GTEG*, chaps. 1 and 2.

3. See chap. 2, where I read *Gorgias* as concerned with property and possessions, with what happiness requires us to have.

4. I have called this territorial gathering Kant's ethical | political | architectural | territorial project See my *GTGG*, especially chaps. 4 and 9. Philosophy as architecture, building as realm *(Gebiet)*, territory *(Bode)*, dwelling *(Aufenthalt)*, habitation (or dwelling-house) *(Wohnhause)*, outhouses, additions *(Anzubauen)*. Here I think of building as annexing and claiming territory, of converting the earth to land, to something occupied and owned. As philosophy.

5. See the general preface, n. 14.

6. "Can it give what it doesn't have?" (Heidegger, *AF*, 43). See the general preface, n. 2, on giving. I interpret giving without having as *plenishment*, linking *cherishment* and *sacrifice*, insisting on the sacrifice of sacrifice, a double betrayal, refusing the possibility of owning or possessing sacrifice, of accumulating the giving into gifts. More of this later. See especially chap. 1, pp. 16–20.

7. If God is male, as if God's gender were not his genitivity in another register.

8. See chap. 1, pp. 16–17, for the full quotation. See also the discussions of Derrida in chaps. 1, 10, 12, 13, 15, and 16.

9. Concern is always *mine* "Dasein's facticity is such that its Being-in-the-world has always dispersed *[zerstreut]* itself or even split itself up into definite ways of Being-in" (Heidegger, *BT*, 83).

10. We may consider Lyotard's words on Heidegger: "The forgetting of Being becomes constitutive of Western philosophy" (Lyotard, *"HJ,"* 146); "But remaining anchored in the thought of Being, the 'Western' prejudice that the Other is Being, it has nothing to say about a thought in which the Other is the Law" (Lyotard, *HJ*, 89). These words appear silent on genitivity, unless we understand this prejudice in

being as genitivity. Things are present to be owned. Human beings are present to own. Yet owning, having, possessing, being in the genitive, all are given from the good without genitivity, a giving with endless responsibility. I raise the question Heidegger avoids, whether coming to presence, being, and genitivity presuppose giving in exposure.

11. Understanding the sacrifice of sacrifice as betrayal, including the genitive.

12. Additional examples:

> The more I return to myself, the more I divest myself, under the traumatic effect of persecution, of my freedom as a constituted, willful, imperialist subject, the more I discover myself to be responsible; the more just I am, the more guilty I am I am "in myself" through the others. (Levinas, *OB*, 112)

> *The infinity of responsibility denotes not its actual immensity, but a responsibility increasing in the measure that it is assumed;* duties become greater in the measure that they are accomplished. (Levinas, *TI*, 244)

13. See chap. 4, pp. 60–66.

14. See chaps. 7 and 9: "the specialist fragments the robust unitary conception of ownership into a more shadowy 'bundle of rights' " (Grey, *DP*, 69).

15. I throw myself down under the curse that doubly curses humanity and nature in the genitive.

> The victim is a surplus taken from the mass of *useful* wealth. . . . Once chosen, he is the *accursed share [part maudite]*, destined for violent consumption. But the curse tears him away from the *order of things*; it gives him a recognizable figure, which now radiates intimacy, anguish, the profundity of living beings. (Bataille, *AS*, 1, 59)

> It is nature transfigured by the *curse*, to which the spirit then accedes only through a new movement of refusal, of insubordination, of revolt. (*AS*, 2, 78)

16. Ascribed to Chief Seattle by David Krell (Krell, *DL*, 317). These words cannot be found in Chief Seattle's published speech (Nerburn, *WGC*). But they have become famous, almost emblematic. In the genitive. I would supplement them with less famous words: "Desert rain is a precious gift from the clouds in the sky. Rain in the desert is a gift of life": giving what no one has.

17. See especially chaps. 7 and 8.

18. As does Spinoza, who speaks of a democracy from which he excludes "women and slaves, who are under the authority of men and masters, and also

children and wards, as long as they are under the authority of parents and guardians" (Spinoza, *PT*, 386). Always authority, insisting on propriety. For "there has never been a case of men and women reigning together, but wherever on the earth men are found, there we see that men rule, and women are ruled, and that on this plan, both sexes live in harmony" (pp. 386–87). The reason lies in the nature of intimacy in the home.

> But if we further reflect upon human passions, how men, in fact, generally love women merely from the passion of lust, and esteem their cleverness and wisdom in proportion to the excellence of their beauty, and also how very ill-disposed men are to suffer the women they love to show any sort of favour to others, and other facts of this kind, we shall easily see that men and women cannot rule alike without great hurt to peace. But of this enough. (p. 387)

In the dwelling, in the home, in the nature of household management. Understanding men's authority in the genitive as property. With an ironic gesture interrupting the authority of male genitality l genitivity. Enough, enough. Permitting us to wonder if property, authority, and genitality are always excessive, always too much.

More of Aristotle and Spinoza later (chaps. 2 and 3). More of economy l ecology as giving without having. More of women and children, kin and kind, the genitality in genitivity—genealogy: marks of blood, sex, kin, class, food, desire, and power, all excessive, where we do not know what bodies can do, where genitality reaches toward ecstasy and where genitivity reaches toward expropriation, dispossessing every possession, unauthorizing every authority, interrupting every interruption, betraying every betrayal.

19. My *GTEG* is an exploration of the expressiveness of bodies in proximity. Here I am concerned with property. I wonder if stones are there to be owned, or if *Dasein* prohibits genitivity, for stones and everything else.

From this moment on, we will be accompanied by Rochelle, who insists that we remember rocks and stones, small and large. Rochelle doesn't speak, but she thinks in French—if she thinks at all—of Pierre, who if he is not *here* is *elsewhere*. Always *here* as well as *there*.

20. See the general introduction, nn. 1, 3, and 5.

21. See chap. 4, p. 60. See also my *IR*, chap. 6.

22. See the general preface, n. 2. See also Derrida's discussion of Heidegger's hand in *G2*, together with discussions of *G2* in my *IR, OT, PE, GB, GA, GTGG, GTEG,* and *GKGA.* See also here chaps. 1 and 12.

23. As Derrida says, *tout autre est tout autre*: every other is entirely other. Every otherness is, I would say, other. Just that. Nothing at all. Impossible to possess, yet in infinite debt. See chap. 15.

## Chapter 1

1. See for example where he speaks of the "two genitives: truth of truth and truth of truth" (Derrida, *TP*, 5): the double genitive of truth's truth; also of Schapiro's truth of Heidegger's truth of Van Gogh's shoes (Derrida, *R*): restitutions to the genitivity of truth. "I owe the shoes, I must return them to their rightful owner, to their proper belonging. . . . But to whom in truth?" (p. 272).

2. See especially Derrida, *SM*, 17, 26, 27, 28, 41, 42, 65, 90, 97, 128, 129, 145, 150, 154, 184.

3. *Mimēsis* as the impossibility of possessing or having meaning, knowledge, and truth in the genitive forever; as the erotic flesh that obscures the transparency of meanings—and keeps them in circulation; as the (general) economy of truth; as the (schizophrenic) economy of desire; as betrayal, the disparate itself betrayed.

4. See especially chap. 8.

5. See the introduction, n. 21.

6. Through chap. 5, perhaps, more obliquely, through chap. 10.

7. See the introduction, p. 4, especially n. 8.

8. Derrida's words:

> Otherwise, justice risks being reduced once again to juridical-moral rules, norms, or representations, within an inevitable totalizing horizon (movement of adequate restitution, expiation, or reappropriation). Heidegger runs this risk, despite so many necessary precautions, when he gives priority, as he always does, to gathering *(rassemblement)* and to the same . . . over the interruption. (Derrida, *SM*, 28)

9. See the introduction, pp. 6, 11–12.

10. A few genealogical citations, repeatedly betraying the genitive:

> What, then, are these *three things of the thing?*

> 1. First of all, mourning. We will be speaking of nothing else. It consists always in attempting to ontologize remains, to make them present, in the first place by *identifying* the bodily remains and by *localizing* the dead. . . . One has to know. *One has to know it. One has to have knowledge [Il faut le savoir].* . . .
> 2. Next, one cannot speak of generations *(générations)* of skulls or spirits *(Kant qui genuit [begets] Hegel qui genuit Marx)* except on the condition of language—and the voice, in any case of that which *marks* the name or takes its place. . . .

3. Finally *(Marx qui genuit Valéry . . . )*, the thing *works*, whether it transforms or transforms itself, poses or decomposes itself: the spirit, the "spirit of the spirit" is *work*. But what is work? (Derrida, *SM*, 9)

11. See Foucault, *NGH*. See also my *GKGA*.

12. I call this history's *lowliness*. See chap. 4, pp. 61–62.

13. Ten plagues, two interpretations, ten ghosts, more interpretations, more genitivity, named and measured:

1. Unemployment. . . .
2. The massive exclusion of homeless citizens. . . .
3. The ruthless economic war among the countries of the European community. . . .
4. The inability to master the contradictions in the concept, norms, and reality of the free market. . . .
5. The aggravation of the foreign debt. . . .
6. The arms industry and trade. . . .
7. The spread of nuclear weapons. . . .
8. Inter-ethnic wars . . . driven by an *archaic* phantasm and concept, by a *primitive conceptual phantom* of community, the nation-State, sovereignty, borders, native soil and blood. . . .
9. . . . the growing and undelimitable, that is, worldwide power of those super-efficient and properly capitalist phantom-States that are the mafia and the drug cartels on every continent. . . .
10. . . . the present state of international law and of its institutions. . . . (Derrida, *SM*, 80–83)

*Gespenst No. 1:* (ghost no. 1): the supreme being *(das höchste Wesen)*, God.
*Gespenst No. 2*: Being or essence *(Das Wesen)*.
*Gespenst No. 3*: the vanity of the world.
*Gespenst No. 4*: good and evil beings *(die guten und bösen Wesen)*.
*Gespenst No. 5*: Being and its realm *(das Wesen und sein Reich)*.
*Gespenst No. 6*: beings, therefore *(die Wesen)*.
*Gespenst No. 7*: the Man-God *(der Gottmensch)*.
*Gespenst No. 8*: man. . . . The most "unheimlich" of all ghosts. . . . Man *makes himself fear.* He makes himself into the fear that he inspires. . . . The ipseity of the self is constituted there. No one will have escaped it, neither Marx, nor the Marxists, nor of course their mortal enemies, all those who want to defend the property and integrity of their home: the body proper, the proper name, nation, blood, territory, and the "rights" that are founded thereon.
*Gespenst No. 9*: the spirit of the people *(Volksgeist)*.
*Gespenst No. 10*: Everything. Marx will have succeeded in transmuting everything, the All itself, into a ghost *("Alles" in ein Spuk zu verwandeln)*. (pp. 143–46)

Ten plagues created the promised land. And now, the new ten plagues. Always ten—genitivity's measure. What promised land, and for which heirs? Which sons? When will daughters inherit? And do they wish to do so? Do I, or you, wish them to do so? By which I do not mean to consider the possibility that they should continue to be disinherited, but that inheritance might become something different with a new arrival, advent, of property. Which might be very old. Disinheriting in the genitive.

14. A brief allusion in anticipation of later discussions, especially chaps. 10, 12–13, 15–16:

> It is no doubt the case that there neither can be nor should be any concept adequate to what we call responsibility. Responsibility carries within it, and must do so, an essential excessiveness. It regulates itself neither on the principle of reason nor on any sort of accountancy. (Derrida, *EW*, 272)

> I believe there is no responsibility, no ethico-political decision, that must not pass through the proofs of the incalculable or the undecidable. (p. 273)

Excessive responsibility interrupting neutrality and genitivity. Property without genitivity. To own and possess by disowning and refusing possession, insisting on circulation, on betrayal. Against every Marxism, perhaps, or Heideggerism and Derridaism. Even Continental philosophy—"continentalism"—which may be too Eurocentric, policing the borders of its empire too insistently. However small the territory. Even Anglo-American philosophy, or philosophy itself—"philosophism"—policing the borders of its non-empire too compulsively.

15. Derrida insists on the genitive, perhaps under a proper name.

> I have my own feeling on this subject (I insist that it is a *feeling, my* feeling . . . : my 'thesis,' my hypothesis, or my hypostasis, precisely, is that it is never possible to avoid this precipitation, since everyone reads, acts, writes with *his or her* ghosts, even when one goes after the ghosts of the other). My feeling, then, is that Marx scares himself, he *himself* pursues . . . a double, thus a diabolical image. A kind of ghost of himself. (Derrida, *SM*, 139)

16. With Plato—another inheritance—in mind: hunting as haunting; philosophy hunting to own or possess. Called by Plato *sophist*, not *philosopher*. "The difference between the two is precisely what tends to disappear in the ghost effect. . . . All the more so in that this rhetoric is in advance devoted to the polemic, in any case to the strategy of a hunt or chase. . . . And even to a counter-sophistics" (Derrida, *SM*, 126). Early in the dialogue the protagonists describe their activity as *hunting*, not individual sophists but their kind(s), their *genos, phulon,* and *eidē, eidos* (Plato, *Sophist*, 219a, c). To which we may add the stranger's words: "One half

of all art was acquisitive . . . half of the acquisitive art was conquest or taking by force, half of this was hunting, and half of hunting was hunting animals; half of this was hunting water animals" (221ab). This is the method by which to catch the sophist, if he (not she) is an artist, a *technōn*, of an acquisitive sort. Except that every genealogy fails to capture the heterogeneity of the sophist's art: "The art of contradiction making, descended from an insincere kind of conceited mimicry, of the semblance-making breed, derived from image making" (268cd). Its general economy.

Hunting, possessing, coercing, selling. If these are sophistry, what is genealogy? What philosophy? All in the spirit of the impossibility of philosophy. Philosophy as hunting not to acquire, own, or possess. Perhaps not hunting at all. Not even the ghost. Or table. Simulacra of simulacra. In another register. "Once the ghost is produced by the incarnation of spirit . . . claiming the uniqueness of *its own* human body, then becomes, . . . simulacrum of simulacra without end" (Derrida, *SM*, 128). Betrayals of betrayal.

I join the hunt for the sophist, philosophy as hunting, in my *GKGA*, chap. 2.

17. See chap. 5.

18. "A commodity appears, at first sight, a very trivial thing, and easily understood. Its analysis shows that it is, in reality, a very queer thing abounding in metaphysical subtleties and theological niceties" (Marx, *C*, 1, 71).

19. I allude to Deleuze and Guattari: "capitalism, through its process of production, produces an awesome schizophrenic accumulation of energy or charge, against which it brings all its vast powers of repression to bear, but which nonetheless continues to act as capitalism's limit" (Deleuze and Guattari, *A-O*, 34).

20. See n. 13.

21. In an extreme and no doubt supplementary coincidence, the first appearance of *larva* as an animal is recorded as 1762, the same year in which Gluck's *Orfeo* first appeared in Italian. Ghosts of the dead returning with Orpheus to the light as animals. Which they had always done, in Greece and India. Even pigs.

## Chapter 2

1. See chap. 1, p. 16, where we begin the dream of property.

2. See the introduction, pp. 9–10.

3. Continuing: "for where some possess much, and the others nothing, there may arise an extreme democracy, or a pure oligarchy; or a tyranny may grow out of either extreme" (Aristotle, *Politics*, 1295b40-1295b45).

4. We might hope today to imagine something different, ecology as the pulsing heart of political economy, political economy as ethical ecology, *ethicoecology*. We might hope to imagine ecology as the betrayal, the *mimēsis*, of economy: *ethicoeconomoecology* or economy|ecology, perhaps *economology* or *ecolonomy* for short. See chap. 5.

5. Like many others, I admire Martha Nussbaum's reading of the role of fortune in Greece, especially in Aristotle. See her *FG*. Yet something is drastically wrong with the image of fortune as it has been instituted historically. In the genitive, I would say, fortune as possession. What of fortune as giving what cannot be had, what must be given again?

6. See chap. 12.

7. To insist that we must own our words is perhaps another blasphemy.

[O]nce a thing is put in writing, the composition, whatever it may be, drifts all over the place, getting into the hands not only of those who understand it, but equally of those who have no business with it; it doesn't know how to address the right people, and not address the wrong. And when it is ill-treated and unfairly abused it always needs its parent to come to its help, being unable to defend or help itself. (Plato, *Phaedrus*, 275de)

8. We may consider two examples, one intensely controversial, especially for women and children, insisting on genitivity.

[T]he possession of wives and marriage, and the procreation of children and all that sort of thing should be made as far as possible the proverbial goods of friends that are common. (Plato, *Republic*, 424a)

These helpers must not possess houses of their own or land or any other property, but that they should receive from the other citizens for their support the wage of their guardianship and all spend it in common. That was the condition of their being true guardians. (464bc)

9. Touching the farthest reaches of thoughts on property.

In the widest sense of the word, property neither can be justified nor needs to be justified, because it is inextricably part of the way we understand the world. In the narrow sense, the problem of property is so unstable that it dissolves into other questions as soon as it is pressed upon by argument. In the contemporary world, the problem resolves itself into a clash between the value of liberty, which in our civilization means a space for individuality, and the value of justice, which for us has a strong component of equality. (Minogue, *CPCS*, 24)

Often when the problem of property is being discussed, some hint of this dream of transcending all the problems associated with property may be discerned. The clearest statement of this dream can be found close to the beginnings of political philosophy in the words of the Athenian Stranger: "if all means have been taken to eliminate everything we mean by the word *ownership* from life. . . ." (Plato, *Laws*, 739; quoted from Minogue, *CPCS*, 24)

10. We may compare Plato and Aristotle on persuasion For if "rhetoric is creator of persuasion" (452e)—and possibly the greatest persuader—Socrates rejects it as insisting on having without generosity. Aristotle admires the authority of persuasion without qualification, ruling over those who have less. Or perhaps it is Aristotle's translators: "for the wise man must not be ordered but must order [*peithesthai*: persuade], and he must not obey another, but the less wise must obey him" (Aristotle, *Metaphysics*, 982a). Perhaps persuasion is a form of owning, without goodness of its own, suggesting a wisdom without authority or genitivity.

Perhaps owning, having the goods of life, creatures and things, even ideas and souls and goodness, do not make a life worth living where for the sake of the owner or the owned. The life worth living is for the sake of the good—which is nothing, nothing to have, nothing to be, nothing to hold, nothing to accumulate. To live finally, to finally learn to live, is to live without finality, giving without having: perhaps nothing at all.

11. See the discussion of duBois, *TT*, in my *GTGG*, chap. 3. Rochelle insists that she has never been and does want to be a touchstone. Especially of torture. She is here to be touched.

12. A vision of happiness—having whatever one needs, whatever one hopes to need, the perquisites of human property—familiar to all societies, expressed by Aristotle. Happiness is an activity whose constituent parts are good birth, plenty of friends, good friends, wealth, good children, plenty of children, a happy old age; health, beauty, strength, large stature, athletic powers, together with fame, honor, good luck, and excellence. All manner of properties and things to be had, acting for the sake of having.

13. Rochelle reminds us of the two meanings of *desert*, barrenness and reward, wondering at their connection. See chap. 6, pp. 101–4.

14. See chap. 9.

15. I take Socrates' ironic words to express admiration for Callicles when he calls him wise—although Callicles warns against too much wisdom.

> You have received a good education, as many Athenians would agree, and you are well disposed toward me. . . . I once overheard you discussing up to what point one should study philosophy. And I know that some such opinion as this prevailed among you, that we should not be zealous to pursue it in the nicest detail, but you advised each other to beware of becoming wiser than you should, for fear of unknowingly becoming corrupted by it. . . . you are my friend, as you yourself claim. In fact, then, any agreement between you and me will have attained the consummation of the truth. (Plato, *Gorgias*, 486e–487e)

16. A brief interpolation in memory of Nietzsche: "What alone can be our doctrine? That no one gives man his qualities—neither God, nor society, nor his parents and ancestors, nor he himself . . . We have invented the concept of 'end': in

reality there is no end" (Nietzsche, *TI*, 500). Including the genitive. In reality there is nothing to own, nothing to have, no end or ideal or goal. Nothing gives humanity its qualities or goodness as if something to possess. Nietzsche's appeal to God is peculiarly Christian, but the great liberation, I suggest, is from property as well as God, from every genitivity. "What is great in man is that he is a bridge and not an end: what can be loved in man is that he is an *overture* and a *going under*" (Nietzsche, *Z*, 127). A rope between, a bridge, a shuddering and stopping, an overture: figures resistant to accumulation. Overcoming is going under, avoiding any possibility of possession. Living is squander. See chap. 12.

17. As Derrida says. See the general preface, n. 2.

## Chapter 3

1. The artifice of persons is linked in Hobbes with possession and authority— "Of persons artificial, some have their words and actions owned by those whom they represent. And then the person is the actor; and he that owneth his words and actions, is the AUTHOR: in which case the actor acteth by authority" (Hobbes, *L*, 218)—so that we may speak of the props of property in the redoubled senses in which, first, authority and law are props whereby property is instituted, and second, property is itself an artifice, a prop. Property is given as *mimēsis*, in betrayal. As if *mimēsis* did not undermine the distinction between mine and yours, did not betray property repeatedly. Together with its ghost.

2. See chap. 2, p. 39, for the full quotation.

3. See chap. 2, n. 4.

4. See chap. 10 for a discussion of the self that is properly one's own.

5. Paraphrasing Hyde, capital must always move—giving more than having See the general preface here, n. 2.

6. See chaps. 11-16.

## Chapter 4

1. The *Essay* is not the place we think of Locke addressing property. Yet he speaks of possessing knowledge and truth as well as goods, riches, pleasure and pain, good and evil, happiness, and power (Locke, *E*, 2, chap. 30, 303, 305). It would appear—perhaps a grammatical feature of Indo-European languages, a relic of God; perhaps something mimetic at the heart of the Indo-European subject—that the relation of the subject, the person, natural or artificial—if *mimēsis* permits these to be distinguished—to itself and to others is by having, possessing, owning them, or at least owning the wherewithal of that relation—language, freedom, law. Locke marks the intimate link between property and *mimēsis*, in the genitive.

2. I again recall the aviary example in *Theaetetus,* which I read to show that knowledge and truth cannot be owned or had, cannot be possessed, locked up, like a bird in a cage If birds can be owned—any more than human beings—though they may be locked up, grasped; if anything in the earth can be owned. See chap. 2, pp. 32–33.

3. Expressed succinctly by C. B. Macpherson. Seven propositions:

(i)   What makes a man human is freedom from dependence on the will of others.

(ii)  Freedom from dependence on others means freedom from any relations with others except those relations which the individual enters into voluntarily with a view to his own interest.

(iii) The individual is essentially the proprietor of his own person and capacities, for which he owes nothing to society. . . .

(iv)  The individual may alienate his capacity to labour.

(v)   Human society consists of a series of market relations. . . .

(vi)  Each individual's freedom can rightfully be limited only by such obligations and rules as are necessary to secure the same freedom for others.

(vii) Political society is a human contrivance for the protection of the individual's property in his person and goods, and (therefore) for the maintenance of orderly relations of exchange between individuals regarded as proprietors of themselves. (Macpherson, *PTPI,* 263–64)

4. Although Locke regards slavery as the worst of human conditions, he grants that human beings—intelligent moral agents—may relinquish their lives and selves to other owners. The right of all to property becomes the right to conquer persons and to make them property. A famous conjunction:

1. Slavery is so vile and miserable an estate of man, and so directly opposite to the generous temper and courage of our nation, that it is hardly to be conceived, that an Englishman, much less a gentleman, should plead for it. (Locke, *TT,* 1, ch. 1, 141)

85. Master and servant are names as old as history, but given to those of far different condition; for a free man makes himself a servant to another, by selling him, for a certain time, the service he undertakes to do, in exchange for wages he is to receive: . . . it gives the master but a temporary power over him, and no greater than what is contained in the contract between them. But there is another sort of servants, which by a peculiar name we call slaves, who being captives taken in a just war, are by the right of nature subjected to the absolute dominion and arbitrary power of their masters. These men having, as I say, forfeited their lives, and with it their liberties, and lost their estates; and being in the state of slavery, not capable of any property, cannot in that state be considered as

any part of civil society; the chief end whereof is the preservation of property. (2, ch. 7, 322)

In this single passage, we find Locke defining what many regard as the determining condition of capitalist economies, the free act whereby individuals make themselves servants to others by exchanging their labor for wages. Locke recognizes that such an exchange is unequal, that workers subordinate themselves, however freely. Might we imagine that the modern nation, filled with modern persons, is linked at its core with hierarchy, subordination, and the seizure of property and person?

5. Rawls, for example, understands talents and abilities to belong to the collectivity (Rawls, *TJ*, 101).

6. See the introduction, pp. 5–12, and chap. 13.

7. I interrupt with a backward gesture toward hands, Heidegger's hands. Reminding ourselves, as Derrida says, of Heidegger's one and only proper hand. Or rather, our hand, mine and yours. In the name of death. "The hand is infinitely different from all the grasping organs—paws, claws, or fangs—different by an abyss of essence" (Heidegger, *WCT*, 357); "Mortals are they who can experience death as death. Animals cannot do so. But animals cannot speak either" (Heidegger, *OWL*, 107) (see the introduction, pp. 5–7). More powerfully, perhaps, in the name of property. Derrida's words: "man's hand *gives and gives itself, gives and is given*, . . . whereas the organ of the ape or of man as a simple animal, indeed as an *animal rationale*, can only *take hold of, grasp, lay hands on the thing*" (Derrida, *G2*, 175) (see the introduction, p. 11). Giving, taking, things as—what else?—property. The hand gives the essence of humanity as language, one hand, never two. In the name of property, one's own arrives by grasping the thing. Heidegger gives us another property, another genitive, having, that makes humanity human. Not things grasped and taken, but given unto themselves, in language and death. Still Ours, in the genitive. Freedom is what each *Dasein* may call his own. Mine and not apes' or birds' or cats'. More of cats later. A warning against understanding giving as the gift, insisting on taking and having.

8. See my *RR*, chap. 7, where I explore at length history's *lowliness*. See also chaps. 11–13 here.

9. Even in Nietzsche—my quarrel with the younger, romantic Nietzsche:

The stronger the roots of the inmost nature of a man are, the more of the past will he appropriate or master; and were one to conceive the most powerful and colossal nature, it would be known by this, that for it there would be no limit at which the historical sense could overgrow and harm it; such a nature would draw its own as well as every alien past wholly into itself and transform it into blood, as it were. What such a nature cannot master it knows how to forget. . . . (Nietzsche, *OADHL*, 10)

10. "[M]an is the final purpose of creation, since without him the chain of mutually subordinated purposes would not be complete as regards its ground. Only

in man, and only in him as a subject of morality, do we meet with unconditioned legislation in respect of purposes, which therefore alone renders him capable of being a final purpose, to which the whole of nature is teleologically subordinated" (Kant, *CJ*, §84, 286).

11. Spelled out as follows: "The aspects of *original* acquisition are therefore: 1) *Apprehension* of an object that belongs to no one; . . . 2) *Giving a sign* of my possession of this object and of my act of choice to exclude everyone else from it; 3) *Appropriation*, as the act of a general will (in Idea) giving an external law through which everyone is bound to agree with my choice" (Kant, *MM*, 80–81).

12. Discussed in the next chapter.

13. Hegel summarizes his view of property as the embodiment of the will as follows: "Property has its modifications determined in the course of the will's relation to the thing. This relation is (A) *taking possession* of the thing directly . . . (B) *use* . . . (C) *alienation*, the reflection of the will back from the thing into itself" (Hegel, *PR*, 46). I see Marx's entire theory of labor value and commodities in this triad, but I will not pursue that understanding here. Instead, I note that the right to alienate, to relinquish one's claim to property, passes into contract and law, giving rise to another, social relation of property. Under contract, Hegel includes gifts, exchanges, rents, and wages. With circulation, we have capital, "the infinitely complex, criss-cross, movements of reciprocal production and exchange, and the equally infinite multiplicity of means therein employed" (p. 130); "In civil society, property rests on contract and on the formalities which make ownership capable of proof and valid in law" (p. 139). I suggest that if there is anything that law and contract cannot regulate it is the infinitely complex and multiply heterogeneous movements of capital. As Deleuze and Guattari and Lyotard suggest.

14. As Bataille says of sovereignty and general economy: NOTHING. See the introduction here, p. 7.

15. We may be reminded of Plato's words in *Phaedrus*, in the genitive. Our products, properties, stand before us as if they were ours, but are silent in their genitivity. Including written words and works. Properties drift all over the place— and why not? They consort with all sorts of people, do not know how to belong only to the right rather than the wrong people. And they need their father to defend them. Or so it seems. The anarchist insists that this wandering is giving from the good, that Socrates' words—*mimēsis*—insist on having and taking rather than giving. We give in writing. We give in living. Giving takes place no matter what, in whatever ways and kinds it does.

## Chapter 5

1. Although Marx and Engels revile industrial civilization and demand its overcoming, savagery and barbarism offer them no paradigms for civilized life. People in Africa, Asia, and South America today who live in uncivilized, undeveloped

societies remain vestigial curiosities for civilized Europeans. Including their women and children—their property. And their writing. The upper stage of barbarism "passes into civilization through the invention of alphabetic writing and its utilization for literary records" (Engels, *OFPPS*, 173). Pre-civilization begins in property of kin and blood, and passes into civilization with the advent of surplus wealth and writing, two forms of *mimēsis*. The props of property mark civilization.

2. See the introduction, p. 7.

3. I pass lightly over the possibility that this is a very contemporary view of the reproductive pressures on social organization, at least in evolutionary circles. The investment is in the genes, guaranteeing with assurance which are mine even as they wander, like writing and *mimēsis*. Props of property.

4. The world-historic defeat of the female sex was "especially manifest among the Greeks of the Heroic and still more of the Classical Age" (Engels, OFPPS, 198).

5. Engels regards polygamy as exceptional, "limited to a few exceptional cases. . . . Polygamy is a privilege of the rich and the grandees, the wives being recruited chiefly by the purchase of female slaves; the mass of the people live in monogamy" (*OFPPS*, 201). Yet it is practiced today in Africa and central Asia. Those who can afford more wives obtain them, as many as the man can afford, if he has enough cattle, enough property and wealth.

6. See the discussion in chap. 11, pp. 169–70, of how prostitution serves as Marx's and Engels's model of capitalist society. Also see the discussion later in this chapter of how Jews serve as such a model. Both betraying something profoundly truthful and deeply aberrant in Marx and Engels.

7. Discussed at length by Sartre in *BN*, "Doing and Having." See the discussion here in chap. 11, pp. 169–70, n. 1.

8. Schizophrenia and capitalism.

9. Of the ten properties that define the Greek gens, eight pertain to descent: kinship and property. Only two pertain to defense and authority. Another interruption in the name of origins, perhaps no interruption at all.

The Athenian gens in particular was held together by:

1. Common religious ceremonies, and exclusive privilege of the priesthood in honour of a definite god. . . .
2. A common burial place. . . .
3. Mutual rights of inheritance.
4. Reciprocal obligation to afford help, defence and support against the use of force.
5. Mutual right and obligation to marry in the gens. . . .
6. Possession, in some cases at least, of common property. . . .

7. Descent according to father right.
8. Prohibition of intermarrying in the gens except in the case of heiresses. . . .
9. The right of adoption into the gens. . . .
10. The right to elect and depose the chiefs. . . . (Engels, *OFPPS*, 232–33)

Expressed throughout in terms of the genitive: *our* gods—and *mine*, *our* cemetery, *our* inheritance—and *mine*, *our* rights, responsibilities, and obligations, *our* marital, family, and reproductive rights and obligations, *our* property—and *mine*, the *father*'s patrimony, *our* rulers. Reiterated in another language, reinforcing the genitive by a mimetic gesture toward *mimēsis*.

At least during the earliest times of the city, the Roman gens had the following constitution:

1. Mutual right of inheritance of the property of deceased gentiles; the property remained in the gens. . . .
2. Possession of a common burial place. . . .
3. Common religious celebrations. . . .
4. Obligation not to marry within the gens. . . .
5. Possession of land in common. . . .
6. Reciprocal obligation of members of the gens to assist and help redress injuries. . . .
7. Right to bear the gentile name. . . .
8. Right of adopting strangers into the gens. . . .
9. The right to elect and depose chiefs is nowhere mentioned . . . we are justified in assuming that the same [election of chiefs] existed in regard to the gentile chiefs. . . . (pp. 249–50)

The Roman gens added the right to bear the gentile name. *Mimēsis* of the name. Together with adoption of the stranger, a crucial property of kinship, to regulate the outsider. Inside and out. Knowing who belongs and who does not, who is owned by the tribe. Insisting on the genitive in the proper name of property. Insisting on the genitive in the state by means of the proper name.

10. See chap. 2, n. 7.

11. Worth another glance at *Phaedrus* on food. Proper food and drink, proper consumption, as perhaps the most improper consumption. For the soul:

Now even as the mind of a god is nourished by reason and knowledge, so also is it with every soul that has a care to receive her proper food; wherefore when at last she has beheld being she is well content, and contemplating truth she is nourished and prospers, until the heaven's revolution brings her back full circle. . . . And when she has contemplated likewise and feasted upon all else that has true being, she descends again within the heavens and comes back home. And having so come, her charioteer sets his steeds at their manger, and puts ambrosia before them and draught of nectar to drink withal. (Plato, *Phaedrus*, 247c–248a)

And for the cicadas:

> The story is that once upon a time these creatures were men—men of an age before there were any Muses—and that when the latter came into the world, and music made its appearance, some of the people of those days were so thrilled with pleasure that they went on singing, and quite forgot to eat and drink until they actually died without noticing it. From them in due course sprang the race of cicadas, to which the Muses have granted the boon of needing no sustenance right from their birth, but of singing from the very first, without food or drink, until the day of their death, after which they go and report to the Muses how they severally are paid honor among mankind, and by whom. (259bc)

Proper food or food forgotten. Forgetting the genitivity of what we need to live, of life itself. Imagining the flourishing and prosperity of cicadas and souls that wander, without holding onto things as property or life itself.

12. A bovine interlude:

> She is a great cow. She stands in the midst of her own soft flesh, her thighs great wide arches, round columns, her hips wide enough for calving, sturdy, rounded, swaying, stupefied mass, a cradle, a waving field of nipples, her udder brushing the grass, a great cow, who thinks nothing, who waits to be milked, year after year, who delivers up calves, who stands ready for the bull, who is faithful, always there, yielding at the same hour, day after day, that warm substance, the milk white of her eye, staring, trusting, sluggish, bucolic, inert, bovine mind dozing and dreaming, who lays open her flesh, like a drone, for the use of the world. (Griffin, *WN*, 67)

> *The Cows Speak*
> *We are the cows. With our large brown eyes and soft fur there was once something called beauty we were part of. . . . We remember that once we stood together in the fields, we remember what we were then, what it was then to be part, to be part of our beauty.*
> *We are Mothers.*
> *When we awaken, there is a child given to us. We are mothers. . . . We fondle the body. We love this body, because we are part of the body. We are mothers.* (pp. 72–73)

Engels tells us that the domestication of animals and women occurred together, but he does not imagine, as does Griffin, that their liberation might also occur together.

13. See Derrida's discussion and mine in chap. 1.

14. See chap. 2, n. 4.

15. Shades of Descartes and Kant—the architectural | ethical | political | epistemological | economic project of regulating desire. See my *GTGG*, especially chaps. 4, 5, and 9.

16. Omitted from the Fowkes translation but present in others, for example, *C3*, translated by Samuel Moore and Edward Aveling.

17. "Just as in the order of representations the signs that replace and analyse them must also be representations themselves, so money cannot signify wealth without itself being wealth. But it becomes wealth because it is a sign; whereas a representation must first be represented in order subsequently to become a sign" (Foucault, *OT*, 177).

18. See my *PE*, 318–22; and my *GKGA*, pp. 170–71. See here also, chap. 16, pp. 241–43.

## Chapter 6

1. See chap. 13 for a discussion of participation as *metaschesis* in Plato, together with *Mitsein* and *partager* in Heidegger and Nancy respectively. Being with others in the earth.

2. Derrida reads Marx as spooked by Stirner who is spooked by Spirit. Stirner's ghost will haunt us throughout our journeys. Rochelle denies that stones can spook.

3. Hardin, *TC*. From the standpoint of maximal individual satisfaction, each member of the commons would overuse it, exploit it. Yet the evidence is that this was largely untrue for the English commons, of which Locke wrote, and entirely untrue for foraging societies. Societies develop complex and nuanced ways to sustain the use of what no one owns in person, perhaps what no one owns at all— earth, air, sky, and water. Living in the earth together calls for social obligations and responsibilities before exploitation. More on foraging, hunting-gathering societies in chapter 7.

4. I foreshadow guidelines b and c to cherishment, sacrifice, and plenishment in the earth, from my *PE*, 318–22, rewritten in my *GTGG*, 207–10 and here in chap. 16, pp. 241–43.

5. I call it *plenishment*.

6. I have always wondered why traditional readings take for granted that the tracklessness and pathlessness of *aporia*—the impassibility of thought—is hated by Plato without reservation when he chooses again and again to enter its wilderness as if under its fascination. The seduction and temptation of *aporia* have always suggested the wandering of *mimēsis* to me, not simply as ways to go wrong, but the ambiguities and deceptions of going wrong in thinking that one was going right. The worst crime is always to think oneself right and be wrong, to think that one knows yet not to know, to think that one follows the way yet not to follow the way, perhaps to imagine a way without betrayal. The truth of *aporia* is its *mimēsis*, that

there is no way out of the wilderness, no way to tell if one is in or out of the wilderness, that wilderness and wandering betray the nature of life and philosophy under the gods. The intermediary figures of *erōs* and *mania* are all figures of wandering, as are writing and refutation, suggesting that philosophy will never escape *aporia*, that the highest life is nomadic, always with a forgotten memory of home.

I would consider the possibility that the Greeks were less fearful of *aporia*, of wandering and landlessness than the Hebrews, who wandered in the wilderness for forty years. I would also consider the possibility that in this way, as in so many others, Plato continues to be read in Judeo-Christian ways beyond the Greek.

## Chapter 7

1. Continued in chap. 8.

2. "The institution called property guards the troubled boundary between individual man and the state . . . [I]n a society that chiefly values material well-being, the power to control a particular portion of that well-being is the very foundation of individuality" (Reich, *NP*, 179). Taken to an extreme: "Like the Bill of Rights, property represents a general, long range protection of individual and private interests, created by the majority for the ultimate good of all" (p. 181). With a single expostulation—*like the Bill of Rights*?!—I postpone the relation between property and freedom to chapter 9.

3. In Derrida's words: "The moral question is thus not, nor has it ever been: should one eat or not eat, eat this and not that, the living or the nonliving, man or animal, but since *one must* eat in any case and since it is and tastes good to eat, and since there's no other definition of the good *[du bien]*, *how* for goodness' sake should one *eat well [bien manger]*?" (Derrida, *EW*, 282). See here chap. 12.

## Chapter 8

1. See my *GKGA*, especially chaps. 5 and 6.

2. "I love to you means . . . I speak to you, I ask of you, I give to you (and not: I give *you* to another)" (Irigaray, *ILTY*, 109).

3. Continuing, "The celebration of rape in story, song, and science is the paradigmatic articulation of male sexual power as a cultural absolute. The conquering of the woman acted out in fucking, her possession, her use as a thing, is the scenario endlessly repeated, with or without direct reference to fucking, throughout the culture."

4. See the discussion in my *GKGA*, chap. 12.

5. See chap. 4, n. 4.

## Chapter 9

1. The infinite will and excessive desire haunt this picture of basic needs with the volatile possibility that what one needs to live is whatever one desires, that the nature of will and desire make it impossible to define a possession that does not become infinite right to infinite accumulation. I have argued that this is a view of capitalism, restricting desire in the name of its lack of restriction. I again postpone this question.

Here I explore the possibility that we may hope to define a sustainable life with modest desires, insisting that the state and other powerful social mechanisms and institutions do not have the right to intrude upon our personal sphere. Personal property, one might say, is and must be regarded as one's own regardless of social forces and the demands of others. Can we determine and defend such a border between the personal and the social, between what human beings need to be free, need to be able to enjoy without interference by others, especially greater powers?

I return to sustenance as generosity in chap. 14.

2. And who will return in most of the remaining chapters.

3. See also chap. 14.

4. Even Harris, whose entire project is one of tracing the shameful history of slavery, finds it possible that personal worth in property might be the route to social and individual salvation, always in the name of the curse.

> Radin argues that, as a deterrent to the dehumanization of universal commodification, market-inalienability may be justified to protect property important to the person and to safeguard human flourishing. She suggests that non-commodification or market-inalienability of personal property or those things essential to human flourishing is necessary to guard against the objectification of human things. (Harris, *WP*, 1733)

5. See chap. 16, p. 241–43.

6. I pause to consider another understanding of general economy.

> The contemporary impulse toward equating the sphere of absolute individual autonomy with the concept of property is, in fact, a radical narrowing of the historical understanding of property. During the American Founding Era, property included not only external objects and people's relationships to them, but also all of those human rights, liberties, powers, and immunities that are important for human well-being, including: freedom of expression, freedom of conscience, freedom from bodily harm, and free and equal opportunities to use personal faculties. (Underkuffler, *OP*, 128–29)

Such a view reaches toward infinity, as Underkuffler implies in quoting Madison on having in the genitive:

In its larger and juster meaning, [property] embraces every thing to which a man may attach a value and have a right; and *which leaves to every one else the like advantage.*

In the former sense, a man's land, or merchandize (sic), or money is called his property.

In the latter sense, a man has property in his opinions and the free communication of them.

He has a property of peculiar value in his religious opinions and in the profession and practice dictated by them. . . .

He has property very dear to him in the safety and liberty of his person.

He has an equal property in the free use of his faculties and free choice of the objects on which to employ them.

In a word, as a man is said to have a right to his property, he may be equally said to have a property in his rights.

. . . Conscience is the most sacred of all property; other property depending in part on positive law, the exercise of that, being a natural and inalienable right. . . . (Underkuffler, *OP*, 135)

Whatever enables human beings to live well may be considered their right to property—but not an absolute or inalienable right, not restricted to a property in things, not against others who may take away what one has by force, but above all, perhaps, including a conscience that dispossesses every property, every right, for the sake of nothing higher. Nothing can bind conscience or responsibility to a place or thing, to genitivity; it does its work by giving. The greatest gift of all is life itself, given to others as well as oneself, for the sake of what cannot be owned or had. The greatest property of all is what cannot be had as property, what is possessed in dispossession, as interruption, in betrayal.

## Chapter 10

1. In German of course, but also in Steven Tracy Byington's wonderful translation.

2. See David Leopold's introduction to *The Ego and Its Own*, xi, xxxvii–xxxviii, with references to Martin, *MAS*, and Tucker, *IB*. If this be anarchism, rather than libertarianism, egoism, or individualism, anarchism would deserve its bad name. Anarchism as theft, so to speak. Stirner dislikes Proudhon as much as he dislikes anyone. Still, Stirner's resistance to outside authorities is salutary, if he does not resist the authority of the self. But that is Wikse's point.

3. His critique of liberalism is more telling, I believe, than Schmitt's, who continues to glorify the state, where Stirner has nothing but contempt for state authority. "The commonalty is nothing else than the thought that the state is all in all, the true man, and that the individual's human value consists in being a citizen of the state" (Stirner, *EO*, 90). Mouffe's and Laclau's return to Schmitt as an avenue to radical democracy seems to me to flirt too much with

authoritarianism, even where we may believe, as I do, that Stirner reinstitutes the authority of the one. Always against church and state, where resistance is required.

> 'Political liberty,' what are we to understand by that? Perhaps the individual's independence of the state and its laws? No; on the contrary, the individual's *subjection* in the state and to the state's laws. (p. 96)

> Political liberty means that the *polis*, the state, is free; freedom of religion that religion is free, as freedom of conscience signifies that conscience is free; not, therefore, that I am free from the state, from religion, from conscience, or that I am *rid* of them. It does not mean *my* liberty, but the liberty of a power that rules and subjugates me; it means that one of my *despots*, like state, religion, conscience, is free. State, religion, conscience, these despots, make me a slave, and *their* liberty is *my* slavery. (p. 97)

Marx is contemptuous of Stirner's ghosts, spooks, and spirits, as if Stirner insisted on another supreme authority without materiality. Saint Max, himself a spirit, plays with spooks. Yet Stirner evokes the possibility, as forcefully as any, that all the causes to which human beings subordinate themselves, including revolution, truth, God, and conscience, are slavery. "What is not supposed to be my concern! First and foremost the good cause, then God's cause, the cause of mankind, of truth, of freedom, of humanity, of justice; further, the cause of my people, my prince, my fatherland; finally, even the cause of mind and a thousand other causes. Only *my* cause is never to be my concern. 'Shame on the egoist who thinks only of himself!'" (p. 5). The human subject subjects himself to authority, throws himself down under its yoke—including the authority of himself. It is not less abject to be slave to oneself.

4. Reminding us of Derrida's suggestion that Heidegger favors something—order, jointure, favor itself—at a point at which it would appear we might refuse favor See chap. 1, pp. 16–19.

5. In Foucault's words, for example, as enigmatic as they have sounded to many readers who look for a relation to power they can understand and possess:

> —Power is. . . exercised from innumerable points. . . .
> —Relations of power . . . have an immediately productive role, wherever they come into play.
> —Power comes from below. . . .
> —Where there is power, there is resistance. . . . These points of resistance are present everywhere in the power network. Hence there is no single locus of great Refusal, no soul of revolt, source of all rebellions, or pure law of the revolutionary. Instead there is a plurality of resistances, each of them a special case. . . . Hence they too are distributed in irregular fashion. . . . (Foucault, *HS*, 94–96)

Power and resistance cannot be owned or possessed, do not have a place, cannot be controlled, dispossess each other.

6. The genitivity of the historical human individual is haunted by the doubled figure of *parousia*, the arrival of genitivity bound to the genitivity of arrival. This is the story of genitivity, which has been considered in its idiocy as a modern phenomenon, speaking Greek. At least, Wikse thinks of it as modern (see this chapter, pp. 156–60). I continue to think of it as human, under the curse. This question, of the arrival of genitivity at a certain point of history, ancient Greek or modern European, I insist on holding in abeyance, perhaps indefinitely. It is the question of the arrival of what appears to have always been present—being, nature, property, truth. Never the good, which never arrives and has never been present, but may haunt arrival itself, presentness itself, as circulation, giving. The good gives what arrives, and what does not arrive, gives from general to restricted economy, from giving to having, where having is impossible without giving and where giving gives gifts of identity, place, and kind that must be had to be present. Or absent.

7. In chap. 12.

8. Of this idiocy: "This book is written out of the pain of my own idiocy, in the root sense of this word from the greek *idiotes*, meaning a private and separate person" (Wikse, *AP*, 1). It is what I call *lownliness*. See chap. 4, pp. 61–62, and chap. 11, p. 162.

9. As Hyde says. See the general preface, n. 2.

## Chapter 11

1. Expressed by Wikse reading Sartre reading Heidegger:

> For Sartre, there are what he calls three "*ekstases*" which characterize being human, three experiences in which the self is separated from, stands out from, itself. The first is that of temporality. . . . The second is that of reflection, in which the self takes itself as its own object. The third *ekstasis* is that of "being-for-others" . . . . (*AP*, 113)

> The identification of contingency and possession means for Sartre that in the very structure of being-for-others, in the experience of being seen, judged, and interpreted by others, in the very presence of others, there is enslavement. (p. 114)

> Man is condemned to appropriate that which is always fleeing from him. (p. 115)

The *ekstases* of time—past, present, and future; the ways in which the self is outside itself—I would say, among others, fallen into historical time *ekstatically*; become *ekstases* of self: temporality, reflection, and being for others. In the *ekstases* of others, seeing and judging *us*, there is enslavement. Instead, Wikse insists, we are always among others as we are with ourselves, neither owning nor possessing, having nor behaving, but living among and with. Instead, I would say, in being with ourselves we are exposed to others in the earth in relationships with endless ramifications. We neither own nor have ourselves; neither do we own nor have others. To mark the *ekstases* of temporal being, human or otherwise, is to mark the impossibility of owning and having—by no means the inevitability of enslavement. To disown the binary of owning and being owned is to disown slavery beyond its abolition—if it could be abolished.

2. As we have seen in chap 4.

3. Yet see chap. 8, n. 2.

4. In short, as *squander* See chap. 12.

5. I allude to Deleuze and Guattari, *A-O*, published in 1972; Wittig, *LB*, published in 1973, and Lyotard, *LE*, published in 1974. I have discussed the first two of these in other places in this project of giving and the good, including the discussion of *A-O* here in chapter 10, and discussions of the continued collaboration, *TP* and *WP*, in my *GTEG* and *GKGA*, and of *LB* in my *PE*, *GBGA*, *GTEG*, and *GKGA*. Here I touch upon another economy of corporeal desire. I intrude the merest sense of interweaving.

> Desire causes the current to flow, itself flows in turn, and breaks the flows. "I love everything that flows, even the menstrual flow that carries away the seed unfecund." Amniotic fluid spilling out of the sac and kidney stones. Flowing hair, a flow of spittle, a flow of sperm, shit, or urine that are produced by partial objects and constantly cut off by other partial objects, which in turn produce other flows, interrupted by other partial objects. (Deleuze & Guattari, *A-O*, 5)

> Open the so-called body and spread out all its surfaces: not only the skin with each of its folds, wrinkles, scars, with its great velvety planes, and contiguous to that, the scalp and its mane of hair, the tender pubic fur, nipples, nails, hard transparent skin under the heel, the light frills of the eyelids, set with lashes—but open and spread, expose the labia majora, so also the labia minora with their blue network bathed in mucus, dilate the diaphragm of the anal sphincter, longitudinally cut and flatten out the black conduit of the rectum, then the colon, the caecum, now a ribbon with this surface all striated and polluted with shit; . . . armed with scalpels and tweezers, dismantle and lay out the bundles and bodies of the encephalon; and then the whole network of veins and arteries, intact, . . . extract the great muscles, the great dorsal nets, spread them out like smooth sleeping dolphins. (Lyotard, *LE*, 1)

> M/y kneecaps appear at m/y knees from which shreds of flesh fall. M/y armpits are musty. M/y breasts are eaten away. *I* have a hole in m/y throat. The smell that escapes from m/e is noisome. You do not stop your nostrils.

> You do not exclaim with fright when at a given moment m/y putrescent
> and half-liquid body touches the length of your bare back. (Wittig, *LB*, 20)

If this exuberant, extravant, moment in French writing appears to have passed, it
may have left a trace of corporeal abundance that is too easy for us to forget despite
finding ourselves constantly immersed within it.

6. *Jouissance,* man's, woman's, or other, is situated at the crux of genitivity.
Sade's words make us tremble, on both sides of desire, in the genitive:

> it is a question of enjoyment *(jouissance)* only, not of property: I have no
> right of possession upon that fountain I find by the road, but I have
> certain rights to its use; I have the right to avail myself of the limpid water
> it offers my thirst; similarly, I have no real right of possession over such-
> and-such a woman, but I have incontestable rights to the enjoyment of
> her; I have the right to force from her this enjoyment *(jouissance),* if she
> refuse me it for whatever the cause may be. (Sade, PB, 319)

Let us give up the right to hold forever and as *mine alone,* but not the right
to grasp securely, if only in the moment. And what if woman's or animal's or even
man's *jouissance* were giving rather than taking?

7. And squander.

## Chapter 12

1. "The singularity of the 'who' is not the individuality of a thing that would
be identical to itself, it is not an atom. It is a singularity that dislocates or divides
itself in gathering itself together to answer to the other, whose call somehow precedes its own identification with itself, for to this call I can *only* answer, have
already answered, even if I think I am answering 'no' " (Derrida, *EW,* 261). The
subtitle of "Eating Well *[Il faut bien manger]*" is "the calculation of the subject," as
if the subject were a calculation or a calculator, perhaps calculating its own identity.
Beyond this calculating subject is something—perhaps nothing—incalculable, immeasurable, not to replace calculation, for nothing can, but that which makes both
subject and calculation possible, intelligible, and meaningful. "Responsibility carries
within it, and must do so, an essential excessiveness. It regulates itself neither on
the principle of reason nor on any sort of accountancy. . . . The subject is also a
principle of calculability—for the political. . . . There has to be some calculation"
(pp. 272-73).

The nature or form—if such terms may be employed here—of this excessiveness,
exceeding excess itself, is the dislocation and interruption of the gathering—gathering itself—that constitutes the singularity, constituted by a call to which *I*—a singular?—can only answer, have already answered. I have responded elsewhere in this
project, first, that the dislocation and interruption of the subject, the individual or
self—*I myself*—are not singular or individual or anything in particular, but constitute

the *I myself* and everything else: interrupting every gathering. Second, the dislocation and interruption express themselves in every kind—not just human selves, persons and subjects, but things gathered and ungathered into kinds. See my *GKGA*.

2. Libidinal economy. "We invent nothing, that's it, yes, yes, yes, yes" (Lyotard, *LE*, 262). See chap. 11, p. 168.

3. See my *GTEG*, where I comment on Socrates' words at the end of *Republic* that "it will save us if we believe it" (621b); that "we must believe in what calls to us from the good even if we do not know the truth of that call or what it says. We should believe in the upward way . . . should always resist injustice and rest in justice" (p. 21). The injustice is betrayal, including the *yes!* of its witness.

4. Diotima's beauty—*phusin kallon*—cannot be weakened or destroyed: "a nature . . . not fair in one point of view and foul in another, or at one time or in one relation or at one place fair, at another time or in another relation or in another place foul, . . . but beauty absolute, separate, simple, and everlasting, which without diminution and without increase, or any change, is imparted to the ever-growing and perishing beauties of all other things" (Plato, *Symposium*, 210e–211a).

5. See the introduction here, p. 6.

6. "[H]uman language, as original as it might be, does not allow us to 'cut' once and for all where we would in general like to cut. . . . We know less than ever where to cut—either at birth or at death. And this also means that we never know, and never have known, how to *cut up* a subject" (Derrida, *EW*, 285). I respond that we have always insisted on cutting—and cutting up—not only the subject, but also The Human and The Animal, that the stakes—where we would in general like to cut—are always humanistic.

7. See chap. 5.

## Chapter 13

1. I explore the self that insists on making the world and itself its own in the next volume of this project, *The Gift of Self: Subjecting the Good*. Here I remain with genitivity.

2. See the introduction, pp. 7–8.

3. Derrida insists that Being's genitivity becomes *Dasein*'s genitivity in a double reversal, possession as dispossession, disowning as owning. Where Heidegger insists that "any Dasein whatsoever is characterized by mineness *(Jemeinigkeit)*," Derrida responds that this *Jemeinigkeit*, this genitivity, is the abolition of self possession, "a singularity, an irreplaceability" (Derrida, *EW*, 271). And where Heidegger insists on "the voice of the friend whom every Dasein carries with it" (Heidegger, *BT*, sect. 34, 206), Derrida reminds us that "The friend is not a man, nor a woman: it is not I, nor a 'self,' not a subject, nor a person. It is another Dasein that each Dasein *carries*, through the voice it hears, with itself" (Derrida, *G4*, 165); and that this nothing that

is the friend absolutely excludes animals, belongs exclusively to humanity: "The animal has no friend, man has no friendship properly so called for the animal. The animal that is 'world poor,' . . . that has no hand, the animal that has no friend, has no ear either" (p. 172). The friend who calls the genitive of *myself* into question is another possession, the friend *I have, my friend, my own*, not others who call every genitivity into question, who can never be *my own* as I can never be *theirs*. "Heidegger does not simply say 'The animal is poor in world *(weltarm)*,' for, as distinct from the stone, it has a world. He says: the animal *has* a world in the mode of a *not-having*. . . . Having-in-the-mode-of-not-having-a-world" (Derrida, *EW*, 277-78). The Animal *has* a world as The Man *has* a world, where the stone—Rochelle stays close by—has no world; but where human beings have a rich and spiritual world, animals are poor in world, *have-in-the-mode-of-not-having-a-world*. Not-having, resistance to genitivity, is evoked to exclude animals absolutely in the form of genitivity—*by an abyss of essence*.

4. See the introduction, p. 6, for the full quotation.

5. See the general preface, n. 2.

6. From which Nancy withdraws "Letting-be, . . . it cannot avoid—and this is wherein freedom is a fact—acceding to the singular dissemination of being, and dividing it. Nor, consequently, can it avoid *exposing* itself as the being-singular of its own decision, exposed to this coming-up of being in its withdrawal . . . " (*EF*, 143). Exposing *itself*, dividing and disseminating being. Freedom gives freedom itself. Letting-be is genitivity.

7. See the introduction here, pp. 6–8.

## Chapter 14

1. Derrida alludes to harm in relation to vegetarianism. "Vegetarians, too, partake of animals, even of men" (Derrida, *EW*, 282); "the complex history of Hinduist culture. . . . Does it not, precisely, set in opposition the political hierarchy—or the exercise of power—and the religious hierarchy, the latter prohibiting, the former allowing itself, indeed imposing upon itself the eating of meat?" (p. 284).

2. I do not disregard recent falling rates of population increase. Perhaps human beings are intelligent and ethical enough to recognize that if they breed like deer when they do not have to, they will die like deer—after destroying the earth around them for future generations of human beings and deer. Perhaps only for human beings.

3. See chaps. 3-5.

4. A vision of democracy, or anarchy, reminiscent of Proudhon and others.

Schumacher's work belongs to that subterranean tradition of organic and decentralist economics whose major spokesmen include Prince Kropotkin,

Gustav Landauer, Tolstoy, William Morris, Gandhi, Lewis Mumford, and, most recently, Alex Comfort, Pool Goodman, and Murray Bookchin. It is the tradition we might call anarchism, if we mean by that much abused word a libertarian political economy that distinguished itself from orthodox socialism and capitalism by insisting that the *scale* of organization must be treated as an independent and primary problem. (Roszak, Introduction to Schumacher, *SB*, 4)

## Chapter 15

1. I lean toward Spinoza and Whitehead, who certainly imagine the great economy, but not as a kingdom of God, who cannot imagine order without disorder, even in relation to God:

> Every definite total phase of "givenness" involves a reference to that specific "order" which is its dominant ideal, and involves the specific "disorder" due to its inclusion of "given" components which exclude the attainment of the full ideal. . . . There is not just one ideal "order" which all actual entities should attain and fail to attain. In each case there is an ideal peculiar to each particular actual entity and arising from the dominant components in its phase of "givenness." (Whitehead, *PR*, 83–84)

Givenness as that which has been given, that which might be given, presupposes giving, I would say. *Creativity*, Whitehead says: "the universal of universals characterizing ultimate matter of fact. It is that ultimate principle by which the many, which are the universe disjunctively, become the one actual occasion, which is the universe conjunctively" (p. 21). Still, perhaps, favoring jointure. Givenness without neutrality, insisting on good and evil. Shades of Anaximander. "The nature of evil is that the characters of things are mutually obstructive. Thus the depths of life require a process of selection. . . . Selection is at once the measure of evil, and the process of its evasion" (p. 340).

2. The burden of my *GTGG*.

3. Reminding us of Heidegger, who does not cite the passage but certainly repeats the obsession. *"No one can take the Other's dying away from him"* (Heidegger, *BT*, 284).

> Of course someone can "go to his death for another." But that always means to sacrifice oneself for the Other *"in some definite affair."* Such "dying for" can never signify that the Other has thus had his death takem away in even the slightest degree. Dying is something that every Dasein itself must take upon itself at the time. By its very essence, death is in every case mine, in so far as it "is" at all. (p. 284)

> Death is a possibility-of-Being which Dasein itself has to take over in every case. With death, Dasein stands before itself in its ownmost potentiality-for-Being. This is a possibility in which the issue is nothing less than Dasein's Being-in-the-world. its death is the possibility of no-longer-being-able-to-be-there. . . . This ownmost non-relational possibility is at the same time the uttermost one. (p. 294)

Entirely in the genitive. The uttermost possibility of being is the death that is in every case mine, that must be mine if at all. As if everything and anything else might not be mine, as if everything might be itself except for the death that is mine alone.

4. Discussed at length in my *GTEG*, chaps. 1 and 2.

5. The story of my *GKGA*.

6. See chap. 12, n. 1.

## Chapter 16

1. Two oblique expressions of betrayal and forgiveness. See chap. 1, pp. 19, 24.

2. See the general preface, n. 10.

3. See chap. 12, p. 177.

4. Derrida's words, broken off in provocation: "irresponsibility insinuates itself wherever one demands responsibility" (Derrida, *GD,* 25). See chap. 15, p. 224.

5. For those who cannot wait, or who have been in this scene before, I close the curtain on this play within a play of ghosts, which brings back another play within a play, and ghosts, and other plays, on p. 238.

6. See chap. 1, p. 23, for the full quotation.

7. Rochelle insists that she is no ghost and does not know death but she returns from where she is buried.

8. See chap. 6, n. 4.

## Chapter 17

1. In Greek, forgiveness is *suggnōmē*, shared feeling and judgment, entirely in the genitive. I would think of forgiving beyond genitivity.

2. See my *IROT*, chap. 6, pp. 144–48.

# Bibliography

Abbott, Sally. "The Origins of God in the Blood of the Lamb" *[OGBL]*. In Diamond and Orenstein, eds., *Reweaving the World*.

Abram, David. *The Spell of the Sensuous: Perception and Language in a More-Than-Human World [SS]*. New York: Pantheon, 1996.

Acker, Kathy. "Against Ordinary Language: The Language of the Body" *[AOL]*. In Kroker and Kroker, eds., *Last Sex*.

Adams, Carol J. *The Sexual Politics of Meat [SPM]*. New York: Continuum, 1992.

Agamben, Giorgio. *Language and Death: The Place of Negativity [LD]*. Minneapolis: University of Minnesota Press, 1991.

Agar, Herbert, and Allen Tate, eds. *Who Owns America? A New Declaration of Independence [WOA]*. Freeport, NY: Books for Libraries Press, 1970.

Allen, Robert. "The Land Monopoly" *[LM]*. *Green Revolution* 9, 10 (October 1971): 7, 16.

Althusser, Louis, and Étienne Balibar. *Reading Capital [RC]*. Trans. Ben Brewster. London: NLB, 1970.

Andersen, Margaret L., and Patricia Hill Collins, eds. *Race, Class, and Gender: An Anthology [RCG]*. 2nd ed. Belmont, CA: Wadsworth, 1995.

Andolsen, Barbara Hilkert, Christine E. Gudorf, and Mary D. Pellauer, eds. *Women's Consciousness, Women's Conscience [WCWC]*. New York: Winston, 1985.

Appiah, Kwame Anthony. "Racisms" *[R]*. In Goldberg, ed., *Anatomy of Racism*.

Aquinas, Thomas. *Basic Writings of St. Thomas Aquinas [BWTA]*. Ed. Anton C. Pegis. 2 vols. New York: Random House, 1945.

———. *Summa Theologica [ST]*. Trans. Fathers of the English Dominican Province. London: Burns, Oates & Washbourne, 1912–36.

Ardener, E. "Belief and the Problem of Women" *[BPW]*. In J. La Fontaine, ed., *The Interpretation of Ritual [IR]*. London: Tavistock, 1975. Reprinted in S. Ardener, ed., *Perceiving Women*.

Ardener, S. *Defining Females: The Nature of Women in Society [DF]*. London: Croom, Helm, 1978.

———, ed. *Perceiving Women [PW]*. London: Dent, 1975.

Arendt, Hannah. *Eichmann in Jerusalem: A Report on the Banality of Evil [EJ]*. Rev. and enl. ed. New York: Viking, 1964.

———. *The Human Condition [HC]*. Chicago: University of Chicago Press, 1958.

Arens, W., and I. Karp, eds. *Creativity of Power [CP]*. Washington, DC, and London: Smithsonian Press, 1989.

Aristotle. *The Basic Works of Aristotle [BWA]*. New York: Random House, 1941.

———. *The Complete Works of Aristotle [CWA]*. Ed. Jonathan Barnes. 2 vols. Princeton: Princeton University Press, 1984. All quotations from Aristotle are from this edition unless otherwise indicated.

———. *Poetics [P]*. Reprinted in part in Ross, ed., *Art and Its Significance*. From *Basic Works of Aristotle*.

Asch, Michael. "To Negotiate into Confederation: Canadian Aboriginal Views on Their Political Rights" *[NC]*. In Wilmsen, ed., *We Are Here*.

Athanasiou, Tom. *Divided Planet: The Ecology of Rich and Poor [DP]*. Boston: Little, Brown & Co., 1997.

Atkinson, Adrian. *Principles of Political Ecology [PPE]*. London: Belhaven Press, 1991.

Augustine. *Basic Writings of Saint Augustine [BWA]*. Ed. and int. Whitney J. Oates. New York: Random House, 1948.

———. *The City of God [CG]*. In *Basic Writings of Saint Augustine*.

Baack, Ben. "The Development of Exclusive Property Rights to Land in England: An Exploratory Essay" *[DEPRLE]*. *Economy and History* 22, no. 1 (1979): 63-74.

Badiner, Allan Hunt, ed. *Dharma Gaia: A Harvest of Essays in Buddhism and Ecology [DG]*. Berkeley: Parallax Press, 1990.

Baechler, Jean. "Liberty, Property, and Equality" *[LPE]*. In Pennock and Chapman, eds., *Nomos XXII*, 269-88.

Balibar, Etienne. "Paradoxes of Universality" *[PU]*. In Goldberg, ed., *Anatomy of Racism*.

Bar On, Bat-Ami, ed. *Modern Engendering: Critical Feminist Readings in Modern Western Philosophy [ME]*. Albany: State University of New York Press, 1994.

Barrow, John D. *The Artful Universe [AU]*. Oxford: Clarendon Press, 1995.

Barthes, Roland. *The Pleasure of the Text [PT]*. Trans. Richard Miller. New York: Hill and Wang, 1975.

Baskin, Yvonne. *The Work of Nature: How the Diversity of Life Sustains Us [WN]*. Washington, DC: Island Press, 1997.

Bataille, Georges. *The Accursed Share: An Essay on General Economy [AS]*. Trans. Richard Hurley. 2 vols. New York: Zone Books, 1988 and 1993. Translation of *La Part maudite, L'Histoire de l'érotisme,* and *La Souveraineté (Consumption [1]; The History of Eroticism [2]; Sovereignty [3])*. In Georges Bataille, *Oeuvres Complètes*. Paris: Gallimard, 1976.

———. *Inner Experience [IE]*. Trans. Leslie Anne Boldt. Albany: State University of New York Press, 1988. Translation of *L'Expérience intérieure [EI]*. Paris: Gallimard, 1954.

———. *Méthode de Méditation [MM]*. In *L'Expérience intérieure*. Quoted in Derrida, "From Restricted to General Economy."

———. "The Notion of Expediture" *[NE]*. In *Visions of Excess*.

———. *Visions of Excess: Selected Writings, 1927–1939 [VE]*. Trans. Allan Stoekl, with Carl R. Lovitt and Donald M. Leslie, Jr. Minneapolis: University of Minnesota Press, 1985.

Batchelor, Martine. "Buddhist Economics Reconsidered" *[BER]*. In Badiner, ed., *Dharma Gaia*.

———. "Even the Stones Smile: Selections from the Scriptures" *[ESS]*. In Batchelor and Brown, eds., *Buddhism and Ecology*.

———. "The Sands of the Ganges" *[SG]*. In Batchelor and Brown, eds., *Buddhism and Ecology*.

Batchelor, Martine, and Kerry Brown, eds. *Buddhism and Ecology [BE]*. New York: Cassell Publishers, 1992.

Baudrillard, Jean. *Forget Foucault [FF]*. New York: Semiotext(e), 1987.

Beauvoir, Simone de. *The Ethics of Ambiguity [EA]*. Trans. Bernard Frechtman. New York: Citadel Press, 1991.

———. *The Second Sex [SS]*. Trans. H. M. Parshley. New York: Knopf, 1971.

Becker, Lawrence C. "The Moral Basis of Property Rights" *[MBPR]*. In Pennock and Chapman, eds., *Nomos XXII*, 187–220.

Bellany, Ian. *The Environment in World Politics: Exploring the Limits [EWP]*. Brookfield, VT: Edward Elgar, 1997.

Bender, Barbara. *Landscapes: Politics and Perspectives [L]*. New York: Berg, 1993.

Benjamin, Walter. *Erfahrung und Armut [EA]*. Passages quoted in Derrida, "Letter to Peter Eisenman."

———. *Illuminations [I]*. Trans. Harry Zohn. New York: Harcourt Brace & World, 1968.

———. "On Language as Such and on the Language of Man" *[LSLM]*. In *Reflections*.

———. *Reflections: Essays, Aphorisms, Autobiographical Writings [R]*. Trans. Edmund Jephcott. New York: Schocken, 1978.

———. "The Work of Art in the Age of Its Technical Reproducibility" *[WAATR]*. Reprinted in part in Ross, ed., *Art and Its Significance*. Selections from "The Work of Art in the Age of Mechanical Reproduction." In *Illuminations*.

Berman, Morris. *The Reenchantment of the World [RW]*. Ithaca, NY: Cornell University Press, 1981.

Bernal, Martin. *Black Athena: The Afroasiatic Roots of Classical Civilization*, Volume 1: *The Fabrication of Ancient Greece 1785–1985 [BA]*. New Brunswick: Rutgers University Press, 1987.

Bernasconi, Robert, and David Wood, eds. *The Provocation of Levinas: Rethinking the Other [PL]*. New York: Routledge, 1988.

Berry, Wendell. *Home Economics [HE]*. San Francisco: North Point Press, 1987.

Bhabha, Homi K. "Interrogating Identity: The Postcolonial Prerogative" *[II]*. In Goldberg, ed., *Anatomy of Racism*.

Birch, Thomas H. "The Incarceration of Wildness: Wilderness Areas as Prisons" *[IW]*. In Oelschlaeger, ed., *Postmodern Environmental Ethics*.

Bookchin, Murray. *The Ecology of Freedom [EF]*. Palo Alto, CA: Cheshire Books, 1982.

———. *Post-Scarcity Anarchism [PSA]*. Berkeley: Ramparts Press, 1971.

———. *Re-enchanting Humanity: A Defense of the Human Spirit against Antihumanism, Misanthropy, Mysticism, and Primitivism [RH]*. New York: Cassell, 1995.

———. *Remaking Society: Pathways to a Green Future [RS]*. Boston: South End Press, 1990.

———. "Social Ecology versus 'Deep Ecology': A Challenge to the Ecology Movement" *[SEDE]*. In *Green Perspectives, Newsletter of the Green Program Project* 4-5.

Bordo, Susan. "The Cartesian Masculinization of Thought and the Seventeenth-Century Flight from the Feminine" *[CMT]*. In Bar On, ed., *Modern Engendering*.

Bormann, F. Herbert, and Stephen R. Kellert, eds. *Ecology, Economics, Ethics: The Broken Circle [EEE]*. New Haven: Yale University Press, 1991.

Botkin, Daniel. *Discordant Harmonies: A New Ecology for the Twenty-First Century [DH]*. Oxford: Oxford University Press, 1990.

Bowden, Ross. "Sorcery, Illness and Social Control in Kwoma Society" *[SISC]*. In Stephen, ed., *Sorcerer and Witch*.

Brace, C. Loring, George R. Gamble, and James T. Bond. *Race and Intelligence*. Washington: American Anthropological Association, 1971.

Brennan, Andrew. *Thinking About Nature: An Investigation of Nature, Value and Ecology [TN]*. Athens, GA: University of Georgia Press, 1988.

Brueggemann, Walter. *The Land: Place as Gift, Promise, and Challenge in Biblical Faith [L]*. Philadelphia: Fortress Press, 1977.

Bryant, Bunyon, ed. *Environmental Justice [EJ]*. Washington, DC: Island Press, 1995.

Bullard, Robert D. "Anatomy of Environmental Racism and the Environmental Justice Movement" *[AEREJM]*. In Bullard, ed., *Confronting Environmental Racism*.

———. "Conclusion: Environmentalism with Justice" *[EJ]*. In Bullard, ed., *Confronting Environmental Racism*.

———, ed. *Confronting Environmental Racism: Voices from the Grassroots [CER]*. Boston: South End Press, 1993.

Burnett, John. *Plenty and Want: A Social History of Diet in England from 1815 to the Present Day [PW]*. London: Methuen, 1983.

Butler, Judith. *Bodies That Matter: On the Discursive Limits of "Sex" [BM]*. New York: Routledge, 1993.

———. *Gender Trouble: Feminism and the Subversion of Identity [GT]*. New York: Routledge, 1990.

Callicott, J. Baird. *In Defense of a Land Ethic [DL]*. Albany: State University of New York Press, 1989.

———. "Traditional American Indian and Western European Attitudes toward Nature: An Overview" *[TAIWEA]*. In Oelschlaeger, ed., *Postmodern Environmental Ethics*.

———, ed. *Companion to* A Sand County Almanac: *Interpretive and Critical Essays [CSCA]*. Madison: University of Wisconsin Press, 1987.

Callicott, J. Baird, and Roger T. Ames, eds. *Nature in Asian Traditions of Thought: Essays in Environmental Philosophy [NATT]*. Albany: State University of New York Press, 1989.

Caplan, Patricia. "Cognatic Descent, Islamic Law and Women's Property on the East African Coast" *[CD]*. In Hirschon, ed., *Woman and Property—Women as Property*.

Capra, Fritjof, and Charlene Spretnak. *Green Politics: The Global Promise [GP]*. New York: Dutton, 1984.

Caputo, John D. *Against Ethics: Contributions to a Poetics of Obligation with Constant Reference to Deconstruction [AE]*. Bloomington: Indiana University Press, 1993.

Card, Claudia, ed. *Feminist Ethics [FE]*. Lawrence: University Press of Kansas, 1991.

Carter, Alan. *The Philosophical Foundations of Property Rights [PFPR]*. New York: Harvester Wheatsheaf, 1989.

Chapman, John W. "Justice, Freedom, and Property" *[JFP]*. In Pennock and Chapman, eds., *Nomos XXII*, 289–324.

Cheal, David. *The Gift Economy [GE]*. New York: Routledge, 1988.

Cheney, Jim. "Eco-feminism and Deep Ecology" *[EDE]*. *Environmental Ethics* 9, no. 2 (Summer 1987): 115–45.

———. "Postmodern Environmental Ethics: Ethics as Bioregional Narrative" *[PMEE]*. In Oelschlaeger, ed., *Postmodern Environmental Ethics*.

Chief Seattle. *The Eyes of Chief Seattle [ECS]*. Exhibition catalogue. Seattle: The Suquamish Museum, 1985.

Christ, Carol P. "Reverence for Life: The Need for a Sense of Finitude" *[RL]*. In Cooey, Farmer, and Ross, eds., *Embodied Love*.

———. "Spiritual Quest and Women's Experience" *[SQWE]*. In Christ and Plaskow, eds., *Womanspirit Rising*.

Christ, Carol P., and Judith Plaskow, eds. *Womanspirit Rising [WR]*. New York: Harper & Row, 1979.

Cixous, Hélène. "Laugh of the Medusa" *[LM]*. In Marks and Courtivron, eds., *New French Feminisms*.

Cixous, Hélène, and Catherine Clément. *The Newly Born Woman [NBW]*. Trans. Betsy Wing. Int. Sandra M. Gilbert. Minneapolis: University of Minnesota Press, 1975.

Clark, Cedric X. "Some Implications of Nkrumah's Consciencism for Alternative Coordinates in NonEuropean Causality" *[SINC]*. In Ruch and Anyanwu, eds., *African Philosophy*.

Clark, Lorenne M. G. "Women and John Locke; or, Who Owns the Apples in the Garden of Eden?" *Canadian Journal of Philosophy* 7, no. 4 (December 1977): 699–724.

Clément, Catherine. "The Guilty Ones" *[GO]*. In Cixous and Clément, *Newly Born Woman*.

———. *Syncope: The Philosophy of Rapture [S]*. Trans. Sally O'Driscoll and Deirdre M. Mahoney. Minneapolis: University of Minnesota Press, 1994.

Clifford, James. "On Collecting Art and Culture" *[CAC]*. Reprinted in Ross, ed., *Art and Its Significance.* From Russell Ferguson, et al., eds. *Out There: Marginalization and Contemporary Cultures.* New York: New Museum of Contemporary Art and Cambridge: MIT Press, 1990, 141–46, 151–65.

Cobb, John, Jr. "Christian Existence in a World of Limits" *[CEWL]*. In Oelschlaeger, ed., *Postmodern Environmental Ethics.*

Cobham, Rhonda, and Merle Collins, eds. *Watchers and Seekers: Creative Writing by Black Women in Britain [WS].* London: Women's Press, 1987.

Codiga, Doug. "Zen Practice and a Sense of Place" *[ZPSP]*. In Badiner, ed., *Dharma Gaia.*

Cohn, Jan. *Romance and the Erotics of Property: Mass-Market Fiction for Women [REP].* Durham: Duke University Press, 1988.

Cole, Eve Browning, and Susan Coultrap-McQuin, eds. *Explorations in Feminist Ethics: Theory and Practice [EFE].* Bloomington: Indiana University Press, 1992.

Comstock, Gary. "Pigs and Piety: A Theocentric Perspective on Food Animals" *[PP]. Between the Species* 8, no. 3 (Summer 1992): 121–35.

Conley, Verena Andermatt. *Ecopolitics: The Environment in Poststructuralist Thought [E].* New York: Routledge, 1997.

Cooey, Paula M. "The Word Become Flesh: Woman's Body, Language, and Value" *[WF]*. In Cooey, Farmer, and Ross, eds., *Embodied Love.*

Cooey, Paula M., Sharon A. Farmer, and Mary Ellen Ross, eds. *Embodied Love: Sensuality and Relationship as Feminist Values [EL].* San Francisco: Harper & Row, 1987.

Cook, Francis H. "The Jewel Net of Indra" *[JNI]*. In Callicott and Ames, eds., *Nature in Asian Traditions of Thought.*

Cooper, David E., and Joy A. Palmer, eds. *The Environment in Question: Ethics and Global Issues [EQ].* New York: Routledge, 1992.

Cornell, Drucilla. *Beyond Accommodation: Ethical Feminism, Deconstruction, and the Law [BA].* New York: Routledge, 1991.

———. *The Imaginary Domain: Abortion, Pornography and Sexual Harassment [ID].* New York: Routledge, 1995.

———. *The Philosophy of the Limit [PL].* New York: Routledge, 1992.

———. *Transformations: Recollective Imagination and Sexual Difference [T].* New York: Routledge, 1993.

Cornell, Drucilla, Michel Rosenfeld, and David Gray Carlson, eds. *Deconstruction and the Possibility of Justice [DPJ].* New York: Routledge, Chapman and Hall, 1992.

Cose, Ellis. *A Nation of Strangers [NS]*. New York: William Morrow and Co., 1992.

Croll, Elisabeth. "The Exchange of Women and Property: Marriage in Post-Revolutionary China" *[EWP]*. In Hirschon, ed., *Woman and Property—Women As Property*.

Curtin, Deane. "Toward an Ecological Ethic of Care" *[TEEC]*. In Warren, ed., *Hypatia*, 60–74.

Daly, Mary. "After the Death of God the Father: Women's Liberation and the Transformation of Christian Consciousness" *[ADGF]*. In Christ and Plaskow, eds., *Womanspirit Rising*.

———. *Gyn/Ecology: The Metaethics of Radical Feminism [G/E]*. Boston: Beacon Press, 1990.

Dawkins, Richard. *The Selfish Gene [SG]*. Oxford: Oxford University Press, 1976.

de Silva, Lily. "The Hills Wherein My Soul Delights: Exploring the Stories and Teachings" *[HWMSD]*. In Batchelor and Brown, eds., *Buddhism and Ecology*.

de Waal, Frans. *Good Natured: The Origins of Right and Wrong in Humans and Other Animals [GN]*. Cambridge: Harvard University Press, 1996.

Delacampagne, Christian. "Racism and the West: From Praxis to Logos" *[RW]*. In Goldberg, ed., *Anatomy of Racism*.

Deleuze, Gilles. *Difference and Repetition [DR]*. Trans. Paul Patton. New York: Columbia University Press, 1994. Translation of *Différence et répétition*. Paris: P.U.F., 1968.

———. *The Logic of Sense [LS]*. Trans. Mark Lester with Charles Stivale. New York: Columbia University Press, 1990. Translation of *Logique du sens*. Paris: Editions de Minuit, 1969.

Deleuze, Gilles, and Félix Guattari. *Anti-Oedipus: Capitalism and Schizophrenia [A-O]*. Trans. Robert Hurley, Mark Seem, and Helen R. Lane. Minneapolis: University of Minnesota Press, 1983.

———. *A Thousand Plateaus: Capitalism and Schizophrenia [TP]*. Trans. Brian Massumi. Minneapolis: University of Minnesota Press, 1987.

———. *What Is Philosophy? [WP]*. Trans. Hugh Tomlinson and Graham Burchell. New York: Columbia University Press, 1994.

Deloria, Vine, Jr. *God Is Red [GR]*. New York: Dell, 1973.

Derrida, Jacques. "Cogito and the History of Madness" *[CHM]*. In *Writing and Difference*.

———. *Dissemination [D]*. Trans. and int. Barbara Johnson. Chicago: University of Chicago Press, 1981.

———. " 'Eating Well,' or the Calculation of the Subject" *[EW]*. Trans. Peter Connor and Avital Ronell. In *Points*.

———. "Economimesis" *[E]*. *Diacritics* 11, no. 2 (June 1981): 3–25.

———. "Force of Law: The 'Mystical Foundation of Authority' " *[FL]*. In Cornell, Rosenfeld, and Carlson, eds., *Deconstruction and the Possibility of Justice*. Reprinted from *Cardozo Law Review* 11, nos. 5-6 (July/August 1991): 919–1045.

———. "From Restricted to General Economy: A Hegelianism without Reserve" *[FRGE]*. In *Writing and Difference*.

———. "Geschlecht: Sexual Difference, Ontological Difference" *[G1]*. *Research in Phenomenology* 13 (1983): 65–83.

———. "*Geschlecht* II: Heidegger's Hand" *[G2]*. Trans. John P. Leavey, Jr. In Sallis, ed., *Deconstruction in Philosophy: The Texts of Jacques Derrida*.

———. *The Gift of Death [GD]*. Trans. David Wills. Chicago: University of Chicago Press, 1994.

———. *Given Time [GT]*. Trans. Peggy Kamuf. Chicago: University of Chicago Press, 1992.

———. "Heidegger's Ear: Philopolemology (*Geschlecht* IV)" *[G4]*. In Sallis, ed., *Reading Heidegger*. Bloomington: Indiana University Press, 1993.

———. "Letter to Peter Eisenman" *[LPE]*. Reprinted in Ross, ed., *Art and Its Significance*. From *Assemblage* 12: 7–13.

———. *Margins of Philosophy [MP]*. Trans. Alan Bass. Chicago: University of Chicago Press, 1982.

———. *Of Grammatology [OG]*. Trans. Gayatri Chakravorty Spivak. Baltimore: The Johns Hopkins Press, 1974.

———. *Of Spirit: Heidegger and the Question [OS]*. Trans. Geoffrey Bennington and Rachel Bowlby. Chicago: University of Chicago Press, 1989.

———. "Parergon" *[P]*. In *Truth in Painting*. Reprinted in part in Ross, ed., *Art and Its Significance*.

———. "Passe-Partout" *[P-P]*. In *Truth in Painting*. Reprinted in Ross, ed., *Art and Its Significance*. Introduction to *Truth in Painting*.

———. "Plato's Pharmacy" *[PP]*. In *Dissemination*.

———. *Points . . . : Interviews, 1974–94 [P. . . ]*. Trans. Peggy Kamuf and others. Stanford, CA: Stanford University Press, 1995.

———. "The Politics of Friendship" *[PF]*. *The Journal of Philosophy* 85 (November 1988): 632–44.

———. "Restitutions" *[R]*. In *Truth in Painting*. Reprinted in part in Ross, ed., *Art and Its Significance*. From *Truth in Painting*.

———. *Specters of Marx: The State of the Debt, the Work of Mourning, and the New International [SM]*. Trans. Peggy Kamuf. Int. Bernd Magnus and Stephen Cullenberg. New York: Routledge, 1994.

———. *The Truth in Painting [TP]*. Trans. G. Bennington and I. McLeod. Chicago: University of Chicago Press, 1987.

———. "Violence and Metaphysics: An Essay on the Thought of Emmanuel Levinas" *[VM]*. In *Writing and Difference*.

———. "White Mythology: Metaphor in the Text of Philosophy" *[WM]*. In *Margins of Philosophy*.

———. *Writing and Difference [WD]*. Trans. Alan Bass. Chicago: University of Chicago Press, 1978.

Descartes, René. *Discourse on the Method of Rightly Conducting the Reason and Seeking Truth in the Sciences [DM]*. In *Philosophical Writings of Descartes*, vol. 1.

———. *Early Writings [EW]*. In *Philosophical Writings of Descartes*, vol. 1.

———. *Meditations [M]*. In *Philosophical Writings of Descartes*, vol. 2.

———. *Objections and Replies [OR]*. In *Philosophical Writings of Descartes*, vol. 2.

———. *Optics [O]*. In *Philosophical Writings of Descartes*, vol. 1.

———. *The Passions of the Soul [PS]*. In *Philosophical Writings of Descartes*, vol. 1.

———. *The Philosophical Writings of Descartes [PWD]*. Trans. John Cottingham, Robert Stoothoff, and Dugald Murdoch. 2 vols. Cambridge: Cambridge University Press, 1985.

———. *Principles of Philosophy [PP]*. In *Philosophical Writings of Descartes*, vol. 1.

———. *Rules for the Direction of the Mind [RDM]*. In *Philosophical Writings of Descartes*, vol. 1.

———. *Treatise on Man [TM]*. In *Philosophical Writings of Descartes*, vol. 1.

———. *The World [W]*. In *Philosophical Writings of Descartes*, vol. 1.

Devall, Bill. *Simple in Means, Rich in Ends: Practicing Deep Ecology [SMRE]*. Salt Lake City: Peregrine Smith, 1990.

Devall, Bill, and George Sessions. *Deep Ecology: Living as if Nature Mattered [DE]*. Salt Lake City: Peregrene Smith, 1985.

Devi, Mahasweta. *Imaginary Maps: Three Stories [IM]*. Trans. Gayatri Chakravorty Spivak. New York: Routledge, 1995.

Dewey, John. *Art and Experience [AE]*. New York: Putnam, 1934. Reprinted in part in Ross, ed., *Art and Its Significance.*

———. "Body and Mind" *[BM]*. In *Philosophy and Civilization.*

———. "Context and Thought" *[CT]*. In *Experience, Nature, and Freedom.*

———. *Experience and Nature [EN]*. 2nd ed. New York: Dover, 1958.

———. *Experience, Nature, and Freedom [ENF]*. Ed. and int. Richard J. Bernstein. Indianapolis: Library of Liberal Arts, 1960.

———. *Human Nature and Conduct [HNC]*. New York: Holt, 1922.

———. *Logic: The Theory of Inquiry [L]*. New York: Henry Holt & Co., 1938.

———. "Nature in Experience" *[NE]*. In *Experience, Nature, and Freedom.*

———. "The Need for a Recovery of Philosophy" *[NRP]*. In *Experience, Nature, and Freedom.*

———. *Philosophy and Civilization [PC]*. New York: Minton, Balch, 1931.

———. *Quest for Certainty [QC]*. New York: Minton, Balch, 1929.

———. *Theory of Valuation [TV]*. Chicago: University of Chicago Press, 1939.

Diamond, Irene. "Babies, Heroic Experts, and a Poisoned Earth" *[BHEPE]*. In Diamond and Orenstein, eds., *Reweaving the World.*

Diamond, Irene, and Gloria Feman Orenstein, eds. *Reweaving the World: The Emergence of Ecofeminism [RW]*. San Francisco: Sierra Club Books, 1990.

Dimen, Muriel. "Power, Sexuality, and Intimacy" *[PSI]*. In Jaggar and Bordo, eds., *Gender/Body/Knowledge.*

Dixon, Vernon J. "World Views and Research Methodology" *[WVRM]*. In King, Dixon, and Nobles, eds., *African Philosophy.*

Dombrowski, Daniel A. *Babies and Beasts: The Argument from Marginal Cases [BB]*. Urbana: University of Illinois Press, 1997.

———. *Hartshorne and the Metaphysics of Animal Rights [HMAR]*. Albany: State University of New York Press, 1988.

———. *The Philosophy of Vegetarianism [PV]*. Amherst: University of Massachusetts Press, 1984.

Dostoevsky, Fyodor. *The Brothers Karamazov [BK]*. Trans. Constance Garnett. New York: Modern Library, 1950.

Douglas, Mary. *Purity and Danger: An Analysis of Concepts of Pollution and Taboo [PD]*. New York: Praeger, 1966.

Douglas, Mary, and Baron Isherwood. *The World of Goods: Toward an Anthropology of Consumption [WG]*. New York: W. W. Norton, 1979.

Dryzek, John S. "Green Reason: Communicative Ethics for the Biosphere" *[GR]*. In Oelschlaeger, ed., *Postmodern Environmental Ethics*.

———. *Rational Ecology: Environment and Political Economy [RE]*. New York: Blackwell, 1987.

duBois, Page. *Sowing the Body: Psychoanalysis and Ancient Representations of Women [SB]*. Chicago: University of Chicago Press, 1988.

———. *Torture and Truth [TT]*. New York: Routledge, 1991.

Du Bois, W. E. B. *A W. E. B. Du Bois Reader [WEBDR]*. Ed. Andrew G. Paschal. New York: Macmillan, 1971.

———. "The Concept of Race" *[CR]*. In Hord and Lee, eds., *I Am Because We Are*.

———. "The Conservation of Races" *[CR]*. In *Du Bois Reader*.

Duerr, Hans Peter. *Dreamtime: Concerning the Boundary between Wilderness and Civilization [D]*. Trans. Felicitas Goodman. Oxford: Blackwell, 1985.

Dworkin, Andrea. *Intercourse [I]*. New York: Free Press, 1987.

———. *Pornography: Men Possessing Women [P]*. New York: G. P. Putnam's Sons, 1981.

Ecker, Gisela, ed. *Feminist Aesthetics [FA]*. Trans. Harriet Anderson. Boston: Beacon Press, 1985.

Eckersley, Robyn. *Environmentalism and Political Theory: Toward an Ecocentric Approach [EPT]*. Albany: State University of New York Press, 1992.

Ehrenfeld, David. *The Arrogance of Humanism [AH]*. New York: Oxford University Press, 1978.

———. "The Management of Diversity: A Conservation Paradox" *[MD]*. In Bormann and Kellert, eds., *Ecology, Economics, Ethics*.

Eliade, Mircea. *Shamanism: Archaic Techniques of Ecstacy [S]*. Princeton: Princeton University Press, 1972.

El Sadaawi, Nawal. *The Hidden Face of Eve: Women in the Arab World [HFE]*. Trans. Sherif Hetata. Boston: Beacon Press, 1980.

Engels, Friedrich. *The Origin of the Family, Private Property and the State [OFPPS]*. In Marx and Engels, *Selected Works*.

Epstein, Richard. *Takings: Private Property and the Power of Eminent Domain [T]*. Cambridge: Harvard University Press, 1985.

Erodes, Richard. *Lame Deer: Seeker of Visions [LD]*. New York: Simon & Schuster, 1976.

Fanon, Frantz. *Black Skin, White Masks [BSWM]*. Trans. Charles Lam Markmann. New York: Grove Press, 1967.

———. *Wretched of the Earth [WE]*. Trans. Constance Farrington. Pref. Jean-Paul Sartre. New York: Grove Press, 1965.

Ferry, Luc. *The New Ecological Order [NEO]*. Trans. Carol Volk. Chicago: University of Chicago Press, 1995.

Fortes, Meyer. "Strangers" *[S]*. In Fortes and Patterson, *Studies in African Social Anthropology*.

Fortes, Meyer, and Patterson, Sheila. *Studies in African Social Anthropology [SASA]*. New York: Academic Press, 1975.

Foucault, Michel. *Archaeology of Knowledge [AK]*. Trans. A. M. Sheridan-Smith. New York: Pantheon, 1981.

———. *The Care of the Self [CS]*. Trans. Robert Hurley. New York: Pantheon, 1986.

———. *Discipline and Punish: The Birth of the Prison [DP]*. Trans. Alan Sheridan. New York: Vintage, 1979.

———. "Discourse on Language" *[DL]*. In *Archaeology of Knowledge*.

———. *Folie et déraison: Histoire de la folie à la l'âge classique [FD]*. Paris: Plon, 1961.

———. *History of Sexuality*, Vol. 1 *[HS]*. Trans. R. Hurley. New York: Vintage, 1980.

———. *Language, Counter-Memory, Practice [LCP]*. Trans. Donald F. Bouchard and Sherry Simon. Ed. and int. Donald F. Bouchard. Ithaca, NY: Cornell University Press, 1977.

———. *Madness and Civilization: A History of Insanity in the Age of Reason [MC]*. Trans. Richard Howard. New York: Random House, 1965. Translation and abridgment of *Folie et déraison*.

———. "Nietzsche, Genealogy, History" *[NGH]*. In *Language, Counter-Memory, Practice*.

———. "On Popular Justice: A Discussion with Maoists" *[OPJ]*. In *Power/Knowledge*.

———. *The Order of Things: An Archaeology of the Human Sciences [OT]*. New York: Vintage, 1973.

———. *Power/Knowledge [P/K]*. Ed. and trans. C. Gordon. New York: Pantheon, 1980.

———. "A Preface to Transgression" *[PT]*. In *Language, Counter-Memory, Practice*.

———. "Questions on Geography" *[QG]*. In *Power/Knowledge*.

———. *Remarks on Marx [RM]*. Trans. R. James Goldstein and James Cascaito. New York: Semiotext(e), 1961.

————. "Theatrum Philosophicum" *[TP]*. In *Language, Counter-Memory, Practice*.

————. "Truth and Power" *[TrP]*. In *Power/Knowledge*.

————. "Two Lectures" *[2L]*. In *Power/Knowledge*.

————. "What Is an Author?" *[WA?]*. In *Language, Counter-Memory, Practice*.

Frederickson, Owen P. *The Psychology of Ownership [PO]*. Washington, DC: The Catholic University of America Press, 1954.

Freud, Sigmund. "Femininity" *[F]*. In *New Introductory Lectures on Psychoanalysis*, vol. 22. From *The Standard Edition of the Complete Psychological Works of Sigmund Freud*. Ed. James Strachey, 24 vols. London: Hogarth Press, 1953–74.

————. "The Relation of the Poet to Day-dreaming" *[RPD]*. Reprinted in Ross, ed., *Art and Its Significance*. From Sigmund Freud, *Collected Papers*, vol. 4. Article trans. I. F. Grant Duff. New York: Basic Books, 1959.

Freyfogle, Eric T. *Justice and the Earth: Images for Our Planetary Survival [JE]*. New York: Free Press, 1993.

Frodeman, Robert. "Radical Environmentalism and the Political Roots of Postmodernism: Differences That Make a Difference" *[REPRP]*. In Oelschlaeger, ed., *Postmodern Environmental Ethics*.

Fry, Tony, and Anne-Marie Willis. "Aboriginal Art: Symptom or Success?" *[AA]*. Reprinted in part in Ross, ed., *Art and Its Significance*. From *Art in America* (July 1989): 111–16, 159–61.

Fuller, Steve. *Controversial Science: From Content to Contention [CS]*. Albany: State University of New York Press, 1993.

————. *Philosophy of Science and Its Discontents [PSD]*. Boulder, CO: Westview Press, 1989.

————. *Social Epistemology [SE]*. Bloomington and Indianapolis: Indiana University Press, 1988.

Gaard, Greta. *Ecofeminism: Women, Animals, Nature [E]*. Philadelphia: Temple University Press, 1993.

Gallop, Jane. *Thinking Through the Body [TTB]*. New York: Columbia University Press, 1988.

Galsworthy, John. *The Man of Property [MP]*. Moscow: Foreign Languages Publishing House, 1950.

Garb, Yaakov Jerome. "Perspective or Escape? Ecofeminist Musings on Contemporary Earth Imagery" *[PE]*. In Diamond and Orenstein, eds., *Reweaving the World*.

Gates, Henry Louis, Jr. "Critical Remarks" *[CR]*. In Goldberg, ed., *Anatomy of Racism*.

————, ed. *"Race," Writing, and Difference [RWD]*. Chicago: University of Chicago Press, 1986.

Gates, Paul W. "Recent Land Policies of the Federal Government" *[RLPFG]*. Section 5 in Forest Service, Department of Agriculture and The Land Policy Section, Agricultural Adjustment Administration for the Land Planning Committee of the National Resources Board, *Certain Aspects of Land Problems and Government Land Policies: Part VII of the Report on Land Planning*. Washington, DC: 1935.

Gilbert, Bil. "Crows by Far and Wide, but There's No Place Like Home." *Smithsonian* 23, no. 5 (August 1992): 101–11.

————. *Our Nature [ON]*. Lincoln: University of Nebraska Press, 1986.

Gilbert, Jess, and Craig K. Harris. "Changes in Type, Tenure, and Concentration of U.S. Farmland Owners" *[CTTCFO]*. In *Focus on Agriculture*. Ed. Harry K. Schwarzweller. Greenwich, CN: Jai Press, 1984.

Gilligan, Carol. *In a Different Voice: Psychological Theory and Women's Development [IDV]*. Cambridge: Harvard University Press, 1982.

Gillis, Malcolm. "Economics, Ecology, and Ethics: Mending the Broken Circle for Tropical Forests" *[EEE]*. In Bormann and Kellert, eds., *Ecology, Economics, Ethics*.

Gluckman, Max. *Politics, Law and Ritual in Tribal Society [PLRTS]*. Chicago: Aldine, 1965.

Godway, Eleanor M., and Geraldine Finn, eds. *Who Is This "We"?: Absence of Community [WW]*. Montréal: Black Rose Books, 1994.

Goldberg, David Theo, ed. *Anatomy of Racism [AR]*. Minneapolis: University of Minnesota Press, 1990.

Golding, Sue. "The Excess" *[E]*. In Kroker and Kroker, eds., *Last Sex*.

Gottlieb, Alma. "Witches, Kings, and the Sacrifice of Identity, or The Power of Paradox and the Paradox of Power among the Beng of Ivory Coast" *[WKS]*. In Arens and Karp, eds., *Creativity of Power*.

Göttner-Abendroth, Heide. "Nine Principles of a Matriarchal Aesthetics" *[MA]*. Trans. Harriet Anderson. Reprinted in Ross, ed., *Art and Its Significance*. From Ecker, ed., *Feminist Aesthetics*.

Gramsci, Antonio. *An Antonio Gramsci Reader: Selected Writings 1916–1935 [AGR]*. New York: Schocken Books, 1988.

————. *Gramsci [G]*. Paris: Seghers, 1966.

————. *The Open Marxism of Antonio Gramsci [OM]*. Trans. Carl Marzani. New York: Cameron Associates, 1957.

Graves, Robert. *The Greek Myths [GM]*. Baltimore: Penguin, 1955.

Gregory, C. A. "The Emergence of Commodity Production in Papua New Guinea" *[ECPPNG]*. *Journal of Contemporary Asia* (1979): 389–409.

Grey, Thomas C. "The Disintegration of Property" *[DP]*. In Pennock and Chapman, eds., *Nomos XXII*, 69-85.

Griffin, Susan. *A Chorus of Stones [CS]*. New York: Doubleday, 1992.

———. *Pornography and Silence [PS]*. New York: Harper & Row, 1981.

———. *Woman and Nature: The Roaring Inside Her [WN]*. New York: Harper & Row, 1978.

Griffiths, Ieuan Ll. *An Atlas of African Affairs [AAA]*. New York: Routledge, 1994.

Grosz, Elizabeth. *Volatile Bodies: Toward a Corporeal Feminism [VB]*. Bloomington: Indiana University Press, 1994.

Gruen, Lori, and Dale Jamieson, eds. *Reflecting on Nature [RN]*. Oxford: Oxford University Press, 1994.

Grunebaum, James O. *Private Ownership [PO]*. New York: Routledge & Kegan Paul, 1987.

Guy-Sheftall, Beverly, ed. *Words of Fire: An Anthology of African-American Feminist Thought [WF]*. New York: New Press, 1995.

Habermas, Jürgen. *Communication and the Evolution of Society [CES]*. Ed. T. McCarthy. Boston: Beacon Press, 1979.

Hallen, Barry. "Phenomenology and the Exposition of African Traditional Thought" *[PEATT]*. In *Proceedings of the Seminar on African Philosophy/La Philosophie Africaine*. Ed. Claude Sumner. Addis Ababa: Chamber Printing House, 1980.

Hallen, B., and J. O. Sodipo. *Knowledge, Belief and Witchcraft: Analytic Experiments in African Philosophy [KBW]*. London: Ethnographica, 1986.

Hamilton, Cynthia. "Coping with Industrial Exploitation" *[CIE]*. In Bullard, ed., *Confronting Environmental Racism*.

Hamilton-Grierson, P. J. "Strangers" *[S]*. In *Encyclopaedia of Religion and Ethics*. Ed J. Hastings. Edinburgh: T. & T. Clark, 1921. Vol. 11: 883–896.

Haraway, Donna. *Simians, Cyborgs, and Women: The Reinvention of Nature [SCW]*. New York: Routledge, 1991.

Hardin, Garrett. "The Tragedy of the Commons" *[TC]*. *Science* 162 (December 13, 1968): 1245–48.

Harding, Sandra. "The Curious Coincidence of Feminine and African Moralities: Challenges for Feminist Theory" *[CCFAM]*. In Kittay and Meyers, eds., *Women and Moral Theory*.

———. "The Instability of the Analytical Categories of Feminist Theory" *[IACFT]*. *Signs* 11, no. 4 (Summer 1986): 645–64.

———. *The Science Question in Feminism [SQF]*. Ithaca, NY: Cornell University Press, 1986.

———. *Whose Science? Whose Knowledge?: Thinking from Women's Lives [WSWK]*. Ithaca, NY: Cornell University Press, 1991.

Hargrove, Eugene C. *Foundations of Environmental Ethics [FEE]*. Englewood Cliffs, NJ: Prentice Hall, 1989.

———, ed. *Religion and Environmental Crisis [REC]*. Athens, GA: University of Georgia Press, 1986.

Harman, Lesley D. *The Modern Stranger [MS]*. Amsterdam: Mouton de Gruyter, 1988.

Harper, Clifford. *Anarchy: A Graphic Guide [A]*. London: Camden Press, 1987.

Harris, Cheryl I. "Whiteness as Property" *[WP]*. *Harvard Law Review* 106, no. 8 (June 1993): 1707–91.

Harris, Leonard. "Postmodernism and Utopia, an Unholy Alliance" *[PU]*. In Hord and Lee, eds., *I Am Because We Are*.

Harrison, Beverly Wildung. "Our Right to Choose" *[RC]*. In Andolsen, Gudorf, and Pellauer, eds., *Women's Consciousness, Women's Conscience*.

Haug, Wolfgang Fritz. *Critique of Commodity Aesthetics: Appearance, Sexuality and Advertising in Capitalist Society [CCA]*. Trans. Robert Bock. Minneapolis: University of Minnesota Press, 1986.

Hegel, G. W. F. *Aesthetics: Lectures on Fine Art [A]*. Trans. T. M. Knox. London: Oxford University Press, 1975. Introduction reprinted in part in Ross, ed., *Art and Its Significance* as "Philosophy of Fine Art" *[PFA]*.

———. *Jenenser Realphilosophie I, Der Vorlesungen von 1803–1804 [JR1]*. Ed. J. Hoffmeister. Leibzig: 1932. Quoted and translated in Agamben, *Language and Death*.

———. *Jenenser Realphilosophie II, Die Vorlesungen von 1803–1804 [JR2]*. Ed. J. Hoffmeister. Leipzig: 1932. Quoted and translated in Agamben, *Language and Death*.

———. *The Logic of Hegel, translated from the Encyclopaedia of the Philosophical Sciences [EL]*. Trans. William Wallace. Oxford: Oxford University Press, 1892.

———. *The Phenomenology of Mind [PM]*. Trans. and int. James Baillie. London: George Allen & Unwin, 1910.

———. *The Philosophy of Right [PR]*. Trans. T. M. Knox. Oxford: Oxford University Press, 1934, 1967.

Heidegger, Martin. "The Anaximander Fragment" *[AF]*. In *Early Greek Thinking*.

———. *Basic Writings [BW]*. Ed. David Farrell Krell. New York: Harper & Row, 1977.

———. *Being and Time [BT]*. Trans. John Macquarrie and Edward Robinson. New York: Harper & Row, 1962. Translation of *Sein und Zeit [SZ]*.

———. *Discourse on Thinking: A Translation of* Gelassenheit *[DT]*. Trans. John M. Anderson and E. Hans Freund. New York: Harper & Row, 1966.

———. *Early Greek Thinking [EGT]*. Trans. D. F. Krell and F. A. Capuzzi. New York: Harper & Row, 1984.

———. *Identity and Difference [ID]*. Trans. and int. Joan Stambaugh. New York: Harper & Row, 1969.

———. *Introduction to Metaphysics [IM]*. Trans. Ralph Manheim. Garden City, NY: Doubleday, 1961.

———. "Language" *[L]*. In *Poetry, Language, Thought*.

———. "Language in the Poem" *[LP]*. In *On the Way to Language*.

———. "Letter on Humanism" *[LH]*. In *Basic Writings*.

———. "Martin Heidegger interrogé par *Der Spiegel*. Réponses et questions sur l'histoire et la politique" (Martin Heidegger Interviewed by *Der Spiegel*: Responses and Questions on History and Politics.) Trans. William J. Richardson S. J. as " 'Only a God Can Save Us': The *Spiegel* Interview." In Sheehan, ed., *Heidegger, the Man and the Thinker*.

———. "The Nature of Language" *[NL]*. In *On the Way to Language*.

———. "On the Being and Conception of *Physis* in Aristotle's *Physics* B. 1" *[OBCP]*. Trans. T. J. Sheehan. *Man and World* 9, no. 3 (August 1976): 219–70.

———. "On the Essence of Truth" *[OET]*. In *Basic Writings*.

———. *On the Way to Language [OWL]*. Trans. Peter D. Hertz. New York: Harper & Row, 1971.

———. *On Time and Being [OTB]*. Trans. Joan Stambaugh. New York: Harper & Row, 1972.

———. "The Onto-theo-logical Constitution of Metaphysics" *[OTLCM]*. In *Identity and Difference*.

———. "The Origin of the Work of Art" *[OWA]*. Reprinted in part in Ross, ed., *Art and Its Significance*. From *Poetry, Language, Thought*.

———. *Poetry, Language, Thought [PLT]*. Trans. Albert Hofstadter. New York: Harper & Row, 1971.

———. "The Question Concerning Technology" *[QT]*. In *Basic Writings*.

————. *The Question Concerning Technology and Other Essays [QTOE]*. Trans. William Lovitt. New York: Harper & Row, 1977.

————. "Time and Being" *[TB]*. In *On Time and Being*.

————. *Was ist das—die Philosophie [WP]*, 1955. Quoted in Derrida, "Heidegger's Ear."

————. "The Way to Language" *[WL]*. In *On the Way to Language*.

————. "What Calls for Thinking?" *[WCT]*. In *Basic Writings*.

Herdt, G. *Guardians of the Flutes: Idioms of Masculinity [GF]*. Stanford: Stanford University Press, 1980.

Hester, Jr., Randolph T. "Sacred Structures and Everyday Life: A Return to Manteo, North Carolina" *[SSEL]*. In Seamon, ed., *Dwelling, Seeing, and Designing*.

Hirschon, Renée, ed. "Introduction: Property, Power and Gender Relations" *[PPGR]*. In Hirschon, ed., *Women and Property—Women as Property*.

————, ed. *Women and Property—Women as Property [WPWP]*. New York: St. Martin's Press, 1984.

Hix, H. L. *Spirits Hovering Over the Ashes: Legacies of Postmodern Theory [SHOA]*. Albany: State University of New York Press, 1995.

Hoagland, Sarah Lucia. "Lesbian Ethics and Female Agency" *[LEFA]*. In Cole and Coultrap-McQuin, eds., *Explorations in Feminist Ethics*.

————. "Some Thoughts about 'Caring' " *[STC]*. In Card, ed., *Feminist Ethics*.

Hobbes, Thomas. *Complete Works [CW]*. Ed. William Molesworth. English Works, 11 vols., 1839. Latin Works, 5 vols., 1845.

————. *De Cive [DCV]*. In *Complete Works*.

————. *Elements of Philosophy [EOP]*. In *Complete Works*, vol. 4.

————. *Leviathan [L]*. In *Complete Works*, vol. 1.

Hölderlin, Friedrich. *Friedrich Hölderlin Poems and Fragments [FHPF]*. Trans. Michael Hamburger. Ann Arbor: University of Michigan Press, 1966.

————. "Patmos" *[P]*. In *Friedrich Hölderlin Poems and Fragments*.

Homann, Margaret. *Bearing the Word: Language and Female Experience in Nine-teenth-Century Women's Writing [BW]*. Chicago: University of Chicago Press, 1986.

Hoppe, Hans-Hermann. *The Economics and Ethics of Private Property [EEPP]*. Boston: Kluwer Academic Publishers, 1993.

Hord, Fred Lee (Mzee Lasana Okpara), and Jonathan Scott Lee, eds. *I Am Because We Are: Readings in Black Philosophy [IABWA]*. Amherst: University of Massachusetts, 1995.

Horovitz, Irving Louis, ed. *The Anarchists [A]*. New York: Dell, 1964.

Hume, David. *An Enquiry Concerning Human Understanding [EHU]*. New York: Prometheus, 1988.

———. "Of the Standard of Taste" *[OST]*. Reprinted in Ross, ed., *Art and Its Significance*.

———. "On National Characters" *[ONC]*. In T. H. Green and T. H. Grose, eds., *Philosophical Works [PW]*, vol. 3. Aalen: Scientia Verlag, 1964.

———. *A Treatise of Human Nature [T]*. London: Oxford University Press, 1888.

Husserl, Edmund. *Ideas: General Introduction to Pure Phenomenology [I]*. Trans. W. R. Boyce Gibson. New York: Collier Books, 1962.

Hyde, Lewis. *The Gift: Imagination and the Erotic Life of Property [G]*. New York: Random House, 1979.

Inada, Kenneth K. "Environmental Problematics" *[EP]*. In Callicott and Ames, eds., *Nature in Asian Traditions of Thought*.

Irigaray, Luce. "Any Theory of the 'Subject' Has Always Been Appropriated by the 'Masculine' " *[ATS]*. In *Speculum of the Other Woman*.

———. "The Culture of Difference" *[CD]*. In *Je, tu, nous*.

———. *An Ethics of Sexual Difference [ESD]*. Trans. Carolyn Burke and Gillian C. Gill. Ithaca, NY: Cornell University Press, 1993. Translation of *Éthique de la Différence sexuelle [ÉDS]*. Paris: Minuit, 1984.

———. "The Fecundity of the Caress: A Reading of Levinas, *Totality and Infinity*, 'Phenomenology of Eros' " *[FC]*. In *Ethics of Sexual Difference*.

———. "He Risks Who Risks Life Itself" *[HR]*. In *Irigaray Reader*.

———. *I Love to You: Sketch of a Possible Felicity in History [ILTY]*. Trans. Alison Martin. New York: Routledge, 1996.

———. "The Invisible of the Flesh: A Reading of Merleau-Ponty, *The Visible and the Invisible*, 'The Intertwining—The Chiasm' " *[IF]*. In *Ethics of Sexual Difference*.

———. *The Irigaray Reader [IR]*. Ed. and int. Margaret Whitford. Oxford: Blackwell, 1991.

———. "Je—Luce Irigaray" *[J]*. Ed. and trans. Elizabeth Hirsh and Gaëton Brechotte. Interview in *Hypatia* 10, no. 2 (Spring 1995): 93–114.

———. *Je, tu, nous: Toward a Culture of Difference [JTN]*. Trans. Alison Martin. New York: Routledge, 1993.

———. *Marine Lover of Friedrich Nietzsche [ML]*. Trans. Gillian C. Gill. New York: Columbia University Press, 1991.

———. "The 'Mechanics' of Fluids" *[MF]*. In *This Sex Which Is Not One*.

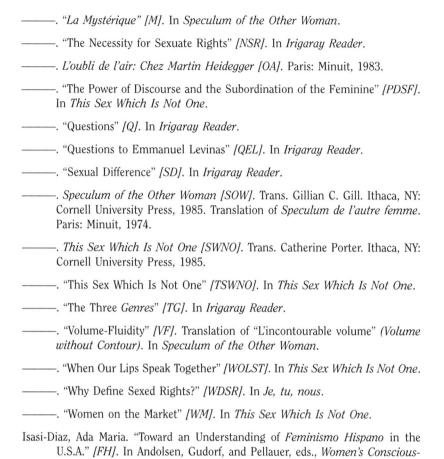

———. *"La Mystérique" [M]*. In *Speculum of the Other Woman*.

———. "The Necessity for Sexuate Rights" *[NSR]*. In *Irigaray Reader*.

———. *L'oubli de l'air: Chez Martin Heidegger [OA]*. Paris: Minuit, 1983.

———. "The Power of Discourse and the Subordination of the Feminine" *[PDSF]*. In *This Sex Which Is Not One*.

———. "Questions" *[Q]*. In *Irigaray Reader*.

———. "Questions to Emmanuel Levinas" *[QEL]*. In *Irigaray Reader*.

———. "Sexual Difference" *[SD]*. In *Irigaray Reader*.

———. *Speculum of the Other Woman [SOW]*. Trans. Gillian C. Gill. Ithaca, NY: Cornell University Press, 1985. Translation of *Speculum de l'autre femme*. Paris: Minuit, 1974.

———. *This Sex Which Is Not One [SWNO]*. Trans. Catherine Porter. Ithaca, NY: Cornell University Press, 1985.

———. "This Sex Which Is Not One" *[TSWNO]*. In *This Sex Which Is Not One*.

———. "The Three *Genres*" *[TG]*. In *Irigaray Reader*.

———. "Volume-Fluidity" *[VF]*. Translation of "L'incontourable volume" *(Volume without Contour)*. In *Speculum of the Other Woman*.

———. "When Our Lips Speak Together" *[WOLST]*. In *This Sex Which Is Not One*.

———. "Why Define Sexed Rights?" *[WDSR]*. In *Je, tu, nous*.

———. "Women on the Market" *[WM]*. In *This Sex Which Is Not One*.

Isasi-Diaz, Ada Maria. "Toward an Understanding of *Feminismo Hispano* in the U.S.A." *[FH]*. In Andolsen, Gudorf, and Pellauer, eds., *Women's Consciousness, Women's Conscience*.

Jackson, Wes, et al., eds. *Meeting the Expectations of the Land [MEL]*. San Francisco: North Point Press, 1984.

Jacobs, Jane. *Systems of Survival: A Dialogue on the Moral Foundations of Commerce and Politics [SS]*. New York: Random House, 1993.

Jacoby, Karl. "Slaves by Nature? Domestic Animals and Human Slaves" *[SN]*. *Slavery and Abolition: A Journal of Slave and Post-Slave Studies* (April 1994): 89–97.

Jaggar, Alison M., and Susan R. Bordo, eds. *Gender/Body/Knowledge: Feminist Reconstructions of Being and Knowing [GBK]*. New Brunswick: Rutgers University Press, 1989.

James, William. *Essays in Radical Empiricism [ERE]*. New York: Longman's Green, 1912.

Jameson, Frederic. "Postmodernism, or The Cultural Logic of Late Capitalism" *[P]*. *New Left Review* 146, no. 4 (July–August, 1984): 53–93.

Johnson, Mark. *The Body in the Mind: The Bodily Basis of Meaning, Imagination, and Reason [BM]*. Chicago: University of Chicago Press, 1987.

Jonas, Hans. "De la Gnose au Principe Responsabilité: Entretien avec Hans Jonas" *[GPR]*. *Esprit* 171 (May 1991): 5–21.

———. *The Imperative of Responsibility: In Search of an Ethics for the Technological Age [IR]*. Chicago: University of Chicago Press, 1984.

Jowett, Donna. "Origins, Occupations, and the Proximity of the Neighbour" *[OOPN]*. In Godway and Finn, eds., *Who Is This "We"?*

Jung, Carl Gustav. *Modern Man in Search of a Soul [MMSS]*. Trans. W. S. Dell and Cary F. Baynes. New York: Harcourt Brace Jovanovich, 1955.

———. "Psychology and Literature" *[PL]*. Reprinted in Ross, ed., *Art and Its Significance*. From *Modern Man in Search of a Soul*.

Jussawalla, Adil. *Missing Person [MP]*. Bombay: Clearing House, 1976.

Kafka, Franz. *The Complete Stories [CS]*. Ed. Nahum N. Glatzer. New York: Schocken, 1971.

———. "In the Penal Colony" *[IPC]*. In Kafka, *Complete Stories*.

Kant, Immanuel. *The Conflict of the Faculties; Der Streit der Fakultäten [CF]*. Trans. Mary J. Gregor. New York: Abaris, 1979.

———. *Critique of Judgment [CJ]*. Trans. J. H. Bernard. New York: Hafner, 1951. Translation of *Kritik der Urteilskraft*. In *Kritik der Urteilskraft und Schriften zur Naturphilosophie*. Wiesbaden: Insel-Verlag Zweigstelle, 1957.

———. *Critique of Practical Reason [CPrR]*. From *Kant's Critique of Practical Reason and Other Works on the Theory of Ethics*. Trans. T. K. Abbott. London: Longman's Green, 1954.

———. *Critique of Pure Reason [CPR]*. Trans. J. M. D. Meiklejohn. Buffalo: Prometheus, 1990. Trans. Norman Kemp Smith *[CPR (NKS)]*. New York: St. Martin's, 1956. Translation of *Kritik der reinen Vernunft [KRV]*. 2 Band. Berlin: Deutsche Bibliothek, 1936.

———. *Fundamental Principles of the Metaphysics of Morals [FPMM]*. In *Kant's Critique of Practical Reason and Other Works on the Theory of Ethics*.

———. *Lectures on Ethics [LE]*. Trans. L. Infield. New York: Harper & Row, 1963.

———. *The Metaphysical Principles of Virtue [MPV]*. Indianapolis: Bobbs-Merrill, 1968.

———. *The Metaphysics of Morals [MM]*. Trans. Mary Gregor. Cambridge: Cambridge University Press, 1991.

————. *Observations on the Beautiful and the Sublime [OBS]*. Trans. John T. Goldthwait. Berkeley: University of California Press, 1960.

Katz, David. *The World of Touch [WT]*. Trans. Lester E. Krueger. Hillsdale, NJ: Lawrence Erlbaum Associates, 1989.

Katz, Eric. "The Call of the Wild: The Struggle against Domination and the Technological Fix of Nature" *[CW]*. In Oelschlaeger, ed., *Postmodern Environmental Ethics*.

————. *Nature as Subject: Human Obligation and Natural Community [NS]*. Lanham: Rowman & Littlefield, 1997.

Keller, Mara Lynn. "The Eleusinian Mysteries: Ancient Nature Religion of Demeter and Persephone" *[EM]*. In Diamond and Orenstein, eds., *Reweaving the World*.

Kheel, Marti. "Ecofeminism and Deep Ecology: Reflections on Identity and Difference" *[EDE]*. In Diamond and Orenstein, eds., *Reweaving the World*.

————. "The Liberation of Nature: A Circular Affair" *[LN]*. *Environmental Ethics* 7, no. 2 (Summer 1985): 135–50.

Kierkegaard, Søren. *Either/Or [E/O]*. Trans. David F. Swenson and Lillian Marvin Swenson. Rev. Howard A. Johnson. 2 vols. Garden City, NY: Doubleday, 1959.

————. *Fear and Trembling/The Sickness Unto Death [FT]*. Trans. W. Lowrie. Garden City, NY: Doubleday, 1954.

King, Deborah K. "Multiple Jeopardy, Multiple Consciousness: The Context of a Black Feminist Ideology" *[MJMC]*. In Guy-Sheftall, ed., *Words of Fire*.

King, Lewis M. "On the Nature of a Creative World" *[ONCW]*. In Ruch and Anyanwu, eds., *African Philosophy*.

King, Lewis M., Vernon J. Dixon, and Wade W. Nobles, eds. *African Philosophy: Assumptions and Paradigms for Research on Black Persons [AP]*. Los Angeles: Charles R. Drew Postgraduate Medical School, 1976. Fanon Research and Development Center Publication, Area 8, no. 2.

King, Roger J. H. "Caring about Nature: Feminist Ethics and the Environment" *[CN]*. In Warren, ed., *Hypatia*, 75–89.

King, Ynestra. "The Ecology of Feminism and the Feminism of Ecology" *[EFFE]*. In Plant, ed., *Healing the Wounds*.

————. "Healing the Wounds: Feminism, Ecology, and the Nature/ Culture Dualism" *[HW]*. In Diamond and Orenstein, eds., *Reweaving the World*.

Kittay, Eva Feder, and Diana T. Meyers, eds. *Women and Moral Theory [WMT]*. Totowa, NJ: Rowman & Littlefield, 1987.

Kline, Linus W., and C. J. France. "The Psychology of Ownership" *[PO]*. *The Pedagogical Seminary* 6, no. 3 (September 1899): 421–70.

Kokole, Omari H. "The Political Economy of the African Environment" *[PEAE]*. In Westra and Wenz, eds., *Faces of Environmental Racism: Confronting Issues of Global Justice*.

Krell, David Farrell. *Daimon Life: Heidegger and Life-Philosophy [DL]*. Bloomington: Indiana University Press, 1992.

———. *Intimations of Mortality [IM]*. University Park: Pennsylvania State University Press, 1986.

Kristeva, Julia. *Black Sun: Depression and Melancholia [BS]*. Trans. Leon S. Roudiez. New York: Columbia University Press, 1989.

———. *Desire in Language: A Semiotic Approach to Literature and Art [DL]*. Trans. Leon S. Roudiez. New York: Columbia University Press, 1980.

———. *The Kristeva Reader [KR]*. Ed. Toril Moi. Trans. Alice Jardine and Harry Blake. New York: Columbia University Press, 1986.

———. *Powers of Horror: An Essay on Abjection [PH]*. Trans. Leon S. Roudiez. New York: Columbia University Press, 1982.

———. "Stabat Mater" *[SM]*. In *Kristeva Reader*.

———. *Strangers to Ourselves [SO]*. Trans. Leon S. Roudiez. New York: Columbia University Press, 1991.

———. "Women's Time" *[WT]*. In *Kristeva Reader*. Published as "Le temps des femmes." *Cahiers de recherche de sciences des textes et documents* 5 (Winter 1979).

Kroker, Arthur, and Marilouise Kroker, eds. *The Last Sex: Feminism and Outlaw Bodies [LS]*. New York: St. Martin's, 1993.

Lacan, Jacques. *Feminine Sexuality [FS]*. Ed. Juliet Mitchell and Jacqueline Rose. Trans. Jacqueline Rose. New York: Norton, 1985.

———. "God and the *Jouissance* of The Woman" *[GJW]*. In *Feminine Sexuality*.

LaChapelle, Dolores. *Earth Wisdom [EW]*. San Diego: Guild of Tudors, 1978.

Lacoue-Labarthe, Philippe. *The Subject of Philosophy [SP]*. Trans. Thomas Trezise, Hugh J. Silverman, Gary M. Cole, Timothy D. Bent, Karen McPherson, and Claudette Sartiliot. Ed. Thomas Trezise. Minneapolis: University of Minnesota Press, 1993. Translation of *Le Sujet de la philosophie [Sp]*. Paris: Aubier-Flammarion, 1979.

Lacoue-Labarthe, Philippe, and Jean-Luc Nancy. *Retreating the Political [RP]*. Ed. Simon Sparks. New York: Routledge, 1997.

Lafferty, William M., and James Meadowcroft, eds. *Democracy and the Environment: Problems and Prospects [DE]*. Cheltenham: Edward Elgar, 1996.

LaFleur, William. "Sattva—Enlightenment for Plants and Trees" *[S]*. In Badiner, ed., *Dharma Gaia*.

Lahar, Stephanie. "Ecofeminist Theory and Grassroots Politics" *[ETGP]*. In Warren, ed., *Hypatia*, 28–45.

Lakoff, George, and Mark Johnson. *Philosophy in the Flesh: The Embodied Mind and Its Challege to Western Thought [PF]*. New York: Basic Books, 1999.

Leibniz, G. W. F. "The Exigency to Exist in Essences: Principle of Plenitude" *[EEE]*. In *Leibniz Selections*.

———. *Leibniz Selections [LS]*. Ed. P. Wiener. New York: Scribner's, 1951. All references to Leibniz are from this edition.

———. "The Monadology" *[M]*. In *Leibniz Selections*.

Leiss, William. *The Limits to Satisfaction: An Essay on the Problem of Needs and Commodities [LS]*. Montreal: McGill-Queen's University Press, 1988.

Leopold, Aldo. *Game Management [GM]*. Madison: University of Wisconsin Press, 1986.

———. "The Land Ethic" *[LE]*. In *Sand County Almanac*.

———. *A Sand County Almanac [SCA]*. New York: Ballantine Books, 1970.

———. "Thinking Like a Mountain" *[TLM]*. In *Sand County Almanac*.

———. "Wilderness" *[W]*. In *Sand County Almanac*.

Levinas, Emmanuel. "Ethics as First Philosophy" *[EFP]*. Trans. Seán Hand. In *Levinas Reader*.

———. *The Levinas Reader [LR]*. Ed. Seán Hand. Oxford: Blackwell, 1989.

———. "Martin Buber and the Theory of Knowledge" *[MBTK]*. In *Levinas Reader*.

———. *Otherwise than Being or Beyond Essence [OB]*. Trans. Alfonso Lingis. The Hague: Martinus Nijhoff, 1978. Translation of *Autrement qu être ou au-delà de l'essence [AÊ]*. The Hague: Martinus Nijhoff, 1974.

———. "The Paradox of Morality: An Interview with Emmanuel Levinas" *[PM]*. With Tamra Wright, Peter Hughes, Alison Ainley. Trans. Andrew Benjamin and Tamra Wright. In Bernasconi and Wood, ed., *Provocation of Levinas*.

———. "Reality and Its Shadow" *[RS]*. Trans. Alphonso Lingis. In *Levinas Reader*.

———. "Substitution" *[S]*. In *Levinas Reader*.

———. *Totality and Infinity [TI]*. Trans. Alfonso Lingis. Pittsburgh: Duquesne University Press, 1969.

———. "The Transcendence of Words" *[TW]*. Trans. Seán Hand. In *Levinas Reader*.

Levine, Donald N. "Simmel at a Distance: On the History and Systematics of the Sociology of the Stranger" *[SD]*. In Shack and Skinner, eds., *Strangers in African Societies*.

Lévi-Strauss, Claude. *The Elementary Structure of Kinship [ESK]*. Trans. James Harle Bell, John Richard von Sturmer, and Rodney Needham. Boston: Beacon Press, 1969.

Lewis, James A. *Landownership in the United States, 1978 [LUS]*. Washington, DC: Natural Resource Economics Division; Economics, Statistics, and Cooperative Services, U.S. Department of Agriculture, Agricultural Information Bulletin 435, April, 1980.

Liddell, Henry George, and Robert Scott. *An Intermediate Greek-English Lexicon, Founded upon the Seventh Edition of Liddell and Scott's Greek-English Lexicon [IGEL]*. Oxford: Oxford University Press, 1991.

Lingis, Alphonso. *Foreign Bodies [FB]*. New York: Routledge, 1994.

Lipietz, Alan. *Green Hopes: The Future of Political Ecology [GH]*. Cambridge, MA: Polity Press, 1995.

Locke, John. *An Essay Concerning Human Understanding [E]*. Ed. Alexander Campbell Fraser. NY: Dover, 1959.

———. *Two Treatises of Government [TT]*. Student ed. Ed. Peter Laslett. Oxford: Cambridge University Press, 1988.

Loewental, Kate. "Property." *European Journal of Social Psychology* 6, no. 3 (May–June 1976): 343–51.

Lorde, Audre. "Age, Race, Class, and Sex: Women Redefining Difference" *[ARCS]*. In Andersen and Collins, eds., *Race, Class, and Gender*.

Lovelock, James. *Gaia: A New Look at Life on Earth [G]*. Oxford: Oxford University Press, 1979.

Lowrie, Robert H. *Primitive Religion [PR]*. New York: Boni and Liveright, 1924.

Lubar, Steven, and W. David Kingery, eds. *History from Things: Essays on Material Culture [HS]*. Washington, DC: Smithsonian Institution Press, 1993.

Lugones, Marìa C. "On the Logic of Pluralist Feminism" *[OLPF]*. In Card, ed., *Feminist Ethics*.

———. "Playfulness, 'World'-Travelling, and Loving Perception" *[PWTLP]*. *Hypatia* 2, no. 2 (Summer 1987): 3–20.

Lyotard, Jean-François. *Le Différend [D]*. Paris: Minuit, 1983.

———. *The Differend: Phrases in Dispute [DPD]*. Trans. Georges Van Den Abbeele. Minneapolis: University of Minnesota Press, 1988.

———. "Europe, the Jew, and the Book" *[EJB]*. In *Political Writings*.

———. "German Guilt" *[GG]*. In *Political Writings*.

———. "The Grip *(Mainmise)*" *[G]*. In *Political Writings*.

———. *Heidegger and "The Jews" [HJ]*. Trans. A. Michel and M. Roberts. Minneapolis: University of Minnesota Press, 1990.

———. "Heidegger and 'The Jews': A Conference in Vienna and Freiburg" *["HJ"]*. In *Political Writings*.

———. *The Inhuman: Reflections on Time [I]*. Trans. Geoffrey Bennington and Rachel Bowlby. Stanford: Stanford University Press, 1991.

———. *Libinal Economy [LE]*. Trans. Iain Hamilton Grant. Bloomington: Indiana University Press, 1993.

———. *The Lyotard Reader [LR]*. Ed. Andrew Benjamin. Oxford: Blackwell, 1989.

———. *"Oikos" [O]*. In *Political Writings*.

———. *Peregrinations [P]*. New York: Columbia University Press, 1988.

———. *Political Writings [PW]*. Trans. Bill Readings and Kevin Paul Geiman. Minneapolis: University of Minnesota Press, 1993.

———. *The Postmodern Condition: A Report on Knowledge [PMC]*. Trans. Geoff Bennington and Brian Massumi. Minneapolis: University of Minnesota Press, 1984.

———. "The Sign of History" *[SH]*. In *Lyotard Reader*.

———. "What Is Postmodernism?" *[WPM?]*. Reprinted in part in Ross, ed., *Art and Its Significance*. From *Postmodern Condition*.

Lyotard, Jean-François, and Jean-Loup Thébaud. *Just Gaming [JG]*. Trans. Wlad Godzich. Minneapolis: University of Minnesota Press, 1985.

MacKinnon, Catharine A. "Feminism, Marxism, Method, and the State: An Agenda for Theory" *[FMMS1]*. *Signs* 7, no. 3 (Spring 1982): 515–44.

———. "Feminism, Marxism, Method, and the State: Toward Feminist Jurisprudence" *[FMMS2]*. *Signs* 8, no. 4 (Summer 1983): 635–58.

———. *Feminism Unmodified: Discourses on Life and Law [FU]*. Cambridge: Harvard University Press, 1987.

———. *Only Words [OW]*. Cambridge: Harvard University Press, 1993.

———. "Sexuality" *[S]*. Chapter 7 in *Toward a Feminist Theory of the State*.

———. *Toward a Feminist Theory of the State [TFTS]*. Cambridge: Harvard University Press, 1989.

———. "Toward Feminist Jurisprudence" *[TFJ]*. Chapter 13 in *Toward a Feminist Theory of the State*.

Macpherson, C. B. "The Meaning of Property" *[MP]*. In Macpherson ed., *Property: Mainstream and Critical Positions [P]*.

—————. *The Political Theory of Possessive Individualism: Hobbes to Locke [PTPI]*. Oxford: Oxford University Press, 1962.

—————, ed., *Property: Mainstream and Critical Positions [P]*. Toronto: University of Toronto Press, 1983.

Maddock, Kenneth. "Involved Anthropologists" *[IA]*. In Wilmsen, ed., *We Are Here*.

Manes, Christopher. *Green Rage: Radical Environmentalism and the Unmaking of Civilization [GRF]*. Boston: Little, Brown and Co., 1990.

—————. "Nature and Silence" *[NS]*. In Oelschlaeger, ed., *Postmodern Environmental Ethics*.

Marks, Elaine, and Isabelle Courtivron, eds. *New French Feminisms: An Anthology [NFF]*. New York: Schocken, 1981.

Martin, James J. *Men against the State: The Expositors of Individualist Anarchism in America, 1827–1908 [MAS]*. DeKalb, IL: Adrian Allen Associates, 1953.

Marx, Karl. *Capital: A Critique of Political Economy [C]*. 4th ed. 3 vols. Ed. Friedrich Engels. Trans. Ben Fowkes. London: Penguin Books in association with New Left Review, 1976.

—————. *Capital: A Critique of Political Economy [C3]*. 3rd ed. 3 vols. Ed. Friedrich Engels. Trans. Samuel Moore and Edward Aveling. New York: International Publishers, 1967.

—————. *The German Ideology [GI]*. In Karl Marx and Friedrich Engels, *Collected Works*, vol. 5. New York: International Publishers, 1976.

—————. "Marx to Schweitzer" *[MS]*. In *Poverty of Philosophy*.

—————. *The Poverty of Philosophy [PP]*. New York: International Publishers, 1963.

—————. *A World Without Jews [WWJ]*. 4th ed. Ed. and int. Dagobert D Runes. New York: Philosophical Library, 1960.

Marx, Karl, and Friedrich Engels. *Selected Works [SW]*. 2 vols. Marx-Engels-Lenin Institute. Moscow: Foreign Languages Publishing House, 1951. London: Lawrence and Wishart, 1953.

Mauss, Marcel. *The Gift: Forms and Functions of Exchange in Archaic Societies [G]*. Trans. Ian Cunnison. Glenco: Free Press, 1954. Also *The Gift: The Form and Reason for Exchange in Archaic Societies*. Trans. W. D. Halls. London: Routledge, 1990.

Maw, Joan, and John Picton, eds. *Concepts of the Body/Self in Africa [CBS]*. Vienna: Afro-Pub, 1992.

May, Todd. *The Political Philosophy of Poststructuralist Anarchism [PPPA]*. University Park, PA: The Pennsylvania State University Press, 1994.

Mbiti, John S. *African Religions and Philosophy [ARP]*. London: Heinemann Educational Books, 1969.

McIntosh, Peggy. "White Privilege and Male Privilege: A Personal Account of Coming to See Correspondences through Work in Women's Studies" *[WPMP]*. In Andersen and Collins, eds., *Race, Class, and Gender*.

McLaughlin, Andrew. *Regarding Nature: Industrialism and Deep Ecology [RN]*. Albany: State University of New York Press, 1993.

Meiling, Jin. "Strangers on a Hostile Landscape" *[SHL]*. In Cobham and Collins, eds., *Watchers and Seekers*.

Merchant, Carolyn. *The Death of Nature: Women, Ecology, and the Scientific Revolution [DN]*. New York: Harper & Row, 1980.

———. *Radical Ecology: The Search for a Livable World [RE]*. New York: Routledge, 1992.

Merleau-Ponty, Maurice. *Eye and Mind [EM]*. Trans. Carleton Dallery. Reprinted in part in Ross, ed., *Art and Its Significance*. From *Primacy of Perception*, 282–98.

———. *Phenomenology of Perception [PhP]*. Trans. Colin Smith. London: Routledge & Kegan Paul, 1962.

———. *The Primacy of Perception [PrP]*. Ed. James M. Edie. Evanston: Northwestern University Press, 1964.

———. *The Visible and the Invisible [VI]*. Ed. Claude Lefort. Trans. Alphonso Lingis. Evanston: Northwestern University Press, 1968.

*Merriam-Webster Dictionary of English Usage [MWDEU]*. Springfield, MA: Merriam-Webster, 1989.

Meyer, Christine, and Faith Moosang, eds. *Living with the Land: Communities Restoring the Earth [LL]*. Gabriola Island, BC: New Society Publishers, 1992.

Mill, John Stuart. *On Liberty; with the Subjection of Women and Chapters on Socialism [L]*. New York: Cambridge University Press, 1989.

———. *Utilitarianism and Other Essays [U]*. New York: Penguin, 1987.

Milton, Katharine. "Real Men Don't Eat Deer" *[RMDED]*. *Discover* 18, no. 6 (June 1997): 46–53.

Minogue, Kenneth. "The Concept of Property and Its Contemporary Significance" *[CPCS]*. In Pennock and Chapman, eds., *Nomos XXII*, 3–27.

Morgan, Lewis. *Ancient Slavery, or Researches in the Lines of Human Progress from Savagery through Barbarism to Civilization [AS]*. London: MacMillan, 1877.

Morgan, Robin, ed. *Sisterhood Is Powerful: An Anthology of Writings from the Women's Liberation Movement [SP]*. New York: Random House, 1970.

Morton, A. I., ed. *Freedom in Arms: A Selection of Leveller Writings [FA]*. New York: International Publishers, 1974.

Mote, Frederick W. *Intellectual Foundations of China [IFC]*. New York: Alfred A. Knopf, 1971.

Mouffe, Chantal. *The Return of the Political [RP]*. New York: Verso, 1993.

———, ed. *Deconstruction and Pragmatism [DP]*. New York: Routledge, 1996.

———, ed. *Dimensions of Radical Democracy: Pluralism, Citizenship, Community [DRD]*. New York: Verso, 1992.

Mudimbe, V. Y. *The Invention of Africa [IA]*. Reprinted in part in Ross, ed., *Art and Its Significance*. From *Invention of Africa: Gnosis, Philosophy, and the Order of Knowledge*. Bloomington: Indiana University Press, 1988.

Munzer, Stephen R. *A Theory of Property [P]*. Cambridge: Cambridge University Press, 1990.

Myers, Fred. "Burning the Truck and Holding the Country: Pintupi Forms of Property and Identity" *[BTHC]*. In Wilmsen, ed., *We Are Here*.

Naess, Arne. *Ecology, Community and Lifestyle: Outline of an Ecosophy [ECL]*. Trans. David Rothenberg. Cambridge: Cambridge University Press, 1989.

———. "The Shallow and the Deep: Long Range Ecology Movement" *[SD]*. *Inquiry* 16 (1973): 95–100.

Nāgārjuna. *Elegant Sayings [ES]*. Ed. Sakya Pandit. Emeryville, Dharma Publishing, 1977.

Nancy, Jean-Luc. *The Birth to Presence [BP]*. Trans. Brian Holmes and Others. Stanford: Stanford University Press, 1993.

———. *The Experience of Freedom [EF]*. Trans. Bridget McDonald. Fwd. Peter Fenves. Stanford: Stanford University Press, 1993.

———. *The Inoperative Community [IC]*. Trans. P. Connor, L. Garbus, M. Holland, and S. Sawhney. Minneapolis: University of Minnesota Press, 1991.

———. "Shattered Love" *[SL]*. In *Inoperative Community*.

Nash, Roderick. *The Rights of Nature [RN]*. Madison: University of Wisconsin Press, 1989.

———. *Wilderness and the American Mind [WAM]*. 3rd ed. New Haven: Yale University Press, 1982.

Negri, Antonio. *Marx Beyond Marx: Lessons on the Grundrisse [MBM]*. South Hadley, MA: Bergin & Garvey, 1984.

———. *Revolution Retrieved: Writings on Marx, Keynes, Capitalist Crisis and New Social Subjects [RR]*. London: Red Notes, 1988.

———. *The Savage Anomaly: The Power of Spinoza's Metaphysics and Politics [SA]*. Trans. Michael Hardt. Minneapolis: University of Minnesota Press, 1991.

*Neither Nationalisation Nor Privatisation: An Anarchist Approach [NP].* London: Freedom Press, 1989.

Nerburn, Kent, ed. *The Wisdom of the Great Chiefs: The Classic Speeches of Chief Red Jacket, Chief Joseph, and Chief Seattle [WGC].* San Rafael, CA: New World Library, 1994.

Nietzsche, Friedrich. *The Antichrist [A].* In *Portable Nietzsche.*

———. "Attempt at a Self-Criticism" *[ASC].* In *Basic Writings.* Reprinted in Ross, ed., *Art and Its Significance.*

———. *Basic Writings of Nietzsche [BWN].* Trans. Walter Kaufmann. New York: Random House, Modern Library Giant, 1968.

———. *Beyond Good and Evil [BGE].* In *Basic Writings.*

———. *Birth of Tragedy [BT].* In *Basic Writings.* Reprinted in part in Ross, ed., *Art and Its Significance.*

———. *Ecce Homo [EH].* In *Basic Writings.*

———. *The Gay Science [GS].* Trans. with comm. Walter Kaufman. New York: Vintage, 1974.

———. *Genealogy of Morals [GM].* In *Basic Writings.*

———. *On the Advantage and Disadvantage of History for Life [OADHL].* Trans. P. Preuss. Indianapolis: Hackett, 1980.

———. *The Portable Nietzsche [PN].* Ed. and trans. Walter Kaufmann. New York: Viking Press, 1954.

———. *Seventy-Five Aphorisms from Five Volumes [75A].* In *Basic Writings.* From *Dawn [D]; Gay Science [GS]; Human, All-Too-Human [H]; Mixed Opinions and Maxims [MOM]; The Wanderer and His Shadow [WS].*

———. *Thus Spake Zarathustra [Z].* In *Portable Nietzsche.*

———. *Twilight of the Idols [TI].* In *Portable Nietzsche.*

———. *The Will to Power [WP].* Ed. Walter Kaufmann. Trans. Robert Hollingdale and Walter Kaufmann. New York: Vintage, 1968.

Nodding, Nel. *Caring: A Feminine Approach to Ethics and Moral Education [C].* Berkeley: University of California Press, 1984.

Nozick, Robert. *Anarchy, State, and Utopia [ASU].* New York: Basic Books, 1968.

Nussbaum, Martha. *The Fragility of Goodness [FG].* Cambridge: Cambridge University Press, 1986.

———. *Love's Knowledge: Essays on Philosophy and Literature [LK].* New York: Oxford University Press, 1990.

———. *Poetic Justice: The Literary Imagination and Public Life [PJ]*. Boston, MA: Beacon Press, 1995.

———. *The Therapy of Desire: Theory and Practice in Hellenistic Ethics [TD]*. Princeton, NJ: Princeton University Press, 1994.

———. *Women, Culture, and Development: A Study of Human Capabilities [WCD]*. Oxford: Clarendon Press, 1995.

Oates, W. J., and E. O'Neill, eds. *The Complete Greek Drama [CGD]*. New York: Random House, 1938.

Oelschlaeger, Max, ed. *The Wilderness Condition: Essays on Environment and Civilization [WC]*. San Francisco: Sierra Club Books, 1992.

———. *Postmodern Environmental Ethics [PMEE]*. Albany: State University of New York Press, 1995.

Omolade, Barbara. "Hearts of Darkness" *[HD]*. In Guy-Sheftall, ed., *Words of Fire*.

Ophuls, William. *Ecology and the Politics of Scarcity [EPS]*. San Francisco: W. H. Freeman, 1977.

Osoro, R. *The African Identity in Crisis [AIC]*. Hudsonville, MI: Bayana Publishers, 1993.

Oudshoorn, Nelly. "A Natural Order of Things: Reproductive Sciences and the Politics of Othering" *[NOT]*. In Robertson, et al., eds., *Futurenatural*.

Outlaw, Lucius. *Philosophy, Ethnicity, and Race: The Alfred B. Stiernotte Lectures in Philosophy [PER]*. Hamden, CT: Quinnipiac College, 1989.

———. "Philosophy, Ethnicity, and Race" *["PER"]*. In Hord and Lee, eds., *I Am Because We Are*.

———. "Toward a Critical Theory of 'Race'" *[TCTR]*. In Goldberg, ed., *Anatomy of Racism*.

Owens, Craig. "The Discourse of Others: Feminists and Postmodernism" *[DO]*. In Hal Foster, ed. *The Anti-Aesthetic: Essays on Postmodern Culture*. Port Townsend, WA: Bay Press, 1983. Reprinted in Ross, ed., *Art and Its Significance*.

*Oxford English Dictionary [OED]*. Compact edition. Oxford. Oxford University Press, 1971.

Pagels, Elaine H. "What Became of God the Mother? Conflicting Images of God in Early Christianity" *[WBGM]*. In Christ and Plaskow, eds., *Womanspirit Rising*.

Parrinder, Geoffrey. *Witchcraft: European and African [WEA]*. London: Faber and Faber, 1970.

Peirce, Charles Sanders. *The Collected Papers of Charles Sanders Peirce [CP]*. 6 vols. Ed. Charles Hartshorne and Paul Weiss. Cambridge: Harvard University Press, 1931–35.

———. *The Philosophical Writings of Peirce [PP]*. Ed. Justus Buchler. New York: Dover, 1955.

Pennock, J. Roland, and John W. Chapman, eds. *Property: Nomos XXII [P]*. New York: New York University, 1980.

Pepper, David. *Eco-socialism: From Deep Ecology to Social Justice [E]*. New York: Routledge, 1993.

Picton, John. "Masks and Identities in Ebira Culture" *[MIEC]*. In Maw and Picton, eds., *Concepts of the Body/Self in Africa*.

Plant, Christopher, and Judith Plant, eds. *Green Business: Hope or Hoax? [GB]*. Gabriola Island, BC: New Society Publishers, 1991.

Plant, Judith, ed. *Healing the Wounds: The Power of Ecological Feminism [HW]*. Philadelphia: New Society Publishers, 1989.

Plato. *The Collected Dialogues of Plato [CDP]*. Ed. Edith Hamilton and Huntington Cairns. Princeton: Princeton University Press, 1961. All quotations from Plato are from this edition unless otherwise indicated.

———. *Phaedo [PP]*. Ed., with int. and notes, by John Burnet. London: Oxford University Press, 1963.

———. *Phaedo*. Trans. Harold North Fowler. Loeb Classical Library. Cambridge: Harvard University Press, 1914. All Greek passages from *Phaedo* are from this edition.

———. *Phaedo*. Trans. Benjamin Jowett. In *The Dialogues of Plato*. New York: Random House, 1920.

———. *Phaedrus*. Trans. Harold North Fowler. Loeb Classical Library. Cambridge: Harvard University Press, 1914. All Greek passages from *Phaedrus* are from this edition.

———. *Protagoras*. Trans. Benjamin Jowett, 3rd ed. London: Oxford University Press, 1982.

———. *Symposium*. Reprinted in part in Ross, ed., *Art and Its Significance*. From *The Dialogues of Plato*. Trans. Benjamin Jowett, 3rd ed. London: Oxford University Press, 1982. All quotations in English from *Symposium* are from this edition.

———. *Symposium*. Trans. W. R. M. Lamb. Loeb Classical Library. Cambridge: Harvard University Press, 1925. All Greek passages from *Symposium* are from this edition.

Poster, Mark. "Postmodern Virtualities" *[PV]*. In Robertson, et al., eds., *Future natural*.

———. *Property: Its Duties and Rights, Historically, Philosophically and Religiously Regarded [P]*. New York: Macmillan, Co., 1922.

Proudhon, Pierre-Joseph. *What Is Property? An Inquiry into the Principle of Right and of Government [WP?]*. Ed. and trans. Donald R. Kelley and Bonnie G. Smith. Cambridge: Cambridge University Press, 1993.

Purchase, Graham. *Anarchism and Ecology [PE]*. Montreal: Black Rose Books, 1997.

Quigley, Peter. "Rethinking Resistance: Environmentalism, Literature, and Poststructural Theory" *[RR]*. In Oelschlaeger, ed., *Postmodern Environmental Ethics*.

Rachels, James. "Why Animals Have a Right to Liberty" *[WARL]*. In Regan and Singer, eds., *Animal Rights and Human Obligations*.

Radin, Margaret Jane. "Market-Inalienability" *[MI]*. *Harvard Law Review* 100 (1987): 1849–1937.

———. "Property and Personhood" *[PP]*. *Stanford Law Review* 34 (1982): 957–1015.

———. *Reinterpreting Property [RP]*. Chicago: University of Chicago Press, 1993.

*Random House Dictionary of the English Language [RHD1]*. Unabridged. New York: Random House, 1966.

———. *[RHD2]*. 2nd ed. Unabridged. New York: Random House, 1987.

Rawls, John. *A Theory of Justice [TJ]*. Cambridge: Belknap Press of Harvard University, 1971.

Regan, Tom. *The Case for Animal Rights [CAR]*. Berkeley: University of California Press, 1983.

Regan, Tom, and Peter Singer, eds. *Animal Rights and Human Obligations [ARHO]*. 2nd ed. Englewood Cliffs: Prentice Hall, 1989.

Reich, Charles. "The New Property" *[NP]*. *Yale Law Journal* 73 (1964): 733–787.

Reiter, Rayna R. ed., *Toward an Anthropology of Women*. New York: Monthly Press, 1975.

Rigby, Peter. *Cattle, Capitalism, and Class: Ilparakuyo Maasai Transformations [CCC]*. Philadelphia: Temple University Press, 1992.

Rigterink, Roger J. "Warning: The Surgeon Moralist Has Determined That Claims of Rights Can Be Detrimental to Everyone's Interests" *[W]*. In Cole and Coultrap-McQuin, eds., *Explorations in Feminist Ethics*.

Roach, Catherine. "Loving Your Mother: On the Woman-Nature Relationship" *[LM]*. In Warren, ed., *Hypatia*, 46–59.

Robertson, George, Melinda Mash, Lisa Tickner, Jon Bird, Barry Curtis, and Tim Putnam, eds. *Futurenatural: Nature, Science, Culture [FN]*. New York: Routledge, 1996.

Robinson, John Manley. *An Introduction to Early Greek Philosophy [EGP]*. Boston: Houghton Mifflin, 1968. All Greek fragments are quoted from this edition unless otherwise indicated.

Rocheleau, Dianne, Barbara Thomas-Slayter, and Esther Wangari. *Feminist Political Ecology: Global Issues and Local Experience [FPE]*. London: Routledge, 1996.

Rolston, Holmes, III. *Environmental Ethics: Duties to and Values in the Natural World [EE]*. Philadelphia: Temple University Press, 1988.

————. " 'Environmental Ethics: Values in and Duties to the Natural World" *[EEVDNW]*. In Bormann and Kellert, eds., *Ecology, Economics, Ethics*.

Rorty, Richard. *Consequences of Pragmatism [CP]*. Minneapolis: University of Minnesota Press, 1982.

————. "Philosophy in America Today" *[PAT]*. In *Consequences of Pragmatism*.

Rose, Carol. "Possession as the Origin of Property" *[POP]*. *University of Chicago Law Review* 52 (1985): 73–88.

Ross, Stephen David. *The Gift of Beauty: The Good as Art [GBGA]*. Albany: State University of New York Press, 1996.

————. *The Gift of Kinds: The Good in Abundance [GKGA]*. Albany: State University of New York Press, 1999.

————. *The Gift of Touch: Embodying the Good [GTEG]*. Albany: State University of New York Press, 1998.

————. *The Gift of Truth: Gathering the Good [GTGG]*. Albany: State University of New York Press, 1997.

————. *Ideals and Responsibilities: Ethical Judgment and Social Identity [IR]*. Belmont, CA: Wadsworth, 1998.

————. *Inexhaustibility and Human Being: An Essay on Locality [IHB]*. New York: Fordham University Press, 1989.

————. *Injustice and Restitution: The Ordinance of Time [IROT]*. Albany: State University of New York Press, 1993.

————. *Learning and Discovery [LD]*. New York: Gordon and Breach, 1981.

————. *The Limits of Language [LL]*. New York: Fordham University Press, 1993.

————. *Locality and Practical Judgment: Charity and Sacrifice [LPJ]*. New York: Fordham University Press, 1994.

————. *Metaphysical Aporia and Philosophical Heresy [MAPH]*. Albany: State University of New York Press, 1989

————. *Perspective in Whitehead's Metaphysics [PWM]*. Albany: State University of New York Press, 1983.

————. *Plenishment in the Earth: An Ethic of Inclusion [PE]*. Albany: State University of New York, 1995.

————. *The Ring of Representation [RR]*. Albany: State University of New York Press, 1992.

————. *A Theory of Art: Inexhaustibility by Contrast [TA]*. Albany: State University of New York Press, 1983.

————. "Translation as Transgression" *[TT]*. In *Translation Perspectives*, vol. 5. Ed. D. J. Schmidt. Binghamton: Binghamton University, 1990.

————, ed. *Art and Its Significance: An Anthology of Aesthetic Theory [AIS]*. 3rd ed. Albany: State University of New York Press, 1994.

Roszak, Theodore. Introduction to Schumacher, *Small Is Beautiful*.

Rousseau, Jean-Jacques. *The Basic Political Writings [BPW]*. Trans. Donald A. Cress. Int. Peter Gay. Indianapolis: Hackett, 1987.

————. *A Discourse on the Origin of Inequality [DOI]*. In *Basic Political Writings*.

————. *A Discourse on Political Economy [DPE]*. In *Basic Political Writings*.

————. *The Social Contract [SC]*. In *Basic Political Writings*.

————. *The Social Contract and Discourses [SCD]*. Trans. G. D. H. Cole. New York: Dutton, 1950.

Rubin, Gayle. "The Traffic in Women: Notes on the 'Political Economy' of Sex" *[TW]*. In R. Reiter, ed., *Toward an Anthropology of Women*.

Ruch, E. A., and K. C. Anyanwu, eds., *African Philosophy: An Introduction to the Main Philosophical Trends in Contemporary Africa [AP]*. Rome: Catholic Book Agency, 1984.

Ruether, Rosemary. *New Woman, New Earth [NWNE]*. New York: Seabury Press, 1975.

Sachs, Wolfgang. *Global Ecology: A New Arena of Political Conflict [GE]*. London: Zed, 1993.

Sade, Marquis de. *Juliette [JUL]*. Trans. Austryn Wainhouse. New York: Grove Press, 1968.

————. *Justine [JUS], Philosophy in the Bedroom [PB], and Other Writings [JPB]*. Compiled and trans. Richard Seaver and Austryn Wainhouse. New York: Grove Press, 1965.

————. *120 Days of Sodom and Other Writings [120]*. Compiled and trans. Austryn Wainhouse and Richard Seaver. New York: Grove Press, 1966.

Salleh, Ariel. "Class, Race, and Gender Discourse in the Ecofeminism/Deep Ecology Debate" *[CRGD]*. In Oelschlaeger, ed., *Postmodern Environmental Ethics*.

Sallis, John, ed. *Deconstruction in Philosophy: The Texts of Jacques Derrida [DP]*. Chicago: University of Chicago Press, 1987.

———. *Reading Heidegger: Commemorations [RH]*. Bloomington: Indiana University Press, 1993.

Sartre, Jean-Paul. *Being and Nothingness [BN]*. Trans. Hazel Barnes. New York: Philosophical Library, 1956.

———. *Nausea [N]*. Trans. Lloyd Alexander. New York: New Directions, 1964.

Scherer, Donald, and Tom Attig, eds. *Ethics and the Environment [EE]*. Englewood Cliffs, NJ: Prentice Hall, 1983.

Schleuning, Neala. *To Have and to Hold: The Meaning of Ownership in the United States [THTH]*. Westport, CT: Praeger, 1977.

Schor, Naomi. "This Essentialism Which Is Not One: Coming to Grips with Irigaray" *[TEWNO]*. *Differences: A Journal of Feminist Cultural Studies* 2, no. 1 (Summer 1989): 38–58.

Schultz, David A. *Property, Power, and American Democracy [PPAD]*. New Brunswick, NY: Transaction Publishers, 1992.

Schumacher, E. F. *A Guide for the Perplexed [GP]*. New York: Harper and Row, 1977.

———. *Small Is Beautiful: Economics As If People Mattered [SB]*. Pref. John McClaughry, Kirkpatrick Sale. Int. Theodore Roszak. New York: Harper & Row, 1989.

Schutz, Alfred. "The Homecomer" *[H]*. *American Journal of Sociology* 60, no. 5 (1945): 369–76.

———. "The Stranger: An Essay in Social Psychology" *[S]*. *American Journal of Sociology* 49, no. 6 (1944): 499-507.

Scott, Russell. *The Body as Property [BP]*. New York: Viking, 1981.

Seager, Joni. *Earth Follies: Coming to Terms with the Global Environmental Crisis [EF]*. New York: Routledge, 1993.

Seamon, David, ed. *Dwelling, Seeing, and Designing [DSD]*. Albany: State University of New York Press, 1993.

Seed, John, Joanna Macy, Pat Fleming, and Arne Naess. *Thinking Like a Mountain: Toward a Council of All Beings [TLM]*. Philadelphia: New Society Publishers, 1988.

Sen, Amartya. "More Than 100 Million Women Are Missing" *[MMWM]*. *New York Review of Books* (December 20, 1990): 61–66.

Senghor, Léopold Sédar. "Negritude: A Humanism of the Twentieth Century" *[N]*. In Hord and Lee, eds., *I Am Because We Are*.

Serequeberhan, Tsenay. *African Philosophy: The Essential Readings [AP]*. New York: Paragon House, 1991.

Serres, Michel. *The Natural Contract [NC]*. Trans. Elizabeth MacArthur and William Paulson. Ann Arbor: University of Michigan Press, 1995.

Sessions, Robert. "Deep Ecology versus Ecofeminism: Healthy Differences or Incompatible Philosophies?" *[DEE]*. In Warren, ed., *Hypatia*, 90–107.

Shack, William A. "Open Systems and Closed Boundaries: The Ritual Process of Stranger Relations in New African States" *[OSCB]*. In Shack and Skinner, eds., *Strangers in African Societies*.

Shack, William A., and Eliot Skinner, eds. *Strangers in African Societies [SAS]*. Berkeley: University of California Press, 1979.

Shantideva. *Bodhicaryavatara [B]* 8:114. Trans. Stephen Batchelor. In *A Guide to the Bodhisattva's Way of Life [GBWL]*. Dharamsala, India: Library of Tibetan Works and Archives, 1979.

Sharma, Ursula. "Dowry in North India: Its Consequences for Women" *[DNI]*. In Hirschon, ed., *Woman and Property—Women As Property*.

Sharper, Stephen D. *Redeeming the Time: A Political Theology of the Environment [RD]*. New York: Continuum, 1997.

Shepard, Paul. *Nature and Madness [NM]*. San Franciso: Sierra Club Books, 1982.

Shiva, Vandana. "Development as a New Project of Western Patriarchy" *[DNPWP]*. In Diamond and Orenstein, eds., *Reweaving the World*.

———. *Staying Alive [SA]*. London: Zed, 1989.

Shiva, Vandana, and Ingunn Moser, eds. *Biopolitics: A Feminist and Ecological Reader on Biotechnology [B]*. London: Zed Books, 1995.

Silko, Leslie Marmon. *Ceremony [C]*. New York: New American Library, 1977.

Sillah, Memuna M. "Bundu Trap" *[BT]*. *Natural History* (August 1996): 42–53.

Simmel, Georg. "The Stranger" *[S]*. In Donald N. Levine, *On Individuality and Social Forms*. Chicago: University of Chicago Press, 1971.

Singer, Joseph W. "The Reliance Interest in Property" *[RIP]*. *Stanford Law Review* 40 (1988): 611–51.

———. "Sovereignty and Property" *[SP]*. *Northwestern University Law Review* 86, no. 1 (1991): 1–56.

Singer, Peter. *Animal Liberation: A New Ethics for Our Treatment of Animals [AL]*. New York: Avon, 1975.

Slicer, Deborah. "Your Daughter or Your Dog" *[DD]*. In Warren, ed., *Hypatia*, 108–23.

Smith, Adam. *An Inquiry into the Nature and Causes of the Wealth of Nations [WN]*. Ed. R. H. Campbell, A. S. Skinner, and W. B. Todd. Oxford: Clarendon Press, 1976.

Smith, Mick. "Cheney and the Myth of Postmodernism" *[CMP]*. In Oelschlaeger, ed., *Postmodern Environmental Ethics*.

Soper, Kate. "Nature/'nature' " *[NN]*. In Robertson, et al., eds., *Futurenatural*.

Sophocles. *Oedipus the King [OK], Antigone [A], Oedipus at Colonus [OC]*. All trans. R. C. Jebb. In Oates and O'Neill, eds., *Complete Greek Drama*.

Soyinka, Wole. *Art, Dialogue, and Outrage: Essays on Literature and Culture [ADO]*. New York: Pantheon, 1994.

Spelman, Elizabeth V. *Inessential Woman: Problems of Exclusion in Feminist Thought [IW]*. Boston: Beacon Press, 1988.

Spencer, Colin. *The Heretic's Feast: A History of Vegetarianism [HF]*. Hanover: University Press of New England, 1995.

Spiegel, Marjorie. *The Dreaded Comparison: Human and Animal Slavery [DC]*. Rev. ed. New York: Mirror Books, 1996.

Spinoza, Benedict de. *Collected Works of Spinoza [CWS]*, vol. 1. 2nd printing with corr. Ed. and trans. Edwin Curley. Princeton: Princeton University Press, 1988.

―――. *Descartes' Principles of Philosophy [DPP]*. In *Collected Works*, vol. I.

―――. *Ethics [E]*. In *Collected Works*, vol. I.

―――. *Ethics [EG]*. Trans. William Hale White. Rev. Amelia Hutchinson Stirling. Ed. and int. James Gutmann. New York: Hafner, 1949.

―――. *A Political Treatise [PT]*. trans. and int. R. H. M. Elwes. New York: Dover, 1951.

Spretnak, Charlene. *The Resurgence of the Real: Body, Nature, and Place in a Hypermodern World [RR]*. New York: Addison-Wesley, 1997.

―――. *The Spiritual Dimension of Green Politics [SDGP]*. Santa Fe, NM: Bear and Co., 1986.

Starhawk [Miriam Simos]. "Ethics and Justice in Goddess Religion" *[EJGR]*. In Andolsen, Gudorf, and Pellauer, eds., *Women's Consciousness, Women's Conscience*.

―――. "Witchcraft and Women's Culture" *[WWC]*. In Christ and Plaskow, eds., *Womanspirit Rising*.

Starr, June. "The Legal and Social Transformation of Rural Women in Aegean Turkey" *[LSF]*. In Hirschon, ed., *Woman and Property—Women As Property*.

Stephen, Michele. "Contrasting Images of Power" *[CIP]*. In Stephen ed., *Sorcerer and Witch*.

―――. "Master of Souls: The Mekeo Sorcerer" *[MS]*. In Stephen, ed., *Sorcerer and Witch*.

―――, ed. *Sorcerer and Witch in Melanesia [SWM]*. New Brunswick, NJ: Rutgers University Press, 1987.

Stirner, Max. *The Ego and His Own [EO]*. Trans. Steven T. Byington. New York: Dover, 1973.

Stone, Christopher D. *Earth and Other Ethics [EOE]*. New York: Harper & Row, 1987.

———. "Moral Pluralism and the Course of Environmental Ethics" *[MPCEE]*. In Oelschlaeger, ed., *Postmodern Environmental Ethics*.

Strathern, Marilyn. "Subject or Object? Women and the Circulation of Valuables in Highlands New Guinea" *[SO]*. In Hirschon, ed., *Woman and Property— Women As Property*.

Sumner, Claude. *The Source of African Philosophy: The Ethiopian Philosophy of Man [SAP]*. Stuttgart: Franz Steiner Verlag Wiesbaden GMBH, 1986.

Tannen, Deborah. *You Just Don't Understand: Women and Men in Conversation [YJDU]*. New York: Ballantine, 1990.

Taylor, Dorceta E. "Environmentalism and the Politics of Inclusion" *[EPI]*. In Bullard, ed., *Confronting Environmental Racism*.

Taylor, Paul. *Respect for Nature: A Theory of Environmental Ethics [RN]*. Princeton: Princeton University Press, 1986.

Tellenbach, Hubertus, and Bin Kimura. "The Japanese Concept of 'Nature' " *[JCN]*. In Callicott and Ames, eds., *Nature in Asian Traditions of Thought*.

Thomas, Elizabeth Marshall. "Reflections (Lions)" *[L]*. *The New Yorker* (October 15, 1990): 78–101.

Thompson, Robert Farris. *Flash of the Spirit; African and Afro-American Art and Philosophy [FS]*. New York: Vintage, 1984.

Tobias, Michael. "Ecological Aesthetics" *[EA]*. In Tobias and Cowan, eds., *Soul of Nature*.

Tobias, Michael, and Georgianne Cowan, eds. *The Soul of Nature: Visions of a Living Earth [SN]*. New York: Continuum, 1994.

Tolstoi, Leo. "What Is to Be Done" *[WD]*. In Horovitz, ed., *Anarchists*.

Trinh, T. Minh-ha. "Nature's R: A Musical Swoon" *[NR]*. In Robertson, et al., eds., *Futurenatural*.

———. *Woman, Native, Other: Writing Postcoloniality and Feminism [WNO]*. Indianapolis: Indiana University Press, 1989.

Trumbull, H. C. *The Threshold Covenant [TC]*. New York: Scribner's, 1896.

Tu Wei-ming. "The Continuity of Nature: Chinese Visions of Nature" *[CN]*. In Callicott and Ames, eds., *Nature in Asian Traditions of Thought*.

Tucker, Benjamin Ricketson. *Instead of a Book, By a Man Too Busy to Write One; A Fragmentary Exposition of Philosophical Anarchism [IB]*. 2nd ed. New York: Gordon Press, 1972.

Turner, Victor. *The Ritual Process [RP]*. Chicago: Aldine, 1969.

Tyler, Edward B. *Primitive Culture [PC]*. New York: Holt and Co., 1889.

Underkuffler, Laura S. "On Property: An Essay" *[OP]*. *Yale Law Journal* 100 (1990): 127–48.

Valiente, Doreen. *Witchcraft for Tomorrow [WT]*. Custer, WA: Phoenix, 1987.

Vattimo, Gianni. *The End of Modernity [EM]*. Trans. J. R. Snyder. Cambridge: Polity Press, 1988.

Veblen, Thorstein. "The Beginnings of Ownership" *[BO]*. *The American Journal of Sociology* 4 (November 1989): 352–65.

———. *The Portable Veblen [PV]*. Ed. Max Lerner. New York: Viking, 1972.

———. *The Theory of the Leisure Class [TLC]*. New York: Modern Library, 1934.

Warren, Karen J. "Feminism and Ecology: Making Connections" *[FEMC]*. *Environmental Ethics* 9, no. 1 (Spring 1987): 3–20.

———. "The Promise and Power of Ecological Feminism" *[PPEF]*. *Environmental Ethics* 12, no. 2 (Summer 1990): 125–46.

———, ed. *Hypatia* 6, no. 1 (Spring 1991). Special Issue on Ecological Feminism.

Warren, Karen J., and Jim Cheney. "Ecological Feminism and Ecosystem Ecology" *[EFEE]*. In Warren, ed., *Hypatia*, 179–97.

Wenz, Peter S. "Just Garbage" *[JG]*. In Westra and Wenz, eds., *Faces of Environmental Racism: Confronting Issues of Global Justice*.

West, Cornel. *Keeping Faith: Philosophy and Race in America [KP]*. New York: Routledge, 1993.

———. "Race Matters" *[RM]*. In Andersen and Collins, eds., *Race, Class, and Gender*.

Weston, Anthony. "Before Environmental Ethics" *[BEE]*. In Oelschlaeger, ed., *Postmodern Environmental Ethics*.

Westra, Laura, and Peter S. Wenz, eds., *Faces of Environmental Racism: Confronting Issues of Global Justice [FER]*. Lanham, MD: Rowman & Littlefield, 1995.

Westwood, Sallie. " 'Fear Woman': Property and Modes of Production in Urban Ghana" *[FW]*. In Hirschon, ed., *Woman and Property—Women as Property*.

Whitehead, Alfred North. *Adventures of Ideas [AI]*. New York: Macmillan, 1933.

———. *Modes of Thought [MT]*. New York: Capricorn, 1938.

———. *Process and Reality [PR]*. Corrected edition. Ed. D. R. Griffin and D. W. Sherburne. New York: Free Press, 1978.

———. *Science in the Modern World [SMW]*. New York: Macmillan, 1925.

Whitehead, Ann. "Women and Men; Kinship and Property: Some General Issues" *[MMKP]*. In Hirschon, ed., *Woman and Property—Women as Property*.

Wikse, John R. *About Possession: The Self as Private Property [AP]*. University Park, PA: The Pennsylvania State University Press, 1977.

Wilcox, Finn, and Jeremiah Gorsline, eds. *Working the Woods, Working the Sea [WW]*. Port Townsend, WA: Empty Bowl, 1986.

Wilmsen, Edwin H., ed. *We Are Here: Politics of Aboriginal Land Tenure [WAH]*. Berkeley: University of California Press, 1989.

Wilson, Edward O. *The Diversity of Life [DL]*. Cambridge: Harvard University Press, 1992.

Wilson, Peter J. *The Domestication of the Human Species [DHS]*. New Haven: Yale University Press, 1988.

Wittgenstein, Ludwig. *The Blue and Brown Books [BB]*. New York: Harper & Row, 1958.

———. *Philosophical Investigations [PI]*. Trans. G. E. M. Anscombe. Oxford: Blackwell, 1963.

———. *Tractatus Logico-Philosophicus [TLP]*. Trans. D. F. Pears and B. F. McGuinness. London: Routledge & Kegan Paul, 1961.

Wittig, Monique. "The Category of Sex" *[CS]*. In *Straight Mind*.

———. *The Lesbian Body [LB]*. Trans. David Le Vay. Boston: Beacon Press, 1973. Translation of *Le Corps Lesbien [CL]*. Paris: Minuit, 1973.

———. "The Mark of Gender" *[MG]*. In *Straight Mind*.

———. "One Is Not Born a Woman" *[OBW]*. In *Straight Mind*.

———. "The Straight Mind" *[SM]*. In *Straight Mind*.

———. *The Straight Mind and Other Essays [SME]*. Boston: Beacon Press, 1992.

Worster, Donald. *Rivers of Empire [RE]*. New York: Pantheon, 1985.

Zimmerman, Michael E. *Contesting Earth's Future: Radical Ecology and Postmodernity [CEF]*. Berkeley: University of California Press, 1994.

———. "Quantum Theory, Intrinsic Value, and Panentheism" *[QTIVP]*. In Oelschlaeger, ed., *Postmodern Environmental Ethics*.

Zizek, Slavoj. "Eastern Europe's Republics of Gilead" *[EERG]*. In Mouffe, ed., *Dimensions of Radical Democracy*.

# *Index*

Abjection, ix, 7, 9, 16, 64, 118, 121, 134–5, 149–52, 177–9, 278, 310; *See also* Subjection

Aboriginal peoples, viii, 63, 105–8, 112–5, 118, 124, 288, 300, 328; *See also* Culture, Foragers

Abraham, 1, 218, 222, 225

Absence, 22, 48, 76, 79, 111, 139, 161, 164, 175, 185, 217, 234–5, 301; *See also* Nothing, Presence

Absent referent, x, 3, 176, 182, 279; See also Adams, *Mimēsis*

Absolute, absolutely, 12, 17, 47, 51–5, 61, 67, 80, 83, 89, 115, 118, 120, 131, 136–8, 141, 144–45, 153, 158, 171, 183–9, 216, 220, 224–5, 228, 234, 255, 268, 275–7, 282–3

Abundance, v, viii, xiv, xvii, 4, 41, 45, 49–51, 56–7, 71, 86–9, 99–104, 108, 128, 138, 143–7, 151, 155, 158–60, 168, 170, 174–5, 183, 187–9, 193, 200–1, 207–9, 212–21, 227, 233–4, 238–46, 249–58, 281, 321; *See also* Cherishment, Earth, Generosity, General economy, Giving, Inexhaustibility, Multiplicity, Plenishment

Accord, accordance, 6, 16–17, 63–6, 96, 108, 143, 188, 204–6, 234; *See also* Jointure, Same

Accumulation, viii–x, xvii, 2–3, 29–30, 33–6, 44–52, 62, 68, 71, 76, 78, 84–8, 93–6, 99, 104, 108–21, 125–7, 133–41, 167, 171, 177, 195, 206–7, 214, 217–21, 235, 241, 243–8, 258, 264–7, 276; *See also* Acquisition, Hoarding, Possession, Property, Squander

Accursedness, 24, 121, 259, 289; *See also* Curse

Acquisition, xiv, 11, 28, 44–6, 49–51, 58, 64, 78, 86, 94–5, 108, 117, 125, 127, 133, 136, 143, 177, 270; *See also* Accumulation, Property

Adams, C., x, 176, 287

Advantage, vi, 31–7, 41, 55–6, 82, 108, 140, 164, 277; *See also* Benefit, Profit, Propriety, Use

Advent, 1–2, 16–9, 22, 29, 55, 59–60, 71–7, 238, 263, 271; *See also* Arrival, Event, *Parousia*

Aesthetic, 122, 204, 229, 240, 298, 301–3, 322, 326; *See also* Art, *Mimēsis, Poiēsis, Technē*

Agathon, 35, 38, 241; *See also* The Good

Agriculture, 66, 76–7, 301, 312

Aliens, 24, 82, 181–3, 199, 269; *See also* Strangers

Alienability, alienation, ix, 15, 49–51, 61–2, 76, 82, 89–90, 94, 130, 144–5, 130, 139, 156, 268–70

Alterity, 183–8, 214, 232–6; *See also* Heterogeneity, Levinas

329